THE

Prophetic Moment

THE

Prophetic Moment

AN ESSAY ON SPENSER

Angus Fletcher

The University of Chicago Press

CHICAGO / LONDON

International Standard Book Number: 0–226–25332–5
Library of Congress Catalog Card Number: 73–130587
The University of Chicago Press, Chicago 60637
The University of Chicago Press, Ltd., London
©1971 by The University of Chicago
Published 1971
Printed in the United States of America

TO
HOWARD

*There is continuall spring, and harvest there
Continuall, both meeting at one time.*

Contents

Acknowledgments   ix

PART ONE

I INTRODUCTION   3

II THE PROPHETIC MOMENT   11

III TYPOLOGICAL MATRICES IN *THE FAERIE
QUEENE*   57

PART TWO

IV JUSTICE, PROPHECY, AND HISTORY   135

V ERROR AND EXPERIENCE   215

VI THE TEMPLE OF TRUTH   259

[vii

CONTENTS

Index of Names: Traditional Sources   305

Index of Names: Modern Sources   309

Index of Subjects: General   315

Index of Subjects: From *The Faerie Queene*   323

Acknowledgments

THIS BOOK CAME INTO BEING SLOWLY AND NOT ALWAYS WITH MUCH ease, but during its composition I received technical advice and spiritual comfort from a number of friendly critics. Among those who read and generously criticized earlier drafts were Jane Aptekar, Calvin Edwards, Northrop Frye, William Nelson, and Phillips Salman. My students, both graduates and undergraduates, at Columbia University and the State University of New York at Buffalo, contributed insight and information to this task of working toward a critique of Spenserian myth. They particularly will see how much the present study leaves to be done, and will forgive any extravagance in it. As an essay on prophetic thought this book owes much to two critics of romantic mythography, Harold Bloom and Geoffrey Hartman, who will recognize their influence over points of theory. Jerome Mazzaro, Lawrence Michel, and Michael Murrin all read the more developed drafts of the manuscript. Professors Mazzaro and Michel raised innumerable questions of detail, and guided me through the final, most difficult stages of rewriting and rethinking. Professor Murrin suggested important structural changes in the book as a whole.

It is doubtful whether any serious intellectual activity is possible without a viable climate of cooperative effort. Many fine essays in criticism have devoted attention to Spenser, and in recent years this quantity of work has been remarkable, matched only by its quality. One reason for the heavy annotation in this book is that, without such notes, my dependence upon other scholars, our agreements and disagreements, and my sense that their work needs continuous recognition, would go unrecorded.

During the decade while I worked intermittently on the composition of this book, I was several times given leisure and the material means for research by generous grants from both Columbia University and the State University of New York. Twice the Humanities Council of Columbia University awarded summer grants for research, which helped immensely. A similar grant and further funds for the preparation of the typescript were awarded by the Graduate Research Committee at Buffalo, and to this agency also I wish to extend my gratitude.

I would like also to thank my typist, Mrs. Jean Robinson Baker, who displayed a speed, accuracy, elegance, and interpretive finesse that was nothing short of wondrous. She produced the final typescript under conditions of great pressure and difficulty, and I am most grateful to her for her efforts.

One acknowledgment I have left to the last, because it is inherent in the dedication of *The Prophetic Moment*. Howard Flock, besides clarifying my notions of phophecy, inspired me to attempt a description of the dialectic of justice and time. If there is balance in the judgments of this book, it derives from conversations with him. He has shared the travails of creation with me, and I hope the book reflects at least a measure of his wit and wisdom. The truth is, of course, that the debts of friendship can hardly be expressed in any terms.

PART ONE

I

Introduction

 *he Faerie Queene* IS A PROPHETIC POEM. IN ITS language and its myth, as we should expect with a work of prophecy, it is momentous. By comparison with previous English narrative poems, perhaps even including those of Chaucer and Langland, this epic has unprecedented vocal resonance and visionary radiance. To call it prophetic is to name these qualities and to draw attention to the ways the poet achieves them, through avenues not unexplored by the subsequent three centuries of English romantic poetry. In our own time the reader will recognize Spenserian vestiges in Yeats, Eliot, and Stevens. A prophetic vocation and a prophetic voice have been primary aims of most romantic poets.

Even so, a prophetic interpretation of *The Faerie Queene* requires at least one initial caution. Our terminology, like an old, much varnished portrait, needs cleaning. The modern era, beginning with the sixteenth century, sees the term "prophecy" gradually pick up a connotation which the critic of Spenser will have to reject: the notion that a prophetic utterance gives a sharp, unequivocal vision of the future. Futuristic prophecy aims to predict events. It often singles out a specific date or year when the prediction will come true. Before the event, the sage Regiomontanus selected 1588—the year of the Spanish Armada—as the target of a European catastrophe. This predictive brand of prophecy had always enjoyed a certain notoriety, as today, under the guise of "futurology," it still may do. Nevertheless, it was fundamentally untrue to the major prophetic writings of the West. Spenser himself appears to reject it. He belongs to the broader tradition, which is only partially predictive, a tradition that balances anticipation of the future with a concern for the past and, even more important, for the present.

Spenser accepts the dictum of Saint Paul in the first Epistle to the Corinthians (13:12): the prophet sees "through a glass, darkly," *per speculum in aenigmate*. Truth comes to him only through "obscure presentations."[1] Because he knows in part, he can only prophesy in part. A final apocalyptic light may at the last end all prophetic doubt, but such permanent wisdom is not given to the seer while he lives and prophesies in this uncertain world. Caught in the "now" of this life, he cannot discern the complete pattern of an apocalyptic "then."[2] Instead, the true prophet accepts his limits and works out his own double perspective on life.

1. Donne, in *Sermon XXIII* (folio of 1640) preached at Saint Paul's on Easter Day, 1628: "for here we see God *in speculo*, in a glass, that is, by reflection, and here we know God *in aenigmate*, says our text [I *Corinthians* 13.12], darkly, so we translate it, that is, by obscure presentations, and therefore it is called a knowledge but in part." Later in the same sermon Donne elaborates the metaphor of the world as a cosmic "theatre," to explicate the image of the mirror: "The whole frame of the world is the theatre, and every creature the stage, the medium, the glass in which we may see God." Paul's prophetic ecstasy is identified with the oral rather than visual medium: "not expressed in a *vidit* but an *audivit;* it is not said that he saw but that he heard unspeakable things . . . the ear is the Holy Ghost's first door . . . therefore to hearing does the apostle apply faith." I quote from the text given in A. M. Witherspoon and F. J. Warnke, *Seventeenth-Century Prose and Poetry* (New York, 1963), 78–86.

2. For apocalyptic use of geometrical imagery, see Austin Farrer, *A Rebirth of Images: The Making of St. John's Apocalypse* (London, 1949).

4]

He contemplates the eternal verities of his faith—his moral, political, and religious principles—which remain his standards of truth.
At the same time he observes the tangle of human experience,
which provides the image of a wayfaring life to be directed by his
prophecy. The method of prophecy is to hold the eternal and the
ephemeral in simultaneous copresence, balancing stable principle
against unstable reality.

Prophetic utterance, in this view, is manifested as "historicism."
Visionary as he may be, the prophet lives with the actual deeds of
men and, like the historian, studies, that he may interpret, the
fragmentary, discontinuous, seemingly irrational succession of
these deeds. History is useful and necessary to the prophet because
it presents him with a theoretical wholeness of past, present, and
future. In prophetic hands, however, the three aspects of time con-
dense into a single moment. The prophet thinks in terms of continual emergencies, if not crises, since for him the past and the future are gathered into an overloaded present.

Yet the prophet is not simply a historicist, content to fabricate
a poetic history. A modern scholar has said that to all intents and
purposes Isaiah "must be reckoned a politician," even though from
the modern perspective "his motives and standards clearly mark
him off from the ordinary politician."[3] Whatever his medium of
expression, the prophet is a man of action. As the name prophet,
from *pro-phemi*, implies, he always "speaks out" for something.

3. H. W. Robinson, *Inspiration and Revelation in the Old Testament* (Oxford, 1962), 129. The prophet is detached from his own
word, speaking as "God's mouth" (*Jeremiah* XV. 19). "This detachment also helps to explain the unique position of the prophet in the
political sphere. He is flinging into this realm something quite different from the necessary expediences and compromises of the ordinary
politician, and he is not concerned to show how his own contribution
is to be incorporated with theirs. Yet, at the same time, he is so conscious of the real and effective power of God that he can boldly enter
with his sole weapon into the arena of *Real-politik*. He is ready both
to claim the service of the inferior weapons of the armies of the
world, and to assert a superior power in the word of God which
goes infinitely beyond theirs." Ibid., 171.

He teaches and preaches sublime interpretations of the meaning of life. Yet this grand objective does not become a glorification of the seer himself. He serves a living community, which for him is a just society.

When the prophet is also a poet, or when in any systematic way poetry and prophecy combine forces, the substance of historicism becomes available to the prophet poet. Spenser writes a "famous antique history," as he says, and this history serves the double function of liberating the mind from excessively narrow vision and constraining it within the bounds of fact. History introduces the idea of limit into the heroic quest, by appealing always to what Herodotus called "the memory of the past." The poet's thought flies up, "above the smoke and stir of this dim spot, / Which men call earth," but at this exact moment a sense of fact restrains his flight and saves him from an exaggerated purity.

Centering upon this moment, the prophetic mode of literature employs two great archetypes, the temple and the labyrinth. More specifically, in the romantic tradition of English poetry a dialectic of the temple and the labyrinth enables the poet to develop a mythological grammar, whereby he can combine myths from various matrices in a large, loose, yet harmonious syncretic union. With Edmund Spenser, "the ancestor of this line,"[4] the mythological grammar is ornate and not entirely stable. The critic interested in the style Spenser invented will find that not all analyses of archetypal form exclude considerations of style. Not only do the temple and the labyrinth imply stylistic choices, but their connection with poetic history tempers the allegorical mode and justifies some of the obvious strangeness of the Spenserian style. When Ben Jonson said that Spenser wrote "no language," he was pointing to a marked Spenserian trait, the archaic backward glance of his poetic diction. This archaism seems necessary to the preservation of the temple. On the other side, Spenser adapted the Italian romantic epic, the chief narrative genre of his own period, so that it would carry a heavy allegorical burden. This thematic weighting of romance, while not a Spenserian innovation, per-

---

4. Harold Bloom, *Yeats* (New York, 1970), 109.

mitted oracular extensions of stories which had begun their literary careers in the service of a more simply entertaining mode. Again, while the image of the temple suggests obvious allegorical meanings, the allegorical narrative of *The Faerie Queene* depends for its naturalness on a highly worked imagery of the labyrinth. Such archetypal forms may well not be the end and summation of all that Spenser's poem achieves, but they do appear to be its imaginative source.

The description of any larger literary work inevitably commits the critic to a series of assumptions which he cannot always place directly before his reader. In the present account of *The Faerie Queene*, which sees it as prophetic, historicist, romantic, and deliberately momentous, the assumed background of the poem is a period of rapid intellectual change. If *Paradise Lost* is an epic written in a "scientific age," *The Faerie Queene* is written in a pre- or protoscientific age, when modern science has only started to roll forward.[5] Concepts of truth and error, so important to the prophetic consciousness, are about to undergo profound alterations of philosophical framework.[6] During the period when Spenser writes the climate of metaphysics becomes increasingly psychological. This is apparent even in a literary treatise like the *Apology for Poetry*, where Sidney is defending the poet's creative inspiration—"that high flying liberty of conceit proper to the Poet," which "did seem to have some divine force in it."[7] Sidney knows that there is a certain "superstition" in the ancient use of the *Sortes*

5. Basil Willey, *The Seventeenth Century Background: Studies in the Thought of the Age in Relation to Poetry and Religion* (New York, 1953; Anchor ed.), chap. 10, "The Heroic Poem in a Scientific Age."

6. D. C. Allen, *Doubt's Boundless Sea: Skepticism and Faith in the Renaissance* (Baltimore. 1964). Eugene Rice, *The Renaissance Idea of Wisdom* (Cambridge, Mass., 1958), especially chap. 4, "The Wisdom of Prometheus"; Ernst Cassirer, *The Individual and the Cosmos in Renaissance Philosophy* (New York, 1964), chaps. 3 and 4.

7. "Apologie" (1595), in Smith, *Essays*, 1:154. For Pléiade thinking on this subject, see Grahame Castor, *Pléiade Poetics: A Study in Sixteenth-Century Thought and Terminology* (Cambridge, 1964), chap. 4, "Inspiration, Nature, and Art."

Vergilianae, with its fortune telling trick, but such ancient fancies concern him because they betoken a psychological freedom the poet's wit seems to possess. "What God creates in the world by His thought, man conceives in himself by intellectual act and expresses in language," as Geoffrey Shepherd reminds us, adding that Sidney and Descartes are separated by little more than a generation.[8] Spenser, however, belongs to the period of transition into this new mentalistic framework, and his words are tinged, like those of Sidney, by what Shepherd has called "resonant religious and transcendental overtones."

The strange mixture of the old world and the new which characterizes *The Faerie Queene* will yield some of its secrets to one critical approach, and some to another. In the following pages the reader will discern the influence of various modern critics, whose own words may often be quoted directly, and will notice a dependence on the critical theory of Northrop Frye. My choice of Book V as a primary field of evidence is not accidental. In that book perhaps more than in any other we can observe the dynamic of Spenserian historicism, which has recently been a subject of Harry Berger's programmatic work on "retrospection" and the realization of myth in the Renaissance.[9] In a remarkable series of

---

8. Geoffrey Shepherd, ed., *An Apology for Poetry* (London, 1965), 62. I owe much to the editor's fine introduction and notes. In citations, however, I have used Smith, who keeps the older spelling.

9. "A Secret Discipline: *The Faerie Queene*, Book VI," in *Form and Convention in the Poetry of Edmund Spenser*, ed. William Nelson (New York, 1961); "The Ecology of the Mind," *Review of Metaphysics* 17, no. 1 (1963): 109–34; "The Ecology of the Mind: the Concept of Period Imagination—An Outline Sketch," *Centennial Review* 8 (1964): 409–34; "The Renaissance Imagination: Second World and Green World," *Centennial Review* 9 (1965): 36–78; "L. B. Alberti on Painting: Art and Actuality in Human Perspective," *Centennial Review* 10 (1966): 237–77; "Spenser's *Faerie Queene*, Book I: Prelude to Interpretation," *Southern Review* (University of Adelaide) 2, no. 1 (1966): 18–49; "Archaism, Vision, and Revision: Studies in Virgil, Plato, and Milton," *Centennial Review* 11 (1967): 24–52; "Ecology of the Medieval Imagination: an Introductory Overview," *Centennial*

essays Professor Berger has analyzed the backward gaze of the prophetic mind, which, since Spenser has an archaizing imagination, provides one key to a valid reading of *The Faerie Queene*. The reader wishing a detailed iconographic analysis of Book V is also fortunate in having two recent monographs on the Legend of Justice: T. K. Dunseath's *Spenser's Allegory of Justice in Book V of the Faerie Queene* and Jane Aptekar's *Icons of Justice: Iconography and Thematic Imagery in Book V of The Faerie Queene*. These two studies have corrected the balance of critical interest by showing that, repelled though the reader may be by some of Spenser's political views, the poetry of the fifth book is far more rich and expert than is commonly thought. As to the specifically prophetic aspect of *The Faerie Queene*, the present work finds support in *The Veil of Allegory*, by Michael Murrin. Professor Murrin has drawn attention to the elitist origins of allegory and the "oral" mode of eloquence by which prophecy redeems that elitism.

The climate of any historical interpretation is double: it derives partly from the critic's world and partly that of his subject. Thus, although Spenserian myth is my subject, I should add that the twentieth century has been no stranger to the archetypes of temple and labyrinth. These figures of thought have acquired almost obsessive force during the period which includes the work of Proust, Mann, Kafka, Yeats, Valéry, Eliot, and Stevens. Many recent authors have, in the manner of Borges, Robbe-Grillet, or Golding, envisioned the change of the temple into the labyrinth, the continuous and often reversible metamorphosis of the shrine into the

---

Review 12 (1968): 279–313; "Two Spenserian Retrospects: The Antique Temple of Venus and the Primitive Marriage of Rivers," *Texas Studies in Literature and Language* 10, no. 1 (1968): 5–25; "The Spenserian Dynamics," *Studies in English Literature* 8, no. 1 (1968): 1–18; "*The Mutabilitie Cantos:* Archaism and Evolution in Retrospect," in *Spenser: A Collection of Critical Essays*, ed. Harry Berger, Jr. (Englewood Cliffs, 1968), 146–76; see also Berger's Introduction to that volume, with his related article, "Poetry as Revision: Interpreting Robert Frost," *Criticism* 10, no. 1 (1968): 1–22.

"circular ruins." Within the English poetic tradition Spenser stands at the beginning of this movement toward a completely ambivalent visionary style. If there is a modern poet who has all the power of the Spenserian vision, it would be Yeats, the poet of the tower, the star-lit dome, and the winding gyre. If there is a modern poet with whom the Spenserian archetypes retain their clarity, their allegorical distinctness, it might be Eliot, who, as a critic, once dubbed Spenser "the master of everybody." Eliot's poetry assumed and assimilated what appears to be an orthodox reading of Spenser. It is important to remember, therefore, that some of the chief romantic inheritors of Spenser would file a dissenting report. This regretful critical opinion, shared by Shelley and Yeats, and perhaps by Blake, holds that Spenser failed to free himself in his prophetic calling, despite a continuous drive toward this freedom. Such romantic poets, so close to Spenser in spirit, did, however, recognize that in his great moments he was a true prophet.

The materials presented in chapters 4, 5, and 6 are those most problematic for the separation of true and false prophecy in Spenser. By looking rather closely at the Legend of Justice, I have tried to show how "timeless" archetypes can accept the burden of the past. To analyze the time-binding of the timeless mythic pattern, these final chapters document the theoretical view of Spenser's prophetic historicism which is presented in chapters 2 and 3.

II

The Prophetic Moment

 S THE AUTHOR OF A ROMANTIC EPIC IN WHICH, AS Richard Hurd claimed in the *Letters on Chivalry and Romance*, a complex design orders an even more complex action,[1] Spenser depends heavily on two cardinal images for his prophetic structure: the temple and the labyrinth. These two archetypes organize the overall shaping of *The Faerie Queene*, and while other archetypal

1. "It is an unity of *design*, and not of action. This Gothic method of design in poetry may be, in some sort, illustrated by what is called the Gothic method of design in gardening"—a view which bears directly on the present concern with the maze. Hurd's criticism perhaps inaugurates the line of thought which culminates in Tuve and Alpers, the former with her theory of Spenserian *entrelacement* (*Allegorical Imagery* [Princeton, 1966], 359–70), the latter with his method of "reading" *FQ*, by stressing its "rhetorical" and formulaic character. Further, it may be useful to notice that critics like Tuve and Alpers are particularly expert in the exegesis of the Spenserian labyrinth, and in this respect their work contrasts with those who are biased toward a "templar" exegesis, for example Frye, Fowler, or even perhaps Nelson. The reader will find selections from a wide range of critics, including those mentioned above, in Paul Alpers, ed., *Edmund Spenser: A Critical Anthology* (Penguin ed., 1969).

images play a part throughout the poem, the temple and the labyrinth, as "poetic universals," are sufficiently large and powerful images to organize an immense variety of secondary imagery, leading thereby to an equally varied narrative.

Temples and labyrinths have a singular advantage to the poet, in that they both imply special layout and a typical activity within that layout. Furthermore, while both images suggest man-made structures—men have built temples and labyrinths—they each have a set of natural equivalents. Temples may rise out of the earth in the form of sacred groves, while labyrinths may grow up as a tangle of vegetation. The cardinal dichotomy of the two archetypes will permit the typical Renaissance interplay of art and nature. For both images the idea of design is crucial, and their stress on pattern as such gives Spenser's intricate poem a certain stability.

Yet design itself may play an ambiguous role when the two great images are set in counterpoint against each other, because whereas the image of a temple is strictly formalized, to frame the highest degree of order, the idea of a labyrinth leads in the opposite direction. The labyrinth allows a place, and would appear to create a structure, for the notable indeterminacy of the textural surface of *The Faerie Queene*. Labyrinthine imageries and actions yield "the appearance, so necessary to the poem's quality, of pathless wandering," which, as Lewis continued, "is largely a work of deliberate and successful illusion."[2]

The image of the temple is probably the dominant recurring archetype in *The Faerie Queene*. Major visions in each of the six books are presented as temples: the House of Holiness, the Castle of Alma, the Garden of Adonis, the Temple of Venus, the Temple of Isis, the sacred round-dance on the top of Mount Acidale. Even the Mutabilitie Cantos display this "symbolism of the center," as the trial convenes at the pastoral *templum* of Diana, Arlo Hill. In many respects the chief allegorical problems of each book can

2. C. S. Lewis, *English Literature in the Sixteenth Century* (Oxford, 1954), 381.

most easily be unwrapped if the reader attends closely to the iconography of such temples, and for that reason Lewis referred to them as "allegorical cores," while Frye calls them "houses of recognition."[3]

Together the temple and the labyrinth encompass the archetypal universe of *The Faerie Queene* and in that sense their meaning is more than allegorical. It is a narrative reality within the epic. Heroes come to temples, which they may enter and leave, and they pass through a labyrinthine faerieland. This archetypal scene of heroic action is not Spenser's own invention, though he develops it with great ingenuity. As Frye argued in the *Anatomy of Criticism*, apocalyptic and demonic imagery polarize the structures of a truly vast number of literary works.[4] On the other hand, for English poetry *The Faerie Queene* occupies a special place, since it is the "wel-head" of English romantic vision. Since it is romance, and not pure myth, it modulates the images of shrine and maze, to fit the scheme of romantic *entrelacement* and its chivalric manner.

In essence the temple is the image of gratified desire, the labyrinth the image of terror and panic. While in its originating form myth is "undisplaced," here the images of temple and labyrinth may be rendered in a more "realistic" or romantic guise, so that, for example, the purity of the temple is represented as the chivalric equivalent, a noble and chaste prowess. Spenser "romanticizes" the apocalyptic temple. Similarly he romanticizes the de-

3. Lewis's habitual epithet, "allegorical core," is from medieval exegesis. Frye suggests that recognition scenes in this vein are the culmination, as with Shakespearian romance, of an educational art in which "providential resolution" is a kind of knowing, re-cognizing. See "The Structure of Imagery in *The Faerie Queene*," in *Fables of Identity* (New York, 1963), 77 and 109. In the same context Berger would speak of an Orphic myth of re-flection, which he has analyzed in depth as the idea of a "retrospect." Memory plays a key role, therefore, in the critiques of Lewis, Frye, and Berger.

4. Frye sets forth the polarity of temple and its opposite, the demonic labyrinth, with their analogical parallels in romantic, realistic and ironic literature, in his "Theory of Archetypal Imagery," in *Anatomy of Criticism* (Princeton, 1957), 141–58.

monic labyrinth, which he does not hesitate to represent in undisplaced myth, as a twining monster or shape-shifting demon, but which he more often displaces into more romantic forms which better suit the romantic level of his mythography.

The archetypal and the displaced treatment of the temple and the labyrinth lead to a rich tapestry. Critics have done much to illuminate the interaction of the two archetypes, but in the following account I shall try chiefly to bring out the fact that when the dichotomy is narrowed, or forced into visionary union, prophecy results. This vatic nexus will be seen to imply a mode of visionary history, which keeps *The Faerie Queene* close to reality even when it seems to be reaching out to a distant world of spirit.

The Temple

A *templum* IS A SACRED, SEPARATED space. It may assume various geometric outlines (four- or five-sided, for example), but ideally it is round. The circularity of the horizon is borrowed, to create the archetypal form of the shrine: "*templum* designates the spatial, *tempus* the temporal aspect of the motion of the horizon in space and time."[5] Within the temple space is said to

---

5. Mircea Eliade, *The Sacred and the Profane* (New York, 1959), 75. Eric Partridge, *Origins* (New York, 1958), 701*b*, associates *templum* with GK *temnein* and thence the Homeric *temenos*, "a piece of land cut off, assigned as a domain to kings and chiefs" and "a piece of land dedicated to a god, the sacred precincts," (Liddell and Scott, *Greek-English Lexicon*). The sacred valley of the Nile and the Acropolis are both referred to in ancient authors as *temenoi*. English "shrine" seems connected to Latin *circus*, and hence Eng. circle (Partridge, *Origins*, 620*a*). Here the originating idea seems to be that of the ring, in view of which, consider Wagner's *magnum opus*. The human body may also be conceived as a self-contained, isolating unity, which, however, is mortal. Thus, in *Death's Duel*, Donne: "Even those bodies that were the temples of the Holy Ghost come to this dilapidation, to ruin, to rubbish, to dust . . . such are the revolutions of the grave." Cf. *Comus*, 461: "the unpolluted temple of the mind."

become "sacred space," or "hallowed ground." One result of the establishment of the sacred space of the temple is that man can thereby exclude the profane world. Generally, in its extreme form, this is an exclusion of chaos. Thus the temple is always a microcosm, or, in the case of a city like ancient Rome, a *mundus*—a cosmos marked out by a sacred line dug or drawn around the edges of the city, within which all is ordered and theoretically indestructible.

The temple, like any major archetype, has a rich iconography. Drawn out of nature and reflecting the original creative powers of God, the temple may be an enclosed garden, a sacred grove of trees, a sacred mountain top, or any other natural eminence. Book I, Canto X of *The Faerie Queene* shows the Redcrosse Knight led to the summit of "the highest mount" after he has done penance in the House of Holiness. There an old man named Heavenly Contemplation shows the knight a vision of the ultimate temple, the City of the New Jerusalem. The quality of sacred centeredness strengthens when the poet, in an aside, compares the "highest mount" with the three other sacred mountains essential to Spenserian myth, Mount Sinai, the Mount of Olives,

> . . . that sacred hill whose head full hie,
> Adorned with fruitfull Olives all arownd,
> Is, as it were for endlesse memory
> Of that deare Lord, who ofte thereon was fownd,
> For ever with a flowring girlond crownd,

and thirdly Mount Parnassus, "on which the thrise three learned Ladies play / Their heavenly notes." The knowledge gained from such a vantage point is too dazzling for mortal eyes, and when Redcrosse comes away from it, he cannot see: "dazed were his eyne, / Through passing brightnesse."

The sacred mountain finds a Renaissance imitation in the works of artful gardeners who, not content with planting gardens, trees and shrubbery, raise at the center of the planting a "mount," an artificial eminence capped, like Belphoebe's "stately theatre," with a pavilion or summer house. In poetry the Ovidian genre of the erotic epyllion gives a free play to such fancies, perhaps most richly exemplified in Drayton's image of Diana's paradise, atop Mount Latmus, in *Endimion and Phoebe*. Drayton first elaborates on the "stately grove" climbing the sides of the mountain, calling it, at one point, a "stately gallery." Though its trees are in the traditional Ovidian order of a catalogue, the grove is also watered by "straying channels dauncing sundry wayes, / With often turnes, like to a curious Maze." Then above the grove there rise steps, or "degrees" of "milk-white Marble," and finally "Upon the top, a Paradise was found." The natural paradise is a model of articulate form. The same tendency toward hierarchic structure appears in the artificial *templum*.

Architecturally the temple may be a palace, a church, a tabernacle, a shrine, a sanctuary, any sacred building built on the plan of a *mundus*. While perhaps originally all such buildings were approximations of the circle, their imaginative extension took innumerable forms in later historical development: the spiral, the square, the polyhedral, the cube, the pyramid, the cross, and so on.[6] Sometimes temples and castles are confused, and for the trench or wall of the *mundus* there is exchanged a "moat defensive." Sometimes, on the model of the Eternal City, the *templum* expands to become a large and complicated urban structure, *urbs* being the microcosmic form of the celestial *orb*.[7] Or, turning back from large to small, the whole vast macrocosm can be reduced to a

6. E.g., the Escorial, on which see René Taylor, "Architecture and Magic: Considerations on the *Idea* of the Escorial," in *Essays in the History of Architecture Presented to Rudolf Wittkower*, ed., Douglas Fraser, Howard Hibbard, and M. J. Lewine (London, 1967), 81–109.

7. The regalia reduce the celestial orb to a microcosmic symbol; Christian kings put a cross on top of the orb, to symbolize the sacred unity of their kingdoms. The reader interested in the further study of the orbic myth should consult J. L. Borges, *Labyrinths* (New York, 1964; also, Penguin ed., 1970), where he may conveniently begin with the "The Library of Babel," which begins with the sentence: "The universe (which others call the Library) is composed of an indefinite perhaps infinite number of hexagonal galleries, with vast air shafts be-

miniature of itself, first to an emblematic shield, like those of Achilles or Aeneas in the *Iliad* and *Aeneid*, then, even smaller, to a sacred *nodus* or knot.[8] The range of magnitude is truly enormous. It may stretch from Herrick's amber bead ("The urn was little, but the room / More rich than Cleopatra's tomb") to the universe itself—"the temple represents the image of the world."[9] John of Gaunt's prophecy in *Richard II* makes the whole realm of England into a temple.

Experientially the temple provides the perfect model for the creation of a home. As such the temple is the resting place of man, the center, the *omphalos*, of his world. The hieratic center of this central place is the hearth fire. The temple is the house of life.

In stressing the vital radiance of the templar form, we should not forget what may be the more basic fact, that through the vision of the temple the hero finds a place, as distinct from the indefinable

---

tween, surrounded by very low railings." See, for similar materials, E. R. Curtius, *European Literature in the Latin Middle Ages* (New York, 1953), ch. 16, "The Book as Symbol;" Arnold van Gennep, *The Semi-Scholars* (London, 1967), tr. by Rodney Needham, chap. 7, "Macl: or, The Complete Epigraphy."

8. Cf. my *Allegory*, 214–19. On the Renaissance symbolism of knots, Edgar Wind, *Pagan Mysteries in the Renaissance* (Peregrine ed., revised, 1967), 38, 89, 118–27, 206, where knotting creates the mazes of the daedalian dance, as in Jonson's *Pleasure Reconciled to Virtue*. The opposite of this labyrinthine knotting exists: e.g., Titian's "The Three Philosophers," where the unification of heaven and earthly reality is symbolized by the knotted belt of the true, middle-placed sage. See Edgar Wind, *Giorgione's Tempesta, with Comments on Giorgione's Poetic Allegories* (Oxford, 1969), 6 and 28–29.

9. Eliade, *Sacred and Profane*, 73. See also 47: the city as cosmos. "The Roman *mundus* was a circular trench divided into four parts; it was at once the image of the cosmos and the paradigmatic model for human habitation. . . . The *mundus* was clearly assimilated to the *omphalos*, to the navel of the earth; the city (*urbs*) was situated in the middle of the *orbis terrarum*. Similar ideas have been shown to explain the structure of Germanic villages and towns. In extremely varied cultural contexts, we constantly find the same cosmological scheme and the same ritual scenario: *settling in a territory is equivalent to founding a world*."

and largely empty space which is excluded by the *mundus*. Among the various attributes of the temple, it may be used to emphasize the concept of limit, edge, margin, boundary or closure. Not only does each *templum* have set boundaries, closing it off from the profane empty space, but it also will usually have reticulated subdivisions which, like the interior arrangement of a cathedral or like the Stations of the Cross, permit secondary closures within the larger closure of the whole templar cosmos. Closure is present at all levels of templar form. Within the Spenserian Garden of Adonis, a true *hortus conclusus*, the "seminal reasons" are sown in distinct orders: "And every sort is in a sundry bed / Set by it Selfe, and ranckt in comely rew." *The Garden of Cyrus* (1658) perhaps marks the culmination of what Browne himself called "inexcusable Pythagorisme," but we should note that its principal method is the analysis of the "net-work plantation" into its mirroring subsections, until the whole templar form of the garden yields a "law of reflexion."[10] During the Renaissance and Baroque periods, Browne and others like him are not so much eccentrics, as extremists in a profession of mystical "analysis" and anatomizing which is in fact a widely common practice. Closure is structurally powerful here, even though the simple outside wall of the temple is suggestively complicated (reticulated) by the intricacy of innumerable inner walls.

Among Spenserian examples the House of Alma may best illustrate this reticulation of the templar form, and it readily suggests the sort of action that typifies the templar scene. Whatever happens to Sir Guyon when he enters this shrine, the structure itself is guarded and tended by ministers of a cult. Their guardianship is an integral aspect of the structure, so that when, in the allegory of the digestive system, there is a "stately hall," there is also a ministering steward, Diet, who takes charge of the menu, while a

---

10. Sir Thomas Browne, *The Garden of Cyrus, Or, The Quincunciall, Lozenge, or Net-Work Plantations of the Ancients, Artificially, Naturally, Mystically Considered*, in *Religio Medici and Other Works*, ed. by L. C. Martin (Oxford, 1964), 167 and 169.

maître d'hôtel, Appetite, walks up and down, bestowing "both guests and meat." With its complete and also comical ordering of its mythic materials, this temple is indeed a "goodly frame of temperance." Similarly with other temples, we find that structure implies a ministry of some kind. When Redcrosse does penance, he is helped or instructed by the servants of the House of Holiness, its angelic ministers. Faith, Hope, and Charity guide and support the hero's confirmation in the sacramental role of *microchristus*. From them and from their temple he acquires the sanctity that will make him Saint George of Merry England.

Because such a strong sense of ritual informs the life of the temple, it is important, with Spenser, not to identify the high degree of structure with a merely external cult. Spenser is a Reformation poet, and during this period the Christian frame of reference alters, bringing the Church and its authority into a closer union with the self of man. By reducing the legitimate scope of the *ecclesia* in its secular establishment, the Reformation opened the way to what must have seemed a new and radically *expanded* individual selfhood. The externally visible temple of Mother Church and her institutionalized cult is in part replaced by an interior shrine, whose great monument in English poetry comes after Spenser, in *The Temple* of George Herbert. The range of human action occurring outside the temple may have seemed to the pious Catholic to have greatly extended, to his distress. The Protestant poet (and later the Counterreformation poet, as a kind of orthodox Protestant) would insist, on the other hand, that by interiorizing his faith he had made it much finer. Herbert's poem "The Window" catches this exalted and expanded sense of a redeeming selfhood.

> Yet in thy temple thou dost him afford
> This glorious and transcendent place,
> To be a window, through thy grace.

Windows open out onto a scene, allowing light to pass through. Rivalries of faith and works cannot obscure the abiding reality of the cardinal image itself: the temple is a place of enlightenment. Argument then follows only over the mystical place and placement of the temple. Its essence remains unchanged, even in Reformation imagery, though it now has a new relation to human consciousness.

Enlightenment is an almost magical access to the truth, and in the temple the ritual ministrations of the priest and beadman, guardian and servant, create an expectant air of teleological form. Every temple subordinates its own rather rigid structure to the promise of a lively flow of energy. This promise it embodies in ceremonial festivity. Thus Herbert, for example, ends *The Temple* with the image of the love feast: "So I did sit and eat." We find that templar rituals often culminate in a ceremony of truth. It has the effect of binding the hero to a fortunate, if strenuous destiny. It may take many forms, but all are types of betrothal, of the kind that inspired Spenser in his two marriage odes, both of which, we might add, display the templar aspiration in their stanzaic forms. The "arithmological stanza" (II, ix, 22) reduces the marriage trope to its absolute microcosm, by fusing masculine and feminine principles in the one theoretical frame of the human body—"O work divine." The conclusion to Book I establishes the ceremony of truth within the narrative form of the whole epic: "Fair Una to the Red Cross Knight / Betrothed is with joy." Truth in the Spenserian setting is always a consequence of betrothal, and at the moment of most intense vision truth *is* betrothal, not merely its consequent.[11] Truth and troth meet at the restoration of Eden, and their meeting generalizes to the scope of a national drama when the monarch, as in Book V, undertakes to protect and judge her people.

Prophecy requires the verbal or visionary expression of this contractual trust based on a betrothal. Because the betrothal is

11. Alexander Welsh, "The Allegory of Truth in English Fiction," *Victorian Studies*, Sept. 1965, 7–28. Noting that OE *triewe*, *treowe* means primarily loyalty or good faith, Welsh quotes the Lockean definition of truth: "the joining or separating of signs, as the things signified by them do agree or disagree with one another."

truly mutual, it accords with the dictates of conscience and it expresses the conscious choice, the deliberate wish, of the parties to the marriage. By its ceremonies of truth the prophetic poem shows that human bonds—the "bonds of society"—will have generative power. Troth is blessed by the benign providence of a higher favoring Being. This favor appears gratuitously in the pleasures of the season, the warmth, light and songs of springtime, the festivity and dancing of a harvest home.

The temporal connotations of the original Latin *templum* suggest this holiday air. Through its roots *templum* grows into a cluster of related terms, "temper," "temperate," and "contemplate" (with their antitype, the "tempest"). The temporal property of the temple resides in the fact that, within it, time, as well as space, is sacred.[12] Thus the name for temple crosses back and forth between the two dimensions of time and space. Spatially the temple breaks into and organizes the endless extension of the labyrinth. Temporally it arrests the ordinary unbroken duration of temporal flow. Inside the temple time shares with space the immutable closure of the perfect circle.

Religious vision sees the temple permitting a perfected symbolic action, as man engages in the ancient rituals of his faith, so that life takes on holiness with the church walls. This we can test easily enough—the feeling of both space and time, when we enter the shrine, is one of removal from the ordinary world we live in, into a life beyond the clock and the marketplace. The

12. Mircea Eliade, *Cosmos and History* [originally published as *The Myth of the Eternal Return*] (New York, 1959), 12–17; *Patterns in Comparative Religion* (New York, 1963), 367–409; Leo Spitzer, *Classical and Christian Ideas of World Harmony: Prolegomena to an Interpretation of the Word "Stimmung"* (Baltimore, 1963), 80–107; Lord Raglan, *The Temple and the House* (New York, 1964), 147–58; Rudolf Wittkower, *Architectural Principles in the Age of Humanism* (New York, 1965), passim. On gothic "aedicular" articulations, away from the round, see John Summerson, *Heavenly Mansions and other Essays on Architecture* (New York, 1963), 1–28, and 203: "Monumentality begins . . . with the temple."

temple is quiet, if not silent. Its perfect song is the Sanctus. It gets its temporal name from the fact that a given ground may be chosen, cut off, structured and consecrated in such fashion that through a sacred blessing (a logos) man isolates time, which then acquires a dimension of stillness.[13] The temple is the still point of the turning world.

Action here is bound to be largely symbolic, as in the Mass. Once within the sacred confines of the church, man is free to reenact the symbolic myths of origin from which his faith springs. Thus the Christian communion reenacts the first giving of the sacrament. (Repetition plays a central role in this, and we find that drama itself seems to have been born in the temple.) The principles enunciated by the inner forms of the templar structure, the "articles of faith," the mysteries of the faith, tend to be associated with the immemorially distant beginnings of a spiritual history. To derive his unchanging principles man goes back to the stage of "once upon a time," *in illo tempore*. Having done so, he can then build up a system of liturgical repetitions of that *arche*, the archetypal beginning. To reinforce the periodic aspect of time in the temple, most religions celebrate hierophanic rituals arranged according to the forms of the liturgical year. The experience of these recurrent rituals (the Easter Week services, for example) collapses ordinary time. The believer feels himself caught up in an "eternal present," a fulfilling contemporaneity.[14] The phenomenology of

13. On Augustinian "space of time," Kenneth Burke, *The Rhetoric of Religion* (Boston, 1961), 154; also, with the works of Georges Poulet, Gaston Berger, "A Phenomenological Approach to the Problem of Time," trans. and ed. Daniel O'Connor, in *Readings in Existential Phenomenology* (Englewood Cliffs, 1967).

14. The philosophical basis for a templar iconography thus is given in Hegel, *Preface to the Phenomenology* III.3, in *Hegel: Texts and Commentary*, trans. and ed. Walter Kaufmann (New York, 1965; Anchor ed.), 70–71: "Philosophy, on the other hand, considers not the inessential determination but the determination insofar as it is essential. Not the abstract or unactual as its element and contents but the actual, that which posits itself and lives in itself, existence in its Concept. It is the process that generates and runs through its moments, and this whole

this collapsed time is entirely paradoxical—emptied of business, it is full; quieted and stilled, it is a breathing, hovering kind of time, the hierophany of stillness in motion.

---

movement constitutes the positive and its truth. This truth, then, includes the negative as well—that which might be called the false if it could be considered as something from which one should abstract. The evanescent must, however, be considered essential—not in the determination of something fixed that is to be severed from the true and left lying outside it, one does not know where; nor does the true rest on the other side, dead and positive. The appearance is the coming to be and passing away that itself does not come to be or pass away; it is in itself and constitutes the actuality and the movement of the life of the truth. The true is thus the bacchanalian whirl in which no member is not drunken; and because each, as soon as it detaches itself, dissolves immediately—the whirl is just as much transparent and simple repose. In the court of justice of this movement, to be sure, the individual forms of the spirit endure no more than determinate thoughts do, yet they are just as much positive and necessary moments as they are negative and evanescent. In the whole of the movement, considering it as repose, that which distinguishes itself in it and gives particular existence is preserved as something that remembers, and its existence is knowledge of itself even as this knowledge is just as immediately existence." (See the fine note of Kaufmann on the "dionysian whirl.") Behind Hegel stand legions of poets, for whom his "court of justice" is an imaginative construct. Harry Berger has shown how this construct appears in the Renaissance. See, with his article on Alberti (chap. 1, n. 8, above): "Introduction," *Spenser: A Collection of Critical Essays*, 4: "The notion of an ideal place or 'space' artificially prepared and rigorously bounded off from actuality, a place where the mind may project its revised and corrected images of experience and where the soul may test and enlarge itself—such a notion lies at the roots of a variety of phenomena identified with the renaissance enterprise. Among them are the theory of perspective in art, the gradual return to the Neoplatonic enhancement of this idea in various descriptions of the diversified unity of the godlike poet's creation, the development of a pastoral as a simplified and experimental play world, and the corresponding development in scientific thought of the idea of experimental method in connection with the idea of a closed world, that is, a specially controlled environment into which the experimenter temporarily has withdrawn."

The Labyrinth

THE OPPOSITE OF the ideal templar form is the "perplexed circle" which a metaphysical poet, Henry King, described in his poem "The Labyrinth."[15]

> Life is a crooked Labyrinth, and wee
> Are dayly lost in that Obliquity.
> 'Tis a perplexed Circle, in whose round
> Nothing but Sorrowes and new Sins abound.

Christian dogma blamed this bewilderment on a blindness beginning with the Fall. Thus Ralegh's *History of the World* speaks of men who, having "fallen away from undoubted truth, do then after wander for evermore in vices unknown."[16] Orthodoxy held that Christ alone could save men from this "home-bred tyranny."

> Thou canst reverse this Labyrinth of Sinne
> My wild Affects and Actions wander in.

Beginning his epic with a Christian version of the classical *in medias res*, Spenser makes a labyrinth crucial to the first episode of *The Faerie Queene*. Redcrosse, the Lady Una, and the Dwarf are caught by a "hideous storme of raine," a tempest, as Spenser twice calls it.

> Enforst to seeke some covert nigh at hand,
>   A shadie grove not far away they spide,
>   That promist ayde the tempest to withstand:
>   Whose loftie trees yclad with sommers pride,

15. *The Poems of Henry King*, ed. Margaret Crum (Oxford, 1965), 173.

16. Sir Walter Ralegh, *The History of the World*, chap. VI, sec. iii (1621 ed.), quoted from Witherspoon and Warnke, *Seventeenth-Century Prose and Poetry*, 26.

24]

> Did spred so broad, that heavens light did hide,
> Not perceable with power of any starre:
> And all within were pathes and alleies wide,
> With footing worne, and leading inward farre:
> Faire harbour that them seemes; so in they entred arre.

> And forth they passe, with pleasure forward led,
> Joying to heare the birdes sweete harmony,
> Which therein shrouded from the tempest dred,
> Seemd in their song to scorne the cruell sky.
>
> (I, i, 7 and 8)

There follows the famous Ovidian catalogue of trees, each given its proper use and therefore brought into line with a human culture. The catalogue is an epitome of order and syntax, and Spenser projects its systematic character by a strict procession of anaphoras and exemplary appositives. If we were not alerted to the overtones of "loftie" and "sommers pride," the rich leafage darkening the light of heaven, we might notice nothing untoward until the last line of the catalogue: "the maple seldom inward sound." Otherwise this would appear a fine plantation. If the forest misleads, it does so in spite of something the travelers can praise, that is, in spite of its mere *nature*. Spenser, however, is playing on the old proverb about not being able to see the forest for the trees. His exceedingly strict stanzaic game disguises the spiritual danger inherent in the darkness of the forest, the *selva oscura*. Instead the stanza becomes an agency in the deception, providing a fine instance, I would think, of the "rhetorical" function of verbal formulas, which Paul Alpers has recently stressed in *The Poetry of "The Faerie Queene."* The deception is gradual.

> Led with delight, they thus beguile the way,
> Untill the blustring storme is overblowne;
> When weening to returne, whence they did stray,
> They cannot finde that path, which first was showne,

But wander to and fro in wayes unknowne,
Furthest from end then, when they neerest weene,
That makes them doubt, their wits be not their owne:
So many pathes, so many turnings seene,
That which of them to take, in diverse doubt they been.

At last resolving forward still to fare,
Till that some end they finde or in or out,
That path they take, that beaten seemd most bare,
And like to lead the labyrinth about;
Which when by tract they hunted had throughout,
At length it brought them to a hollow cave,
Amid the thickest woods.

(I, i, 10 and 11)

Una, the embodiment of Truth, at once recognizes the labyrinth
for what it is: "This is the wandring wood, this *Errours* den, / A
monster vile, whom God and man does hate." The turbulence of
the "hideous storme of raine" persists in the description of the
monster Errour. Like the tempest that wrapped itself around the
travelers, the dragon would surround them in natural or unnatural
fury.[17] Spenser gains something at once by making his first antagonist a dragon whose "huge long taile" is a grotesque incarnation
of the twists and turns of the maze: "God helpe the man so wrapt
in *Errours* endlesse traine." Errour can so tie herself in knots that
she creates her own "desert darknesse."

17. The tempest is emblematically associated with Fortuna, as
chance events are the maze-happenings. Donne plays with this idea in
"The Storm" and "The Calm." As demonic parody of the temple, the
tempest (Spenser's "hideous storme") creates its opposite, the calm of
the shrine. *The Tempest* thus shows, in the Boatswain's phrase, how
men "assist the storm." The entrance of Master and Boatswain in act V,
i, 216 ff. prepares us for Alonzo's final admission:

This is as strange a maze as e'er men trod,
And there is in this business more than nature
Was ever conduct of. Some oracle
Must rectify our knowledge.

The encounter with the dragon links the ideas of error and wandering, suddenly fixing the malevolent aspect of the maze. This forest is ominous, threatening, and should produce a wise, dwarfish panic. Seen in this light the labyrinth is a purely demonic image, the natural cause of terror. So strong is the aftertaste of this terror that the reader may at once forget how pleasantly the forest had beguiled the unwary travelers. This is our first introduction to an ambivalence that colors almost every episode in the poem. As to the baffling form of the maze there can be no doubt, once one is "in" it. Though all avenues are promising, none ever gets anywhere. While some winding passages enter upon others, those others turn into dead ends, or twist back to return the seeker to his starting point. In the garden of forking paths an opening is often the barrier to an openness.

The artist of the maze may, reversing the idea of a temple, grow high and formal walls of hedge, or he may baffle the quester by thickening and complicating a natural outgrowth of trees, plants, rocks or streams. Spenser is aware of both the artificial and the natural maze, both of which are models in *The Faerie Queene* for a rich iconography of motion. The sinuous lines of the maze can be reduced to a mythic essence, with such characters as Pyrochles or Cymochles, whose names and behavior imply the motion of waves and furious, redundant turbulence. (This Milton later chose as a metonymy for both Eve and Satan.) More largely, when the maze provides a perverse map, the hero finds himself following the antitype of the direct and narrow "way" of salvation. In the phrase of Spenser's early *Tears of the Muses*, the blinded hero deserves Urania's complaint, since he has gone astray: "Then wandreth he in error and in doubt." Even Truth itself, as Una, is forced to wander.

> Now when broad day the world discovered has,
>> Up *Una* rose, up rose the Lyon eke,
>> And on their former journey forward pas,
>> In wayes unknowne, her wandring knight to seeke,
>> With paines farre passing that long wandring *Greeke*,

That for his love refused deitie:
Such were the labours of this Lady meeke,
Still seeking him, that from her still did flie,
Then furthest from her hope, when most she weened nie.

(I, iii, 21)

The allusion to Odysseus sets two kinds of wandering against each other, the erroneous wandering of Redcrosse against the "true" wandering of Una, who is patterned partly on the hero who refused immortal life with Calypso ("the hider"). The *Odyssey*, with its inset tales of utopian vision, joins the idea of wandering with the idea of a finally targeted quest, the return home. Thus wandering may satisfy a benign form of nostalgia.

More usually Spenser associates the state of wandering with the idea of blank extension—words that typically accompany wandering are "wide," "deep," "long," and "endless." Wandering may also be "vain." To wander is to live in a state of continuous becoming (if such a paradox can be imagined), so that Spenser keeps errantry and error in process, by preferring the present participle, "wandering," to other grammatical forms.[18] Like Hob-

18. In "Milton's Participial Style," *PMLA* 83, no. 5 (1968): 1386–99, Seymour Chatman shows that older poets, among them Marlowe, Shakespeare, and Spenser, preferred the present participle to the past, while Milton's marked preference for the past participle creates effects of finality, absolute loss, etc., in *Paradise Lost*. The general principle of participial usage applies to Spenser: ". . . participles are derived from underlying complete sentences, including the subjects, even when subject-deletion has taken place; and . . . more than any other parts of speech, the participles are characteristically subject to ambiguity of interpretation" (1386–87). Thus Josephine Miles, in *Eras and Modes in English Poetry* (Berkeley, 1964), 15: "But Biblical richness and the Platonic tradition early offered to such poets as Spenser and Sylvester, and then Milton, the idea of a poetic language as free as possible from clausal complication, as resilient as possible in richly descriptive participial suspension." Not all of Miss Miles's "signs of such a mode" are to be found in Spenser, but the participial is very much there. On sentence structure in Spenser, see Paul Alpers, *The*

binol in the June Eclogue, the hero suffers from a "wandring mynde," and he must govern his "wandering eyes." The strange and the monstrous, like blindness and vanity, are further associations of the image of errantry, and it is not long before the reader forges a yet larger associative link with this wandering motif: resemblances met in this meandering life often strike the hero as uncanny, *unheimlich*.

By dramatizing the "image of lost direction," as Frye has named this archetypal cluster, Spenser is following long centuries of traditional iconography. Besides the dense forest, where the labyrinth is all tangle, mythology can pursue this sinister logic to its conclusion, where it discovers the image Eliot used for his microcosmic epic of the modern world, the wasteland. If the labyrinth is the archetypal order of things outside the temple, if it is the basic image of profane space, then its form is to be defined not so much as a material setting (trees, rocks, streams, etc.) as a general condition of unmapped disorder. The poet born into a Christian world will often suggest that outside the temple lies the desert, the place of inevitable wandering. Without a guide, like a Guyon without his Palmer, man appears destined to wander forever. In the desert he may die horribly, alone, or he may fade away in gradual exhaustion. The wasteland is an unmarked wilderness. The Children of Israel would surely have been lost but that "the Lord went before them by day in a pillar of a cloud, to lead them the way; and by night in a pillar of fire, to give them light; to go by day and night." Without such signs a man deserted cannot choose but lose his way, and wandering becomes his destiny.

Poetry of The Faerie Queene (Princeton, 1969), 74–94. Alpers does not stress the controlling function of the present participle; in general he agrees with Empson that Spenser engages in deliberate syntactic mystification. H. W. Sugden, *The Grammar of Spenser's Faerie Queene* (1936; repr. New York, 1966), 141, cites "With pleasaunce of the breathing fields yfed" (I, iv, 38.2) as "a striking example of the license which Spenser allowed himself in the construction." The freedom resides in one central term of chivalry, the infinitive and participial errantry of the knight.

Common to these images of the deserted profane space, with their burning sands and feeble, inadequate shade "under the red rock," is a cosmic emptiness, a terror that man and god have withdrawn from the evil represented by the unbounded horizon. When the sea is depicted as an element of chaos, it too shares in this iconography of cosmic desertion, for then sailors wander over its "pathless wastes." In a somewhat comic vein Spenser suggests this sea-born confusion in his myth of Phaedria, who pilots her "wandring ship" over the Idle Lake until she reaches the floating island. How much more fearful is the waste sea that imprisons Florimell, or the mythologized Irish Sea crossed by the shepherd in *Colin Clouts Come Home Again*.

> And is the sea (quoth *Coridon*) so fearfull?
> Fearful much more (quoth he) than hart can fear:
> Thousand wyld beasts with deep mouthes gaping direfull
> Therin stil wait poore passangers to teare.
> Who life doth loath, and longs death to behold,
> Before he die, alreadie dead with feare,
> And yet would live with heart halfe stonie cold,
> Let him to sea, and he shall see it there.
> And yet as ghastly dreadfull, as it seemes,
> Bold men presuming life for gaine to sell,
> Dare tempt that gulf, and in those wandring stremes
> Seek waies unknowne, waies leading down to hell.
>
> (200–211)

If the terror of infinite space may be realized on land and sea during the Renaissance, an even wider sense of the vastness of outer space grows apace, and poets may now envision the receding horizon through the yet larger forms of space travel, as in *Paradise Lost*. During the Renaissance material horizons were rapidly expanding, notably those of the tiny island power into a world explorer and world trader. In *The Merchant of Venice* the profane world is mapped by an inversion of the stillness of a perfect Belmont—the wandering of lost merchant ships.[19]

The Spenserian meditation might be expected to come down heavily on a pessimistic note, but it does not. The poet opposes his own demonic imagery. Because the labyrinth comes to be his dominant image for the profane space lying outside the temple, the labyrinth becomes the largest image for faerieland as a whole. Logically then, if we except the final apocalypse of the New Jerusalem, the heavenly City, the sacred temple space will always be found *inside* the labyrinth. The human temple assumes the existence of the labyrinth, where it finds itself. The labyrinth specifies the large and open extensions of faerieland, the temple its perfect enclosures. As in a Western, without the desert there can be no stockade, no Fort Bravo, not even a Dodge City.

In principle, therefore, the profane world is simply the world outside, or before, the temple; it is *pro-fanum*. It thus has a neutral aspect, into which we must briefly inquire. On this level the profane world appears to be the arena of business, of mundane commerce, of the Rialto, the marketplace, the undistinguished, ordinary, everyday scene of man's mortal life. News here means largely the ups and downs of gain and loss. Such was the "profit and loss" of Eliot's drowned Phoenician sailor, and such "the motive of action" in *East Coker*. On the whole, on this level, life

19. See D. W. Waters, *The Art of Navigation in England in Elizabethan and Early Stuart Times* (New Haven, 1958); E. G. R. Taylor, *Tudor Geography 1485–1583* (London, 1930); G. B. Parks, *Richard Hakluyt and the English Voyages* (New York, 1930), especially chap. 15, "The English Epic"; and R. V. Tooley, *Maps and Map-Makers* (1949; repr. New York, 1962), chap. 7, "English Map-makers; English Marine Atlases." Tooley reproduces various maps of the Elizabethan era, including the map of Dorset in Christopher Saxton's *Atlas*, 1579, (plate 38) and one plate from Robert Adams, *Expeditiones Hispanorum in Angliam vera descripto* (1590) (plate 39), showing the Spanish and English fleets ranged opposite each other during the Armada engagement. The Spanish fleet (Spenser's Soldan, V, viii) here appears in a crescent formation.

simply goes on, with the individual and the species seeking its own survival, if not its fortune.

The truth is complicated here, as with other archetypal clusters. What emerges from *The Faerie Queene*, as from *The Wasteland* and the *Four Quartets*, is a labyrinth imagery which is only apparently dualistic. As a picturesque beauty may be intricate so may the beauty of this poetic maze called faerieland. Edward Dowden wrote that "*The Faerie Queene*, if nothing else, is at least a labyrinth of beauty, a forest of old romance in which it is possible to lose oneself more irrecoverably amid the tangled luxury of loveliness than elsewhere in English poetry."[20] Loveliness is not the whole story, but the tangle and luxury are truly Spenserian, and their form is mazelike. They are basic Spenserian facts chiefly because the labyrinth itself permits an ambivalence. The temple may perhaps be unreservedly benign and desirable. The labyrinth is, by contrast, suspended between contraries.

The labyrinth is not a polarity, but a continuum joining two poles. It might be constructed according to the formula: Terror—neutrality (indifference?)—Delight. The terrifying is readily understandable as one pole. The delightful is less easy to account for. But even here the poet is traditional. Military defenses had been early transformed into the fanciful form of magical protections thrown up around a sacred spot.[21] Hostile beings and influ-

20. "Spencer, the Poet and the Teacher," from Paul Alpers, ed., *Edmund Spenser*, 164–65.

21. I am paraphrasing W. F. Jackson Knight, *Vergil: Epic and Anthropology*, ed. J. D. Christie (London, 1967), 202. The protective labyrinth is familiar to Elizabethans through the story of the Fair Rosamond, as retold in Daniel's *Complaint of Rosamond* and Drayton's *Heroical Epistle* of Rosamond to King Henry. The original notes to the latter include the statement that "some have held it to have beene an Allegorie of Mans Life: true it is, that the Comparison will hold; for what liker to a Labyrinth, then the Maze of Life? But it is affirmed by Antiquitie, that there was indeed such a Building; though *Dedalus* being a name applied to the Workmans excellencie, make it suspected: for *Dedalus* is nothing else but, Ingenious, or Artificiall. Hereupon it

ences cannot penetrate the web of mazed spells cast by the medicine man. Such visionary defenses are understandable enough, since the defenders of a real city surrounded by an intricate outwork, would know its turns and twists intimately, while the attackers would not. Eliade has observed that frequently the labyrinth protected the temple by providing a trial of initiatory access to the sacred world within. Perhaps on this analogy it could be argued that the "delightful land of faerie" is a maze surrounding the series of temples which comprise the heart of each successive book, and that in this sense faerieland "protects" each temple. The labyrinth implies a rite of passage. "The labyrinth, like any other trial of initiation, is a difficult trial in which not all are fitted to triumph. In a sense, the trials of Theseus in the labyrinth of Crete were of equal significance with the expedition to get the golden apples from the garden of Hesperides, or to get the golden fleece of Colchis. Each of these trials is basically a victorious entry into a place hard of access, and well defended, where there is to be found a more or less obvious symbol of power, sacredness and immortality."[22] This perspective on the continuum gives faerieland a double value which Spenser's readers have often observed, that while its lack of structure is threatening to the hero, he still persists in his quest, as if delighted by his good fortune in being awarded the heroic trial. Though each quest moves ambiguously "forward" in the manner of Redcrosse and Una ("at last resolving forward still to fare"), each quest also assumes the goal of a homecoming. Not surprisingly we find that the most Spenserian of the Metaphysicals, Andrew Marvell, is fascinated by the idea of the protective labyrinth. This image governs the form of "The Garden" and makes it a lyric temple never fully detached from the profane

---

is used among the ancient Poets, for anything curiously wrought." Michael Drayton, *Works*, ed. J. W. Hebel (Oxford, 1961), 2:138–39. Cf. Jonson's masque, *Pleasure Reconciled to Virtue*.

22. Mircea Eliade, *Patterns in Comparative Religion* (Cleveland and New York, 1963), 381.

world, where men, amazed, wander about, seeking fame and fortune. The truly green nature that surrounds one in England lends substance to this mythography.

In a revealing passage of his autobiography C. S. Lewis caught this natural perspective on the problem of the protective labyrinth. He was talking about youthful walks in Surrey, which he contrasted with walks in Ireland, his homeland. "What delighted me in Surrey was its intricacy. My Irish walks commanded large horizons and the general lie of land and sea could be taken in at a glance; I will try to speak of them later. But in Surrey the contours were so tortuous, the little valleys so narrow, there was so much timber, so many villages concealed in woods or hollows, so many field paths, sunk lanes, dingles, copses, such an unpredictable variety of cottage, farmhouse, villa, and country seat, that the whole thing could never be clearly in my mind, and to walk in it daily gave me the same sort of pleasure that there is in the labyrinthine complexity of Malory or *The Faerie Queene.*"[23] Physical perambulation here provides a model for reading Spenser.

Such walking tours of *The Faerie Queene* will generate a growing atmosphere of centeredness, as each picture of the picturesque scene is framed in the mind's eye, becoming a momentary symbol of the center. At such times the essential emptiness of Faerieland fills with structured shapes, and the reader will feel the presence of the temple as the tempering harmony of order in disorder.

Parodic Transformations

THE AMBIVALENCE OF THE LABYRINTH is a prominent case of the mythological "parody" whereby, for example, a de-

23. *Surprised by Joy: The Shape of My Early Life* (1955; repr. London, 1969), 118–19.

monic image provides a travesty of an apocalyptic image.[24] The wasteland is the demonic parody of the delightful maze. Similarly with the temple: the Bower of Bliss and the House of Busirane are demonic parodies of temples of pleasure and love. The Caves of Despair and Mammon are demonic parodies of the temples of Holiness and Temperance. In such "waste houses," as Lewis called them, one often finds "no living creature," and in that case the hero has Britomart's experience of "wastefull emptinesse."[25] Demonic parody is a fully developed Spenserian technique. The

24. Northrop Frye, *Anatomy of Criticism* (Princeton, 1957), 157; *Fables of Identity* (New York, 1963), 74. Frye's view of the parodistic forces in romantic poetry stems in part from his analysis of Blake.

25. C. S. Lewis, *Spenser's Images of Life*, ed. Alastair Fowler (Cambridge, 1967), 71. Cf. the stanza of *Astrophel*, where Spenser describes the fatal wood where Astrophel/Sidney is imagined as meeting the boar:

> It fortuned, as he that perilous game
> In forreine soyle pursued far away,
> Into a forest wide and waste he came,
> Where store he heard to be of salvage prey.
> So wide a forest and so waste as this,
> Nor famous Ardeyn, nor fowle Arlo, is.
>
> (lines 91–96)

Such woods are places to get lost in, like the wood in which *The Divine Comedy* begins. In them the hero experiences error. For the archetypal case in Christian myth, see Burke, *Rhetoric of Religion*, 223–24, on Exodus; A. B. Giamatti, in *The Earthly Paradise and the Renaissance Epic* (Princeton, 1966), 187, observes that Rinaldo in *Jerusalem Delivered*, XIV, 17 and 18, is said to be in "errore," while he is also called one of Goffredo's "compagni erranti," because he is with Armida: "Wandering, which for all Renaissance epic poets was the emblem for spiritual uncertainty, is here linked to a definite moral code." The tradition continues, with neoclassic interruptions, right up through *The Excursion*. John Freccero gives the Christian background in "Dante's Firm Foot and the Journey without a Guide," *Harvard Theological Review* 52 (1959): 245–82.

narrative consequence of this technique is a continuous creation of ambiguous choices for the hero. Everywhere the hero must decide whether he is looking at the real thing, or at a double of the real thing. He is rarely given a choice between flatly different things. He can never take the forms of being for granted. He can only hope that, with his memory of principles holding firm and his love of the good remaining strong, he will continue in the process of discovery.

Parody is, however, a symmetrical effect. The parodic process enters the poem as the testing of good by evil, but it may be reversed. The neutralizing of the labyrinth is a case of a benign, if not exactly apocalyptic, parody. A certain amount of comedy will arise out of the apocalyptic transformation of the fearsome labyrinth. And with a poetic imagery thus loosened up, the reader will have to look for the means of knowing the direction of parody. Whatever means it is, it will be an emergent attitude, a superordinate.

The key to the direction of parodic change will be the hero's freedom to continue his quest. If he is free to go forward, for him at that moment the labyrinth is benign or at least neutral. If he is held or trapped in place, like the lovers in Busirane's palace or like the obsessed Furor, then he is a creature of the sinister maze. Similarly, if a "paradise" like the Bower of Bliss prevents free exit to its denizens, then it is a demonic parody of a true paradise. The defining principle is freedom to enter and leave. The demonic parody of the temple, that is, the sinister form of the labyrinth, is thus always a prison.

Again the genre of romantic epic makes it easy to narrate the testing of mythic parodies. The freedom of entry and departure is an issue as soon as the hero begins to move about in faerieland. The labyrinth assumes the function of a necessary medium through which the hero must pass in his life of continuous initiation. "The supreme rite of initiation is to enter a labyrinth and return from it, and yet every life, even the least eventful, can be taken as the journey through a labyrinth. The sufferings and trials undergone by Ulysses were fabulous, and yet any man's return home has the value of Ulysses' return to Ithaca"[26]—a value on which Joyce placed considerable stress. There is no completely Odyssean hero in *The Faerie Queene*, but there is a little of Odysseus in many of Spenser's protagonists, especially insofar as they are seeking to respond to the transformations of an endlessly shape-shifting scene. Held in the maze, the hero emerges from it suddenly in the middle of the way. Suddenly he gets a perspective on the perspectiveless tangle. Daedalus, who made the inescapable labyrinth, in which even he might get lost, was not accidentally a mythic inventor of human flight. With Proteus, he is the master of transformations. He invents wings, the parody of a bird's wings, and he invents the maze. It seems important that Daedalus is thus the inventor of the original prison, which he could redeem or transform by his parodic invention of the means of freedom. Something of the equivocal nature of this double achievement inheres in the rich overtones of the terms "daedal" and "daedalian," with their implication of endless but slightly sinister prolixity.

Prophecy and History in The Faerie Queene

PROPHECY IS A VISIONARY interpretation of the life of the spirit. A vocation rather than a job, prophecy gives the poet an inspired voice, and with this voice he utters, not words, but the Word, the Logos. A divine spirit speaks through him, informing his human speech with a rare selfpossession. The prophetic poet is uniquely sure of himself, and this he shows by allowing his utterance to be enigmatic and obscure on its surface, knowing that the immediate surface of the riddle is supported by an underlying clarity. The prophet seeks to be the clear medium of the divine wisdom—Blake held that he wrote his poem by "dictation."[27] His

26. Eliade, *Patterns in Comparative Religion*, 382.

27. Letter to Thomas Butts, April 25, 1803. Reprinted in Geoffrey Keynes, *The Complete Writings of William Blake* (London, Nonesuch edition), 823. Blake's phrase is, "from immediate Dictation, twelve or sometimes twenty or thirty lines at a time, without Premeditation & even against my Will."

task is literally a calling. In *The Faerie Queene* the strangely automated ritualism of the verse is one familiar sign of this vocation. In general such "dictated" speech displays a freedom from material reference. The prophet seeks "the liberation of a word of God, which becomes objectively powerful far beyond the personal range of the prophet's activity. Once spoken and current, his word is, as we might almost say, depersonalized, and enters upon its own independent history. . . . The word will be more or less detached from its human speaker, and become an independent event."[28] Even though the Old Testament prophets are highly individual in their styles of utterance, their prophetic speech abandons the typical aims of personal communications (self-expression) and takes on the role of a communal and, if need be, impersonal eloquence.

The prophet may be opposed to the futurist predictor, but he is even more unlike the mystic, whose passive, quietistic, contemplative resignation and removal from the hurly burly of life are expressed as a strong distrust of history. The mystic shuns the life of man in time, seeking a withdrawn perfection. Prophets reject withdrawal. "Their inspiration did not make the prophets [of the Old Testament] independent of the historical conditions of their time. They did not desire or conceive any such independence. The notion of them as mystical dreamers brooding in a realm above space and time, and forecasting the remote future in riddles to be deciphered by an amazed posterity, is wholly misleading. They were intensely men of the hour. . . . Their interests were particular and not general, concrete and not abstract."[29] And yet, as Dodd goes on to say, "they spoke eternal truth." The paradox may be resolved if we think that the prophet utters an eternal truth that is immanent in the daily affairs of men. This daily life is contained in the notion of history.

With Spenser the varieties of history are threefold, but only one of these has major force in his poetry. There is, to begin with,

28. H. W. Robinson, *Inspiration and Revelation*, 170–71.

29. C. H. Dodd, *The Authority of the Bible* (New York, 1958), 124.

the cyclical historiography of the ancient Greeks, which tends to discern a periodic order in "the spectacle of incessant change."[30] Great men perform great actions, and these are complete, like the plots of plays. But history in this view has no overall structure or unity that can be conceived developmentally. During the Renaissance this historiographic mode persists in longer poems like *Albion's England* and the *Mirror for Magistrates,* and we find that the periodic image of life gives the poet an arsenal of cyclical images.[31] Samuel Daniel catches this tone of inevitable cycle in his

30. R. G. Collingwood, *The Idea of History* (New York, 1957), 22; Karl Löwith, *Meaning in History* (Chicago, 1949); Raymond Klibansky and H. J. Paton, *Philosophy and History* (New York, 1963). Generally, on Renaissance philosophy of history, see: Frank Manuel, *Shapes of Philosophical History* (Stanford, 1965); George H. Nadel, "Philosophy of History before Historicism," in *Studies in the Philosophy of History,* ed. G. H. Nadel (New York, 1965), 67–73; C. A. Patrides, *The Phoenix and the Ladder: Rise and Decline of the Christian View of History* (Berkeley and Los Angeles, 1964), 36–58.

31. F. S. Fussner, *The Historical Revolution: English Historical Writing and Thought, 1580–1640* (New York and London, 1962), 28; F. J. Levy, *Tudor Historical Thought* (San Marino, 1967), 217; Christopher Hill, "Sir Walter Ralegh and History," in his lectures, Intellectual Origins of the English Revolution, in *The Listener,* 14 June 1962: "Ralegh's work then helped to establish the rule of law in history, as against the more arbitrarily providential and moralizing chronicles of Foxe and his like; and yet Ralegh also helped to break the cyclical theories with which a conception of historical law had hitherto usually been associated. He thus prepared the way for the more modern sociological history of Harrington." For exemplary history: Myron Gilmore, "The Renaissance Conception of the Lessons of History," in *Facets of the Renaissance,* ed. W. H. Werkmeister (Los Angeles, 1959; repr. New York, 1963), 73–102; Gilmore, *Humanists and Jurists: Six Studies in the Renaissance* (Cambridge, Mass., 1963), chaps. 1–4; Gilmore, *The World of Humanism: 1453–1517* (New York, 1952; repr. New York, 1962), chap. 7. On mythologizing of history: Isabel Rathborne, *The Meaning of Spenser's Fairyland* (New York, 1937; repr. 1965), chaps. 1 and 2; O. B. Hardison, *The Enduring Monument: A Study of the Idea of Praise in Renaissance Literary Theory and Practice* (Chapel Hill, 1962).

valedictory couplet addressed to the "great men," Essex and Mountjoy: "And therefore leave, sad muse, th'imagined good, / For we must now return again to blood."[32] Doom is almost casual, and destiny automatic.[33]

A second, more tentative historiographic style, that of modern historical study, is beginning to gain momentum during the period when Spenser wrote. According to such a model—and it remains very much an infant discipline—the historian's interest attaches, not to vast and impressive mythographic structures, but to the statement of limited chains of causal connection. The mapping, the surveying, the anatomizing of contemporary Elizabethan Britain and furthermore of English overseas voyaging play a major part in this development. Speculations on the growth of law and justice, we shall discover, share this same interest in record and research, and here too the concern for historical *conditions* will undermine belief in mere cyclical repetition. Nevertheless, although Spenser reflects this critical outlook in his *Vewe of the Present State of*

32. *The First Fowre Bookes of the Civile Wars* (1595), Book II, stanza 131. I quote from H. E. Rollins and Herschel Baker, *The Renaissance in England* (Boston, 1954), 19.

33. Note the dedication to Essex, in the *Seaven Bookes of The Iliades* (1598), in Allardyce Nicoll, *Chapman's Homer* (New York, 1956), 1:504. A similar view is presented in the 1611 dedication to Prince Henry, which is in the same volume, as also the address to the reader. We should note, not simply the rhetoric, or propaganda, of a prophetic appeal, but the imagery Chapman disposes, to show that Homer is a prophetic poet, e.g., lines 114–24 of the address to Prince Henry:

> And, as in a spring
> The plyant water, mov'd with any thing
> Let fall into it, puts her motion out
> In perfect circles, that move round about
> The gentle fountaine, one another raising:
> So Truth and Poesie worke, so Poesie, blazing
> All subjects falne in her exhaustlesse fount,
> Works most exactly, makes a true account
> Of all things to her high discharges given,
> Till all be circular and round as heaven.

Ireland, it exerts only a secondary influence on his poetry, giving it a Machiavellian hardness of attitude toward the pieties of mythographic history.

The third shape of history, somewhat misleadingly called "linear," finds its remoter origins in the Old Testament. "The Hebrews saw their whole past as a revelation of the purposes of Jahweh. Christianity, going on from there, makes world-history in its entirety a single, transcendentally significant story with a well-defined plot pivoted on Creation, Fall, Redemption, and Judgment."[34] Seemingly chaotic and unrelated events are shown to have a progressive character; history appears to move in a certain direction. Because wandering bulks large in this story, the form of history in this tradition should be called "linear" only with the express understanding that with it the line is not a very straight line. Lewis and others have referred to this mode of thought as "historicism," by which is meant "the belief that by studying the past we can learn not only historical but also metahistorical or transcendental truth."[35] The governing drive in this historicist view seems to be the desire for a sense of direction.

The Old Testament shows how the Children of Israel are chosen to enact the central role in a providential drama. During the reign of Elizabeth this shaping view of a "linear" history would characterize the thinking of most Puritans, and Englishmen generally to the extent that they imagined England was chosen in a manner similar to the election of Israel. Prophecy arises out of such soil almost automatically. The prophet confronts a heterogeneous mass of deviations from a straight line—which come about in the nature of almost any personal or corporate existence. He gives these deviations a meaning. Moses shows how the errors, wanderings, trials of the Exodus demand a reduction to order, and he achieves this reduction by demonstrating that the apparently random omens of the desert are the natural signs of a divine ordinance. By showing that the wanderings of the chosen ones are momen-

34. Lewis, *Discarded Image*, 174. See also, on metahistory, Frye, "New Directions from Old," in *Fables of Identity*, 52–66.
35. Lewis, *Discarded Image*, 174–75.

tously linked to the all-known but veiled design, the prophet "straightens" the twisting, labyrinthine shapes of profane time. When the children are lost, he unveils his prophetic gift, an inspired sense of direction.

Spenser is a Christian poet and he subordinates the insights of cyclical and scientific history to the Christian revelation of a prophetic historicism. When Coleridge remarked that *The Faerie Queene* showed "a marvellous independence and true imaginative absence of all particular space or time," he was only partly right.[36] Like *The Shepheardes Calender* the epic may allude to topical events, but it does so in a universalizing way, so that allusions to current happenings tend to go *through* their historical particularity, till they reach a level of transcendent meaning.[37] From each ephemeral contact with history there emerges a larger pattern, a providential British destiny. Emergency here has the intentionality of the Logos. Each particular crisis advances a single great argument.

The poet's "acceptance of history—this reduction of dream to providential event"[38] is uttered as prophecy. The stories told in *The Faerie Queene* have their natural narrative form, each to its

36. Coleridge, *Course of Lectures*, III (Feb. 3, 1818): "It [*FQ*] is in the domains neither of history or geography; it is ignorant of all artificial boundary, all material obstacles; it is truly in land of Faery, that is, of mental space. The poet has placed you in a dream, a charmed sleep, and you neither wish, nor have the power, to inquire where you are, or how you got there." I quote from Coleridge, *Essays and Lectures on Shakespeare and Some Other Old Poets and Dramatists* (Everyman, ed., 1919), 233–34.

37. An important start has been made by David Bevington, *Tudor Drama and Politics: A Critical Approach to Topical Meaning* (Cambridge, Mass., 1968). Bevington's formal interests may be judged from his statement that "the artist's conception of the genre in which he writes is frequently the product of his political intent" (5). One could wish that, as often in the best criticism of Book V of *FQ*, the critic would develop such a principle in terms of the underlying idea, which is that "political intent" implies a theory, a myth, or an aesthetic of the ephemeral.

38. Frank Kermode, "Spenser and the Allegorists," in Paul Alpers, ed., *Edmund Spenser*, 298.

own, but the larger mythos of the poem as a whole acquires the providential form of an historicist dream. Romantic narrative aids this development. Each temple holds out an intermediate promise of final recognition. All intermediate errantry becomes a metaphor for the search for structure in a disordered world. Errantry modulates into cognitive error, which in turn may extend into theology, as in Book I, where error is from time to time lack of faith, of law, of joy. Una, "representing" the Temple, stands for that special "oneness with" which is the mark of a transcendental faith in the true God. Error denotes a mistaken deviation from a right line of thought or conduct, and in this broader sense of deviation from correct judgments error is the symbolic action that typically occurs in the labyrinth. In addition, although error permits the wildest wandering once the deviation has started, the radical assumption of error is always a way (the *via* of the *homo viator*) from which the deviation departs. When judgment corrects an error, the symbolic act of correction is a return to the right way. These spatial metaphors are standard in the imagery of prophetic historicism.

Spenserian heroes are always learning something, and sometimes they gain corrected visions of their lives, when they receive enshrined wisdom. Sir Guyon and Prince Arthur, for example, are given a short course in history. Redcrosse learns who he is, Saint George, when Heavenly Contemplation leads him to reflect on the difference between the City of God and the City of Man. This reflection divides and yet also unites the temple with the labyrinth. Such recognitions are the basis of the internal prophetic structure of the poem at large. Even so, it is also possible to call *The Faerie Queene* a prophetic poem because it goes beyond these periodic visions vouchsafed to the hero. It does include these moments of truth. But *The Faerie Queene*, like all legitimate prophecy, is a larger unity. It is a "constitutive" vision. It builds "the constant incorporation of past, present, and future events into that which claims to be a word of the everlasting God."[39] The constitutive aim of prophecy amounts to an inbuilding function, an assimilation

39. Robinson, *Inspiration and Revelation*, 126.

of the poetic narrative to a steadily emerging vision of a final, guiding Logos. Each episode of knight errantry adds its material substance to the accumulated argument of a higher truth, the revelation of a providential will. Because Spenser is a Christian poet, writing in the tradition laid down by the Old and New Testaments, this higher revelation usually ends up as a vision of justice.

Poetically the superordinate vista is revealed as the gradual marriage of the poem with its message. *The Faerie Queene* may at first appear a random collection of heroic quests—we have six Legends, but we might as well have twelve, ten, or twenty-four. The poem, looked at "from a distance," itself finally becomes a heroic quest, the poet's myth of prophetic historicism. Berger has shown this in some detail, as a property of Book VI. But of Book I he has given a similar account: "We might approach the first Book in this light as a dialectic between hero and poet: the knight, through weakness of will and mis-placed confidence in self, permits the evil to grow and to dominate the poem; the poet illuminates the growing evil, catches and controls it as image, through the widening network of allusion, the delicate modulations of symbolic reference. What happens to the knight becomes clearer as well as more more critical. It even seems that Redcrosse gets well *in order to* make the evil luxuriate, tempt it to assert itself and so expose its true nature."[40] Some readers may object that this process would contaminate Spenser's muse. But reflexive virtuosity is the natural condition of prophetic utterance. The more reticulated the poem becomes, the more it reflects the poet's exuberant involvement with his own genius and freedom. Orpheus, rather than Narcissus the suicidal beauty, is the spirit of this poetry. An Orphic enthusiasm lends grace and a kind of permanence to the ephemeral glory of the native ground marked out by the temple and the labyrinth.

In such wise a prophetic poetry may serve a community. It localizes the source, the spring, of inspiration. The "famous antique

40. "Spenser's *Faerie Queene*, Book I: Prelude to Interpretation," 42.

history" of *The Faerie Queene* "takes place" in a mythical, imaginative, intensely felt placement. Traditional iconography here supports the poet as usual. Genius is tied to place, in order that creative powers may draw on the sense of belonging and "belonging to." Drayton, following and extending the Spenserian model, perfectly expresses the nature of this prophetic power. He begins the *Poly-Olbion* by invoking a local muse.

> Thou Genius of the place, this most renowned ile,
> Which livedst long before the all-earth-drowning flood,
> Whilst yet the world did swarm with her gigantic brood,
> Go thou before me still thy circling shores about,
> And in this wand'ring maze help to conduct me out.

The Prophetic Moment

THE PROPHETIC MOMENT is that critical juncture when the prophetic order of history is revealed. It is a *kairos* or marked occasion, and as an event it is a privileged meeting between two undifferentiated spans of time. It is the hour, in the phrase "man of the hour." Prophetic tradition understands it as the "right time," the suitable season, the auspicious moment. We can add that it is an inspired moment, such as Dr. Johnson envisioned, when he said that Denham's couplet on the Thames must have been composed in "some hour propitious to poetry." During the prophetic moment the genius of the poet collaborates with all the forces of the world spirit, which breathe into him recognition of his inborn powers and their connection with the present time.

The structure of the prophetic moment is given by the dialectic of the temple and the labyrinth, between which there is a theoretical threshold, corresponding spatially to the temporal crossover defined as a moment.[41] Thresholds are openings or doorways be-

41. Harry Berger, Jr., "Two Spenserian Retrospects: The Antique Temple of Venus and the Primitive Marriage of Rivers," *Texas Studies in Literature and Language* 10, no. 1 (1968): 5–25, argues that the

tween two spaces or places. Moments are doorways between two spaces of time. These metaphors diagram the emergence of vision. At the theoretical meeting place between the temple and the labyrinth there bursts forth a higher order, which the great syncretist of ancient allegory, Philo Judaeus, would call "the Immanent Logos."

As a temporal threshold, the prophetic moment is not without its antecedents in Christian and Classical iconography. The Christmas season is full of the expectancy before a great visionary truth is revealed to man, and this *Kairos* has origins far back in the

---

Spenserian *discordia concors* is dynamic, i.e., a flux that cannot be identified as a static world picture. "First, the main thrust of Spenser's concern is not toward the depiction of a world or world view in which characters find themselves; it is rather toward characters in development and toward the ways in which they project the phases of their development as aspects of environment. Spenserian landscape for the most part evolves from the projection of inscape, emerging out of the problems and actions of his characters. Thus, for example, where Dante's cosmos is hierarchically organized in terms of *up* and *down*, the dominant Spenserian vectors are *in* and *out*, and these vectors control both the psychic or allegorical and the topographic elements (plains, forests, houses) of experience." From this view Berger derives his second main principle, that the Spenserian thought is *evolutionary*. In Spenser, therefore, we see the first stage of the Miltonic myth of the lateral fall: The failure of Eve and Adam occurs in the beguiling maze of the Garden, where her mazy locks of hair are the chief symbol of her error, which by transumption or metonymy becomes an effluence of the labyrinthine garden. Milton combines the lateral of Spenser with the vertical of Dante, and it may be that the combination could only happen in an age that saw the first truly deterministic, scientific account of bodies falling, that is, the development of the Galilean-Newtonian theory of gravity. Newton's apple is the first thing to really fall, in history. This fall liberates Milton to analyze, freely for the first time, the imponderables of the metaphysical fall. Newton is not free from his own religious culture, in fact is bound to it, as Frank Manuel has shown in *Isaac Newton, Historian* (Cambridge, Mass., 1963); yet Newton had driven the wedge between physics and metaphysics, thus making it possible for a major, in some ways scientifically-minded, poet to show up the paradox of a physical

Hebraic prophetic sources. Saint Luke catches the readiness perfectly by the simple statement, otherwise realistic enough, that the shepherds were "keeping watch over their flock by night." Milton, initiating the full advance of his career as a prophetic poet, began by singing the "Hymn" whose subject is precisely this prophetic moment. The vision, "On the Morning of Christ's Nativity," is unusually reflexive in that the birth of Christ provided a new spiritual context for the art of prophecy, marked by the cessation of the pagan oracles and the inception of the Christian revelation.

---

representation (gardens, humans, serpents, etc.) of a metaphysical loss. Spenser lives and writes before this position is reached.

With various threshold symbolisms, Spenser constructs *FQ* so as to enhance the horizontal effect, by beginning each book with a Proem. Joan Webber's description of the formal proem and division of the Donne sermons will apply here: "In proem and sermon division, a special effort is made to provide the listener with a kind of doorway. By means of symbol and metaphor, the sermon itself is presented as a penetrable thing. It is distinctly suggested that the listener can enter and move about within its borders, to explore the content of a text, or to participate in the unfolding of a symbol." *Contrary Music: the Prose Style of John Donne* (Madison, 1963), 148. The beauty of Spenser's proems, as distinct from those of the sermon, lies in their indeterminacy—they do not always "divide" the theme of the book—which gives them a greater sense of threshold, less determinate than the sense of gateway. The difference may be important: "Gates and doors mark the division between the sacred and the profane world, and so do thresholds, but precautions taken at the latter are far more numerous and widespread than at gateways, and at doors and doorways as distinct from thresholds. It seems not to matter how you go through a gateway, but in most parts of the world you must not go through a doorway without observing the threshold ritual." Raglan, *Temple and House*, 26. Herbert is aware enough of this need. *The Temple* effectively begins, after "The Church Porch," with the two stanzas of the "Superliminare," the second of which expresses the taboo: "Avoid, Profanenesse; come not here: / Nothing but holy, pure, and cleare, / Or that which groneth to be so, / May at his peril further go." F. E. Hutchinson, ed., *The Works of George Herbert* (Oxford, 1941), 25.

[47

Classical poetry, like the historiography of Herodotus, had known an equivalent myth of prophetic threshold. The oracles of the ancient world were variously trusted, consulted, and feared. Their poetic forms of utterance were important enough to Plutarch for him to write at length on the subject. The pagan notion of visionary threshold was also a familiar experience. Roman religion associated the oracular threshold with the deity, Janus. He is a god of gates. (Spenser in the *Vewe* calls them the "ingate" and the "outgate.") Janus is depicted with double-faced head, and in times before the bifrontal Janus emerges, the god is more simply represented as a simple arch—Cicero calls the *Iani* "transitiones perviae." The daimon is equally a god of beginnings, a numen of passage.[42] Janus finds one origin of his worship in lunar symbolism, suggesting the search for the propitious moment. A typical god of the heroic wayfaring journey and its beginning, Janus presides over "the uncertainty of his setting forth."

Thresholds face two ways, but if a choice must be made between the inward and the outward passage, for prophecy the inward is primary, the outward secondary, since the motion to the center (even if sometimes the center does not hold) is the defining motion toward the temple.[43] Yeats, adopting his own version of this dialectic, says in a note for *Michael Robartes and the Dancer* that "The Second Coming" has to use the double cone or gyre, because "the human soul is always moving outward into the objective world or inward into itself; and this movement is double

---

42. L. A. MacKay, *Janus*, in *University of California Publications in Classical Philology* 15, no. 4 (1956): 157–81. MacKay observes: "The idea of 'beginning' in general is, however, a rather advanced abstraction." This is important, for Roman religion, as for Spenserian allegory, because the personification of abstractions is the chief mechanism of detailed ornamentation in the allegorical narrative or ritual vision.

43. John Freccero, "Dante's Pilgrim in a Gyre," *PMLA* 76 (1961): 168–81, a study to which T. K. Dunseath refers in an important passage of his *Spenser's Allegory of Justice in Book V of The Faerie Queene* (Princeton, 1968), 70–71.

because the human soul would not be conscious were it not suspended between contraries, the greater the contrast the more intense the consciousness."[44]

Already in the Yeatsian formulation (which derives from Blake) one can see that the threshold and the moment are capable of various figurative changes. Yeats himself used several—the flight of the circling bird, the gyring motion of the great tree, the twisting stairway of the tower, and so on. Perhaps at the head of this tradition of a threshold transformed into a three-dimensional volume is the immemorial image of the "time-serpent," the helical snake wound around the god Serapis, who is a prophet king in the Hermetic and "Egyptian" pantheon. Such an image grows into the triform head of Titian's "Allegory of Prudence," with its extra theriomorphic triplet of dog, lion and wolf—here the "three ages of man" are joined in one emerging moment by a weird, metamorphosing twist of the head.[45] There is really no limit to the 'pataphysical imagination, and it can perceive time as a spiral, a gyre, a helix, a set of double intersecting cones.

The main dynamic quality of the the threshold is an elusive betweenness. There is probably a measure of repose in the juncture of temple and labyrinth. The shepherds of Milton's "Hymn" were "simply chatting in a rustic row" (stanza 8). But there is also an opposed sense of crisis, which lessens repose. The moment is more like a calm before the storm, or the stillness as one enters the eye of the hurricane. A whole cluster of unstable "Conradian" states would pertain to this experience: transience, vacillation, fluidity and rushing fluency, drop-off, falling, wavering, hovering, simple mobility, vertigo perhaps, even mere restlessness. Here the idea of balance, a "justifying" poised stance precisely at the doorstep between two realms, is translated into an affectively loaded

44. *The Variorum Edition of the Poems of W. B. Yeats*, ed. Peter Allt and R. K. Alspach (New York, 1965), 824.

45. Erwin Panofsky, "Titian's *Allegory of Prudence*: A Postscript," in *Meaning in the Visual Arts* (New York, 1955; Anchor ed.), 157. See also the revised ed. *Pagan Mysteries in the Renaissance*, where Wind analyzes this figure as a "vestige" of the Trinity.

expectancy.[46] Various polarities of the to and fro will enter the reader's mind here, and they cannot fail to include alienation/homecoming, divorce/marriage, betrayal/promise, and even the more physical dualities of cohabitation and coition. One has only to read the end of Book III of *The Faerie Queene*, with its original ending, to sense the degree to which threshold was for Spenser an intense physical as well as metaphysical reality. He suspends the templar and the labyrinthine modes of being in a continuous, unresolved, but always promising flux, whose place of measurement is the imaginative gateway between the two. Janus-like, the vatic poet stands watching his hero experience the rite of passage.

Spenserian prophecy depends, as we might expect, on the educational myths common to his time. After the fashionable *Cyropaedeia*, with its myth of royal education, we might invent a new name for Spenser's knights—cyropedic heroes. The Spenserian plan sends them out in search for heroic knowledge and wisdom. This becomes a search for an idealized imperial domain. Heroic life is then reducible to a myth of continuous initiation. The heroic *vita activa* is one of wandering, trial, and discovery. Initiation affirms the heroic self, by instructing the cyropedic hero, and he may not long remain in the temple. At the House of Holiness Redcrosse is told that he must "turne againe / Back to the world,"

46. Freccero, 174: "It is not incarnation which disrupts the soul of Dante's pilgrim, for the soul did not pre-exist as far as Christians were concerned. Man's calamity in a Christian context was not therefore a fall from the heavens, but rather the fall from Grace. The Platonic life cycle is recapitulated in a single moment of the Christian's moral existence [my 'prophetic moment'], for at any time after the stain of Original Sin has been removed, the soul may fall from Grace, and through Grace be reborn." Then, as Freccero shows, 175: "By virtue of the analogy between the movements of the macrocosm and the interior movements of the microcosm, we may say that the three cosmic movements perceived by the ancients were the ultimate source of the medieval and Neoplatonic doctrine of the three movements of the mind, the most famous expression of which is to be found in St. Bonaventure's *Itinerarium Mentis:* conversion *extra nos* (linear), *intra nos* (spiral), and *supra nos* (circular)."

that maze "whose joyes so fruitlesse are," or that seem at first so fruitless to him when he contemplates a return to service. The poem acts out the hero's reluctance to break the spell of the temple. The poem is well designed to prolong the pèriod of betweenness.

The need for prophetic suspension may account for the deliberate, flowing, almost glutinous continuity of Spenserian verse. How well Hazlitt described it: "It is a labyrinth of sweet sounds, 'in many a winding bout of linked sweetness long drawn out'— that could cloy by their very sweetness, but that the ear is constantly relieved and enchanted by their continued variety of modulation—dwelling on the pauses of the action, or flowing on in a fuller tide of harmony with the movement of the sentiment. It has not the bold dramatic transitions of Shakespeare's blank verse, nor the high-raised tone of Milton's; but it is the perfection of melting harmony, dissolving the soul in pleasure, or holding it captive in the chains of suspense."[47] Hazlitt is here in the grip of Milton's theory of prosody and is articulating it with new energy, but he might also be articulating the idea Blake intended by his phrase "The labyrinthine Ear" (*Jerusalem*, chap. 4, plate 98). Twice in the passage Hazlitt alludes to the withholding power of Spenserian verse. This is a restraint upon the impatient wish to get back to the world of heroic encounter and excitement. Instead, the poem holds the labyrinthine ear "captive in the chains of suspense."

Less like a point in time than a seasonal stretch, the prophetic moment appears to last forever. And yet being only a moment, it must also be infinitesimal. Such is the paradox of immediate apprehension, when the mind takes in the truth of some puzzle. Ariel embodies the spirit of this apprehension, as *The Tempest* enacts most of its archetypal conditions. Prospero's farewell to the masque almost perfectly describes the mystery of the mixed extension and instantaneity of the prophetic moment. Prolongation of the moment gives a special place to the often noted Spenserian preference for masque-like effects. Spenser (and the Shakespeare of the late

47. "Lectures on the English Poets" (1818), in Paul Alpers, ed., *Edmund Spenser*, 138.

romances) may have decided that the best art-form for the prophetic moment is the masque or pageant. These employ the *tableau vivant*, the slow-motion procession, the *joyeuse entrée*, the marvelous vision, the spectacular theatrical epiphany. Theatrical dazzle has a mysterious effect. In posthumously edited notes for his lectures, we read that Lewis sought the forming principles of *The Faerie Queene* in the pageant, which he understood in several ways, common to all of which there was a union of epiphanic fixation and processional flow.[48] No law prescribes exactly when or how this union will occur, and it may happen briefly or at length. The Marriage of the Rivers occupies many stanzas, but a sense of betrothal may animate the single stanza, for example the arithmological stanza (II, ix, 22), and may even illuminate a phrase or a word that suddenly "rings a bell," sending the mind off on a flight toward some other distant word or phrase.

The social purposes of masque recur here too. The prophet begins in critical withdrawal, but his withdrawal, unlike that of the mystic, ends in a return, affirming a festive hope. His *kairos* or season promises truth in the measure that any betrothal is a union of opposites and can hope for an offspring. The festivity is rich with hope because infused by faith. Prophecy, representing its vision in ceremonial pageant, can enforce a feeling of local topocosmic unity among a varied people, creating a court, a family, a city, a culture.[49] Elizabethans appear to have been great celebrators, but their festive comedy is perhaps more vigorous in its

48. C. S. Lewis, *Spenser's Images*, 2–7.

49. "The essence of the topocosm is that it possesses a twofold character, at once real and punctual, and ideal and durative, the former aspect being necessarily immerged in the latter, as a moment is immerged in time. If it is bodied forth as a real and concrete organism in the present, it exists also as an ideal, timeless entity, embracing but transcending the here and now in exactly the same way that the ideal America embraces but transcends the present generation of Americans. The successive leases of its life therefore exist not only in the reality of the present but also in a kind of infinite continuum of which the present is but the current phase. Accordingly, the seasonal ceremonies which mark the beginnings and ends of those leases possess at once a punctual and a transcendent aspect." T. H. Gaster,

faith than the more delicate art of masque, which includes doubt in its promises of rebirth. Spenser did not need to be told that prophecy itself needs always to be redeemed from the false hopes of millennial anticipation.

Prophetic uncertainty and betweenness would be undesirable if they prevented heroic action. But they are, as the shaping of Faerieland suggests, its prerequisite. The disciplining experience that lies before the hero is an uncertain role in the enactment of historical destiny. The goal of the quest is justice and peace. In its six books *The Faerie Queene* examines the spiritual conditions under which this providential quest is pursued. The quest takes varied forms, all of which demand the persistance of a heroic energy, that "great puissance" which characterizes the several heroes of the six books and which is finally gathered into the person of Prince Arthur.

Heroic Energy

THE ENACTMENT OF THE HEROIC QUEST in *The Faerie Queene* is, though a history, rendered in as abstract and conventional a style as possible, without destroying the sense of human involvement. The latter requires verbal energeia, the stylistic equivalent of "forcibleness."[50] The bulk of Spenserian criticism devotes itself to the definition of the precise level of ab-

---

Thespis: Ritual, Myth, and Drama in the Ancient Near East (New York, 1961), 24. Cf. Leo Spitzer, *Classical and Christian Ideas*, 74–78, et passim, on "temper" as basis of peace, the most desirable topocosmic "atmosphere."

50. See chap. 10, "Energeia," in Neil Rudenstine, *Sidney's Poetic Development* (Cambridge, Mass., 1967). The prime examples of "forcibleness" are precisely those that characterize the prophetic language of the psalms of David, and though parallels can be found in Aristotle's *Rhetoric* and Scaliger's *Poetics*, Rudenstine is surely right to join these biblical instances from the *Apologie* with the Vergilian instances Scaliger gave, as examples of "activity" and of "the sense of things being present before one's eyes." See *Sidney's Poetic Development*, 153–57.

straction the poem engages at any particular moment, and the extreme trickiness of hitting the exact level has long been the greatest challenge to Spenserians. Most such criticism is concerned with the mythography of *The Faerie Queene*, not merely as allusion to external sources, but more profoundly as articulation in its own terms. Almost every critic has maintained that Spenser draws on multiple sources of symbolism, although the dominant influence on the narrative style of his poem comes from romance and romantic epic.

Perhaps the most insistent worry in our critical literature is the matter of narrative surface. In his own alternately heroic and rustic style Spenser does tell stories. But many criticis would agree with Lewis's lecture notes: "Spenser, however, is only superficially a narrative poet. He is much more concerned with the state of being a good or bad man, than with the actions by which we become so. In his 'bad' places, the poet gives us, not merely images of the baits to sin, but much more pictures of the mental atmosphere in which the sinner is trapped. We may add, and in his good places, pictures of the large room into which the good man is liberated. He shows us not what it is like to murder Duncan, but what it is like, in the long run, simply to *be* Macbeth."[51] The chief formal problem in criticizing Spenser would from this angle appear to be the question, How do we understand the paradoxical nature of a narrative whose aim is to unfold states of being? Elsewhere Lewis described Spenser's epic in specifically atmospheric terms: "There is a real affinity between his *Faerie Queene*, a poem of quests and wanderings and inextinguishable desires, and Ireland itself—the soft, wet air, the loneliness, the muffled shapes of hills, the heart-rending sunsets. It was of course a different Ireland from ours, an Ireland without potatoes, whitewashed cottages, or bottled stout: but it must already have been the 'land of longing'. *The Faerie Queene* should perhaps be regarded as the work of one who is turning into an Irishman."[52] "Longing" may be a helpful term, since, besides ro-

51. Lewis, *Spenser's Images*, 97. Lewis is quoting Janet Spens.
52. Lewis, *Studies in Medieval and Renaissance Literature* (Cambridge, 1966), 126.

mantic nostalgia, it suggests the state of potential change, and then the problem of potentiality itself.

Lewis took the view that evil in Spenser is almost always represented as a deprivation of energy, while "normally, it is the image of good that is active"; "Evil means starvation, good glows with what Blake calls 'the lineaments of gratified desire.' Evil imprisons, good sets free. Evil is tired, good is full of vigour. The one says, Let go, lie down, sleep, die; the other, All aboard! kill the dragon, marry the girl, blow the pipes and beat the drum, let the dance begin."[53] Spenser's giants might seem to put Lewis in error, but his notes remind us that Spenser always relates his morality to an idea of courage, of heart, almost in the Italian sense: *corragio!* The poem attempts to show the conditions under which the heart and the passions are enlisted in "fierce warres and faithfull loves."

Allegory makes the "pleasing analysis" of heroic energies. Tasso expressed this interest in his account of *Jerusalem Delivered:* "allegory respecteth the Passions, the Opinions and Customs, not only as they do appear (the province of Imitation), but principally in their being hidden and inward; and more obscurely doth express them with notes (as a man may say) mystical, such as only the Understanders of the Nature of things can fully comprehend."[54] Allegorical narration is always daemonic, which is to say, it accepts and depicts the irresistible drives of men's actions.[55] These drives are distinct from the actions that ensue, but are their psychological prerequisite, and energy in this Spenserian system is predominantly psychic energy, though important cases like the fainting of Sir Guyon indicate Spenser's awareness that soul and body are, in action, one.

Spenser pursues each action to the point at which it is clear

53. *Spenser's Images,* 95.

54. Quoted in William Nelson, *The Poetry of Edmund Spenser* (New York, 1963), 129.

55. See Harry Berger, Jr., *The Allegorical Temper: Vision and Reality in Book II of Spenser's Faerie Queene* (New Haven, 1957), chap. 10, "The Demonic Allegorist;" also, my *Allegory* (Ithaca, 1964), chap. 1, "The Daemonic Agent."

how energies are distributed. Few incidents have a discursive interest of their own, as they might in a novel. But every ornament in the tapestry implies a power. It is exactly because the poem is so "overdetermined" in this way that it needs, and gets, an exceedingly complex structure. Its stability comes largely from its multiplication of sources and its deep strain of imagistic relativism. The mythic surface of *The Faerie Queene* arises from these sources in such a way that their separateness is at once both affirmed and denied. Different critical conclusions may be drawn from this paradox, but insofar as the poem is prophetic—our concern in the present essay—it draws on five large banks or matrices of myth. Spenser, like Milton, writes as if he too had "infinite remembraunce," and so strong is the sense of this memory that *The Faerie Queene* affirms the idea of typological matrix itself. In any event, by accepting the internal relativism of the five matrices, their continual giving way to each other unexpectedly, we find that the larger construct of the six books gains in coherence.

III

Typological Matrices in
THE FAERIE QUEENE

 T IS HARD TO AVOID THE IMPRESSION THAT SPEN-
ser completed his epic to the extent it needed
completion; the open-ended sixth book seems to
close a circle begun in Book I, while the Mutabilitie Cantos—Spenser's Apocalypse—share a
similar satisfactory assertion of closure. A timeless circle of continual change, the poem rounds
off typologically, within its six books displaying the most obvious symmetries of narrative.[1] Book I shares

1. The use of the term "typology" is problematic. Strictly speaking, the vogue of biblical typology—figural allegory, with its strong
historical bent—is a seventeenth-century phenomenon in England. My
reasons for believing Spenser anticipates this vogue are set forth in the
present chapter. But perhaps only one reason need be given, to start
with: that the heroic poem during the Renaissance always has strong
local, national, or historical overtones, whether through the Euhemerist
tradition or not. One fundamental typological aspect characterizes all
five of the matrices adduced below: their yield of the hopeful image
of rebirth, in time, "that true glorious type of thine." The situation
following the seventeenth century is similar; here too poets probably
kept the typological perspective alive through their continuing interest in the heroic poem.

with Book VI the analysis of the problem of grace (spiritual holiness and courtly graciousness). Books II and V share the problem of balance, whether the interior balance of temperance or the exterior balance of justice. Books III and IV share the theme of love, whether attachments to a single object or to a group of objects (chastity and friendship). Taking the first three books as parallels to the second three, we have another symmetry: private virtues are set off against their public equivalents. Critics furthermore have shown that such linkages join books in sequential pairs, 1 plus 2, 3 plus 4, 5 plus 6. One is faced with various concentricities, circles within circles, and although the poem opens out at the edges and quests are left unclosed, the thematic structure of *The Faerie Queene*, as it stands, may be plotted in a large concentric mandala design. This fact suggests at once that the poem is basically templar in form, which I believe to be the case, but that its narrative intention presses vagrant images of error into the foreground. Further, as we know, the narrator can imagine errantry in a benign form:

> The waies, through which my weary steps I guyde,
>> In this delightfull land of Faery,
>> Are so exceeding spacious and wyde,
>> And sprinkled with such sweet variety,
>> Of all that pleasant is to eare or eye,
>> That I nigh ravisht with rare thoughts delight,
>> My tedious travell doe forget thereby;
>> And when I gin to feele decay of might,
> It strength to me supplies, and chears my dulled spright.
>
>> (VI, Pr., 1)

This wandering refreshes weary steps, but significantly the lines occur towards the end of the epic, where the poet has already established the golden meaning of his vision. He has, in our terms, redeemed the maze of error which was the locus of the first adventure, Redcrosse's encounter in the Wood of Error. But this achievement has been long in happening.

One reason for wanting to account for the overall style and form of *The Faerie Queene* in prophetic terms is the powerful teleological drive which accounts for Spenser's success in arriving at the perspective of the Proem to Book VI. By centering the whole poem around the image and person of Gloriana, Spenser has let the whole complex mythos depend, finally, upon the idea of glory—a secular (or not so secular) equivalent of the magnificence of Divine Providence. Glory is a *telos* so powerful that it permits the ambiguous suspension, often in mid-career, of innumerable stories and scenes, just as God's providential designs allow the myriad trials and errors of the City of Man. In the words of Fulke Greville's *Inquisition upon Fame and Honor*, "glory doth containe / some supernaturall sparke, or apparition, / More than the common human can attaine." Through her glory the Faerie Queene controls the doom of her dependents, her knights and ladies, as indeed her title tells us. In tune with this providential myth, Spenser can in the Letter to Ralegh describe himself as a "poet historicall" who, "recoursing to the thinges forepaste, and divining of thinges to come, maketh a pleasing Analysis of all." This is a vatic conception of the heroic poem.

Biblical Matrix

MUCH THE MOST OBVIOUS TYPOLOGY to Spenser's earliest readers would have been the biblical. This mode of prophecy has been frequently noted as the basis of Milton's epics and of his *Samson Agonistes*, and increasingly it is seen to be a major force in seventeenth-century poetics.[2] It is based, generally, on the doubling of Old and New Testaments, with their Old and

2. W. G. Madsen, *From Shadowy Types to Truth* (New Haven, 1968); Northrop Frye, "The Typology of *Paradise Regained*," *Modern Philology* 53 (1956), reprinted in *Fables of Identity;* Frye, *The Return of Eden: Five Essays on Milton's Epics* (Toronto, 1965); Michael Fixler, *Milton and the Kingdoms of God* (London, 1964); Barbara Lewalski, *Milton's Brief Epic: The Genre, Meaning, and Art of Paradise Regained* (Providence, 1966); C. A. Patrides, *Milton and the Christian Tradition* (Oxford, 1966); F. M. Krouse, *Milton's Samson and the Christian Tradition* (Princeton, 1949).

New Laws, Old and New Covenants: "Yea al the old Testament is a general prophecie, and foreshewing of the New, which . . . is conteyned, and lieth hid in the old."[3] Central to this "typological perspective" is the mythic equation drawn between the first Adam and Christ, the second Adam. Whereas a positive equal sign could be placed between, let us say, Joshua and Jesus, both manifestly heroic fighters, "Adam was a rather special type in that his figural relation to Christ was defined chiefly through contrasts rather than, as is the usual emphasis, through resemblances, though of course in all typological symbolism both elements are present."[4]

The *discordia concors* of the old and new Adam contains in little the ratio of temple and error. Saint Ambrose had observed that "it is fitting to be recorded that as the first Adam was ejected from Paradise into the desert, so the second Adam returned from the desert to Paradise."[5] This interpretation fixes the view that the errors of Adam are due to his acceding to temptation, whereas the victory of Christ is specifically his victory over the tempter "in the wildernesse." Paradise, the garden, is the original *templum* for the Hebraic-Christian tradition, while the desert is the archetypal profane space. Thus it is easy to give Moses or David or Solomon or Joshua a typological role, since they attempt an archetypal return from the wilderness to a Promised Land. In seventeenth-century theology and poetry the parallelisms between Old and New Testaments could be ramified in great complexity. Henry Vertue, for example, held that "Adam was a King, a Prophet, and a Sacrificer."[6] What was fully articulated in

3. The Douai reading, quoted in Lewalski, 170.
4. Lewalski, 176.
5. Quoted in Lewalski, 176.
6. Ibid. Thomas Traherne, meditating on the Psalms in *Centuries* III, calls David a prophet. Donne assumes this commonplace in his sermons on the Psalms. On his exegetical methods, see E. M. Simpson, ed., *John Donne's Sermons on the Psalms and Gospels* (Berkeley and Los Angeles, 1963), 7–8; cf. C. S. Lewis, *Reflections on the Psalms* (London, 1958) especially 9–19 (on "judgment"); 44–53 (on the Temple).

Paradise Regained and *Paradise Lost* could hardly receive such complete "analysis" in *The Faerie Queene*, and yet readers of Spenser have long known that the quest of Redcrosse was an *imitatio Christi* and thus belonged to this same typological tradition.

The redemptive myth of Redcrosse begins on a plain, edged by a labyrinthine Wood of Error which the hero and his companions enter to escape from a sudden storm. The omen of the tempest heralds the first, but only partial, victory over "Foule Errour." When Redcrosse spills her inky blood, he might be thought to have achieved a permanent advantage over falsehood, but as we discover, his quest is only beginning. In what is perhaps the most disgusting epiphany in literature, Spenser paints the portrait of Errour, "most lothsome, filthie, foule, and full of vile disdaine."[7] This envious creature, half serpent, half woman, is an apocalyptic summary of all that is evil in the abuse of prophecy, as one of its sources, Revelation 16:13, suggests: "And I saw three unclean spirits like frogs come out of the mouth of the dragon, and out of the mouth of the beast, and out of the mouth of the false prophet." Spenser likes to overreach in his monstrosities, and here he overreaches even himself, so that one can hardly begin to tie the mistakenness of Errour to any particular fault or vice of knowledge. On the other hand, besides the continuous association of Errour with her own muck and filth, Spenser strongly suggests her immense procreative power (her "fruitfull curses spawne"), which he compares with the progeny of the swollen Nile. Further, her "cole black bloud" sustains a hellish obscurity, which can only be called "inky," and which the poet identifies as the perversion of language. Errour's poisonous vomit is full of unchewed, uncooked, and undigested lumps of meat; it is full of "bookes and papers;" it is full of blind, loathsome frogs and toads. Blind, printed, and undigested! If one were a Puritan

7. See J. M. Steadman, "Spenser's *Errour* and the Renaissance Allegorical Tradition," *Neophilologische Mitteilungen* 62 (1961): 22–38. Alpers, *The Poetry of The Faerie Queene*, 230 n., consigns the said "tradition" to outer darkness: "There is no justification for imposing these commentaries on the poem."

reader, one probably thought the books were Romanist. Whatever one's faith, the Spenserian aition of error seems strongly connected with his own mode of literary existence, since he too is writing a book. One aim of Book I is to widen the scope of the opening apocalypse, to include more human or more natural sources of error than the source in verbal untruth.

Error thereafter assumes more virulent forms, when Redcrosse suffers a separation from Truth in the person of his lady, Una. Both Duessa and Archimago are named for their divisive, delusive functions. To reinforce the sense that error is a widening gyre separating man from God, Spenser allows Redcrosse to escape from the demonic parody of the temple, Lucifera's court, the House of Pride.[8] He can defeat despair in the person of Sansjoy, a limited despair, the lack of a Christian sense of well-being at having put on the whole armor of God. Yet this victory is not complete (Sansjoy, merely wounded, gets treatment from the pagan doctor and magus, Aesculapius), and pride still haunts the hero, who later succumbs to its more deadly effects in the double assault of Duessa's seduction and Orgoglio's tyranny. Here in pride's dungeon (which must be the "keep" of the House of

---

8. Spenser uses "gyre" in a pejorative sense, e.g., III, i, 23, where it rhymes with "yre" and is used for a battle of six knights against one; Britomart, in her first adventure, "perforce disparted their compacted gyre." Cf., the more interesting usage, at II, v, 8:

> Deadly dismayd, with horrour of that dint
> *Pyrochles* was, and grieved eke entyre;
> Yet nathemore did it his fury stint,
> But added flame unto his former fire,
> That welnigh molt his hart in raging yre,
> Ne thenceforth his approved skill, to ward,
> Or strike, or hurtle rownd in warlike gyre,
> Remembred he, ne car'd for his saufgard,
> But rudely rag'd, and like a cruell Tygre far'd.

Other poets of the time use "gyre" more neutrally, or with a kinder sense, e.g., Drayton, *Eclogue II*, 71; Peele, *Polyhymnia*, 36 (for which see *OED*, "gyre").

Pride) the hero's distance from his Savior is greatest, and yet exactly at this occasion Prince Arthur, the type of Christ as Redeemer throughout the poem, makes his appearance and saves Redcrosse. Fittingly, Arthur tells us at once of his devotion to the Faerie Queene, and we know that he shares directly in the *telos* of her glory. His intervention, providential for Redcrosse and Una, prepares the way for the hero's successful battle against the suicidal Despair, if we can call such dark ruminations a "battle," and it prepares us for the subsequent demonstration that Redcrosse has a true but temporary home, the House of Holiness, which is the preparatory temple of instruction and vision. Whitaker reminds us that this episode of sacred pedagogy, "certainly the most conservative part of Book I . . . will reveal how much medieval Catholic thought remained in Spenser, as indeed it did in Anglicanism."[9] Whitaker further has observed the inherent complications, even ambiguities, that surround such moments of prophetic instruction. He argues that a vision of mystical truths, though prophetic, may involve Spenser in a contradiction here, since his hero cannot enjoy the contemplative ascent to Holiness but must pursue the *vita activa* in his role as defender of the faith. Yet it may be that Redcrosse's "deeds of armes" are theologically not simply identical with "good works," since such martial deeds are not only a costly purchase of salvation; they are also the Protestant's preparation for salvation through trial; the "care" of Una is not a "work" in the old sense. The virtues of monastic retreat Spenser handles with unconcealed doubt, if not suspicion; one distrusts a hermit, even an honest one, in *The Faerie Queene*. Even so, "it should be noted, by way of caution, that it was the contemplative life—the life of mystical union with God—and not the intellectual life that Spenser was relegating to heaven,"[10] that is, to a future paradise.

The redemption of Eden, announced by the betrothal of Red-

9. Virgil K. Whitaker, *The Religious Basis of Spenser's Thought* (Stanford, 1950), 54.

10. Ibid., 56.

crosse and Una at the close of Book I, is, however providential in form, a human quest—never perfected, but always in the process of perfection. The reunion of Redcrosse and Una thus comments directly on history, which we have found to be one requirement of the prophetic vision. If the conclusion of the typological action of Book I is the defeat of death the ultimate error, if Redcrosse at the end is no longer "wrapt in Errour's endless train," one might suppose that this first portion of the poem *predicts* a fully confident future for the reborn British nation. But that would be the demonic parody of the prophetic moment, and the aim of the poem is a proper, limited aim. This "other Eden" is yet only a demiparadise. In keeping with the mode of most Old Testament prophecy, Spenser wants perspective on the ongoing present in the visionary life of England. He is generally opposed to millenarian speculations and promises.[11] He admits historical uncertainty. He wishes in his prophetic role merely to be a free spokesman of God and Man. Biblical prophecy as a basis for explaining the mode of symbolizing in Book I means something like "scriptural interpretation" or "vision based on an inspired understanding of scriptures." It does not mean *l'art de conjecture*. When, during the reign of Elizabeth, "prophesyings" were held, these public meetings mainly allowed congregations to discuss various readings of the scriptures; only in their abuse did they become political meetings, and were thus suppressed by Elizabeth.[12] The chief problem for a poet living in an age of "prophe-

11. Harry Berger, Jr., *The Allegorical Temper*, 102: "Commentators who, like Greenlaw, emphasize the idea of an Elizabethan millennium are going against the major tendency of Book II, which, in its view of man's earthly state, is much more traditional." True enough, but this in part is possible because Book II, as opposed to Book V, is relatively closed off from the actual world of error. Its vision of *krasis*, as Berger shows, can be projected as an interiorizing temple, the Castle of Alma. It is also true that Spenser would like to deny millennial impatience in general.

12. "Prophesying" here has roughly the same sense as in Jeremy Taylor's *Liberty of Prophesying* (1647), which could be rendered, *Freedom to Interpret the Scriptures according to the Dictates of Con-*

syings" would be to steer a middle course between futurism and abject conservatism.

Throughout the history of prophecy, beginning with the Old Testament, there had been an inherent tendency in scriptural and natural interpretation to look to the future, if only because the Old Testament heritage assumed the election of the Children of Israel.[13] They were a small and embattled people whose voca-

---

science and the Wisdom of Inherited Authority. Suppression of Elizabethan prophesyings was at first entrusted to Archbishop Whitgift; on which, see P. M. Dawley, *John Whitgift and the English Reformation* (New York, 1954), 131–34; also E. T. Davies, *The Political Ideas of Richard Hooker* (London, 1948), 7, where it is shown that only Grindal's death prevented Elizabeth from dismissing him for his defense of the prophesyings. Narrowing the definition of the term to mere political prediction, we find that suppression of prophecy has an earlier origin: cf. Statute 33, Henry VII, c. XIV, proclaiming it a felony "to declare any false prophecy upon occasion of arms, field, letters, names, cognizances, or badges." After repeal in Edward VI's reign—reenacted in Statutes 3, 4, Edward VI, c. XV—Statute 5, Elizabeth, c. XV (clause 2) spells out the feared intent of "false prophecy": "to make any rebellion, insurrection, dissension, loss of life or other disturbance within this realm or other the Queen's dominions." These statutes are discussed in Rupert Taylor, *The Political Prophecy in England* (New York, 1911), 105–6. Taylor is largely concerned with Galfridian prophecy, its rise, development, and decline.

13. On prophecy and history, and typology: H. W. Robinson, *Inspiration and Revelation in the Old Testament* (Oxford, 1962); John Skinner, *Prophecy and Religion* (Cambridge, 1961); T. J. Meek, *Hebrew Origins* (New York, 1960); Martin Buber, *The Prophetic Faith* (New York, 1960); Rudolf Bultmann, *History and Eschatology* (Edinburgh, 1957); Erich Auerbach, "Figura," in *Scenes from the Drama of European Literature* (New York, 1959); R. P. C. Hanson, *Allegory and Event* (London, 1959); E. Lampert, *The Apocalypse of History* (London, 1948); Stanislas Giet, *L'Apocalypse et l'histoire* (Paris, 1957); Paul Vuillaud, *La Fin du monde* (Paris, 1952); M. C. D'Arcy, *The Meaning and Matter of History* (New York, 1961); Herbert Butterfield, *Christianity and History* (New York, 1949); T. F. Driver, *The Sense of History in Greek and Shakespearean Drama* (New York, 1960). Within the frame of Christian historiography the aim of life is participation in a cosmic education; Löwith

tion could only be justified by the future; their present was too hazardous to seem like home. Furthermore, two major books of the Bible lent weight to the futuristic drive of prophecy, the Book of Daniel and the Book of Revelation. As a modern scholar has said of Daniel, "the device adopted by its author of addressing his contemporaries through the medium of an ancient sage has encouraged the erroneous notion that prediction rather than proclamation was the primary business of the prophet."[14] Yet this was an immensely popular text during Spenser's time, and it may only be because he follows an argument (by his own intuition if not directly from his reading) set forth in Jean Bodin's *Methodus*, that Spenser is, as it seems to me, resolutely opposed to apocalypse, in spite of his periodically apocalyptic symbolism. Bodin had felt obliged to refute the theory of the four monarchies which drew so much authority from Daniel. "A long-established, but mistaken, idea about four empires, made famous

---

calls it "divine pedagogy." Orosius, *Seven Books of History against the Pagans*, trans. I. W. Raymond (New York, 1936), 33, is perhaps typical: "We hold that if the world and man are directed by a Divine Providence that is as good as it is just, and if man is both weak and stubborn on account of the changeableness of his nature and his freedom of choice, then it is necessary for man to be guided in the spirit of strict justice. Everyone who sees mankind reflected through himself and in himself perceives that this world has been disciplined since the creation of man by alternating periods of good and bad times"—the rewards and punishments of a divine schoolmaster.

14. E. W. Heaton, *The Old Testament Prophets* (Penguin ed.), 17–18. The antipredictive view of prophecy is apparent in Campanella's remarks on Tasso: "Certain people think that Tasso chose such a subject in order to reanimate our minds to reconquer the Holy Land through the examples of the virtue of our men, and to generate concord among Christians. . . . Such a poem as Tasso's is very profitable and almost prophetic (*quasi profetico*), because the true prophet is one who not only says future things, but who scolds princes for their wickedness and cowardice and peoples for their ignorance, for sedition, and for bad behaviour." *Poetica*, quoted in Bernard Weinberg, *A History of Literary Criticism in the Italian Renaissance* (Chicago, 1963), 2:1068.

by the prestige of great men, has sent its roots down so far that it seems difficult to eradicate. It has won over countless interpreters of the Bible. . . . Shaken by their authority, I used to think it ought not to be doubted. I was stirred also by the prophecy of Daniel, whose reliability it is a crime to disparage, whose authority it is wicked to question. Yet afterwards I understood that the obscure and ambiguous words of Daniel could be twisted into various meanings; and interpreting the prophecies I preferred to take that formula of the courts, 'It doth not appear' . . . I do not see how we are to relate the wild beasts and the image discussed by Daniel to those empires which flourish everywhere nowadays and have flourished for so many centuries."[15] Obscure as the Daniel prophecy may be, it seems to have been lurking in Spenser's thought when he wrote Canto II of Book V, where the Egalitarian Giant resembles the "great image" of Daniel 2:31, the giant moulded in gold, silver, brass, iron and clay. Like Daniel's giant the Spenserian monster advances or implies a theory of linear time. Spenser wants to show that the apocalyptic hope for a future which would return men to a material golden age is an empty, brittle, idolatrous hope, while the true apocalypse can reveal only a spiritual state. The mainstream of Old Testament prophecy tends to reinforce such a view since Isaiah, Jeremiah, and Ezekiel seek the moral invigoration of their people as they live in the present. On the other hand the eighth-century prophets show political motivations, and these were open to chiliastic interpretation. One such bias is present in Foxe's *Book of Martyrs*, the "history" of the

15. Jean Bodin, *Method for the Easy Comprehension of History*, trans. and ed. Beatrice Reynolds (New York, 1944), 291–96. In *Daniel: A Commentary* (Philadelphia, 1965), 44, N. W. Porteous observes that the first thing Daniel tells King Nebuchadnezzar about his dream (in Daniel 2) is "that it is eschatological in character. It concerns what is to happen at the end of the present age. . . . The king is being told by God how history is moving towards its consummation. . . ." The passage uses a phrase, "in the end of days," which seems to denote "the end of a perspective of history," or, in another formulation, "the *closing period* of the future so far as it falls within the range of view of the writer using it."

Marian martyrs. Haller has said that *"Actes and Monuments* in 1562 was the most elaborate expression of the apocalyptic expectancy with which the returned exiles and their party greeted Elizabeth at her accession."[16] This expectancy was kept alive during her long reign, and any use of prophetic language by a poet, even a conservative like Spenser, would gather some of the millennial passion attached by Protestants to Elizabeth's rule. The poet can only reduce the futurist, determinist pressure of his myth. Within the orthodox Christian providential framework there is no problem in this: the hero moves within a sacramental universe where all events, persons, and things are what Spenser calls "sacred symbols."[17] Looking before and after, the *vates* reveals the mystery of what *is*.

Since the biblical tradition of prophecy is God-centered and book-centered at the same time, it extends the relevance of a true reading to the widest possible scope. The prophet who speaks for the Deity also tries to make his vision available to the ordinary believer by translating the Word of the Lord into vernaculars. Even to translate vision into speech is a great step, and it employs the full resources of metaphor. Boccaccio, with other Renaissance mythographers, imagines that classical myth translates Christian mystery.[18] *The Faerie Queene* makes a similar translation of sacred myth and vision into its own poetic variant, which touches the lay reader. The lively oracles of God exercise that skill which is the basis of Reformation faith, the independent power of reading and interpreting a text, such as Erasmus had

16. William Haller, *The Elect Nation: The Meaning and Relevance of Foxe's Books of Martyrs* (New York, 1963), 124; also Helen White, *Tudor Books of Saints and Martyrs* (Madison, 1963). The martyr, like Thomas More (White, 120–21), was often believed to have prophetic powers, as indeed any man at the point of death, e.g., John of Gaunt in *Richard II*.

17. *F.Q.*, II, ii, 10. Cf. D. C. Allen, *The Harmonious Vision: Studies in Milton's Poetry* (Baltimore, 1953), chap. 1, "The Search for the Prophetic Strain: 'L'Allegro' and 'Il Penseroso.'"

18. Boccaccio, *Genealogia Deorum Gentilium*, XIV, viii, xiii; XV, vii–viii. Translated as *Boccaccio on Poetry*, by C. G. Osgood (Princeton, 1930; repr. New York, 1956).

contemplated when editing the New Testament. As a divine poem *The Faerie Queene* picks up an immense surplus of literary energy which comes through as a steady allusive recollection of the Bible, most prominently of the psalms, the prophetic books, and the Book of Revelation. The epistles of Saint Paul underpin much of its Christian doctrine.

For the ordinary Elizabethan reader the New Testament was, moreover, a presage of political destiny, even though its more sublime purpose was to tell the Redeemer's spiritual history. Modern critics have perhaps overemphasized the instructive contrast between nature and grace in *The Faerie Queene*, so that we should insist on the politics of grace, to correct the balance. In Elizabethan England, Tudor England, the quest for a true faith was informed by the continual search for myths of power and authority. Men found these in the idea of a New Jerusalem, a "City of God" which in more extreme leveling and digging moods some might wish to locate on earth, but which more usually was located in a heavenly afterstate. Jerusalem kept its Hebrew sense, "city of peace," or, in Gilson's translation, "vision of peace." This afterstate served as the model against which to measure the present life; the two "lives" were not synonymous. Even so, and in spite of any reservation which Spenser himself might have, we cannot too strongly emphasize the apocalyptical beliefs of common men during the last years of the sixteenth century, when with the aid of astrology, numerology, and magical omens they might well believe that 1588 would be a terrible year,[19] or that the end of the world would come with the turn

19. Garrett Mattingly, *The Armada* (Boston, 1962), 400: "When the Spanish Armada challenged the ancient lords of the English Channel on their own grounds, the impending conflict took on the aspect of a judicial duel in which, as was expected in such duels, God would defend the right. The solemnity of the occasion was heightened by the portentous prophecies about the year of the conflict, prophecies so ancient and respectable that even the most enlightened and skeptical could not quite ignore them. So, when the two fleets approached their appointed battleground, all Europe watched." When the "Protestant

of the century. Any natural disaster would add its ominous fuel. The Mutabilitie Cantos are one answer to such faiths. Mutabilitie is denied her apocalypse. God's "sabbath" is yet to come at some divinely withheld moment, but certainly not to be ordained by a rebel princess. Rebellion, we shall see, is the sublunar attempt to anticipate and hasten the apocalyptic moment, and that, above every other crime, must be prevented and punished. There can be no materially self-fulfilling prophecies.

To write the full account of Spenser's dependence on biblical symbolism would therefore be to describe an imagery that transcends materialist or determinist notions of linear progress. In that sense *The Faerie Queene* is against progress. Biblical thought animates the whole poem, while biblical imagery lends itself to Spenser's present-centered mythmaking. To take only the most obvious example: the Gardens of Adonis are capable of interpretation entirely within the terms of Ovidian and Neoplatonic thought; but the typology of the Song of Songs enters here, complicating our sense of the possibilities. The connection of the Canticles with ideas of time and history had long been established by the commentary of Saint Bernard, and the epithalamic "enclosed garden" shades and guides the poem here, to fulfill its commentary upon the nature of time. Old Testament prophecy animates because it uses a language of animation (David's "notable prosopopeias"), and the effect is almost that of a modular unit of animation, which Sidney called "the often and free changing of persons." Robinson's summary applies: revelation in the Old Testament operates in three general realms, in Nature, "which to the Hebrew mind was alive even in those forms which we regard as inanimate," in Man, "both in the individual and social aspects of human nature," and, most obvious of all, in History, where

---

wind" sprang up, "the English welcomed a material proof that God was with them," while on their side the Spaniards equally accepted the prophecies, for them a sign of God's inscrutable, providential displeasure. The prophecy of Regiomontanus links the Armada with the Spenserian prophecies of Merlin, since Merlin was the sage on whom Regiomontanus drew.

"prophecy found its chief material and from [which it] derived its most significant content. . . . The changing events of political and social circumstance always admitting a secular interpretation, were transformed by the prophets into firmly controlled activities of God. He was shown as often using human agencies, just as he used those of physical force and nature, in fulfillment of his purpose."[20] The political role of the prophet, once fixed by the Old Testament, never faded, and a ruler had to take his prophets seriously, for they were among his most powerful propagandists. Queen Elizabeth came close to dismissing Archbishop Grindal (Spenser's Algrind in the *Calender*) because he defended the "prophesyings," which fears about the royal succession made only more threatening to Elizabeth's peace of mind. Guided by the radical interpreter of scriptures, the average man might betake himself to a radical cause. But rightly used, prophecy instructed him to believe that he had joined in the Tudor vocation. Lampert has well expressed this compromise of God's timeless purpose and the historical aims of man: "Providence, therefore, is a theandric mystery which requires a world where God is active and where man is active too. In short this is not a block universe nor one in which God's providence is exercised *ab extra* after the fashion of an earthly architect or moral governor who imposes his laws upon men, but a realm of divine-human activity —the realm of History. And freedom under God's providential care belongs only to him who no longer knows providence and History as an extraneous force, but begins to apprehend them as an inward event, as the expression of God's and his own freedom."[21] Spenser writes in Book V this Christian allegory of "realization of types finding their consummation and oracles their fulfillment and events their ordained re-enactment."[22] Under these conditions, as Richard Hooker had said, "nature there-

20. Robinson, *Inspiration and Revelation*, 161–63.

21. Lampert, *Apocalypse of History*, 142.

22. Hanson, *Allegory and Event*, 36. For the literary student Auerbach's "Figura" essay may be the best introduction.

fore is nothing else but God's instrument."[23] All significant events of history are given typological value, instead of timeless moral value. Nor is there any barrier to syncretic use of pagan materials. As Hooker could allow the pantheon of natural deities (Jupiter, Juno, and the rest) to become God's agents, so Spenser, in the manner of other Renaissance poets and philosophers, could conflate Christian and pagan divinities to make one large and varied army of spirits.[24]

The crudest effect of a Christian prophetic reading will be to show that *The Faerie Queene* is an epic of England's election to the sacred defence of the Protestant faith. The election comes at a "definite point of time which has a fixed content," the *kairos* or *occasion* of New Testament hermeneutics.[25] This is not equal to,

23. *Ecclesiastical Polity*, I, iii, 4. Faerieland, a kingdom of spirit, may be contrasted with the mythical kingdom of "Britain." Thus Thomas Roche states: "Spenser's apparent confusion of Britain and Faeryland is in reality a careful poetic discrimination. The poem is a fulfillment of the ideal of civil life that is to occur historically during the reign of the Tudors. From the point of view of the narrative Elizabeth is only a descendant of Britomart, still far off in the future. From the point of view of the poet Elizabeth is the fulfillment of the prophecy in the chronicle of British kings. The action of the poem is the evolution of the civil ideal and is conceived as a reciprocal interchange between England and Faeryland." *The Kindly Flame: A Study of the Third and Fourth Books of Spenser's Faerie Queene* (Princeton, 1964), 46; also 31–50 on prophecy.

24. E. g., Tommaso Campanella, *Del Senso delle cose e della magia*, ed. A. Bruers (Bari, 1925), 3:201 (chap. 2). See D. P. Walker, *Spiritual and Demonic Magic from Ficino to Campanella* (London, 1958). On prophecy in the *De incantationibus* of Pomponazzi, see Ernst Cassirer, *The Individual and the Cosmos*, 106–9.

25. Oscar Cullmann, *Christ and Time* (Philadelphia, 1964), 51–52: "Because in Greek thought time is not conceived as a progressing line with beginning and end, but rather as a circle, the fact that man is bound to time must here be experienced as an enslavement, as a curse. Time moves about in the eternal circular course in which everything keeps recurring. . . . For the Greeks, the idea that redemption is to take place through divine action in the course of events in time is impossible." Here one must, however, raise the question of the mystery

but it is analogous to, the coming of the Messiah, as the Marian martyrdoms corresponded to the moment of his Crucifixion. It is a sacred *season*, or, alternatively, when Redcrosse lives through his trials in the world of error, he lives through an undifferentiated period prior to and necessary to the coming of the true season of his betrothal to Una. Through trial of an otherwise "fugitive and cloister'd virtue" he emerges from the flux of the

---

religions and their temporal meaning. Cullmann continues: "In the Primitive Christian preaching, on the contrary, salvation, in keeping with the Bible's linear understanding of time, is conceived strictly in terms of a time process. The expectation of the coming Kingdom of God is not to be so dissolved that it means 'always standing in the situation of decision.' (Bultmann, *Jesus*, 1926, 49–54) Were that done, the event of the coming of God's reign would not be 'an event in the course of time.' The coming consummation is a real future, just as the past redemptive deed of Jesus Christ, in spite of the fact that it is the interpreting mid-point of all times, is from the standpoint of the Church a real past, and just as the present of the Church, stamped as it is with a thoroughly time-conditioned character, is bound back to this past and forward to that future. The New Testament knows only the linear concept of Today, Yesterday, and Tomorrow; all philosophical reinterpretation and dissolution into timeless metaphysics is foreign to it. It is precisely upon the basis of this rectilinear conception of time that time in Primitive Christianity can yield the framework for the divine process of revelation and redemption, for those kairoi which God in his omnipotence fixes, for those ages into which he divides the whole process. Because time is thought of as a progressing line, it is possible here for something to be fulfilled; a divine plan can move forward to complete execution; the goal which beckons at the end of the line can give to the entire process which is taking place all along the line the impulse to strive thither; finally, the decisive mid-point, the Christ-deed, can be the firm hold that serves as a guidepost for all the process that lies behind and for all that lies ahead." For a useful discussion of the terms *kairos* and *chronos*, see Frank Kermode, *The Sense of an Ending: Studies in the Theory of Fiction* (New York, 1957); also, Edward Said, "A Meditation on Beginnings," *Salmagundi* 2, no. 4 (1968): 36–55; Harry Berger, Jr., "*Paradise Lost* Evolving: Books I–VI," *Centennial Review* 11, no. 4 (1967): 483–531 (on certain problems of "happy ending").

aion, the endless duration of linear time. The critical notion is the idea that his *kairos* has a fixed content; that is, the season of Redcrosse's final redemption at the Well of Life gives stable, templar form to his earthly existence, though he has glimmerings of this freedom and order earlier in his doubtful career. (The quest imposed on him by Gloriana prefigures an endless cycle of such careers.) The happy season celebrated at the end of Book I is another *kairos* because it is "the moment in time which is especially favorable for an undertaking; it is the point of time of which one has long before spoken without knowing its actual date."[26] The prophetic moment here is coeval with the beginning of the epic quest, with the annual feast at the Court of Maidenhead. That feast was a "wellhead" of the poem, a moment of conception. Viewed in this light, the end of each heroic quest is its beginning, and by returning to the sacred origin, to Eden, Redcrosse establishes the initial concentricity of the whole vision, enabling it to include variant quests in the books that follow.

The reader may well ask, then is the prophetic moment only that promised end, when "his owne two hands the holy knotts did knitt, / That none but death for ever can divide?" (I, xii, 37). In a final, perfected sense, perhaps our answer should be yes, the marriage of heroic Christian man with Truth is a complete union. But we come closer to Spenser, and I think to the biblical tradition of typology, if we imagine that *many* moments are conceived as prophetic, if only in a limited sense. What counts

---

26. *Christ and Time*, 51–52. Aquinas: "Philosophers call every work of nature the work of intelligence. Consequently, the world is ruled by the providence of that intellect which gave this order to nature; and we may compare the providence by which God rules the world to the domestic foresight by which a man rules his family, or to the political foresight by which a ruler governs a city or a kingdom, and directs the acts of others to a definite end." Thomas Aquinas, "Providence, Article 2," in *Providence and Predestination*, trans. R. W. Mulligan from *De Veritate* (Chicago, 1961), 18–19. *Ecclesiastical Polity*, I, iii, 4, calls Providence a "divine efficiency," while V, xx, 1, reminds us of the traditional diad, "the Law and the Prophets."

rather is the sense of threshold, the sense that great deeds contain within their forms the seeds of great truths. Viewed in this more provisional light, every episode in Book I, since it involves the alternatives of temple and error, of spiritual virtue or depravity, possesses a typological direction. Book I differs from subsequent books in that it officially recognizes relations of temple and error in theological terms. Here, since the Christian system of providential time is openly the basis for the *templum*, the House of Holiness, the poet can at the same level of narrative treat error as a matter of truth versus falsehood. Error here, we might say, is pure error; later it will be transformed into variant modes, excess, impurity, promiscuity, and so on. Una as truth offsets Errour as falsehood. Partly then, because its myth projects ideas of true and false knowledge, in short a fundamental set of choices which governs all other choices, Book I creates a particularly strong sense of trust and expectation.

Through his readiness for grace and good tidings, joy and glory, Redcrosse exposes himself to the hazard of despair and disgrace.[27] His exposure is complete and continuous, with no let-up, and this creates a governing tension. Any phenomenon may be an omen, so that eternal alert is the price the hero pays. The style of the poem is therefore not sententious, which would imply a reference to the classical world view of endlessly historical cycles. Here continuous novelties—the wonders of romantic encounter—promise rebirth into the New Covenant of grace and

27. Cf. Donne, Sermon 4 (for 29 Jan. 1625/6), in *Sermons on the Psalms and Gospels*, 112: "If you looke upon this world in a Map, you find two Hemispheares, two half worlds. If you crush heaven into a Map, you may find two Hemisphears too, two half heavens; Halfe will be Joy, and halfe will be Glory; for in these two, the joy of heaven, and the glory of heaven, is all heaven often represented unto us." Because the text of this sermon includes the word "shadow," the exordium turns into an analysis of biblical typology: "*David* was not onely a cleare Prophet of Christ himselfe, but a Prophet of every particular Christian: He foretels what I, what any shall doe, and suffer, and say."

at the same moment offer the occasion of a fall from grace. As in the famed "Choice of Hercules," heroism is a response to emergency and spiritual crisis.

Vergilian Matrix

Spenserian anxiety has another source, insofar as its origin is literary: the Vergilian mode of typology. Spenser early announces the Vergilian affinities of his poem and follows Vergil by combining mythic elements from multiple sources in one single heroic framework.[28] As the *Aeneid* made a single diptych of the *Odyssey* and *Iliad*, so *The Faerie Queene* makes an even more complex union of earlier sources.[29] With his contemporaries Spenser doubtless would assume that the *Aeneid* was a model for the "heroic poem," not least because it had enjoyed a long and vigorous treatment in Christian exegesis. Further it was the source, with a few other major works which Spenser mentions in his Letter to Ralegh, of the new mode of romantic epic. Finally, the *Aeneid* is a prophetic work written in strictly epic form, so that it combines the figural style of Christian prophecy with the classical mode of a narrative poem. Di Cesare has well described this mode of prophecy: "In Homer and Virgil, and to a lesser extent in Apollonius of Rhodes and the minor Latin poets, prophecy serves to focus attention on particular characters and incidents; to heighten suspense; to unite the narrative proper with

28. The opening lines, "Lo I the man . . . ," etc., are derived from the opening of the *Aeneid*, in the Renaissance version Spenser would have read. William Nelson, *The Poetry of Edmund Spenser*, 117, and throughout the chapter, "That True Glorious Type."

29. Macrobius, the early fifth-century author of the *Dream of Scipio*, set forth this view of the double "source" of the *Aeneid* in his *Saturnalia*, V, ii, et passim. Since Macrobius is writing a paean to the *Aeneid*, it is revealing that he could praise it for being a perfect "mirror" (*speculum*) of Homer (V, ii, 13). *Saturnalia* would be a main text for the study of literary collage.

matters relative to it but not strictly in its compass; to expand the legitimate scope of the action beyond the poem's conclusion and thus suggest broader implications; and finally to suggest larger areas of the heroic world by the projection of the divine connection with human life."[30] Again we notice the mixture of two seemingly antithetical drives, toward focus and toward expansion.

Yet the chief structural or mythic drive may reduce all counterpulls to a single vector, the *fatum* that draws Aeneas toward the founding of a Latin state. This fatalism often permeates works influenced by Vergil, focusing our interest on the founding of a nation. The Letter to Ralegh recounts the classic line of descent

30. M. A. Di Cesare, *Vida's Christiad and Vergilian Epic* (New York and London, 1964), 107. Di Cesare cites G. E. Duckworth, *Foreshadowing and Suspense in the Epics of Homer, Apollonius, and Vergil* (Princeton, 1933) and C. H. Moore, "Prophecy in the Ancient Epic," *Harvard Studies in Classical Philology* 32 (1921): 98–175; to which add Duckworth, *Structural Patterns and Proportions in Vergil's Aeneid* (Ann Arbor, 1962). A brief, convenient account of Vergil's historiography appears in C. M. Bowra, *From Virgil to Milton* (London, 1961), 74–77, where Bowra describes the three main Vergilian excursions: Jupiter's prophecy in Book I, the vision of the famous Romans which the spirit of Anchises shows to Aeneas in Elysium, and the vision contained in the shield of Aeneas, "where the scenes depicted show those occasions when the existence of Rome seemed to be imperilled, either physically or morally, and yet somehow it survived." An excellent treatment of this subject is Nancy Lenkeith's *Dante and the Legend of Rome* (London, 1952); the actual existence of oracles in the ancient world complicates the literary idea thereof, on which see, among other sources, Robert Flaceliere, *Greek Oracles*, trans. Douglas Garman (New York, 1965); C. A. Patrides, "The Cessation of the Oracles: the History of a Legend," *MLR* 40 (1965): 500–507. *Georgic III* speaks of a temple to Caesar, which is in part the poem itself, and which foreshadows the temple Aeneas vows to build in *Aeneid 6*. In the dedicatory sonnet to Christopher Hatton, the Lord Chancellor, Spenser compares himself to Ennius and Vergil, Hatton to Caesar. The dedicatory sonnets deserve closer attention than they have received, since each appears to present a different aspect, not merely of the Elizabethan court circle, but also of the poet's own muse.

within this epic tradition: Homer, Vergil, Ariosto, and "lately Tasso." Book II of *The Faerie Queene* imagines a spread of empire within the political framework these "poets historicall" provided. In his Proem, Spenser would have the reader of "all this famous antique history"

> . . . with better sence advize,
> That of the world least part to us is red;
> And dayly how through hardy enterprize,
> Many great Regions are discovered,
> Which to late age were never mentioned.
> Who ever heard of th' Indian *Peru*?
> Or who in venturous vessell measured
> The *Amazons* huge river now found trew?
> Or fruitfullest *Virginia* who did ever vew?

This is an age when Sidney can write that Xenophon's "absolute heroical poem," the *Cyropaedeia*, "did imitate so excellently as to give us *effigiem justi imperii*, 'the portraiture of a just empire.' "[31] Imperialism means discovery of a God-given inheritance, which (through an oxymoron) is sanctified by taking the name of the "fruitfullest," sacred princess Virginia.[32] Throughout Book II, as Hamilton has shown, there run fleeting or full-scale allusions to *Iliad* and *Odyssey*, the final canto being, in effect, a microcosmic reduction of the whole of the *Odyssey*, while a continuing challenge to the aggressive Sir Guyon (the wrestler,

31. "Apologie for Poetrie," in *Elizabethan Critical Essays*, ed. G. G. Smith, 1:160.

32. Since Book V, Proem, invokes the Ovidian myth of the Flood, Book V may be commenting on the legend of the repeopling of the earth. A myth of justice has to take this legend into account, if only because the Flood is a millenarian nightmare adduced by many radical proponents of revolutionary change. See D. C. Allen, *The Legend of Noah: Renaissance Rationalism in Art, Science, and Letters* (1949; repr. Urbana, 1963), 113–38; Margaret T. Hodgen, *Early Anthropology in the Sixteenth and Seventeenth Centuries* (Philadelphia, 1964), 207–53.

as one iconography suggests) is the demand that he moderate a wrath very similar to the wrath of Achilles. The effect of these typological parallels is to double the spiritual questing of Book I with a geopolitical questing, as in the classical and Italian romantic epics. While Guyon's sensual trials parallel those of Odysseus, who flees Calypso and escapes from Circe and the Sirens, and Aeneas, who flees Troy and escapes from Dido, and therefore constitute an allegory of the soul, they have a purpose similar to the strivings of the classical heroes: a return home, or a voyage to the place where the national unity and destiny will be affirmed. Thus Spenser creates a demonic parody of Eldorado (which his Proem might have led us to expect), and in the Cave of Mammon presents hell as a variant of the Plutonian underworld to which both Odysseus and Aeneas descended, where the hero achieves a new level of visionary insight into his own true destiny. As with the *Odyssey* Spenser's poem associates the power of prophetic vision with memory and gives it final authority over the transformational magic of Circe, which hovers everywhere in Book II and is suggested darkly in its first and last cantos.[33] In the Vergilian mode, Spenser's underworld is a nursery of allegorical vices (Revenge, Despite, Treason, Hate, Jealousy, Fear, and Sorrow), while in the Cave itself we discover a pageant of fortune hunters, the doomed princes of classical legend, whose lack of a Redeemer brings them to their dark fate. The allegorical figure of Philotime reminds us that fame may be an infirmity of noble mind, a limiting and secular parody of sacred aspiration. The Cave is one kind of antitemple, the Bower of Bliss another. Between them lies the genuine temple of the Castle of Alma, where Spenser fully explicates the idea that the human body, the human soul, the divine "mystical body," and the perfect artifacts of the poet cohere in a vast architectural allegory. By making this temple (or "house of Temperance") into a castle, Spenser strengthens

33. Cf. *Comus*, where the figure of the false prophet is played by Circe's child. In the *Odyssey* Circe has a priestly position at the threshold of the other world. (Cf. *FQ*, II, i, 54; xii, 84–87.)

our sense that to enter it one has to have sought and practised a kind of athletic prowess. The chief virtue to be gained is tonus; Guyon is not a prig, though his tastes are delicate. He responds to anything impinging on his senses. Here the clarity he seeks, and the poet through him, is not truth, as before, but responsiveness, freedom from the prison of the body and the senses.

It is interesting, as a kind of narrative metonymy, that the final episode of Book II is preceded by Arthur's battle with Maleger, a resonant episode which is structured as the archetypal wrestling match between Hercules and Antaeus. Boccaccio typically enough allegorized Antaeus as the lust of the flesh. The myth itself goes deeper and suggests something of the essential nature of the virtue sought throughout Book II. Maleger is a "dead-living swain," revived continuously by contact with "th' earth his mother"—Spenser's word "usury" (stanza 45) implies that conditional immortality is a kind of unearned increment—and although the myth is complex we can say that Maleger's death by water is *not* a baptism (though perhaps a travesty of one), but is death by contact with the chaos of his own birth. The "standing," dead lake of water is the poetic image for the womb of Mother Earth, denied her blind procreative power. Maleger is the child of darkness, and though he cannot be killed by being committed "to grave terrestrial," the blind waters "in the earth" can kill him. He can be thrust back to his monstrous chthonic source, once the precise dynamic of that source is remembered by Prince Arthur. Maleger, complex in iconography, suggests that sin deprives man of good, and, as Augustine held of evil, is not something but a lack of something. This is the implication of his association with the blind womb of earth and water, the "womb of all, tomb of all, home of all, hearse of all night." Blindness, then, is an absolute sensory deprivation. Clear perception is the essence of the prudent act, according to a Platonic view; Spenser indeed must add the work of the will, to empower this structuring ability. Thus, when we arrive at the opening of Canto XII and Guyon is ready to attack the "perilous stead" of Acrasia's Bower, the *templum* of prudence is both a philosophic structure (that implied by the Castle of Alma and its apocalypse) and a perceptual order, or ordering process.

> Now gins this goodly frame of temperance
> Fairly to rise, and her adorned head
> To prick of highest praise forth to advance,
> Formerly grounded and fast setteled
> On firm foundation of true bountihead.
>
> (xii, 1)

Charity here as always within the Christian epic is the governing Pauline virtue, but "true bountihead" is only the foundation of Guyon's power. Above this foundation rises the head adorned (and this word is technically precise), while the whole "goodly frame" gives focus and form to the hero's actions. As frames yield perspective, they yield control over the chaos of fallen nature. There is here almost an identification of mental cybernetic powers with the framing process. The temperate hero, his virtue symbolizing the human attainment of the *templum*, can navigate freely. The last person to appear in Book II is Gryllus, the metamorphosed victim of Circe/Acrasia, who, in his own darkness, lives in a sty which resembles a temple in reverse. Willingly transformed, Gryll will "have his hoggish mind," that is, will never think his way out of that sensual prison. The freedom of the hero to act in his own true interest is a precondition, though not a full enactment, of political freedom, and it is in that sense that Book II prefigures its antitype, Book V. It was this same prefiguring liberation that occurred in the *Aeneid*, where the Odyssean quest for Aeneas' own rebirth foreruns the Iliadic battle for a land he wants to claim for his descendants.[34]

34. On the prefiguring orders of *Odyssey* and *Iliad* see Howard Porter, intro. to *Odyssey*, trans. G. H. Palmer (New York, n.d.); Cedric Whitman, *Homer and the Heroic Tradition* (Cambridge, Mass., 1958). Whitman's theory of "geometric structure" is a typological theory, allowing not only for fulfillment of positive prophecies, but also for "inversion of prophecy" (282). Besides the "Messianic Eclogue," *Georgic III* and the *Aeneid* throughout, there is the strong

Through allusion to the sea voyages of the heroes in Vergilian tradition, Spenser flatters the Elizabethan sea captains, to be sure. He also creates a new mythic basis of error. Redcrosse wandered in the desert of the land, surrounded by forests whose most "accomplished Snare" is darkness. As Redcrosse was able through his own "light" to illuminate his own way, well or ill, so Guyon through his sense of balance—which is equated in Canto VII with the Pilot's magnetic compass—can "the steady helme apply," that is, can navigate the seas of chaos and intemperance. In an iconography of error that Milton was to exploit even more fully, Spenser develops throughout Book II the notion that sinuosity, wave motions, redundancy, are types of human error. Death here is drowning, and survival is passage safe across an Idle Lake, a Lethe of oblivion, while one of the great Spenserian moments occurs when Guyon sails over the "Perilous Poole," past Keats's favorites, the spring-headed hydras and sea-shouldering whales. Such scenes should remind us that a classical iconography does not exclude reference to biblical typology, since behind these fishy threats there lurks the terrible vision of Leviathan. Throughout these sections of the poem, and perhaps also in earlier moments when image and action involve the ideas of gyring and wavy motions (for example, with Pyrochles and even more clearly with Cymochles), the hero's task is to steer a straight course. The magnetic compass is a modern and in its way magical instrument for this purpose, but its mechanism does not solve the cybernetic problem entirely. The Palmer is making an important correction when he sees Sir Guyon gazing at the two naked siren girls of Canto XII: "He much rebuked those wandring eyes of his, / And counseld well, him forward thence did draw." The phrase anticipates or echoes one of the most famous of Dowland's

---

sense of prophetic involvement in the political odes of Horace, on which see Steele Commager, *The Odes of Horace: A Critical Study* (New Haven, 1962), 13 ff., and 160–234. Commager describes a technique of suspension which, through its syntax, creates prophetic expectations (51–52).

songs, where we find the same notion of constancy and magnetic steadiness:

> Now cease, my wand'ring eyes,
>   Strange beauties to admire:
> In change least comfort lies,
>   Long joys yield long desire.
> One faith, one love
> Makes our frail pleasures eternal,
>   and in sweetness prove.
>   New hopes, new joys
> Are still with sorrow declining unto deep annoys.
>
> One man hath but one soul,
>   Which art cannot devide;
> If all one soul must love,
>   Two loves must be deni'd.
> One soul, one love,
> By faith and merit united cannot remove.
>   Distracted spirits
> Are ever changing and hapless in their delights.
>
> Nature two eyes hath given
>   All beauty to impart
> As well in earth as heaven,
>   But she hath given one heart,
> That though we see
>   Ten thousand beauties, yet in us one should be:
> One steadfast love
> Because our hearts stand fix'd although our eyes do move.[35]

Wandering in Book II is often this perceptual, spiritual error, a misuse of the senses as perceptual systems. By clearing and steadying these eyes, the Palmer instructs his charge in the larger task

---

35. Text from *The Second Book of Songs or Airs* (1600), given in Hyder Rollins and Herschel Baker, *The Renaissance in England* (Boston, 1954), 261.

of navigating (in Guyon's case "guiding") the ship of self, which is the microcosm of the ship of state.

Most Elizabethan readers doubtless would experience in the destruction of the Bower another figural effect, the duplication of the triumph of Redcrosse over the Dragon of the *Apocalypse*. Insofar as Book II seems grossly analogous to Book I it has always been read in a typological way, and its details have always elicited a backward look to determine their sacred "shadowy types" in Book I. The same diadic form connects the instructional myths of the temples of holiness and temperance, while every contrast between realms of grace and nature further invigorates this overarching shape of a typology.

Spenser is finally specific about the direction of Vergilian prophecy: it associates the hero with the vision of a native history. For this reason he goes out of his way to educate both Guyon and Prince Arthur in the history books of their respective destinies. Guyon, though an Elf, has a "history," paralleling that chronicle of Briton Kings which tells Arthur who he is and what his life portends for the nation he must govern. By the combination of the double vision, elfin and heroic, Spenser further complicates the earlier vision of Cleopolis, a secular complement to the New Jerusalem, Britain's "Eternal City."

> Yet is *Cleopolis* for earthly frame,
> The fairest peece, that eye beholden can:
> And well beseemes all knights of noble name,
> That covet in th' immortal booke of fame
> To be eternized, that same to haunt,
> And does their service to that sovereigne Dame
> That glorie does to them for guerdon graunt:
> For she is heavenly borne, and heaven may justly vaunt.
>
> (I, x, 59)

In the tradition of Chaucer's *House of Fame*, *The Faerie Queene* is able to secularize the quest for glory without abdicating the "heavenly" purpose entirely, since the hero is sent upon his quest by one who herself may justly vaunt heaven, "for she is heavenly born."[36] To a degree *The Faerie Queene* itself is the "immortal booke of fame," though here it talks about that "booke" as if it were an ideal literature thrown out into a visionary sphere. Simply because the "immortal booke of fame" exists for a world of courtly readers (or would-be courtiers), it asserts, through its own fact of existence, a new and more settled mode of prophetic hope than even Book I had promised. For the Legend of Temperance transforms the mystical shape of time, Rédcrosse's history, into a palpable, material, natural history. Spenser moves closer to the Elizabethan power structure in Book II, closer to ideas of economy, wealth, maritime exploration, imperial expansion, political dominion. The elusive choices between appearance and reality which so plague the Redcrosse Knight give way to equally difficult, but more technical choices forced upon Sir Guyon. Already visionary trust in holiness (faith) is giving away to the need for a good memory, and the two Histories (Canto X) make this explicit. It is hard not to see in Alma's castle a kind of "memory house," a vast mnemonic device, and if indeed allegory makes us think about things we already know, this suggests a further point, that allegories may be formed in the shape of the hermetic memory theaters. Memory is the chief treasure of the House of Alma. Old Eumnestes creates a mental space in which British and Elfin destinies unfold, recalling the role of memory in the *Confessions* of Augustine and the medieval *ars praedicandi*. By recourse to memory the vision of a future is settled upon an epic, heroic course.

While in Book II Spenserian prophecy *settles down*, prophetic anxiety scarcely diminishes. It may even increase, because much of the tension of the first book carries over into the sec-

36. Isabel Rathborne, *The Meaning of Spenser's Fairyland* throughout, on the typologies of the city in *FQ*. Cf. B. G. Koonce, *Chaucer and the Tradition of Fame: Symbolism in the House of Fame* (Princeton, 1966). In "To Rosamunde," Chaucer calls the lady a shrine and map of the world (playing on her name). Fame is celebrated in the *Trionfi* of Petrarch; also, in the final cantos of Hawes's *Pastime of Pleasure*. Spenser in Book V attacks the enemies of fame.

ond, as if this heavenly footrace were a relay and the baton had passed to Sir Guyon from an exhausted Saint George. The epic accumulates its effects. One of these is the ambiguity of the relation between faery and Briton, described in Isabel Rathborne's monograph, *The Meaning of Spenser's Fairyland*, a work which suggests that from faerie lore there derives a subset of Vergilian prophecy. Her thesis may be summarized in her own words: "Spenser's Fairyland is a land of fame, resembling the classical Elysium. The fairies are the race of gods and heroes who in their earthly lives anticipated the fame of Arthur and the future worthies who were destined to revive it. Arthur's visit to Fairyland, like the similar visits of classical epic heroes to the lower world, is preparatory to his accomplishment of his earthly mission and the *Faerie Queene*, like the *Divine Comedy*, is a literary descendant of the Sixth Book of the *Aeneid*."[37] This daring hypothesis turns out to permit a flexible theory of Spenser's historical allegory in which, to take only the most obvious of problems, Miss Rathborne can explain the presence of an impersonation of a living monarch (Gloriana/Elizabeth) in the midst of "a mythical land of fame inhabited largely by dead heroes." The argument and evidence are complex, but here I shall only adduce two points from them, first that they anticipate an argument recently made from a quite different point of view by Professor Berger. Miss Rathborne (and Greenlaw's attack upon Cory supports her view) suggests that the marriage of Arthur and Gloriana "might fittingly symbolize the mystical 'return' of the ancient British dynasty in the person of Elizabeth, sprung 'of Arthur's rase and lyne.' The importance of this 'return motif' in determining Spenser's choice of Arthur as hero can hardly be exaggerated, and it is extremely probable that the genealogical connection between Elizabeth and Arthur had some influence upon their relationship in the *Faerie Queene*."[38] This "return motif" plays an important part in Berger's recent discussions of the Mutabilitie Cantos and the Spenserian manner in general. He has observed that "the subjec-

37. *Meaning*, p. vii.
38. Ibid., 222–23.

tive mode of Spenser's historical vision is retrospective,"[39] and by this he means more than simply the historian's typical interest in the past. "Again and again we come upon instances of one-sided development in early phases of the career of a character or of a culture and also upon instances of premature union and fulfillment that must be undone, destroyed, or transcended so that they may be re-enacted in more adequate form in a later, more appropriate phase of relationship." Berger gives numerous and varied examples, and continues, "this family of instances comprises a subclass of a more general category in which a first or instinctive form of behavior must be experienced, felt as insufficient, then corrected and revised. The new context and usage confer on earlier, simpler forms a destiny more inclusive than their own, a more universal and organic function, allowing them to transcend themselves in a manner not possible to them in their first isolated thrust toward the premature fulfillment that they hope will end suffering and pain. The second chance, however, is never construed as the final resolution, for Spenser sees every triumph as precarious and momentary, and all his happy endings are carefully 'unperfited.' His vision is developmental in an evolutionary rather than a progressive sense, and the development is everywhere tempered or beset by interruptions, regressions, lapses into despair, and momentary yearnings toward the vanished glory of an archaic golden age."[40] I am not certain to what extent Berger's term "evolutionary" is problematic for the present argument. Certainly it implies the intellectualized primitivism that gives *The Faerie Queene* its visionary force.

Such primitivism, as it was defined and documented by Lovejoy and Boas,[41] leads to what I should call a prophetic interaction

39. "The *Mutabilitie Cantos:* Archaism and Evolution in Retrospect," in *Spenser: A Collection of Critical Essays*, ed. Harry Berger, Jr., 147.

40. Ibid., "Introduction," 10 and 11.

41. A. O. Lovejoy and George Boas, *Primitivism and Related Ideas in Antiquity* (Baltimore, 1935), especially chapter 2, "Chronological primitivism in Greek and Roman Mythology and Historiography."

between the halves of a double vision, faery and Briton. This is the second point to be introduced from *The Meaning of Spenser's Fairyland*. It is perhaps not always interesting to speculate on the role of Arthur, since he plays a relatively small part in the extant poem. But it is crucial to ruminate on the differences between the two races of heroes. Rathborne observes, for example, that the two cardinal virtues, Justice and Temperance, are represented by a Briton and a fairy, respectively. This may not be entirely simple to explain. But Rathborne argues then that such worthies as Arthur, Britomart and Artegall "belong not to the past or to the future, like the fairies, but to the present. They are the living heroes, like Odysseus and Aeneas, who are permitted to visit the land of the dead and of the unborn. And, like Odysseus and Aeneas, they must return to earth, and win their right to a permanent dwelling in the heaven of heroes by their great exploits in their native countries, over which their 'famous progenie' is to rule." In these terms Saint George holds an intermediary place. (Rathborne remarks on the fact that both Saint George and Artegall come into fairyland as changelings.) The main rule, however, is clear: the interaction of the two modes of heroic existence, faery and Briton, is an interaction of two aspects of time, its recurrent forms and its linear, evolutionary forms. Out of the two aspects of heroism we can derive the prophetic shaping of time.

To the extent, then, that *The Faerie Queene* may be said to descend from the *Aeneid* and specifically *Aeneid VI*, Spenser is continuing the medieval tradition that allowed a mantic voice to the Roman poet. Vergil provides Spenser with an epic model which narrows the life of the hero to a single destiny, and this destiny is held to be prophetic. Fame, renown, monumentality, even sublimity are the marks of the Vergilian hero, who is so much less of a blusterer than Achilles, so much less cunning than Odysseus. Aeneas is a burdened, melancholy man, possessed by his imperial mission which, as T. S. Eliot argued in "Virgil and the Christian World," is humbling yet significant. Aeneas seeks to transplant a culture that will give meaning to history; for him, Eliot observes, "this destiny is something not to be desired and not to be avoided." And also the Vergilian matrix of prophetic vision leads to a cold heroism, a struggle drained of human warmth.

At the same time the *Aeneid* sets up an epic structure of ideas, a narrative mechanism, which might be called the myth of creative fatalism. In "Virgil and the Christian World" Eliot showed how the Vergilian *fatum* arose out of the twin activities of *labor* and *pietas*. If heroic labor is the work of man caught in the maze of life, piety is his devotion in and towards the temple. The resolution of these two ways of being occurs, for the Vergilian hero, when he gradually or momentarily discovers his role as Eliot's "original Displaced Person." This wanderer comes at last to a new home, which he battles for and establishes, as the legendary Brutus had established Britain, and then, having saved his household gods from destruction, having cultivated the soil of a new culture, gains endless fame. (One perceives that the Vergilian tradition is also influential as a model for the poet's career and persona, since the full prophetic Vergilian matrix is the accumulated canon, including the *Eclogues*, the *Georgics* and the *Aeneid*.) The Vergilian hero may create an empire, because he participates in destiny. Aeneas is the natural prototype of the Christian hero in the Reformation. Kermode has defended Spenser from the charge of mythic reductionism, that abject loss of selfhood which is said to result whenever a poet drowns himself in the oceanic matrix of cyclical myth. And a Vergilian historicity seems to be a major element in this defence. "The achievement of Spenser in that heroic First Book is not to have dived into the archetypes, but to have given them a context of Virgilian security—to have used them in the expression of an actual, unique, critical movement of a nation's culture and history. He looks backward only to achieve ways of registering the density of the central situation: the reign of Elizabeth. . . . His mood is acceptance; he welcomes history, not seeking to lose his own time in some transhistorical pattern. Such patterns of course exist; but only the unique and present moment can validate them. As to that moment, Apocalypse prophesied and history foreshadowed it; the mind of Europe— not merely that of Virgil and Constantine, Dante and Marsilius, Ariosto and Foxe, but of the people—expected its coming. Spenser

[89

celebrates the Elizabethan *renovatio* with something of Virgil's sober exaltation. It is a phase of no temporal cycle but a once-for-all historical event, like the Incarnation itself—however cruel the claims of Mutability and the certainty of suffering in the Last Days."[42] This description of Spenser gives a lighter weight to the cyclical theory of history than it may deserve in the full account of his mythmaking. On the other hand, Spenser does subordinate cyclical to dialectical symbolism, and his acceptance of a Vergilian matrix implies that he accepts the trauma of modern man, who must live with the endless forwarding of profane time, ever more bereft of sacred cyclicality, suspended cruelly between the temple and the labyrinth, like the surveyor hero of *The Castle*.

If the prophetic burden of Christianity is guilt sprung from the Fall, the Vergilian burden, equally a consequence of the prophetic vision of human history, is the hero's belief that he owes a debt (his duty) of heroic labor and piety to the culture which it is his destiny to serve. Weighed down by the burden of the past and the ominous specter of the future, the prophetic destiny is yet experienced as a singleminded mission. Were the Vergilian model allowed to overpower the other prophetic matrices in its influence upon *The Faerie Queene*, its fatalistic myth-making would perhaps narrow the lively variegation of the other modes Spenser draws on. But this narrowing does not occur. Spenser remains an irrepressible syncretist. As Nelson has observed, dealing with the scope of Spenserian narrative units, the poet unremittingly displays a "hunger for complexity, for binding into one the multiple and for revealing the multiple in the one."

Ovidian Matrix

THE CHIEF PROCESS by which Spenser unifies the diverse matrices of his myths of Faerieland is the Ovidian typol-

42. "Spenser and the Allegorists," in Paul Alpers, ed., *Edmund Spenser*, 298.

ogy. Sometimes, of course, an Ovidian spirit is clearly manifest—
throughout Books III and IV one senses it—but the exact nature
of this spirit has never been clearly defined. To make this definition would in principle require a massive study of the metamorphic process itself, a task beyond the range of the present essay.[43]
And yet we may achieve a purchase on the subject by bringing
it into a typological context. To begin with, the notion that Ovid,
poet of the *Fasti* and the *Metamorphoses*, was a prophet did not begin with Renaissance interpretations of the speech of Pythagoras
(Book XV); it had been current in medieval moralizations of the
Metamorphoses, and, as Commager has observed, Ovid himself
"invokes the name of *vates* or *sacerdos* repeatedly" to describe his
own poetry.[44] In Golding's introductory Epistle to Leicester the
translator draws continuous comparisons between the visionary
form of Ovidian cosmogony and the writings of Moses; he is able
easily to show "How Ovids scantlings with the whole true pat-

43. For standard works on Ovid's *Metamorphoses*, see the bibli-
ography in Simone Viarre, *L'Image et la pensée dans les "Metamorphoses" d'Ovide* (Paris, 1964); on metamorphosis more generally,
G. B. Ladner, *The Idea of Reform: Its Impact on Christian Thought
and Action in the Age* (1959; repr. New York, 1967).

44. Commager, *Odes of Horace*, 14. On Graeco-Roman prophecy,
see Duckworth, *Foreshadowing and Suspense* and *Structural Patterns;*
Moses Hadas, *Hellenistic Culture: Fusion and Diffusion* (New York,
1959), 238–63, where connections between Vergil's Messianic Eclogue
and the *Libri Sibyllini* and thence between these and Jewish prophetic
sources are discussed, and where Hadas also notes the prophetic form
of Livy's history: "Livy's Romans are in the natural order of things
children of destiny, lords of creation, fated to prevail over all other
peoples"—precisely what interested Machiavelli. See also Hadas, "Livy
as Scripture," *American Journal of Philology* 61 (1940): 445 ff.; Hadas
and Morton Smith, *Heroes and Gods; Spiritual Biographies in An
tiquity* (New York, 1965), 13–16, and in the Philo "Life of Moses" reproduced therein, 156–60; on the Livy of the Renaissance, Myron Gilmore, *Humanists and Jurists*, 46–47; that he was preferred to Tacitus
during this period, R. R. Bolgar, *The Classical Heritage and Its Beneficiaries: From the Carolingian Age to the End of the Renaissance*
(Cambridge, 1954), 281.

terne doe agree." There is a perfect coincidence between the Renaissance belief in the "conditional immortality" of fame and Ovid's concluding lines: " . . . And Tyme without all end / (If Poets as by prophesie about the truth may ame) / My lyfe shall everlastingly bee lengthened still by fame."[45] *Metamorphoses* XV had envisioned a glorious Augustan Rome, significantly following the lengthy prophecy of Pythagoras, that "sum of all the former woorke." Like the Bible itself, the *Metamorphoses* begins with a cosmogony and includes primal myths of beginning-again such as the Four Ages, the Flood, Deucalion and Pyrrha, and ends with a prophetic tableau resembling the Apocalypse of Saint John. These parallels introduce a scriptural typology not unlike that between Old and New Testaments. Boccaccio and other apologists for classical myth maintained that parallels from such sacred sources were a prime basis for justifying vernacular poetry. But here the parallel goes further: it is a formal doubling between two whole sacred texts. The consequent sense of inevitability in myth is overwhelming. Not even the literary prefigurations of the Vergilian or Galfridian types possess this encyclopedic force and form. Ovid becomes a kind of biblical prophet.

Large as may be the subject of Ovid's influence upon Spenser, one aspect of it stands out more prominently than others. As a poem the *Metamorphoses* makes a larger direct claim for the importance of myth than any other surviving classical document the Renaissance knew; unlike the classical epics of heroic suffering and discovery, such as the *Aeneid* and the *Argonautica*, the *Metamorphoses* bring myths together in clusters so that they begin to develop myth itself as a language. Compendiously, and with ex-

45. *Metamorphoses*, XV, 877–79 (Golding's translation):

> quaqua patent domitis Romana potentia terris
> ore legar populi, perque omnia saecula fama,
> siquid habent veri vatum praesagia, vivam.

I quote from the edition of Golding by John F. Nims (New York, 1965).

traordinary variegation, the Ovidian poem imagines that all possible kinds of reality may be seen as mysterious changes. The range being cosmic, the resultant mode of speech has a grammar, a syntax, a semiotic sufficient unto itself. Metamorphosis becomes a universal principle of transformation, radically metaphoric and therefore radically poetic. For this reason the *Metamorphoses* provide a groundwork for something Spenser absolutely requires: a self-reflexive theory of his own poetic process. He is clearly not a naïve allegorist and equally clearly he imagines the interplay of images and agents according to a Pythagorean theory of metamorphic flux.

There is no wall between the typological modes we have discussed and this third Ovidian type, but it concentrates on what seems to be, from the poet's point of view, an essential creative moment within the larger prophetic season. This moment is a *reformatio*, the instant of rebirth, or rather, the instant at which the vision asserts that life (which here is always a rebirth) is possible. Not only Plutarch's *Of Isis and Osiris*, but another probable source for Book V, *The Golden Ass*, had portrayed this possibility. Ovidian prophecy tends to stress the cyclical shape of time, even though the *Metamorphoses* ends with a vision of the stellification of Julius Caesar and the reign of "our Augustus," who "beares / Dominion over all the earth." Ovid, it is true, thinks that "how farre so ever / The Romane Empyre by the ryght of conquest shall extend, / So farre shall all folke read this woork," so that his belief in his own fame as a prophet depends upon the linear destiny of Roman arms. On the other hand, the bulk of the poem involves changes occurring *in illo tempore*, and the dominant mode is a recurrent temporality. This mode reappears in *The Faerie Queene* in many places, but the Ovidian masterstroke of the poem is the Gardens of Adonis, while the most familiar *magus* of this type of recurrent change is the daimon who controls much of what happens in Books III and IV, Proteus. He is a shapeshifter, but also traditionally a prophet, and in the trials of Florimell and Marinell he introduces them into a cyclical scheme of seasonal change. Spenser therefore makes an important distinction when he gives Proteus his familiar role of villain.[46] By denying Proteus his claim to authority over Florimell, over the principle of flourishing life and its image, beauty, Spenser allows himself to come to her rescue. The poet's *persona*, opposed to Protean guile, becomes the shapeshifter the poem needs. He is, as Durling has shown,[47] present throughout the whole epic and is everywhere its formative power (which he lets us know through asides and hints), but here he enters quite directly into competition with a prophet.

The Gardens of Adonis have been more written about than almost any scene in Spenser, so that here I need only remind the reader it is a poetical garden, a nursery of forms, the archetypal anthology. It projects the triumph of poetry as the prophetic moment, symbolized by the triumph of Psyche in her marriage with Cupid, a victory over Death in the person of the imprisoned Boar.[48] As such, the Gardens are a temple of creativity, and

46. In *The Jonsonian Masque* (Cambridge, Mass., 1965), Stephen Orgel discusses Francis Davison's *The Masque of Proteus and the Adamantine Rock* (1595), where Proteus is the villain. On Proteus as prophet—Abraham Fraunce, quoted in Roche, *Kindly Flame*, 159. His parallel in Hermetic lore: Serapis, or Osiris; cf. Erwin Panofsky, "Titian's *Allegory of Prudence*; a Postscript," in *Meaning in the Visual Arts*, figs. 28–44.

47. Robert M. Durling, *The Figure of the Poet in Renaissance Epic* (Cambridge, Mass., 1965). The chief caution to be observed in regard to the poet's *persona* is that Spenser's tone is finally so even that in spite of subtle rises and falls it creates a large sense of unity, which is a major reason for accepting what traditional criticism at once understood, that *FQ* is a cosmos of some kind. Word counting in allegory is a suggestive critical approach. Spenser's markedly most frequent usage of "world" occurs in Book III, where, with eight uses of "world's," it occurs 51 times. This compares significantly with the 42 uses in *Antony and Cleopatra*, Shakespeare's highest frequency of the term, which Dryden recalled in his redaction.

48. See Donald Cheney, *Spenser's Image of Nature: Wild Man and Shepherd in "The Faerie Queene"* (New Haven, 1966), chap. 3,

naturally enough the enemy of the sacred space and time is Time itself, imagined, however, as the grim reaper, the monstrous saturnian deity of profane temporality. Time is *in* the garden only in the sense that, as sacred time, it defines the temple; as profane linear time it is excluded. The same sacred space and time characterize Belphoebe's "stately Theatre" in the forest, "as it an earthly Paradize had beene" (III, v, 40). Venus is in some sense the goddess of all earthly paradises. Later in the poem Spenser presents her sacred completeness of being in the image of the Hermaphrodite Venus.[49] Yet if we sought the most magnificent Spenserian tapestry of metamorphic rebirth, it would be elsewhere, larger and more local, the Marriage of the Rivers in Book IV.[50] There, at the climax of the Legend of Friendship, space (as geography mapped by the banks of the rivers) merges with time (defined by the streaming of the water.)[51] This epi-

---

"Man in the Cycle of Generation." Kermode, *Sense of an Ending*, 70, shows how the Thomist notion of *aevum* (duration, distinct from time and eternity) enters *FQ:* "In the Garden of Adonis canto, Spenser is talking about the *aevum*, the quasi-eternal aspect of the world. . . . Broadly speaking, Spenser is talking about the quasi-immortality of the generative cycle." In my own terms, the epiphany of the Garden is the projection of the prophetic moment, which arises out of, in some sense sublimes, the *aevum*. In this way it is perfectly correct for Kermode to say that here Spenser is "talking about" the *aevum*. On the other hand, dispute about these matters reaches the proportions of the dispute about what's wrong with Hamlet.

49. IV, x, 40–41. See Alastair Fowler, *Spenser and the Numbers of Time* (London, 1964), 162–70; Nelson, *Poetry of Spenser*, 233–55; R. V. Merrill and R. J. Clements, *Platonism in French Renaissance Poetry* (New York, 1957), chap. 5, "The Androgyne"; Donald Cheney, "Spenser's Hermaphrodite and the 1590 *Faerie Queene*," (forthcoming article).

50. See Harry Berger, Jr., "Two Spenserian Retrospects: The Antique Temple of Venus and the Primitive Marriage of Rivers," *Texas Studies in Literature and Language* 10, no. 1 (1968): 5–25.

51. In the Fifth Song of the *Polyolbion* Drayton recounts the birth of Merlin (and Selden in his notes speaks of "the vulgar tradition of

sode takes the form of a pageant or masque, whose "mystery" is the sacralizing of space and time. The names of the rivers are magical, first because as Coleridge observed they have a bright, national ring to them, but also because they come from the matrix of Ovidian typology.

Perhaps more clearly than with the other modes we discern the importance of naming to the Ovidian mode. A magic name attempts to fix an essence, and when, as with the rivers, Spenser shows the merging of names he shows the essential fluency of mythic speech, the interinanimation of such language. In like manner, viewed purely as a literary exercise the imprisonment of Amoret is significant because it shows that the pageant and the masque are liable to profane abuse. They may fixate meanings, and the task of the Ovidian poet is to liberate language from this impersonating fixation. Busirane is an idolatrous tyrant whose language is the repressive allegory of the Mask of Cupid, with its nightmare images and its obsessive cruelties represented by Reproch, Repentaunce, Shame, and "a rude confused rout / Of persons . . . whose names is hard to read." (III, xii, 24–25) His castle, which we have already noted as one of Lewis's "waste houses," presents time in the specious order of a locked-step. With a pun

---

Merlins conception.") The Song also includes the story of Sabrina and Severn, and we get these lines:

> O yee Pegasian Nymphes . . .
> Conduct me through these Brooks, and with a fastned clue,
> Direct mee in my course, to take a perfect view
> Of all the wandring Streames, in whose entransing gyres,
> Wise Nature oft her selfe her workmanship admires
> (So manifold they are, with such Meanders wound,
> As may with wonder seeme invention to confound)
> That to those *British* names, untaught the eare to please,
> Such relish I may give in my delicious layes,
> That all the armed Orks of *Neptunes* grislie Band,
> With musick of my verse, amaz'd may listning stand;
> As when his Trytons trumps doe them to battell call
> Within his surging lists to combat with the Whale.
>
> (83–100)

on "wondering," Britomart spent her day "in wandering / And gazing on that Chambers ornament." The Castle at last shakes like the temples that crack when Christ's transfiguration occurs, revealing the essential unreality of the fixated world of images when "those goodly roomes, which erst / She saw so rich and royally arayd, / Now vanisht utterly and cleane subverst / She found, and all their glory quite decayd." Britomart's triumph occurs because she can go back to the right starting point, "that perlous porch," the threshold of the vicious shrine which she, having tested herself by the wanderings of her vigil, can now easily pass over. In the canceled original ending of Book III the triumph of metamorphosis was sealed by the sexual embrace of Amoret and Scudamour, but in the poem as rewritten to permit linkage with Book IV, this hermaphroditic union was withheld, perhaps for use at a later instant. The canceled passage was too much like a fulfilled prophecy, and already Spenser was seeking ways of counterpointing the concentricities of his themes by opposed narrative lines.

His Ovidian style, in Books III and IV most prominently,[52] conventionally requires him to explore the ramifications of love and its social equivalent, friendship. The idea of chastity permits love and metamorphosis to enter a dialectical relationship, since the question about the chaste virgin is, Will she change her virgin state? Virginity is simply the fixated state of which chastity is the perfected flowing form. As such virginity is much more mysterious, more veiled, and less natural. Britomart is a heroine of nature, and her unveilings are always momentous. But even the

52. Drayton created the largest such vatic form, in *Polyolbion*, but owing to the massive pedantry of Drayton's love of his native land "this strange *Herculean* toyle" does not often take wing in mantic enthusiasm. Yet the poem intended, through an image of the "Ile of Wonders," to establish the full meaning of the idea of English "Genius." Thus the First Song (8–10) invokes "Thou *Genius* of the place (this most renowned Ile)," and every river bounds a particular location of this varied spirit. Songs Nine and Ten, glossed by Selden, deal directly with the prophetic knowledge of the Druids and of Merlin.

Faerie Queene will eventually marry Prince Arthur, at which time all nature in her kingdom will have been redeemed by the various quests of her Knights of Maidenhead.

Yet even more important than the allegory of love which Ovid largely supports in *The Faerie Queene*, there is another literary consequence of the Ovidian preference: the creative use of parody.[53] Critics have often noted that the Malbecco-Hellenore episode is a self-contained unit of narration, in style somewhat different from the usual Spenserian story. Yet, as parody of a Trojan-Achaian myth it may fit easily the method of a Renaissance poem. So far I have mentioned only demonic parodies, travesties of genuine visions of the good, which define that good dialectically through antithetical images and events. To a degree the Malbecco-Hellenore fabliau belongs to this category, since it reduces the grandeur and significance of Homeric myth to a level of almost bourgeois domesticity. The passions of Paridell of course reflect an original Homeric irony, for even in the *Iliad* Paris has little of the heroic energy of Hector or Achilles. But in Homer that may be due to the fact that Paris and Helen are not central figures, while Hector and Achilles are. By contrast the reduction of Hellenore to a wandering strumpet and Malbecco to personified Jealousy contributes to the whole Spenserian fable. More important than the humor, the charm, even the moral of their domestic tribulations is the effect which telling the story in this way has on the poem as a whole. It gives a very obvious place

53. See the important study, Calvin Edwards, "Spenser and the Ovidian Tradition," unpublished Ph.D. dissertation, Yale University, 1958. Possibly, Ovid in Spenser is analogous to other classical influences, in that the Ovidian influx is partly direct, and partly indirect. Here one indirect source is Ariosto, of whom Professor Bush has said: "Ariosto . . . might be called the Ovid of the Renaissance; along with many specific debts, he had his own large stock of Ovidian inventiveness, buoyancy, and irony, and, we must add, the predominant lack of seriousness of a pure Ovidian artist." In *The Renaissance Image of Man and the World*, ed. Bernard O'Kelly (Ohio State University Press, 1966), 67.

to the use of parody as a device of mythic recreation, or mythic "displacement."[54] Spenser knew that to create an epic at all he would have to retell old stories, and he knew that, logically, the only way to do this would be to parody them. Every retelling is a transvestism of an old costume. This is especially true in the tradition of romantic epic, but Milton himself is aware of it when he retells the story of Adam and Eve. To make certain, among other things, that his reader knows that he knows what he is doing, he quotes directly from Genesis. With Spenser we do sometimes get quotations, as in the Song of the Rose from Tasso, but in the main his procedure suggests free-style parodic imitation. Not surprisingly, for the Renaissance theory of imitation is a highly refined theory of parody, taking that term in a broad and unsatiric sense. Thus, Spenser imitates Chaucer, and we (with Ben Jonson) feel the imitation to be parody, stylistic Sir-Thopism, and unless we are careful we condemn the tonal rusticity in the Spenserian renewal of Chaucer's "antique" diction. But the method resembles rather that of Pound and Eliot, where the rendition of a cruder speech than the poet seems absolutely to need comes from his higher demand for a mythic source which he can "make new." Spenser himself learned this parodic style from Ariosto no doubt, but behind Ariosto lies the greatest poet of love, Ovid, whose own major work is a continuous parody of Greek sources. Furthermore, the humor of it all is quite intentional, a natural lightening of the tone which comes from the openly imitative dependence upon an older style; the child is humorous when he imitates the motions of his father.

Much of the humor in Spenser, and I think his tone is intermittently humorous throughout, comes from his habit of using "bad puns," as on the word "Christal," or on "chaste" and "chased" with Florimell. The apparently accidental nature of the pun does something for poetic texture. It affirms our sense

54. The stylistic tradition of this episode is described in Charles Muscatine, *Chaucer and the French Tradition* (Berkeley, 1964), chap. 3, "The Bourgeois Tradition."

of what we might call "nominal constancy," the feeling that although names refer apparently at random to more than one thing, we are not really in doubt about their meanings, because as I. A. Richards would say, we can maintain their "systematic ambiguity." Critics have recently noted one source for this behavior, in Plato's *Cratylus*, where, as Arnold Williams puts it, "language is not at all conventional," whereas "each word carries within it, entirely apart from the conventions of reference, its own meaning. Thus, in one example Socrates gives, man is called ἄνθρωπος because he is the only creature that looks up, considers what he sees; he looks up (ἀναθρεῖ) at what he has seen (ὄπωπε)."[55] The parallel Spenserian case would be the etymological punning on the name of *Ignaro* (I, viii, 31): "His name *Ignaro* did his nature right aread." Given such a theory of language, the bad pun becomes a good pun, since the referential oddity is submerged in Cratylan nominalism.

The difficulty with referring to the *Cratylus* lies not in the insight of the perception, but in working out the meaning, for Spenser, of such a generalized technical procedure. What then, is the meaning of the "bad puns" in Spenser? In answering this question, which Martha Craig has done much to illuminate, we would perhaps arrive at a viable outline of the problem of Spenser's diction. Clearly, a congeries of elements must be brought into relation with each other: Spenser's rusticity, his humor, his theory of pastoral, his archaism, his visionary intensity, his mode of narration, his primitivism, his theory of literary borrowing ("influence"), his authoritarian bias, his cosmic ambitions, his aestheticism, his love-hate relationship to mystery and secrecy, and doubtless a number of other matters. The concordance to Spenser would reveal that such elements cohere because the

55. Arnold Williams, *Flower on a Lowly Stalk: The Sixth Book of the Faerie Queene* (Michigan State University Press, 1967), 63; Martha Craig, "The Secret Wit of Spenser's Language," in *Elizabethan Poetry*, ed. Paul Alpers (New York, 1967), 447–72, an article based on the author's unpublished dissertation, "Language and Concept in *The Faerie Queene*," Yale University, 1959.

cross-referencing within the poem is obsessively rich and varied. "Badness" in punning seems to mark a special kind of verbal accident; it seems to prove coherence where there is no "reason" to expect it. This "badness" of punning is marvelous, a source of wonder, a fairly miraculous proof of providential order.

It proves another thing, the poet's implicit confidence in language. Nelson has in effect drawn our attention to this Spenserian trait: "He calls Chaucer his master, but he dares to take the central plot of his great poem from the burlesque *Tale of Sir Thopas*. He models himself on Vergil, but he parodies the speech of Aeneas recognizing his mother Venus by putting it into the mouth of the ridiculous Trompart. He draws freely from the literary traditions available to him, and always with a superb disregard for the intention of the writers from whom he borrows."[56] This is prideful theft, surely, but under the inspired guidance of Hermes. One way of handling the problem of the superb disregard is to deny its relevance to the evolved text as it stands. One can mock the researches of iconographers, graciously or otherwise, thereby achieving a fresh vision of Spenser as an earnestly boring rhetorician bent on changing our moral attitudes. Another way, perhaps it is the opposite of the Alperian shift toward a "rhetorical mode," would be to entertain all the past mythic meanings ascribable to a presented mythic person or event. This latter procedure complicates the poem beyond endurance, and I would not be unwilling to imagine that as one of Spenser's own intentions. But I think the lighter approach may help, since it balances these two extremes. The lighter approach says, roughly: Well, Spenser wanted this iconographic "bit" precisely because in a way it does *not* fit the place where he is using it; its irrelevance is "conspicuous," and I would add, perspicuous. Critical resistance to the parallel phenomenon of "bad punning" may be explained as a preference for an Arnoldian high seriousness. It is not impossible that Spenser knew of the *doubles entendres* latent in Old Testament Hebrew naming, but he may

56. Nelson, *Poetry of Spenser*, 29.

have discovered these word games quite on his own. Perhaps his puns undermine the sobriety of Homeric Narrative.

Yet the fact remains, fair Florimell is chased, and we need a theory of such punning and its function in a work of extended scope. It may possibly come from a field of art, which, though modern and very familiar to us, was not without its Renaissance exemplars, in the field of anamorphoses.[57] These were grotesque distortions of alien objects, placed on the picture plane of paintings, which could only be perceived for what they were by adopting a specific viewing position. The most famous of these is the Holbein painting of two ambassadors. In the foreground to the left, floating in space, is a cloudy shape, of no distinct form or meaning, which, nevertheless, viewed from a certain position, suddenly turns into a perfectly shaped human skull (the *memento mori*). Thus, it depends on one's point of view. I think that it may help to shift from such an example to the more complicated Spenserian situation if we consider the modern equivalent of anamorphic art, the use of collage. In a word, Spenser's "conspicuous irrelevance" and his "bad puns" and the other devices of bizarre iconographic dislocation which he truly assembles with "superb disregard" for original intention—these are the uses of collage. They are like the artwork which attaches a piece of rope, a swatch of cloth, a can opener, a watch chain, a typewriter ribbon, to the painted pictorial surface. (They have affinities with the picturesque.) This process, as I see it, is parodistic. Collage is parody drawing attention to the *materials* of art and life. It denies the neutrality and transparency of medium. It can even create a psychic barrier between the representing aesthetic surface and the world represented; it relocates bodily, it does not mediate. Collage deliberately subverts communication and tends also to destroy "style," or "stylishness" at any rate. Through collage the medium itself replaces metaphor as the prime aesthetic concern, and the method therefore plays an important part whenever the media of art are under general pres-

57. See Jurgis Baltrusaitis, *Anamorphoses ou perspectives curieuses* (Paris, 1955).

sure to change, to adapt beyond their means, to retain attention when people are bored with the old skills and styles. Spenserian archaism is a collage device, as Ben Jonson testily recognized when he said it amounted to "no language." For years now Empson has been exploring such oddities as Spenserian diction and poetic language, and has shown up most of the problems, among them this one. The Empsonian position requires individual words always to be interpreted in relation to their structural context. But to return: if we think of Spenserian diction as often employing a technique of verbal collage, we arrive at a simple and immediately clear version of his strangeness with regard to the sources. Like the alien piece of string on the surface of the Picasso, the word or image from Vergil or Ovid or the Bible does not attempt to produce an effect of new "good sense" or "intellectual generosity." It does attempt to annex the materials of a distant artifact, and it does this for at least two reasons. The first we have seen. Bad puns and the like show good faith in language. But that is the poetical angle on the matter.

The more important aspect of the collage technique is its structural implication. Martha Craig's study of Spenser's "secret wit" needs to be seen in this way. The *Cratylus* is a treatise largely based upon etymological grounds. As she puts it: "Through his theory of language Plato in fact acts out the etymology of 'etymology': the true explanation of words is in their origin."[58] This is not the place to go into the matter in any depth, but two things at least can be said. If it is true that Spenser plays on verbal origins, as on other retrospective materials, he does so through etymological means, as Craig has so clearly shown and as Ruthven has argued on a much wider scale, referring to other English poets as well.[59] This means that puns generated from such a ground have the properties accruing to it, chief of which is a rooted characteristic of *structure in time*. The main aim of etymology

58. Alpers, *Elizabethan Poetry*, 451.

59. K. K. Ruthven, "The Poet as Etymologist," *Critical Quarterly* 11, no. 1 (1969): 9–38. Ruthven distinguishes between false or popular etymologies and the stricter definition of etymology attempted by

is to give temporal form to the endless becoming of linguistic units. This structuralism through archaeology is present even, perhaps rather more strongly, when the etymologies are false or "popular," for then there is no excuse other than the sense of security conferred by the apparent structure one is thereby giving to one's "incorrect" reading. Only if we keep the inherent structuralism of etymology clearly in mind can we assess the fantastic detail of the Cratylan reading of Spenser, for otherwise we should have chaos produced by the total dominance of materials randomly stuck together on a grotesque and barbarous surface. But his collage is capable of "secret wit," and it is too bad to see Miss Craig's work misappropriated in the service of a moralizing theory of Spenser's "rhetorical mode." He is rhetorical, but then so is everyone.

The second thing to be said of the *Cratylus* and its relevance is that Cratylus himself was a follower of Heraclitus, as Hermogenes (Plato's first interlocutor here) followed Parmenides. There is therefore through the dialogue a constant play upon the problem of the flux, which culminates in the discussion of the letter *rho*, which is associated with words for running, flowing, whirling, etc. (sec. 37). It seems no accident that Cratylus, questioned by Socrates, says he believes the theory that words are "as much as possible like the things they represented," that is, their meanings are discoverable through etymology as then defined. A telephone, as in German, is thus a "far-speaker." For the Heraclitan position on nature is that the flux produces an endless amount of what we might call "reified ideas," or, reversing the formula, we could say that such etymological linguistics are an

---

the historian of language; he refers to Yakov Malkiel, for example. Since this poetic tradition comes through Isidore of Seville from Varro, in the main, it will be useful to consult the volume of the Fondation Hardt devoted to Varro: *Varron* (Vandœuvres-Genève, 1962), ed. C. O. Brink, Jean Collart, et al., especially the paper of Antonio Traglia, "Dottrine etimologiche ed etimologie varroniane con particolare riguardo al linguaggio poetico" (33–78). Traglia wishes to show there can be a poetic function for a given etymology "che è senza dubbio falsa."

attempt to bring order, a taxonomy, to the poetical superabundance of the Heraclitan system. This system, of course, gave rise to one of the earliest bodies of allegorical imagery we have. I do not mean that Spenser is a Neoheraclitan, but that he shares that philosopher's overwhelming sense of fluency. He resorts to etymological puns and the like from much the same demand. If one is a scientifically distant observer of the world in motion, if one can abstract motion from the world, instead of instilling motion into the world or instead of believing motion simply to *be* the world, one can become a nominalist of some kind. One can, like Hermogenes in the *Cratylus*, "claim that names are convention . . . and that convention is the sole principle of correctness in names"[60] (sec. 40). But Spenser has none of that distance, and his language is in that sense the opposite of conventional. He flouts convention. But he adores pattern, even to the point of making a mystery of it. He pushes etymology to such an extreme that he reaches its folly, wanton structuralism. If one does not object to the excess, one discovers that *The Faerie Queene*, in parody, pun, false transformation, and bizarre mythic etymology, possesses an absolutely recreative poetic style, a style beyond style, which again Ben Jonson recognized (and fought against).

The penchant for punning spreads out into larger compositional techniques. It is as if Spenser wanted every part, every feature, every partial form within the poem, to be a pun of some kind, a parody of some other form somewhere else. His originality has long been recognized to lie in his devotion to other poets

60. Plato, *Cratylus, Parmenides, Greater Hippias, Lesser Hippias*, ed. and trans. H. N. Fowler (1926; Cambridge, Mass., 1963), 169. A useful inquiry here would be to converge upon Renaissance etymologizing, from the classical and medieval side (Presocratics, Cratylus, and Isidore's *Etymologiae*) forward, and backward from Heidegger's late studies of Hölderlin. The double interest of a transcendental phenomenology seems to lead to the etymological exploration of language as an ontological voice, so that "language is not something that man, among other faculties or instruments, *also possesses*, but *that which possesses him*." An unpublished statement by Heidegger, quoted in Pierre Thévenaz, *What is Phenomenology?*, ed. and trans. J. E. Edie (Chicago, 1962), 62.

and to myths he recombined from other sources. He can make up his own myths, but we suspect that even the myths of Arlo Hill or the streams in *Colin Clouts* belonged to an inherited Irish folklore. His originality lies in the cosmic extension of the principles of verbal echo.

The poem creates an impression of endless reduplication, which permits each narrative unit to mirror every other unit—much less subtly than with the reflexive interplay of Milton's verse-paragraphs (though Milton can use exact mirror forms when he wishes). The intricacy of Spenserian rhyme has a similar echoic effect.[61] Through an unrelenting concentricity of shape, books mirror books, cantos cantos, stanzas stanzas, lines lines, alexandrines alexandrines, words words—a phenomenon which on the one hand creates a general anesthesia which keeps the pressure down, or keeps the poem under continuous control, depending on how one looks at the reader's response, and on the other hand creates an impression of endless fertility. A total relativism animates the language, and much as England becomes a temple in the marriage of the rivers, the poem itself becomes a temple in the similar confluence of so many echoing verbal elements. Only a method of complete parodic freedom, in the Ovidian manner, could enable a poet to write so long so well on such a scale of moral, mystical, historic intensity.

Galfridian Matrix

ENGLAND THE TEMPLE and British history as the experiential framework of that temple are major elements in the fourth matrix of prophecy Spenser employs. Geoffrey of Monmouth's Arthurian writings, in the *Prophecies of Merlin* and the

---

61. Samuel Daniel, in *A Defence of Ryme* (1602?) repr. in *Poems and A Defence of Ryme* (Chicago, 1965), 132: [Ryme] "is likewise number and harmonie of words, consisting of an agreeing sound in the last silables of severall verses, giving both to the Eare an Eccho of a delightfull report & to the Memorie a deeper impression of what is delivered therein."

History of the Kings of Britain, provide the Galfridian matrix.
We have already noted that in Book II Arthur is exposed to his
own destiny through a chronicle which attaches him to the heroic
line of Aeneas and Brute. As one of the Nine Worthies, Arthur
was already implicated in typological thinking, since it was possible to compare his doings with those of the three Paynims, the
three Jews, and the other two Christians (Charlemagne and Godfrey of Boulogne, Tasso's hero). Caxton prefaced Arthur's story
with a moral "to the intent that noble men may see and learn the
noble acts of chivalry," in short, as an exemplary history of "the
gentle and virtuous deeds that some knights used in those days,
by which they came to honour, and how they that were vicious
were punished and oft put to shame and rebuke."[62] Yet the Arthurian legend retained a strong folkloric strain, and it was here
that it suggested prophecy. Geoffrey's *Vita Merlini,* for example,
encouraged the popular tradition that King Arthur, sleeping in
Avalon, would someday come again to restore a golden age.[63]
This belief had considerable political allure, owing to its basis

62. Preface to *Morte Darthur,* in O. B. Hardison, *English Literary
Criticism: The Renaissance* (New York, 1963), 23. In "Les Douze
triomphes de Henri VII" (perhaps by Bernard André), twelve deeds
of King Henry are paralleled to the twelve labors of Hercules; Margaret of Burgundy is the envious Juno who imposes the labors. In
*Rerum Britannicarum Medii Aevi Scriptores, or, Chronicles and Me-
morials of Great Britain and Ireland during the Middle Ages,* ed.
James Gairdner (London, 1858). When Gascoigne produced the
Princely Pleasures at the Courte at Kenilworth (1576), he naturally
invoked Merlyne the Prophet to assist at "the delivery of the Ladie of
the Lake." Arthurian lore is typical on state occasions, because Arthur
is the great British "worthy."

63. E. K. Chambers, *Arthur of Britain* (Cambridge, 1964), 217–
27; Roberta Brinkley, *Arthurian Legend in the Seventeenth Century*
(Baltimore, 1932), 9–10, gives several cases of the equation between
the new king and King Arthur; see also the more recent "Contribution
de Ben Jonson et de Dekker aux fêtes de couronnement de Jacques
Ier," by Glynne Wickham, in *Les Fêtes de la renaissance,* ed. Jean
Jacquot (Paris, 1956 and 1960), 1:279–84. The return of the sleeping
Arthur is a popular prophetic motif in the myth of the social bandit,
on which see below, chap. 4.

in an original foundation myth. In fact, although Spenser masks this tradition by associating Merlin and Britomart in an allegory of love, such Galfridian prophecy is the most markedly political of all types available to the English Renaissance poet.

Spenser uses Arthurian material pivotally: Arthur is the titular hero of the poem, its chief deus ex machina; the Knights of Maidenhead are a recollection of the Round Table; the chief magus of the poem is Merlin, Arthur's instructor and guardian in the original *Historia*. Merlin can read "the streight course of heavenly destiny, / Led with eternall providence"; he can assert that "the fates are firme, / And may not shrinck, though all the world do shake." He prophesies the doom of Britomart, the fullest *persona* of the poem, and the effects of his prophecy will resonate through long ages, until men's good endeavours "guide the heavenly causes to their constant terme." His mirror is a magical *speculum historiale*.

Among the more familiar uses of Galfridian prophecy is the political oracle in which a succession of the line of kingship is predicted in obscure terms.[64] So troublesome was the folklore of Merlinesque vision and the succession it foreboded, that both Henry VIII and Elizabeth forbade the publication of prophetic poems and broadsides. Since Arthur was the archetypal British prince, and since the Tudors were "descended" from him, it was natural to invoke Merlin to foretell the destiny of the Crown. Dr. Dee, who seems to have aped the Merlin of legend, assiduously proved Elizabeth's genealogical descent from Arthur, and since Dee was a great favorite of the queen's and a great advocate of "the prosperity of this Brytish Impire under our most peaceable Queen Elizabeth," the genealogy was at last somewhat acceptable, if only as myth, to Lord Burghley.[65] But then the obscurity of Galfridian visions was such that almost anything could be proved

64. On the popularity of Arthurian lore in Elizabeth's reign: C. B. Millican, *Spenser and the Table Round* (Cambridge, Mass., 1932).

65. Millican, 42–46; also Richard Koebner, *Empire* (Cambridge, 1961), 62: "When in 1577 Francis Drake set out to snatch the supposed *Terra Australis* in the South Sea—assumed to be King Solomon's *Ophir*—from the Spaniards, the promoters of the voyage took Dr.

by them. Furthermore, the Arthurian material was not a simple, happy image of Augustan peace. On the contrary, a profound disharmony troubled the stabilizing order of the Round Table, since to serve the king and one's peers would be to disserve the lady. Malory had dramatized this conflict of *philia*, and the story of Arthur became in his hands a tragic political drama, which an Elizabethan dramatist called *The Misfortunes of Arthur*.[66] Service is the form of courtly action by which a knight achieves honor, but Spenser, like Malory, has to deal with divergent pulls on the allegiance of the knight. Much of the poem's finest art is spent on this conflict—the triangle of Britomart, Radigund, and Artegall presents the political flaw of chivalry, showing the human element, especially a sexual component, at the center of that ideal system. Both Malory and Spenser have myths through which they break the political scene and the historical scene

---

John Dee into their confidence." It should be remembered that "leading promoters of discovery—Leicester, Gilbert and Dee's patron, Edward Dyer, even Cecil (now Lord Burghley)—were members of the Society of the New Art, which sought to transmute copper into gold." K. R. Andrews, *Drake's Voyages: a Re-assessment of their Place in Elizabethan Maritime Expansion* (New York, 1967), 45.

66. Irving Ribner, *The English History Play in the Age of Shakespeare* (Princeton, 1957), 229–36: "The play is a warning against the civil war and the annihilation of England which would inevitably follow the joining of Englishmen with foreign powers against their queen, just as Modred had allied himself with foreign powers against his king." Cf. *Misfortunes of Arthur*, V, ii, 11–38, for parallel with Proem to Book V. Of Merlin's role in the *Morte Darthur*, T. L. Wright says "it is manifest that Merlin assumes a special task—that of bringing about the reign of Arthur. In this respect Malory's treatment of Merlin is by no means a mere copy of earlier traditions; it marks the start of a new version of the legend. In his opening subdivision Malory portrays Merlin in two important offices: he is the agent through whom God's will and 'grace' are expressed, and he is an omniscient strategist who leads Arthur to victory over the rebel kings. These functions are, it is true, derived from the French tradition which came to Malory through the *Suite du Merlin*, where Merlin appears as a prophet, semipriest, shapeshifter, and strategist." In *Malory's Originality*, ed. M. Lumiansky (Baltimore, 1964), 23–24.

down to their essentials, by looking retrospectively, as Berger might say, at the large familial structures of the Round Table and the Order of Maidenhead. The mythic structure of Galfridian prophecy is then useful for the political science of the poem, which through Britomart's story reduces the fundamental political order to the family unit.

Furthermore, Arthurian myth had a broader relevance to British history, because it told, in legend, of the unification of the state and of imperial conquest. Arthur in Geoffrey had even defeated the pope and had become, like Charlemagne, the ruler of the world. He was the British Hercules. His partnership in Book V with Artegall is entirely proper to this Herculean pattern. Both are culture bringers, and differ only in the degree of their providential grace and power. Artegall struggles to attain the providential Arthurian ideal, and like the Arthur of legend fails mainly because of his entanglements with woman as fury.

The Galfridian magus, Merlin, has charge of the love quest of Books III, IV, and V, and over these his magic has a measure of control, bringing Britomart to Artegall by means of the magic mirror he makes for her father, King Ryence. Merlin the Welsh wiseman is also a culture bringer, a Hephaestus, who makes armor, shields and spears, and gives secret powers to the chosen ones of the elect nation. His power is also alchemical. Through him the wisdom and foresight of God contract into a pagan system of thought, engineered by the good magician, who conveniently predicts the future. Merlin's political wisdom stands behind governance, for besides looking in his mirror and conjuring up the future, Merlin is a teacher to the prince. He instructs Britomart. Like Dr. Dee he is a patriot and knows all. Of his magic mirror we are told by Spenser that "round and hollow shaped it was, / Like to the world it selfe, and seem'd a world of glas."[67] Thus the nurse Glauce could plead with the Enchanter:

67. The mirror is the emblem of wisdom, as displayed in the woodcut from Carolus Bovillus' *Liber de sapiente* (1511), reproduced in E. F. Rice, *The Renaissance Idea of Wisdom* (Cambridge, Mass., 1958). Fortuna here is a blindfold, crowned woman who in her left

And sayd, Sith then thou knowest all our griefe,
  (For what doest not thou know?) of grace I pray,
  Pitty our plaint, and yield us meet reliefe.
  With that the Prophet still awhile did stay,
  And then his spirite thus gan forth display;
  Most noble Virgin, that by fatall lore
  Hast learn'd to love, let no whit thee dismay
  The hard begin, that meets thee in the dore,
And with sharpe fits thy tender hart oppresseth sore.

---

hand holds the Wheel of Fortune; Sapientia, holding a mirror in both hands, sees her own reflection at the center of the disc, which is bordered by the sun, moon, and stars. The Promethean and hermetic sense of the iconography is apparent in the mottos of the thrones of either: *Sedes fortune rotunda—Sedes virtutis quadrata.* The mirror symbolizes this Promethean wisdom in that "all wisdom is self-knowledge"—the motif of Davies' *Nosce teipsum.* Bovillus enobles the mind as a reflecting power. Thus, Rice paraphrases *De sapiente:* "Man, therefore, passes from ignorance to knowledge, from potency to act, as the mirror of his soul is polished by and impregnated with the reasons or species of things." (*Renaissance Idea*, 114) Spenser's Merlin is not far removed from the image in Bovillus: "a Renaissance culture hero, heroic in his self-achieved perfection, his universality of knowledge, his esoteric isolation and self-sufficiency, and his capacity for ruling men" (122). Merlin serves King Ryence, but his powers of foresight are those a ruler requires. His figural character owes much, on the other hand, to the person and professional extravagance of Dr. Dee, for whom, as Trattner has shown, "overseas exploration (the field of his geographical and navigational writings) was part of a search for something deeper; it was a probing for the heart of all knowledge, for the Infinite, for the Unknowable." W. I. Trattner, "God and Expansion in Elizabethan England: John Dee, 1527–1583," in D. L. Stevenson, ed., *The Elizabethan Age* (New York, 1966), 162–85. Dr. Dee was self-consciously a prophet of empire, and it seems possible that Merlin's mirror in *FQ* is intended to suggest, among its more obvious magical meanings, the "monad" of Dee's treatise *The Hieroglyphic Monad Explained Mathematically, Cabalistically, and Anagogically* (1564), on which see Trattner, "God and Expansion," 171. Cf. A. L. Rowse, *The Expansion of Elizabethan England* (1955; New York, 1965), especially chap. 5, "Oceanic Voyages."

For so much all things excellent begin,
   And eke enrooted deepe must be that Tree,
   Whose big enrooted braunches shall not lin,
   Till they to heaven hight forth stretched bee.
   For from thy wombe a famous Progenie
   Shall spring, out of the auncient *Troian* blood,
   Which shall revive the sleeping memorie
   Of those same antique Peres, the heavens brood,
Which *Greeke* and *Asian* rivers stained with their blood.

Renowmed kings, and sacred Emperours,
   Thy fruitfull Ofspring, shall from thee descend;
   Brave Captaines, and most mighty warriours,
   That shall their conquests through all lands extend,
   And their decayed kingdomes shall amend:
   The feeble Britons, broken with long warre,
   They shall upreare, and mightily defend
   Against their forrein foe, that comes from farre,
Till universall peace compound all civill jarre.[68]

68. Note the similarity with *Amoretti*, 44, with its allusion to the Argonauts, "those renoumèd noble Peres of Greece," whose internecine quarreling made them "forgetfull of the famous golden fleece," till Orpheus calmed them with song. In both the sonnet and *FQ* Spenser associates civil war and mental conflict. See Nelson, *Poetry of Spenser*, 124–27, on the distinction between "ethical" and "political" realms, a distinction probably already in Spenser's mind when writing the *Amoretti*—see Nelson, 324, n. 12. Spenser did not need to know the *Argonautica* of Apollonius Rhodius; Jasonian lore was commonplace: see Douglas Bush, *Mythology and the Renaissance Tradition*, new rev. ed. (New York, 1963), 31, on Caxton's rendering of the medievalized French *Jason* (ca. 1477). Milton, on the other hand, as Bush observes, 284, n. 50, knew the *Argonautica* in detail. The idea of the quest of the golden fleece, from whatever source, may be interesting to Spenser since it embodies what Paul Diel has called "the fight against banalization." In *Le Symbolisme dans la mythologie grecque* (Paris, 1952), 131–75, Diel describes the processes of the mythological "death of the soul," and shows three forms of this "banalization": conventional (the simple platitudinous failure of any

spiritual exaltation), dionysiac (the letting go, liberation through a loss of ascetic inhibition), and titanic (the tendency toward social or political aggression). The second and third types of banalization are involved in Book V particularly. Of the third, Diel says: "Every form of banalization is a state of underlying psychic tension [*de sous-tension psychique*]. However, the underlying tension here, as with the Dionysian form, involves the essential desire [or, the essence of desire: *le désir essentiel*], the evolutionary thrust [*l'élan évolutif*]. In so-called titanic banalization, energy is dispersed into a multitude of anguished desires, cares, which generate each other and which tend to regroup around an obsessive ambition which, however, remains materialistic, a center of overwhelming and destructive agitation." This is the inner turmoil of social banditry. It is thus important, as Diel then argues, that "for the most part the heroes menaced by banalization are reunited in the adventure of the Argonauts." Besides their leader, Jason, the most important are: Orpheus, Heracles, Theseus. "The color of gold represents spiritualization, while the fleece—the sheep, figuring innocence—is a symbol of sublimation. The golden fleece to be won suggests that the goal of the enterprise is the conquest of spiritual force (truth) and the purity of the soul." Diel, 176. This idealization of the quest might be drawn from Christian syncretic exegesis. Hercules cuts the finest figure of the lot; after many *erga* and *parerga*, he is transfigured at Mount Oeta. In the Herculean myth we discern two complementary motifs: the traveler (the Christian form of which is *homo viator*) and the warrior. Hercules becomes the archetype of the *ambulatory* social bandit. The traveling aspect of this model is modified in the story of Jason and the golden fleece, which provides one of the great *frissons* of literature: the terzina at the close of the *Divine Comedy*. "Un punto solo m'è maggior letargo / che venticinque secoli alla 'mpresa / che fè Nettuno ammirar l'ombra d'Argo" (XXXIII, 94–96). ("A single moment makes for me deeper oblivion than five and twenty centuries upon the enterprise that made Neptune wonder at the shadow of the Argo.") Text and translation from J. D. Sinclair, *Dante's Paradiso* (New York, 1961), 482–83. Sinclair's version does not greatly clarify this compacted scene, but we can isolate at least three translating problems: (1) The contraposition of *punto* and *letargo*: the range of *letargo* is great—it implies a swooning lethargy, a forgetfulness as of Lethe, and is thus here refracting ideas of truth (Gr: *alethes*); but along with the river/ocean of time and other ideas of eternity, it also has overtones of breadth and width, and suggests that in oblivion there are no points, no punctate distinctions of place or moment, i.e., space and time (in oblivion) are undifferentiated continua. (2) How to convey the proportional metaphor—*punto : letargo* equals *secoli : impresa? Impresa*, as rhetorical term for *figura*, is roughly synonymous with *ombra*. The point is being made by Dante that figures, impresas, types, and shadows—the imagery of Christian typology—are subject to temporal change, or scansion, while retaining their continuous freshness as of the moment when they were first conceived. (3) To preserve the bad pun on *ammirar*, a word whose literal sense of wondering, gazing, admiring, etc., is picked up by Dante in the next terzina, which analyzes the psychology of the prophetic moment at which Dante/Neptune gazes at the shadow of the Argo on the ocean floor. The bad pun is simply the fact that Jason is the great "admiral" of myth, and this sense is from Arabic *amir*, commander. Dante gets the pun working because he can juxtapose *ammirar*, with *mirava* and *mirar* in the next terzina. But English *admire* has lost its religious sense and would not work well here.

Why insist on these details? Because they illustrate the echo principle that Spenser introduces into English poetry in full force (though again I believe Chaucer had known it). And further, because the quest of Jason, through the Argo/Ark pun, has important overtones for the notion of the poem as vessel, which Spenser himself exploits: he thus ends Book I, "Now strike your sails ye jolly Mariners . . . " and Book II, "Whilest wether serves and wind." The ark, of Noah or of the Covenant, is the original ambulatory form of the *templum*, since it is one ramification of Latin *arcere* (to contain or maintain, hence to maintain at a distance, to keep or ward off; Eric Partridge, *Origins*, 25b), and is related to *arcanum* and *exercere* (to keep someone moving) and *exercitare* (to practice or exercise diligently). The ark is the moving home of Jason, Odysseus, Noah, Guyon, and in the Elizabethan period its force increases, through the mythmaking of sailors who explored the oceans and landed on "otherworldly" shores. See W. T. Jewkes, "The Literature of Travel and the Mode of Romance in the Renaissance," in *Literature as a Mode of Travel*, ed. with intro. by W. G. Rice (New York, 1963). In English pageants the Golden Fleece makes a useful topos for the Guilds of Drapers, e.g., at the 1522 triumphal entry of the Emperor Charles V into London, where the scene was mounted on London Bridge, complete with an armored Jason, firebreathing dragon and bulls, Medea—all in honor of the Emperor as Grand Master of the Knights of the Golden Fleece. See *Fêtes de la Renaissance*, 2:173. On the legend of Jason in France, Jean Seznec, *Survival of the Pagan Gods*, trans. Barbara Sessions (New

It was not, Britomart, thy wandring eye,
  Glauncing unwares in charmed looking glas,
  But the streight course of heavenly destiny,
  Led with eternall providence, that has
  Guided thy glaunce, to bring his will to pas:
  Ne is thy fate, ne is thy fortune ill,

York, 1953), 24–25; Seznec notes that Gideon seconded Jason as patron of the Order of the Golden Fleece. Among other values, such imagery expresses the expansion of an *imperium*, the extension of heroic control to cover the mythologized Mediterranean or the seas beyond the pillars of Hercules. Thus, in Dante, and in Spenserian allusions to Jason, there will be an Ovidian overtone, insofar as both recall the end of *Metamorphoses* 6 (Golding):

And finally when childhod once was spent
And youth come on, togither they with other Minyes went
To Colchos in the Galley that was first devisde in Greece,
Upon a sea as then unknowen, to fetch the golden fleece.

Mythic *experience* is travel across the *mare non notum*, the unknown sea. Given such a point of departure, we can see how in the Renaissance there developed a pastoral of the sea, and Ralegh became the "shepherd of the ocean," etc. A crossover to Christian myth is possible through the identification of the Argo as the *fatidicam ratem* (Valerius Flaccus, *Argonauticon* I, 2), based on the fact that a timber in the bow of the ship, which could speak to the Argonauts, was taken from the sacred oracular oak of Dodona. Camoens in the *Lusiads*, IV, 83, recalls the myth of the prophetic bark, the *fatidica nao*. Milton seems to be reversing this figure, in *Lycidas*, 100–103, "It was that fatal and perfidious bark / Built in the eclipse and rigged with curses dark, / That sunk so low that sacred head of thine." As noted in the edition of *The Poems of John Milton*, of John Carey and Alastair Fowler (London, 1968), M. Lloyd, *Modern Language Notes* 75 (1960): 103–8, suggests that here the "bark" is "the human body, subject to death ('fatal'), and built in the eclipse man has endured since Adam's fall." This double sense will help in the reading of the nautical imagery of *FQ* II. Eliot's rubric, "death by water," will be a useful entry into the whole subject.

> To love the prowest knight, that ever was,
> Therefore submit thy wayes unto his will,
> And do by all dew meanes thy destiny fulfill.[69]
>
> (III, iii, 21–24)

Much of the suffering, Vergilian in tone, that Spenser later projects in his myths of justice appears here. The prophecy shows, not only the substance of the providential order of Britomart's love, but also some of the violence that passes through the prophet's hands, when, like Merlin, he enjoys in microcosm all knowledge of whatever is going on presently in the macrocosm. More interesting to the prince, the mirror can discover treasons, rifts in the inner fabric of the state, and can defeat foreign enemies, attack from without. With such powers at his disposal Merlin can, and according to Spenser does, guarantee the happiness of the realm. This happiness is raised to the sphere of a providential care. The only area where Merlin lacks complete second sight is the

---

69. Kathleen Williams, *Spenser's World of Glass: A Reading of "The Faerie Queene"* (Berkeley, 1966), 94: "Britomart's mistake is understandable, for the mirror in Elizabethan symbolism could be of a kind to reflect false unreal shadows. But it could also be the mirror of truth, penetrating the false appearance of things, and is often an attribute of pictured Truth itself. . . . The globe, a sign of power over the world, is another attribute of Truth. Thus in seeing Artegall in the armour of Achilles Britomart sees not an illusion, as she supposes, but a truer vision of his essential quality than she could gain from a sight of the man himself." It is not clear to what extent Spenser is here also playing on the idea of art holding the mirror up to nature; this was the period of Gascoigne's *Glass of Government* and *The Steele Glass*. If Spenser means this, the text of Leonardo will fit: "The mind of the painter should be like a mirror which always takes the colour of the thing that it reflects and which is filled by as many images as there are things placed before it. . . . You cannot be a good master unless you have a universal power of representing by your art all the varieties of the forms which nature produces." Quoted from the *Notebooks* by M. H. Abrams, *The Mirror and the Lamp: Romantic Theory and the Critical Tradition* (New York, 1953), 32. Leonardo here betrays the imperialist theory of Renaissance art, which leads eventually to the theory of melancholic genius, in Ficino, and others.

realm of love and chivalric service, where Arthurian lore presents a notably grim story. Spenser is most deliberate in portraying a Britomart shaken by anxiety over her capacity to love or to find a true lover, and the use of an Arthurian background makes her doubtful story plausible.

Finally, Spenser observes decorum when stressing the Galfridian prophecy, because Merlin belongs to the world of native faery.[70] He is the mythic seer of *British* legend and a popular Elizabethan ectype associated with an extravagant animal symbolism which had served oracular purposes in *The Book of Merlin*. To use the figure of Merlin meant to guarantee a popular style of Elizabethan prophecy. Partly because of the Tudors' Welsh descent, Henry VIII had named his son "Arthur," so that Merlin's prophecies were grounded in the political destiny of the kingdom, purporting to show its unity as a separate, insular, self-sufficient state, a holy island, joining Welsh, British, Scotch, and their invader-conquerors, the Saxons and Normans. Galfridian vision is England's equivalent of the vocation of the chosen people in the Old Testament and the Vergilian election of Rome as the new

70. "Geoffrey, like the Old Testament, contains catalogues of names and other forms of vaguely understood vision, also the oracular prophecies of Merlin, snatches of folklore, legends of ferocious female wills like the Gwendolen who flung Sabrina into the Severn [cf. *Comus; FQ*, II, x, 19], references to underground labyrinths in which hidden loves are imprisoned, and other jigsaw pieces with suggestive contours. Further, he associates the events in legendary English history with Biblical events which are asserted to be contemporary with them, and some later histories founded on Geoffrey, such as Warner's *Albions England*, complete the Anglo-Biblical parallel by beginning with the Book of Genesis and working down through the Trojan War to Brutus. It may be noted for its general interest that this parallelism is more common in English literature than the casual reader may think—particularly, of course, during the period when the Geoffrey legends were accepted as historical." Northrop Frye, *Fearful Symmetry* (1947; reptd. Boston, 1962), 373. The battle over Geoffrey's historicity is itself a classical instance of demythification. On Geoffrey, see R. W. Hanning, *The Vision of History in Early Britain: from Gildas to Geoffrey of Monmouth* (New York, 1966).

Troy. Spenser is evidently uniting all three traditions. Under-lying this national destiny is a deep desire for national freedom. The idea that Englishmen were free, which was to become leg-endary throughout Europe, had ancient roots, and the *Historia* of Geoffrey of Monmouth was an early document in that founda-tion myth. In the *Historia*, to be free means resistance to Rome and the aboriginal giants of the island; in Spenser it means to be free from Rome, Catholic France, and Spain. This prophetic tradition is narrower than either the Christian-Hebraic, which entails a higher freedom entirely, the belonging to God, or the Graeco-Roman, which expands the destiny of the hero to include the destiny of an exfoliating Mediterranean empire, the Roman hegemony over all Europe. Galfridian prophecy mainly supports the British kingdom, the narrowly national state within the island and its immediate appendages, Ireland and sometimes parts of France or the Low Countries. The vision of Merlin is focused on resistance to foreigners without and traitors within.

In formal terms, by incorporating Arthurian matter into a Christian and Vergilian poem, the poet is enabled to write of these Christian and classical materials in romantic terms.[71] A romantic plot has advantages for the epic of prophetic history,

71. Conflict of service in the terms of courtly love is transmuted in *FQ*, V, xii, into the religious conflict which led to Henry of Navarre's apostasy (Burbon's losing his shield). A. B. Gough, in *The Works of Edmund Spenser, Variorum Edition* (11 vols. Baltimore, 1932; hereafter cited as *Variorum*), 5:259–60, observes that "this action finds a suitable place in the book as an example of a form of in-justice not elsewhere dealt with—the desertion of the religious faith that one has pledged onself to maintain. The conversion of King Henry to Catholicism (which was obviously due to self-interest rather than conviction) was no merely personal matter, it was an act of faith-lessness toward the Reformed Church of France of which he was the protector." Agrippa d'Aubigné could maintain that Henry's assassina-tion marked Divine retribution for the crime; elsewhere d'Aubigné took Henry's career as exemplifying "the scales in which the mercy and justice of Him who reigneth above the kings should be weighed." See Samuel Kinser, "Agrippa d'Aubigné and the Apostasy of Henry IV," *Studies in the Renaissance* 11 (1964): 245–68.

since the digressive form of the romantic epic opens up gaps in the narration at periodic intervals, planting enigmas and ominous changes of the expected course of things, raising suspense and a low-level anxiety. Ariosto and Tasso combine magic and romance with ease, through the discontinuity of their plots. The later pre-romantic defense of the Ariostan form and Tasso's digressions seems to me partly a defense of devices which are congenial to prophetic utterance.

In typological terms, the iconography of error in this Galfridian tradition seems to involve the passions, most notably those fears and anxieties of the love-struck Britomart, but also the more serious backslidings of her lover Artegall. The Malbecco-Hellenore episode presents in little a travesty not merely of the causes of the Trojan War (which leads therefore back to the Vergilian frame), but also of Arthurian scandal. At least once, in the troubled relationship of Timias and Belphoebe, Spenser hints at the tricky state of royal love affairs, but generally he guarantees a reversal of the Arthur-Guinevere tragedy by making his central heroine Gloriana, who is entirely stable because she is a "magnifique virgin." Not only is she stable, but she is for the present unapproachable, untouchable, as befits her virgin state. In this she is symbolically kept distinct from Britomart, who, though a virgin like Gloriana, is lauded for a chastity that will include her married state when finally she is joined in royal betrothal to Artegall. Britomart enjoys the help of Merlin, while her nurse, Glauce, associates her upbringing further with the powers of foresight, since the name Glauce suggests the owl eyes of Minerva. Finally, to the extent that Artegall is a surrogate for Arthur, her promised future is to be blessed by providential favor. By restraining the role of Prince Arthur in all this Galfridian material, Spenser keeps him more effectively providential than he would be if he intervened at every crisis. Secondly, by making him a prince, Spenser averts any suspicions of later amorous scandals, though a reader need not imagine these to be inseparable from all retellings of the myth. Ironically, something threatening in this iconography of error broods over the decision Milton finally made not to write an Arthurian epic. But the prophetic modality of such stories had in the first place suggested the topic to Milton, as well as the apparently unfinished nature of the Spenserian treatment of Arthur.

It might be said, to conclude, that the temple of this system is Merlin's laboratory, where he does his alchemical business like Doctor Faustus. But surely the temple is the spherical glass Merlin creates to foresee events. The perfect home of second sight is a mirror, as the Proem to Book III reminds us: "Ne let his fayrest Cynthia refuse / In mirrours more then one her selfe to see." This mirror is a druidical, all-seeing eye, and an uncanny gleam hangs over the story it initiates, Britomart's love for Artegall. For in this mirror, as in all true alchemical processes, magic triumphs over time and space, reducing them to the dimensions of a purified consciousness.[72] Although the tone of such legends is steeped in

72. Mircea Eliade, *The Forge and the Crucible* (New York, 1962), describes the mythic interrelations of alchemists (the "masters of fire"), shamans (prophets and seers), smiths, heroes, mythical kings (founders of dynasties). Eliade argues an even more pertinent role for the alchemist, for Merlin: "Alchemy has bequeathed much more to the modern world than a rudimentary chemistry; it has left us its faith in the transmutation of Nature and its ambition to control Time." p. 174. "Although he put himself in the place of Time, the alchemist took good care not to assume its role. His dream was to accelerate the tempo of things, to create gold more quickly than Nature; but like the good 'philosopher' or mystic that he was, he was afraid of Time. He did not admit himself to be an essentially temporal being, he longed for the beatitude of paradise, aspired to eternity and pursued immortality, the *elixir vitae*. In this respect, too, the alchemist was behaving like pre-modern man. By all sorts of means he tried to conceal from himself his awareness of the irreversibility of Time, either by regenerating it periodically by a re-enactment of the cosmogony, or by sanctifying it in the liturgy, or even by 'forgetting' it, that is, by refusing to acknowledge the secular intervals between two significant (and hence sacred) acts. Above all we must bear in mind that the alchemist became master of Time when with his various apparatus, he symbolically reiterated the primordial chaos and the cosmogony or when he underwent initiatory 'death and resurrection.' Every initiation was

romance, and although the false futurism of Galfridian predictions was in fact condemned by the state, the use of this prophetic mode permits Spenser to speculate on the genuine possibility of knowledge of the future. Through Merlin he can write a plausible science fiction, at the very least.

Hermetic Matrix

ONE OF THE MOST EXOTIC critical events in the history of our literature has been the recent discovery that Spenser engaged in number symbolism. Both Hieatt and Fowler have come in for some heavy questioning, both as to the main drift of their work and for the detail of its execution.[73] On the second of

---

a victory over death, i.e., temporality; the initiate proclaimed himself 'immortal'; he had forged for himself a post-mortem existence when he claimed to be indestructible. . . . But the moment the individual dream of the alchemist might have been realized by a whole society, and on the plane on which it was collectively realizable (the physico-chemical sciences and industry), the defense against Time ceased to be possible. The tragic grandeur of modern man is bound up with the fact that the first to take on the work of Time in relation to Nature." pp. 174–75.

73. A. K. Hieatt, *Short Time's Endless Monument* (New York, 1960); Fowler, *Spenser and Numbers;* the addendum to Hieatt's monograph: "The Daughters of Horus: Order in the Stanzas of Epithalamion," in *Form and Convention in the Poetry of Edmund Spenser* ed. William Nelson. It seems to me possible that Spenser's instinctive numerology is what might be called Augustinian; it need not be considered unusually elitist. Hence, here in the *Epithalamium*, where fertility is a theme of some importance, number symbolism evokes the craving of Christians for the order of *rationes seminales*. Thus David Knowles, in *The Evolution of Medieval Thought* (New York, 1964), 49: "For him [Augustine] number is the intelligible formula which describes the qualities of being and the manner of change, so that all change throughout the universe, which presents so much philosophical difficulty, can in a sense be 'controlled' by numbers, just as an algebraic formula might express an electrical transformation or an en-

these questions I have little to say, except that within limits of common sense it is possible to hold that even if only a certain percentage of Fowler's numerosities are correctly counted, the phenomenon itself would be sufficiently amazing. At first, if I may recall my own impression of *Spenser and the Numbers of Time*, it seemed impossible that Spenser could have contained such systematic variables in his mind as he wrote. This response, I now realize, was wrong for the literary period in question. It was also wrong in terms of the poetic process generally. Later reflection suggested, on the contrary, that nothing could be easier than to keep to a system of numerical symbols. Such processes become readily habitual, once indulged, and for a poet like Spenser, whose stanzaic inventions indicate his fascination with the fact of number itself, the feat seemed finally not so unbelievable. The matter is a little like the apocryphal story about Artur Schnabel, who for his students used to play fiendishly difficult passages from Liszt and pronounce, "That is easy!" and then follow such bravura displays with a simple melody of Mozart, to which he would add, "Now, *that* is hard!"

The first sort of question is more to the point, even though no amount of special pleading can take the place of sound proofs —fortunately Hieatt's analysis of *Epithalamium* provides one highly suggestive, and apparently unassailable, demonstration that in fact Spenser could organize his work on the most complex numerological basis. Yet the critics who ask whether it is generally right to seek such tropical plants in Spenser's northern garden perhaps are asking a more serious question. In thinking about the possibility of this kind of symbolism in Spenser we need to keep to the broad reasons for such a procedure and to the positive values it might have. Perhaps, as a starter, it might help to recall that the first two extant criticisms of Spenser and the Spenserian vision of any magnitude, Digby's *Observations* and Reynolds'

---

gineering stress. Numbers are, in fact, a rationalization of the seminal reason of things." This, of course, was Hieatt's point about the *Epithalamium*.

Mythomystes, both support the magical symbolism of numbers. Digby refers the "mystical" senses of Book II, Canto IX, stanza 22 (the arithmological stanza) to the prophetic theory of inspired "enthusiasm" which we have found basic to such modes of speech, and he proceeds to show that, in this idealized description of the Castle of Alma, Spenser employs geometric symbols of circle, square, and triangle to establish the mystical relationship between man's soul and God.[74] Fowler has shown how this interpretation joins with other similar readings to convey a much larger sequence of mathematical omens. Digby concludes, we might say, where Fowler begins; he admits he might have done better "if either I had afforded my selfe more time or had had the conveniencie of some other books apt to quicken my Invention, to whom I might have been beholding for enlarging my understanding in some things that are treated here, although the Application should still have been mine own: With these helps perhaps I might have dived further into the Authors Intention (the depth of which cannot be sounded by any that is lesse learned than he was). But I perswade my self very strongly, that in what I have said there's nothing so contradictory to it, and that an intelligent and well learned man proceeding on my grounds might compose a worthie and true Commentarie on this Theme: Upon which I wonder how I stumbled, considering how many learned men have failed in the Interpretation of it, and have all at the first hearing, approved my opinion."[75] Digby says that "it was Fortune that made me fall upon it, when first this *Stanza* was read to me for an indissoluble Riddle," and we might be led to admire Digby therefore for uncommon good luck and remarkable learning.

Yet the whole point of his elaborate disclaimer is the fact that such lore as Spenser used was very common fare indeed, and

74. The fullest account of the stanza: Fowler, *Spenser and Numbers*, 260–88.

75. "Observations on the 22 Stanza in the 9th Canto of the 2d. Book of Spensers Faery Queene, Written by the Request of a Friend" (1628?), repr. in Tayler, *Literary Criticism*, 213.

any "intelligent and well learned man" was not only likely to know what Spenser's arcane stanza meant, but would enjoy the little parade of Hermetic lore. Such "Pythagorean" numberings were not confined to the "curious learning" of Sir Thomas Browne, as anthologies have led us to believe. Quite the contrary: they were indispensable to Neoplatonic speculations and, as the researches of Yates and her colleagues have shown, were filtering into England during the latter half of the sixteenth century.[76] Giordano Bruno was not an eccentric foreigner whose wierd ideas were the property of an arcanum; they were known to the circle around Sir Philip Sidney, some of his major works were published in England, his *Expulsion of the Triumphant Beast* and *Heroic Frenzies* may have directly influenced Spenser, and his work possessed a natural charm for scholars and poets who sought enthusiasm and inspired understanding wherever they could find it. The court masques, although yet far from their utmost elaboration, were another seedbed of such materials, and these cannot be regarded as out of the ordinary, When even such a sane and sensible poet as Sir John Davies employs the symbolism of the number 26 because it may rightly be associated with the Queen, we know we are looking at a common enough fashion of image making.[77] The symbolism is not half so curious or

76. Frances Yates, *Giordano Bruno and the Hermetic Tradition* (Chicago and London, 1964). Egyptian materials play a major role here; K. H. Dannenfeldt, "Egypt and Egyptian Antiquities in the Renaissance," in *Studies in the Renaissance* 6:7–27. Bodin, for example, was interested in Egyptian chronology, and Egyptian iconography (real or supposed) enjoyed a vogue as the source of true hieroglyphics.

77. Fowler, *Spenser and Numbers*, 199, observes that "26" is associated with the constellation Virgo, according to the mythic number system of Ptolemy. Davies' *Hymns to Astraea* consist of twenty-six poems, each an acrostic on *Elisabetha Regina*. Yates has studied the Elizabeth-Astraea iconography in her article "Queen Elizabeth as Astraea," *Journal of the Warburg and Courtauld Institutes* 10 (1947). Yates, *Bruno*, 392: "The atmosphere of imperialist mysticism surrounding Elizabeth I, which I have analyzed in my study of her symbol of

odd as it appears to us, and that is the historical fact we need to insist on. Something made this kind of abracadabra truly forceful, took it from the closure of the private séance, and made it available to a poem with large public pretensions, such as *The Faerie Queene*.

This "something" is the strong sense of *telos* that animates the Hermetic mode. Since the antiquity of Hermes Trismegistus was thought to place him even before the Old Testament patriarchs in position of authority, and since a syncretic theory of myth could harmonize Hermetic lore with the prophecies of the Old Testament, the whole body of Hermetic writing enjoyed that same sense of inevitability that informed the orthodox visions of biblical prophets. Hermetic magic shared in this same purposive drive; it became one more mode of sacred revelation, and its adepts could, by an almost mathematical conversion, bring its cabalistic pronouncements and visions into line with Christian belief. We have an instance of this Hermetic tendency in the Proem to Book V, where Spenser couches the vision of world history in the language of astrology, not because he wishes to benumb his reader with a strange vocabulary, but because, in the manner of his master Chaucer, he wants his work to possess the greatest mythic authority. Of a parcel with this tendency is the belief that the whole cosmos moves according to the Pythagorean principles of harmony, a belief brought down to human scale by means of the image of the dance, which Davies exploited for

---

Astraea, the just virgin of the golden age, is a transfer to the Tudor Monarchy of the sacred imperial theme. Uniting, as it did, the spiritual and the temporal headship, this monarchy might well have qualified as 'Egyptian.' Bruno knew of chivalry and joins in it in the *Eroici Furori*." Replying to the Venetian Inquisitors, Bruno explained that he called Elizabeth "diva," not "as a religious attribute, but as that kind of epithet which the ancients used to give to princes, and in England where I then was and where I composed this book (*De la causa, principio ed uno*), this title 'diva' used to be given to the Queen." See also Yates, "Elizabethan Chivalry: The Romance of the Accession Day Tilts," *Journal of the Warburg and Courtauld Institutes* 20 (1957).

his major work, the *Orchestra*. All symbolisms of music, as music, whether in the *Merchant of Venice* or *Comus* or *The Faerie Queene*, get their power from the commonly accepted belief that cosmic order is a kind of supernal music. The most affecting instance of this music is one of the last in *The Faerie Queene*, the vision of the Dance of the Graces, where symbolisms of number organize the scene. The dance and music are obvious in the magic Spenser invokes. What is perhaps at first less obvious is his own awareness that he is using a number symbolism. Having praised his wife, the fourth Grace, Spenser continues as follows:

> Sunne of the world, great glory of the sky,
>> That all the earth doest lighten with thy rayes,
>> Great *Gloriana*, greatest Majesty,
>> Pardon thy shepheard, mongst so many layes,
>> As he hath sung of thee in all his dayes,
>> To make one minime of thy poore handmayd,
>> And underneath thy feete to place her prayse,
>> That when thy glory shall be farre displayd
> To future age of her this mention may be made.
>
> (VI, x, 28)

A minim, the half note of musical time, will be only a footnote to the endless temporality of Gloriana's fame. By contrast, through a mystery, that endless fame preserves the image of eternity, vanquishing time.

The "minime" is only a touch, yet it tells its story of consciously musical symbolism; the poem celebrating Colin's wife is part of a larger harmony, to which it bears the musical relation of exactly one minim. The technical term alerts the reader to a Hermetic reading because it picks out the Pythagorean aspect of the scene of dancing, namely its musical aspect. If one were to choose an instance of the prophetic moment expressed by a single word, this "minime" would serve as well as any in *The Faerie Queene*.

Such scenes and details imply the rage for order, the delight in magic, the Apollonian system-building that Pico had celebrated in his *Oration on the Dignity of Man.* Mount Acidale is a natural arcadian scene, and appropriately its musical atmosphere is "re-creative," to use E.K.'s term in *The Shepeardes Calender.*

Hermetic symbolism is not exhausted by the use of numbers and geometry, or their applied forms, dance and song. It recurs wherever there is a strong appeal to "pagan mystery." The temple in this tradition may simply be a shrine, an oracular center, as with the other religious modes. But it appears that with Hermetic thinking there is no need to present the temple as a built object; it may be a shrine in the mental process of coming into being. Thus the circular form of the round dance will suffice to create an Hermetic temple, as a musical "round" would suffice. Architecture becomes purely "architectonic," to use Sidney's word for it. This leads to a view that we have already broached, that the whole of *The Faerie Queene* is somehow attempting to be a templar structure. Certainly the Spenserian stanza, like the stanzas of his marriage odes, has conveyed to many readers the impression of a prosodic shrine of meaning. Thinking in these terms we do not really seek meanings through iconographic research. We prefer the pure form of the templar idea, its implication of a promise of completed steps, all taking part in a dance of larger scope. This is Eliot's idea of Spenser, which leads him to allude to the *Prothalamium* in *The Waste Land.* Eliot's later work appears to round out a circle of Spenserian prophecy, by innumerable allusions and a borrowing even deeper than allusion. A Spenserian sense of cosmic harmonies, which we know are not rare in the Elizabethan period, illuminates the "musical" form of the *Four Quartets.*

Similarly the notion of error thins out to evanescence in this Hermetic mode. Instead of imagining human or heroic error in the "historical" forms common to the epic and biblical traditions, Hermetic philosophy envisions error in itself, as the pure form of erring. Thus, astrology provides one archetype in the "wandering" of the wayward planets to which Spenser refers in the Proem to Book V, while the poet's own imaginary wandering through "this delightful land of Faery," considered purely formally, symbolizes the possibility that the poet's inspired knowledge must go through its own profane trials before it reaches home. The many disordered "routs" of the rabble have political implications, but their "uncontrolled freedome" operates with its own demonic magic to define the pure idea of disorder.[78] The unredeemed falsity of prowess in Braggadochio and Trompart is a similar parody of the true order of chivalric expression. Instances of error in this mystical vein often occur when the poem presents error of grosser kinds, and it is perhaps only as an *aspect* of gross error that we perceive the Hermetic variety of profane existence in the poem.

Hermetic readings of *The Faerie Queene*, then, are proper only when they subserve other solider readings, of which they are only the most purely aesthetic variant. For it was the glory of Florentine Neoplatonists and the Hermetic philosophers of the period that they sought, not material forms of the good, but in-

---

78. Hooker's *Laws of Ecclesiastical Polity* gives a relevant background to Spenserian ideas of law in general and to the "idea of disorder." Only because "with us one society is both Church and commonwealth" (VIII, 1, 340) does the notion of political disorder generalize to a spiritual realm, and vice versa. Disorder is antinomian, wherever it asserts itself, and for that reason, "in Hooker's system there is no ground for a claim to a right of forcible rebellion in any case." J. W. Allen, *Political Thought in the Sixteenth Century* (London, 1928), 194. Hooker gives law the range of a universal harmony: "Her seat is the bosom of God, her voice the harmony of the world; all things in heaven and earth do her homage, the very least as feeling her care, and the greatest as not exempted from her power; both Angels and men and creatures of what condition soever, though each in different sort and manner, yet all with uniform consent, admiring her as the mother of their peace and joy" (I, xvi, 8). Hooker's image of law as a matrix or maternal figure is a continuing image in Book V, where, as Fowler has shown, the number five is the Pythagorean number of marriage and justice. Wedding in this sense is always "holy matrimony." To prove the point, Spenser always insists that evil demons have a terrible, false progeny, a demonic parody picked up in Milton's portrayal of Sin and Death.

tellectual forms. Thus, for them the idea of a redeemed court is truly an *idea*, a form not present to the mind's eye except as the shadow of a "true type." By admitting such exegesis to our reading we return all prophetic types to their ideal Platonic sources. The poem exploits an intellectual raptus, enthusiasm in the imaginative realm, where prophetic vision encompasses the sphere of the mind reaching out toward the infinity of the Divine Mind. The Graces vanish when Sir Calidore interrupts their dance, and this whole mode of insight disappears before the intruding eyes of the uninitiated. At heart the Hermetic typologies of *The Faerie Queene* are always secret, that is, in the strictest sense they are mysteries. The details of the Hermetic iconography matter far less than the reader's willingness to open up his mind to a degree of mystery in the poem. Spenser's earliest readers had no problem doing this; why should we? Conceivably if we were to accept such magical lore more readily, we would know better when to apply and when not to apply a Hermetic reading.

To a degree the Hermetic style of prophecy sums up the influence of all prophetic tendencies within the epic. All had drawn the poem forward toward one kind of fulfilling experience or another. Only here in this evanescent realm of Pythagorean and arcane symbolism can the drive toward verbal pregnancy find its complete fulfillment, for only here is language freed *entirely* from any need to communicate particular referential meanings. Only here can the poet create unmediated images of pure order, with no admixture of sense. That Renaissance poets sought often for this freedom is apparent from many cases. That Spenser sought it is perhaps less important for a simple, powerful reading of his poem than is his recapitulation of biblical or Vergilian or Ovidian traditions of prophecy. They provide the main strength and substance of his vision. But the Hermetic mode of thought provides a measure of his style and visionary intensity. Only by wanting to go beyond meaning can the poet achieve a truly free vision, which, through his absolute control of number, Spenser achieves in a manner we may loosely call Hermetic.

Spenserian Stanza

OTHER EPICS, including some of Spenser's models, had employed a stanzaic unit of narration. Yet no other epic before or since (with the possible perverse exception of *Don Juan*) has used the stanza with so much sense of its own determining purpose. The prosodic qualities of the Spenserian stanza are well known: the intricacy of rhyme, the evenness of tone, the regularity of line length and the fall of beats, the strong sense that each stanza is a unit, enhanced by the alexandrine closing off each "room" from the next. If indeed Spenser varied the stanza of "The Monk's Tale" to produce his own type, he did so in the direction of greater magnitude and greater cohesion and greater closure. He adjusts the first eight lines of each unit to lead easily into the longer, ninth line. One result of this adjustment is the well-known languor of the style. The poem flows, in general, with unprecedented ease and fullness. The poem does not lightly tolerate dramatic interchanges of dialogue or sudden shifts in the action, nor does the poet want it to. Every motion of the verse leads to vibration of sound and sense.

In such fashion, without claiming that the Spenserian stanza is numerologically ordered—though its nine lines lend themselves to such a purpose—we may say that the stanza is the sine qua non of Spenserian hermeticism. It deploys a numerous magic in prosodic form, that is, it articulates the magic of numbers in the palpable realities of verse. As one dives deeper into the intention of the poem, recalling Sir Kenelm Digby's phrase, one enters deeper and deeper into each stanza, into each prosodic room. These rooms are the ultimate templar monuments of which the whole templar vision is made. Without going so far as to hold that the "Spenserian matrix" of prophecy in *The Faerie Queene* is the Spenserian stanza and its overtones of rhythmic order, it would be tempting to hold that such perfect constructs are miniature memory houses, perfect sacred spaces, microcosms of the vaster templum of the whole poetic vision. But as very likely there is an interpenetration of temple and labyrinth through the whole poem, an interpenetration occurs here too.

Temple meets labyrinth in ideal union. Spenser seems to have wished to make the merging more palpable, and for that reason as the poem progresses, especially in Books IV, V, and VI, there is an increased use of enjambment. This prosodic phenomenon seems at first a metrical equivalent of the iconographic wanderings of error, and of course it is limited in Spenser by the overall form of the stanza; it cannot proceed to the seemingly endless degree to which Milton deliberately led it. But Spenser increasingly allows error into the temple of the stanza, and the effect is one of interpenetrating gyres. Frye and Empson have both stressed the technical mastery of the poet over his stanza, an almost automated process. Fully automated, it might have become as rigid as only the architectonic forms of a temple would permit; but it is not a "frozen labyrinth," and the enjambment reveals the poet's involvement in his own uttering powers. Wearisomely sometimes, sometimes with exuberant joy, with every stanza the poet rededicates his voice. Probably no formal unit in English poetry has received a finer response than Empson gave the Spenserian stanza, when he adduced it as a case of ambiguity; Empson conveys the fixating effect of "the size, the possible variety, and the fixity of the unit," and it is hard to see how a description could be better than that provided in *Seven Types.*

Nevertheless, Empson may be a little misleading, since we may hastily assume that "the scale" of Spenser's rhythm is fully defined by the fact that "Spenser concentrates the reader's attention on to the movement of his stanza." This concentration is the essence, granted. But the stanza serves an expansive as well as concentrative purpose. It is true that with Spenser one learns to attend rather closely to the particular word—as we shall see with Book V the language may even be technically intricate—but this particularity of focus depends upon a structural method of frames within frames, a segregation of parts, and this in turn can widen the reader's scope of attention. Like the inverted cones of Yeats's gyre, the framing technique of the stanza can lead either toward or away from the center. With such a technique at work, there is a sense in which the center need not hold. But in all this the stanza abides, the essential modular unit of *The Faerie Queene*. If this view of Spenser's poetic language is correct, his commitment to free rhythmic flow is continually checked. By the same token the stanza makes possible that sense of withheld fulfillment which all prophecy expresses. The famed couplet of another visionary poem defines the quality of the Spenserian stanza, almost as well, perhaps, as it was defined in *Seven Types of Ambiguity:*

> Though deep, yet clear, though gentle, yet not dull,
> Strong without rage, without o'er-flowing full.

PART TWO

IV

Justice, Prophecy, and History

 I N A PROPHETIC MOMENT SPENSER TRANSFORMS a mythical city of London into the City of Man, where justice is embodied in a beautiful, awesome, human innovation.

> It *Troynovant* is hight, that with the waves
>   Of wealthy *Thamis* washed is along,
>   Upon whose stubborne neck, whereat he raves
>   With roaring rage, and sore himselfe does
>   throng,
>   That all men feare to tempt his billowes strong,
>   She fastned hath her foot, which standes so hy,
>   That it a wonder of the world is song
>   In forreine landes, and all which passen by,
> Beholding it from far, do thinke it threates the skye.
>
> (III, ix, 45)

This third Troy fulfills the promise of the imperial quest of Aeneas and it displays proof, as if defying the City of God, that heroes will create a *civitas* to harness brute energy. In the largest sense justice may be conceived as the spirit of this creation, and our first critical response to Book V, taking quite seriously its commentary on divine providence, should be to attend to its cosmogonic form.

Every prophetic poet will try to originate an order. Typically he arrives at a scene of confusion, which he tries to clarify. He reduces wilderness to order. Prophecy is by nature cosmogonic. Thus we discover an affinity between Blake and Hesiod, the forgotten prophet of ancient Greek poetry. Within the Hebraic-Christian tradition the cosmogonic aims of prophecy are embodied in the person of Moses, who creates an order in history and creates the mythic order of the first books in the Bible. With Spenser every Book of *The Faerie Queene* narrates the origination of an order in time, but the most graphic instance may be the Fifth Book, where the panoramic virtue of Justice expands into a cosmogonic framework, which may indeed be influenced by Hesiod's *Theogony*. As the *Theogony* sets forth an archetypal reduction of the history of the original cosmogonic movement, so Book Five is a planlike document, much more spare than many readers have wished it. Book Five is nonetheless an historicist myth, a blueprint for the historical dimension of the mythology elsewhere in the poem.

The Fifth Book plots a troubled movement from chaos to cosmos, from desolate piratical violence to a cruel, taut, repressive, yet ever hopeful political settlement, which in turn will yield to the promise of Book VI: an order of ceremonial grace. Every stage of this advance is threatened by divisive forces, and because (lacking utopian conditions) government remains balance of power, this poem of justice itself remains tragically poised between hope and despair. Book V recounts the liberation of Irena, but does not predict, though it does prophesy or "speak out for," a final peace. Beginning with its frequently ambivalent mythic materials, Book V enjoins an attitude of prophetic understanding, we might even say, prophetic sympathy. Yet even this impatient, wide-ranging fiction cannot contain all the main forces of political change in Spenser's imperialist world. The story of Artegall and Talus is flawed with doubt and ominous uncertainty, and while these are the normal tones of all major prophetic utterance, they have never comforted Spenser's readers. They testify that in the Legend of Justice, truly a "legend," Spenser wants to enforce the interdependence of justice and man's historical awareness. Book V may be aesthetically lean and muscle-bound at times, but it no less than other Books of *The Faerie Queene* is involved with the problem of conscience.

The Bible had shown man to be responsible for his actions, though overarched by Providence, and had defined history as the unfolding through time of that responsibility. Judaeo-Christian apologetics had long insisted that "justification" must occur in time and must be purgatorial.[1] This view of cosmic justice does not result solely from the prophet's wish to predict future courses of action. Rather it follows from an early awareness, notably in Jeremiah, that a religious cult of the Temple could degenerate into an empty series of external rites, with no significance for spiritual growth. Growth through time, monitored by prophetic wisdom, is the ideal Judeo-Christian image—the "divine pedagogy"—of human destiny. This biblical framework has parallels in the four other traditions of prophetic thought, each of which favors its own typical context.

Talus and Time:
The Tragic Instrument of Justice

In Book V, Spenser's most striking creation is Talus, whose resistless force and impermeable being betoken certain well-known characteristics of the law. Talus is a monster, and yet Spenser depicts him and his actions as necessary to the

1. Thus, John Freccero, "Dante's Pilgrim in a Gyre," *PMLA* 76 (1961): 177: "Justice is achieved in the pilgrim's soul when he reaches the Earthly Paradise and his will is at last enabled to follow his reason's discernment." T. K. Dunseath makes use of Freccero's argument in analyzing the westward movement of the Labors of Hercules; see *Spenser's Allegory of Justice*, 70–71. Artegall's journey to the west is a kind of purgatory. It may be that there is more of Dante, in Spenser, than we have tended to assume; but this Dante would come through Ariosto, Tasso, and other Italian poets.

pursuit of justice. We need therefore to remind ourselves of the iconography of the Iron Man.

Talus cannot act without orders from someone over him, whether his master Artegall, or Britomart, or Prince Arthur. He thus corresponds to any so-called "instrument of the law," that is, an order given out by some higher officer of justice to a lower constabulary which then carries it out. Talus also performs the policing function of the law, as Padelford showed,[2] and when he ferrets out criminals, he resembles the police detective whose officious labors are in modern romances of crime undercut and even opposed by the "private eye." The robot's relentless and cold rage also suggests the mechanism of bureaucratized justice.

But certain mythic overtones, Hesiodic and Ovidian, complicate this personification, and I think they give Talus a special relevance to the prophetic historicizing of justice. Since, with certain variations, he is modeled on the *Talos* who according to legend carried the Tables of the Law in triannual circuits about the island of Crete, he may be associated with processes of legal codification. But Minos' giant was .bronze or brass, whereas Talus is iron, which may rust like Mercilla's sword. Spenser may be suggesting that through the change of element the bronze age shifts directly into the iron age. The third, bronze age of Hesiod's cosmogony had been a time of giants who destroyed each other by violent deeds; the fourth age had been the heroic era of the *Iliad* and Theban saga; the fifth age, to which the iconography of Talus makes an immediate leap, is of iron. This iron age inaugurates human labor and care. It inaugurates human suffering but at the same time mythically it represents the time of transition to the beginnings of human, as opposed to divine culture. Talos, whose movements about Crete associate him with a cult of the sun, seems to belong to this transition period.[3] It is distinct from the

2. *Variorum*, 5:276–80.

3. *Variorum*, 5:165–67, for Apollodorus, I, ix, 26 (119); On the "conditional immortality" of Talos see Francis Vian, *La Guerre des géants: le mythe avant l'époque hellénistique* (Paris, 1962), 192–93. Apollonius Rhodius, *Argonautica*, IV, 1622–95, tells how Medea was

golden time when men and women simply culled the free gifts of nature, which were not of their own willing or making.

The Golden Age was by tradition identified with the world or idea of Eden and with a time *ante legem*, which, we remember,

---

able to cast deadly spells against the Cretan Talos, whose "body and . . . limbs were brazen and invulnerable, except at one point: under a sinew by his ankle there was a blood-red vein protected only by a thin skin which to him meant life or death." Latin *talea*, heelpiece, extends also to mean "set," "layer," and then a "bar," "rod" (flail?). This heel associates Talos with Achilles, and in Book V with Artegall, who is seen in vision by Britomart to be wearing the armor of Achilles. On Artegall and Achilles, see Kathleen Williams, *Spenser's World of Glass*, 134–35; Dunseath, *Spenser's Allegory*, 52 and 59, where we are reminded that Achilles (with Hercules, Jason, and Aesculapius) was reared by Chiron, the Golden Age centaur. The Achilles-heel death of Talos in *Argonautica* resembles Spenser's account of the death of the Egalitarian Giant, with revealing differences; Spenser arranges things to focus on the political iconography of the "ship of state." Thus, in *Argonautica*, the narrator says he is appalled by the thought that a being like Medea can kill with magic: "Is it true then, Father Zeus, that people are not killed only by disease or wounds, but can be struck down by a distant enemy?" Talos, getting ready to throw boulders at the Argo, to keep it from safe anchorage, "grazed his ankle on a sharp rock and the ichor ran out of him like molten lead. He stood there for a short time, high on the jutting cliff. But even his strong legs could not support him long; he began to sway, all power went out of him, and he came down with a resounding crash. Thus a tall pine up in the hills is left half-felled by the woodman's sharp axe when he goes home from the woods, but in the night is shaken by the wind, till at last it snaps off at the stump and crashes down." Translation by E. V. Rieu, *The Voyage of the Argo* (Penguin ed., 1959), 192. Among the semantic overtones of the name Talus there is a sustained play on the idea of paying back, the old *talio* (Old Irish *tale*, Welsh *talu*, etc.), as a form of compensation, which gets mixed in with ideas of weighing, as in Latin *talentum*, and Greek *talanton*, a pair of scales. Spenser imposes the latter image on the Egalitarian Giant, but the ancient myth of Talos also suggests the balancing process, by the way in which he finally loses his balance and falls over the cliff. On "the talion and the idea of balance," see J. P. Guepin, *The Tragic Paradox: Myth and Ritual in Greek Tragedy* (Amsterdam, 1968), 151–59. Spenser, compressing the meanings of the episode, compares the fallen Giant to a

was finally succeeded by the expulsion of man and woman from the garden, a fall corresponding to Astraea's withdrawal from the earth.[4] The iron age man, Cain, plows the land and after his crime

---

wrecked ship, i.e., to a foundered Argo. He is the natural victim of the "cruell tempest," the demonic reversal of the *templum*. At the same time Spenser's Talus engages one in thoughts about the "ages of man" and the Hesiodic "ages of the world," on which see Donald Cheney, *Spenser's Image of Nature*, 150–56; Jane Aptekar, *Icons of Justice: Iconography and Thematic Imagery in Book Five of the Faerie Queene* (New York, 1969), 110–15; and for more general background, C. G. S. Farnell, *The Cults of the Greek States* (Oxford, 1896–1909), 1:125 ff. The original source would seem to be Hesiod, *Works and Days*, 109–201 (Loeb Classics ed., 11–17); thereafter, typically, Ovid, *Metamorphoses*, I, 89 ff., and Vergil, *Georgics*, I, 125 ff. Modern studies: Frederick C. Osenburg, *The Golden Age and the Decay of the World in the English Renaissance* (Urbana, 1939); D. C. Allen, "The Degeneration of Man and Renaissance Pessimism," *Studies in Philology*, 35 (1938): 202–27; S. C. Chew, *The Pilgrimage of Life* (New Haven and London, 1962), 144–73; Adalbert Schoele, *Zeitaltersage und Entwicklungstheorien: Die Vorstellungen vom Werden von Hesiod bis Lukrez* (Berlin, 1959); Walter Veit, *Studien zur Geschichte des Topos der Goldenen Zeit von der Antike bis zum 18. Jahrhundert* (Cologne, 1961); and on Saturn's reign, Erwin Panofsky and Fritz Saxl, *Saturn and Melancholy* (London, 1964). The end point of the decay of the world is a renewal at some apocalyptic moment. Thus, it seems important that, as noted in Loomis, "The Legend of Arthur's Survival," in *Arthurian Literature in the Middle Ages*, ed. R. S. Loomis (Oxford, 1959), 71, Plutarch had reported that, according to British legend, Cronus (Saturn) is confined by Briareus to an island near Britain, and a deep sleep brought upon him "in order to chain him," while "round about him were many daemons for his guards and servants." This would make Arthur into a sleeping Father Time.

4. Astraea's educational program is described in Lactantius, *Divine Institutions* 5. 5–9; Natalis Comes, *Mythologiae* 2.2; H. G. Lotspeich, *Classical Mythology in the Poetry of Edmund Spenser* (Princeton, 1932), 40. Astraea abandons the world, as Diana Arlo Hill—cf. Sherman Hawkins, "Mutabilitie and the Cycle of the Months," in *Form and Convention in the Poetry of Edmund Spenser*, ed. William Nelson, 86.

becomes an outlaw: "And I shall be a fugitive and a vagabond in the earth; and it shall come to pass, that every one that findest me shall slay me." Thus the *lex talionis* enters its second phase; after Adam's primal fall a murder and then retribution become the general human lot. It is not long before races of giants, archetypes of rebels and tyrants, spring up on the earth, and the stage is set for an initial phase of protective social organization. While Talus resembles a giant or Titan, he is in fact a *sub lege* destroyer of giants and Titans, appropriately seconding Artegall, whose Christian sword Chrysaor gets its name in part from the weapon that in ancient mythology had repulsed the Titans. But Talus's flail is significant in another direction: it is an instrument of harvest. It was "never wont in war" (IV, 44), and thus we know it is not identical with Mars' flail. This instrument at first suggests Biblical typology, for in the Bible truth is the winnowed harvest of God's divine justice, working through the heroic acts of men.

There is also a biblical suggestion that the Iron Man shares in the allegorical idea of the "four ages," which, as we have seen, did not convince Bodin of anything he wanted to believe. In the dream of Nebuchadnezzar Daniel had discovered a monstrous giant made of gold, silver, bronze, iron, and clay, starting from the head and working downward to the feet. The crucial gloss on this image was given by Daniel himself: "And there shall be a fourth kingdom, strong as iron, because iron breaks to pieces and shatters all things; and like iron which crushes, it shall break and crush all these" (Daniel 2:40). The mixture of iron and clay in the feet was interpreted as a "divided kingdom . . . partly strong and partly brittle." As is well known, this prophecy gave rise to innumerable millenarian visions, including in part those of Joachim of Flora and later chiliasts. The point to be made is not, however, that Talus has a specific millenarian overtone in his iconic makeup, but that the mere use of the metallic image is enough, in this context, to raise the specter of millenarian possibilities. Time is introduced as a theme, and with some ambivalence of meaning. This occurs without our needing to know exactly the extent to which, in the words of a modern commentator on Dan-

iel, Spenser wants Talus to symbolize the "brutality and ruthless-
ness of the fourth kingdom."[5] There seems to be no difficulty in
the fact that Spenser is conflating the fourth and fifth ages of
Hesiod's account, since he does so generally, with his fiction of
the fairy world.

Talus, furthermore, is associated with his master's Herculean
model, though the mythic linkage may seem tenuous, except of
course that Talus is so powerful physically. Nevertheless, in the
Irish *Stair Ercueil*,[6] a Gaelic life of Hercules, the hero wields not
his club but a flail. The club of Hercules, which Spenser refers
to but Artegall does not carry (suitably, for it would be an odd
weapon even for a "salvage" knight), still exists in Book V,
though displaced into the shape and function of Talus's flail. The
frequent portraiture of Mars showing him carrying a flail, re-
minding us here of Talus, enhances our sense that in its quest
for truth justice may require violent means, though we can distinguish these from actual war.[7] Mars takes revenge on men for
their sins, and the scourge of his cruelty is the most violent retaliation, the form nemesis takes when it carries its judgments
beyond the seas in wars of liberation. This would fit the Belge
episode, perhaps. Yet there is a more interesting allegorical significance to the flail, one which allows Talus to embody the main
theme of Book V, that justice works through time.

As an instrument of harvest the flail has a mythic connection
with the chronography of Hesiod, which in turn finds parallels
in the Bible. After the laborious cultivation of the land comes
the reaping and raking and winnowing of the grain. Man, like
Cain, is a digger and harvester who depends upon the apparent

5. N. W. Porteous, *Daniel: A Commentary*, 106.

6. *Stair Ercueil Ocus a Bas* (*The Life and Death of Hercules*), ed.
and tr. Gordon Quin (Irish Text Society 38; Dublin, 1939), 83, 111,
246.

7. Jean Seznec, *The Survival of the Pagan Gods*, figs. 74, 75, 76,
77. Osiris is shown in Egyptian art holding a shepherd's crook and a
flail, for which see S. H. Hooke, *Middle Eastern Mythology* (Penguin
ed., 1963), fig. 3.

(to him real) motion of the sun. Here the image of Talus comes into focus. He has a mythic analogue, even closer than Hercules or Mars. Since Panofsky first exposed the error by which the mythographers confused Kronos and Chronos, thus allowing a conflation of the figures of Saturn (Kronos) and Time (Chronos), we have known that the scythe of Father Time usually represents the destructive effects of temporal change, but had once simply been the harvest god's chief implement.[8] Saturn was originally a cereal god, as we should expect from his connection with the Golden Age. The story of Talus contains a similar conflation of several myths originally separable (as his name appears complex in etymological overtones). By changing his external attributes of body and weapon, Spenser creates a Talus who can subsume the several ideas of martial law, divine nemesis, annual rebirth in the organic world, temporal passage and decay, and finally titanic power. Imaginatively we must exchange the scythe for the flail. This syncretism enables Talus to embody more than mere executive police power. It shows us the connection between that power and the evolution of justice.

For throughout the Renaissance, as Panofsky, Chew, and others have shown in great detail, Father Time—or at least, Time—had a daughter, Truth, who was inseparably linked with the principles of Justice.[9] *Veritas filia temporis*, Truth is the daughter of Time, and we arrive finally at one consequence of this *topos:* Spenser must be looking forward to the reconciliation of Truth with the other three daughters of god—Justice, Mercy,

8. Erwin Panofsky, *Studies in Iconology: Humanistic Themes in the Art of the Renaissance* (New York, 1939; repr. New York, 1962), chap. 3, "Father Time," and especially n. 47. S. C. Chew, *The Virtues Reconciled: An Iconographical Study* (Toronto, 1946), 141, n. 57, describes Barten Holyday, *Texnogamia: the Marriages of the Arts* (1618), where Time is an ornament on the crown worn by the character Historia.

9. Fritz Saxl, "Veritas Filia Temporis," in *Philosophy and History: Essays Presented to Ernst Cassirer* (Oxford, 1936; repr. New York, 1963), 197–222.

and Peace. Truth is shown in a woodcut bearing the attributes of Time—the torch, the hourglass, and the scythe.[10] Allegories of justice show Old Father Time aiding the discovery of error, "truth brought to light and discovered by time." And Time himself, as, for example, he appears in the woodcut of Gilio's *Topica Poetica* of 1580, bears the scourge of justice, a scourge remarkably like a flail.[11] The connections of Time and Justice, in short, are well established in Renaissance emblematic literature. Talus also, associated as he is with emblems of Time's harvest, discovers truth through time.

The trial of Duessa fixes this interpretation of Talus. For although Canto IX idealizes Mary's trial and sixteenth-century treason trials in general, its immediate antecedent gives truth-versus-falsehood a major place in the allegory. Before the trial can take place, Talus must kill Malengin, or Guile, who may be associated with Dolon, another deceiver. The trial itself consists of a conflict between two types of evidence: the defense witnesses all testify to character rather than actions, while the prosecution has a clear, if unexamined, field and calls witnesses only to the bad conduct of the queen. She appeals to Arthur by her romantic appearance, and he must learn to see through it into the true identity. The outcome is a triumph of truth, as perhaps all trials will be when they are just, but here the poet enlarges on the role played by deceit. For in historical fact, Mary of Scotland never openly renounced plans to get rid of Elizabeth. (This is not to deny Elizabeth's intrigues.)[12] The strange allegory of the poet, Bonfont, whose name was changed to Malfont, gives a

10. Chew, *Virtues Reconciled*, fig. 10, "Truth with the attributes of Time"—from Meisner, *Sciographia Cosmica* (Nuremburg, 1637).

11. Ibid., fig. 13, "Time with the scourge of Justice," from Gilio, *Topica Poetica* (Venice, 1580).

12. See J. E. Phillips, *Images of a Queen: Mary Stuart in Sixteenth-Century Literature* (Berkeley and Los Angeles, 1964); J. E. Neale, *Queen Elizabeth: A Biography* (London, 1934; repr. New York, 1957), speaks of a particular situation as being "after Elizabeth's own heart, demanding caution, secrecy, and valiant lying."

perspective to this reading; a court poet purveyed an image of the sovereign, and a false poet might be a false propagandist, a false image maker.

Mercilla's three attendants, Dice, Eunomie, and Eirene (Justice, Good Law, and Peace), as the daughters of Themis are also identified with the passage of time; the sacred three were popularly known as the Hours, the *Horai*. Like other trinitarian mythic groupings, this one embodies a triune mystery, analogous to the unity of "arithmetic," "geometric," and "harmonic" justice, which, as Bodin observed, is a summation of the first two within the third, thus constituting "the onely scope and summe of all the lawes and judgements as also of the true Royall government."[13] Peace and harmony are obvious synonyms. The effect of the triple grouping is musical as well as mathematical. To think of peace as harmony, a common enough equivalence during this period, is to give peace a groundwork for development through time. Dunseath observes that Duessa's trial itself is "completely stylized." Stylization quells motion, or, in the present terminology, settles upon harmonic structures which provide a *basis*. These structures, forms of justice conceived with fixed iconographies, provide the foundation (musically, the bass line or "ground"), which itself does not change, though it may move in order that secondary voices be supported and driven by its cadences. This musical analogy has a temporal aspect: the Hours here are emblems of cyclical order—they govern time; time does not govern them.

There is an important, if obvious, difference between unique historical events and recurring events, so that while the sentencing of Duessa is "historically" unique in time, the presence of the Hours shows it is also a ritual defeat of evil. Perhaps justice meets history proper in its relation to the *persons* of the trial, and ritual

13. Dunseath, *Spenser's Allegory of Justice*, 211, quoting this passage from the 1606 translation of Bodin's *Six Books*. Dunseath continues: "Bodin explains that just as the line contains the point and the surface contains the line, so the geometrical justice contains arithmetical and harmonical justice contains geometrical."

in the *forms* of the trial, for these latter are templar. The markedly cosmic, ornamental, hierarchical arrangement of Mercilla's
Court gives it ritual authority, the authority of customary habi-
tude, while the intrusion of Artegall and Arthur, following
Talus's destruction of Malengin, gives it a punctate relation to the
flux of historical time. Though it is not easy to decide whether
here and elsewhere Book V shows "the subordinating of cyclical
symbols to dialectical ones,"[14] the stress on rebellion in Book V
would appear to require this subordination. Yet everywhere in
Book V "historical allegory," whatever it includes in the way of
topical reference, always has a strong ritual coloration. Ritual
itself is one harvest of time.

Social Banditry:
Prophetic Origins of Justice

THE COSMOGONY OF JUSTICE assumes a special sort
of hero, exemplified here in Artegall. The vision of justice, which,
as vision, is a static ideal, has also to be lived, though at first under
confusing conditions. The Proem to Book V sets this beginning
in the vast temporal perspective of astrology, but the reader must
not think that Spenser has committed his hero to a deterministic
pattern. The Proem is mainly intended to provide the broadest
possible temporal frame for its hero's rejuvenating actions. The
world has grown old and unjust; Artegall will make it new and
fair again. To do so, as mythic figure, he begins at the beginning.
Through him the reader returns, looks back, to the *arche*.

Artegall, the chief instrument of justice in Book V, belongs
to a category of archetypal figures which Spenser is able to identify with the prophetic role of England's patron saint, Saint
George. But along with the association of the two changelings,
Artegall and Redcrosse, Artegall is likened by Spenser to other

14. Northrop Frye, "Structure of Imagery in *The Faerie Queene*,"
in *Fables of Identity*, 79.

figures of myth and history: Bacchus, Hercules, Achilles, Osiris, Samson, even Antony. With all their differences these figures may be said to conform to the type of the "social bandit," which means that they bring justice to a world where laws either do not yet exist or have failed somehow to work, usually through a governor's malfeasance. "Social bandit" is a technical term for the Robin Hoods of history, the good badmen whose *de jure* wrong aims at *de facto* right. Robbing the rich to pay the poor—this proverbial English expression amounts to a primitive definition of equity in the area of distributive justice, while the second half of Robin Hood's fame, that "he never killed but in self-defence or just revenge," defines a primitive mode of Aristotle's corrective justice.

Two points should at once be observed: such social bandits are surrounded by an aura of prophecy and often millennial expectation, and secondly, they are hard to distinguish from all sorts of bandits who are *not* social. "Naturally Robin Hood, the archetype of the social rebel 'who took from the rich to give to the poor and never killed but in self-defence or just revenge,' is not the only man of his kind. The tough man, who is unwilling to bear the traditional burdens of the common man in a class society, poverty and meekness, may escape from them by joining or serving the oppressors as well as by revolting against them. In any peasant society there are 'landlords' bandits' as well as 'peasant bandits' not to mention the State's bandits, though only the peasant bandits receive the tribute of ballads and anecdotes. Retainers, policemen, mercenary soldiers are thus often recruited from the same material as social bandits."[15] Obviously, then, we shall have no easy time distinguishing the precise characters of heroes in such a mythography. It was the need to preserve this telling ambiguity that prompted Swift to suggest to John Gay that he write

15. E. J. Hobsbawm, *Social Bandits and Primitive Rebels* (Glencoe, Ill., 1959), republished as *Primitive Rebels* (New York, 1965). I quote from the 1965 edition, here from 13. On prophecy and social banditry, see Hobsbawm, 11, 19, 60, 63, 69, 83, 87, 92, 101, 127, 143, 181–82, and below in my remarks on the Egalitarian Giant, 242–46.

a "Newgate Pastoral," to which Gay responded by creating the new, urban social bandit, Captain MacHeath. Pastoral provides a sophisticated mythographic technique for projecting, in rather abstract form, the conditions of banditry, social banditry, and evolved justice. For this reason the most celebrated classical prophecy of a just world returning to the Golden Age, Vergil's in *Eclogue IV*, is set in a pastoral framework of vision.

Here myth and history, as in the address to Pollio of *Eclogue IV*, merge indistinctly, creating a mode of "legend." The interpenetration of myth and history is broadly typological, given a wide interpretation of prophecy. Thus, according to ancient and medieval tradition, Alexander the Great assumed the divinity of Bacchus. Many actual rulers claimed descent from Hercules— Henry of Navarre is called the Hercules of France.[16] In both

16. Seznec, *Survival of Pagan Gods*, 26. King and pope alike might be equated with Hercules because the latter, "the champion of Virtue and conqueror of evil in all shapes and forms, had long been accepted as the model of the *miles Christianus* or even as a prefiguration of Christ." Erwin Panofsky, *Albrecht Dürer* (Princeton, 1948), 190. See Eugene Waith, *The Herculean Hero in Marlowe, Chapman, Shakespeare, and Dryden* (New York and London, 1962). Marcel Simon, *Hercule et le christianisme* (Paris, 1955), 83: "Apotheosis in this context [Dio Chrysostomos] is no longer the automatic consequence of a divine parentage. It appears rather to be the recompense for an exceptional human quality. Or at least, if Hercules becomes a god after his death, it is above all because he knew, insofar as he was a man, how to achieve a flourishing of the divine seed planted in him at birth." The Herculean Henry of Navarre seems a commonplace— he appears in a poem of Joshua Sylvester, "The Trophies of the Vertues and Fortune of Henry the Great," lines 23 ff.

> I' th' winter Solstice (when the yeare is worne)
> Within Pau Castle This young Mars was born:
> Born for the World's Good: as his Enterance
> Presag'd him then the Hercules of France.

And also in "The Battail of Yvry," lines 217 ff:

> Goe, happy Soule, goe tell the news beneath,
> How thou wert honour'd to have had thy death

Shakespeare and Plutarch's *Life*, Antony (like Artegall) is identified with Bacchus and Hercules. Hallett Smith has observed that "to the Elizabethans Hercules was a figure in early history who was particularly interesting because he was supposed to have liberated England from a tyrant, the Albion from which the country took one of its early names. This notion is given prestige by appearing in William Harrison's *Description of England* which was the introduction to Holinshed's *Chronicle* (1596)."[17] Renaissance mythographers revel in hyperbolic praises of Herculean legendary justice. Similarly, during this period there is a tendency to make Osiris a euhemerized god, an actual ruler so admired and worshiped that he finally becomes a god. Typically, for Christian readers of the Old Testament Samson played a role in history precisely because he was a prototype of later figures, preeminently Christ himself, as Judith was the type of Queen Elizabeth when she resisted oppression. By alluding typologically to such figures, Spenser recalls that in ancient times history is crossbred with mythology. Book V is a brief History of the World which begins by rehearsing the doings of gods and demigods, of planets

---

By th' onely hand of th' *Hercules* of *France*,
Th' invincible; (for, such a death, perhaps,
Shall more extoll thy famous Memory,
Then to have won some other Victory);
Say, here revives a *Martel*, Foes to maul;
And that Orlando rules again in Gaul.

From *The Complete Works of Joshua Sylvester*, ed. A. B. Grosart (Edinburgh, 1880), vol. 2.

17. Hallett Smith, *Elizabethan Poetry: A Study in Conventions, Meaning, and Expression* (Cambridge, Mass., 1952; repr. Ann Arbor, 1968), 296. See 293–303 on the "Choice of Hercules" and associated myths. The particular interest of the myth of Omphale, and of Iole, whom Spenser parallels to Radigund (V, v, 24), resides in their countering the heroic asceticism. Boccaccio, *Concerning Famous Women*, trans. G. A. Guarino (New Brunswick, N.J., 1963), 45–47: "Then the enemy of chastity [whoever is seduced by Iole] and encourager of crimes casts shame and honor aside, makes ready the pigsty, and, grunting, gives himself up to the allurements of copulation."

and constellations. Artegall, who is not a god or demigod, nor even a child of faery, is a legendary person. His story is a sequence of episodes unified by their prophetic, typological coherence in a providential scheme.

Plutarch's *Of Isis and Osiris*, a major source for Book V, shows the outlines of this typology. It paints the portrait of Osiris the social bandit. But the portrait is difficult to read through this extremely dense symbolic commentary on Osirian cult, and we may more conveniently examine the parallel *Lives* of Theseus and Romulus, where Plutarch depicts the beginnings of civilization. In this matter insufficient credit has been given to Richard Hurd's *Letters on Chivalry and Romance*. Hurd explains the giants and savages of gothic romance as follows: "These Giants were oppressive feudal Lords; and every Lord was to be met with, like the Giant, in his strong hold, or castle. Their dependents of a lower form, who imitated the violence of their superiors, and had not their castles, but their lurking-places, were the Savages of Romance. The greater Lord was called a Giant, for his power; the less, a Savage, for his brutality. All this is shadowed out in the Gothic tales, and sometimes expressed in plain words." Hurd's legendary account may appear fantastical to us, who are far away from both the age of romance and its gothic revival. But there is some wisdom in the theory, and rough though it is, Hurd can say, "For this interpretation we have the authority of our great poet," as exemplified in Book V, Canto II, stanza 1. "Even Plutarch's life of Theseus reads, throughout, like a modern Romance: and Sir Arthegal himself is hardly his fellow, for righting wrongs and redressing grievances. . . . Accordingly, Theseus is a favourite Hero (witness the *Knight's Tale* in Chaucer) even with the Romance-writers."[18]

In the parallel lives of Theseus and Romulus, Plutarch shows that justice does not spring full-blown into the world, but must be forcibly established. Not long after the passing of the Golden Age (which also sets the scene in Book V) the world is overrun with bandits, outlaws, local strongmen, giants, monstrous tyrants.

18. *Variorum*, 5:169–70.

In response to this violence Theseus and Romulus, the archetypal city builders, rise up to defend mankind. Theseus, for example, begins his career by journeying to Athens and on his way destroying the bandits who terrorized that countryside.

> . . . the waye by lande from TROEZEN TO ATHENS was very daungerous, all the wayes being besett by robbers & murderers. For the worlde at that time brought forth men, which for strongnesse in their armes, for swyftnes of feete, and for a generall strength of the whole bodye, dyd farre passe the common force of others, and were never wearie for any labour or travell they tooke in hande. But for all this, they never employed these giftes of nature to any honest or profitable thing, but rather delighted villanously to hurte and wronge others: as if all the fruite and profit of their extraordinary strength had consisted in crueltye, and violence only, and to be able to keepe others under & in subjection, and to force, destroye, & spoyle all that came to their handes. Thincking that the more parte of those which thincke it a shame to doe ill, and commend justice, equitie, and humanitie, doe it of fainte cowardly heartes, bicause they dare not wronge others, for feare they should receyve wronge themselves: and therefore, that they which by might could have vauntage over others, had nothing to doe with suche quiet qualities.[19]

Some of these bandits, who like Albion, are conceived as giants, met destruction in older time at the hands of Hercules, who is the model for both Theseus and Romulus.[20] But other bandits escaped Hercules and went into hiding. While he served

19. Plutarch, *The Lives of the noble Grecians and Romanes*, trans. Sir Thomas North (London, 1579). I have used W. H. D. Rouse, ed., Nonesuch Press Edition (London, 1929–30), 1:6–7.

20. On gigantomachia: Roger O. Iredale, "Giants and Tyrants in Book Five of *The Faerie Queene*," *Review of English Studies* 17 (1966): 373–81; Vian, *La Guerre des géants*. Hercules allies himself with the Olympian gods to put down the Titans (as in Apollodorus). Hercules becomes an Olympian auxiliary in Euripides, *Heracles*, 1192–94; Diodorus Siculus, I, 24:2; IV, 15:1; Seneca, *Hercules Furens*, 444–46; *Hercules Oeta*, 1137–1217; Aelius Aristides, *Heracles* XL, 7; Macrobius, *Saturnalia*, I, 20:8–9; and is a giant killer in Pindar, *Nemean Odes*, VII, 90; Sophocles, *Tracchiniae*, 1058–59.

Omphale as penance for killing his friend Iphitus, there was no
hero to quell the banditry which at once broke out again. Such
was the situation when Theseus journeyed to the site of Athens,
and in his deeds as before in the deeds of Hercules, we discover
the peculiar reflexes of the social bandit. For Theseus and Hercules freely enter the bandits' world, triumphing over them by
violent, extralegal means closely resembling the bandits' own devices. Theseus and Hercules are "social" in that they both "purge
both land and sea from wicked men," but they are bandits in
that they act within the terms of the outlaw world. Their justice
enacts, though it does not codify, a primitive *lex talionis*. As
Plutarch puts it,

> He slewe also *Cercyon* the ARCADIAN, in the cittie of ELEVSIN,
> wrestling with him. And going a little further, he slewe *Damastes*,
> otherwise surnamed *Procrustes*, in the cittie of HERMIONIA: and that
> by stretching on him out, to make him even with the length and
> measure of his beddes, as he was wont to doe unto straungers that
> passed by. *Theseus* dyd that after the imitation of *Hercules*, who
> punished tyrannes with the selfe same payne and torment, which
> they had made others suffer. For even so dyd *Hercules* sacrifice
> *Busiris*. So he stifled *Antheus* in wrestling. So he put *Cycnus* to death,
> fighting with him man to man. So he brake *Termerus* heade, from
> whom this proverbe of *Termerus* evill came, which continueth yet
> unto this daye: for this *Termerus* dyd use to put them to death in
> this sorte whom he met: to jolle his head against theirs. Thus pro-
> ceeded *Theseus* after this selfe manner, punishing the wicked in like
> sorte, justly compelling them tabyde the same payne and torments,
> which they before had unjustly made others abyde.[21]

21. Plutarch, *Theseus*, 12. On the parallel biblical tradition of the
giants as bandits and usurpers, see, besides Iredale, Dunseath, *Spenser's
Allegory of Justice*, 108. The text was Genesis 6: "There were gyantes
in the earth in those days," specifically glossed in the Geneva Bible as
men who "usurped authoritie over others." Iredale quotes a more
comprehensive indictment, from Abraham Fraunce's *Third Part of
the Countess of Pembroke's Ivychurch* (London, 1592), sig. 9: "These
allegorically are seditious and rebellious subjects in a common wealth,

The distinction between the good and the bad bandit is tenuous, since in these legendary days which we may call both "prehistorical" and "prejudicial" the main need of society is not for a lawyer or judge, but rather for some one man of great power and natural goodness who uses the most violent means to establish or restore a basic social order. But the native goodness of the social bandit is an uncertain thing, and Plutarch says, for example, that according to some ancient writers one of the worst bandits put down by Theseus, Sciron (who resembles Spenser's Egalitarian Giant) "was never any robber, nor wicked persone, but rather a pursuer and punisher of the wicked, and a friend and a kynseman of the most honest, and justest men of Greece." Plutarch discounts this, but the contradictory legend hints that between bandit and social bandit no clear line exists, a point Eric Hobsbawm has documented in his study of modern social banditry. Indeed, the two types merge at that very moment when justice itself is evolving from chaos and is therefore in flux.

One reason why the myths of Bacchus and Osiris are so complex and why they parallel each other, is that they both include strictly prehistoric legends of the hero who will later become the euhemerized social bandit. (Possibly, as gods, though Dionysus is a "younger god" in the Pantheon, the two might come from an older stratum of myth than the demigod culture-hero Hercules.) Although, in typical encyclopedic fashion, Linche's Cartari knows that Bacchus has a nefarious history, he also begins his account with praise: "Histories doe deliver unto us," as the Elizabethan translator had it, "that this Bacchus (of whome wee now entreat) was held among the Auncients in great repute and esteeme for a most valerous, hardie, and well-approved Captaine,

---

or schismaticall and haereticall seducers in the Church. Iupiter, the King or supreame governour: the Giants, rebells or heretikes: the hills, their aspiring deseignes and accursed stratagems: Ioves lightning, the iust plague and confusion of such attempts: their serpentine feete signifie their pernicious and poysonable policies, and their monstrous and most degenerate deformitie in opposing themselves against the commonwealth."

performing in those his times many worthie, haughtie, and gallant services, which gained unto him the report and title of a victorious and all-conquering commander: as *Diodorus Siculus*, and many other autentic Authours have written."[22] The account that follows periodically contradicts the valiant legend, and if we did not know that this is the norm for social banditry, we should perhaps ask how a heroic poet could choose such protagonists. Rage, venery, effeminacy, drunkenness and a long list of other doubtful qualities have to be accepted, if this archetype is to function for what it is. For contained in the almost chaotic life style of the social bandit is the flexibility that makes him responsive enough to produce change before there are any rules and regulations of change.

The most familiar example of the social bandit in English lore is Robin Hood. The mere mention of his name recalls a vendetta in which Robin's conflict with men of law and with rich ecclesiastics allows him to restore a social justice. Keen has shown in some detail how strong is this legalistic element of the medieval ballads: "the heroes of the earlier outlaw stories made their names fighting for the cause of right against known oppressors."[23] Even more bitter than the outlaws' traditional enmity against rich monastic landholders and their clerks is the enmity against false lawmen. Discussing the relationship between the Robin Hood stories and the actual medieval revolts of the peasants, Keen observes that "modern historians who have examined the causes of these revolts have diagnosed them in economic terms. But because the rebels were medieval men living in an age which tended to see everything in terms of law their demands were largely legal, which is what we would expect from the outlaw poems with their persistent bitterness against men of law. . . . When (in the Peasants Revolt of 1381) the rebels reached London, they broke into the Temple and burned all the books of the lawyers that they could

22. Vincenzo Cartari, *The Fountain of ancient Fiction. Wherein is lively depictured the images and statues of the ancients . . . Done out of Italian into English by Richard Linche* (London, 1599), sig. X. ii.

23. Maurice Keen, *The Outlaws of Medieval England* (London, 1961), 209.

lay hands on."[24] If we remember that the bandit is an outlaw, lawless as well as outside the law, he becomes a paradoxical (we might say mythical) figure when he overthrows the established legal machinery, because in effect he does this in order to establish, if not new laws, a new justice. Otherwise he would not bother to burn the law books.

Robin Hood's legend, like that of Hercules and Theseus, is one long, dramatic examination of the postulates underlying legal and judicial process. Thus Robin's chief enemy is the Sheriff of Nottingham. Thus Gamelyn, in the *Tale of Gamelyn*, takes the king's Justice and his jurymen prisoner—they are about to hang Gamelyn's good brother, Sir Ote—and himself assumes the role of Justice, sitting in the judgment seat, arraigning a panel of jurymen from his own outlaw band, himself passing sentence of death when his men returned the verdict.[25] Once more the proximity of bandit and social bandit is inherent in the legend: the sheriff in this case is Gamelyn's oldest brother.

This overlap complicates Book V of *The Faerie Queene*, where Artegall repeats some of the labors of Hercules. Spenser could learn of an ambivalent Hercules from Plutarch and the classical and Renaissance mythographers. He could read in Jean Bodin that Hercules was "the greatest of pirates," who "allied Theseus and Pirithous with him in criminal association."[26] Spenser shares Bodin's doubt about the perfection of his hero. He knows, with Bodin, that no one was "stronger in all kinds of lust than Hercules."[27] A poet wishing to use such a hero will have to doctor his myth, or else, as with the Robin Hood type of ballad, show that the bandit hero is really a social bandit. As a

24. Ibid., 161–62.
25. Ibid., 85–87.
26. Jean Bodin, *Method for the Easy Comprehension of History*, trans. and ed. Beatrice Reynolds, 297.
27. Ibid., 298. This tradition was problematic for Christianity on account of the reputed deification of Hercules. Lactantius, *Epitome*, chap 7, concludes: "The result is that, even if for his courage he might have been credited as a god, he is seen, by reason of his evil deeds, to have been but a human being."

scientific historian Bodin had followed Thucydides in noting that brigandage, piracy, and banditry were a fact of ancient Greek life, as piracy was one aim of Queen Elizabeth's privateers, and Spenser himself knew England and the remote regions of Ireland well enough to supply his own equivalent of the stories Bodin had found in Thucydides. The Desmonds and Fitzgeralds were, in their own defence, model social bandits.[28] There is some irony in the fact that Spenser's Kilcolman house was burned down by bandits who considered themselves "social," while his last official appointment in the service of Queen Elizabeth, which he was destined never to fulfill, was to the office of sheriff.[29]

28. See Edmund Curtis, *A History of Ireland* (London, 1936; repr. 1961), chap. 12, especially 190–91, on "a curious bit of antiquarian buccaneering [that] drove Sir Edmund Butler with others into revolt." "The chief motives of rebellion under Elizabeth were destined to be: the insecurity of land-titles among the Old English of Leinster and Munster, threatened by English-born adventurers and planters, the attack upon feudal and chiefly lordships, and the religious grievance." Note that Spenser's views and actions were incendiary on all three counts. Precisely his own involvement in the system he is defending has called his poetic integrity into question, and the present argument about Spenser's mythistoria is forced to show that "distinterest" is not one of the properties of his prophetic art.

29. A. C. Judson, *Life of Edmund Spenser* (Baltimore, 1945), 200. Eudoxus, in the *Vewe* (Renwick ed., 180–81), fears that "as for these garrissons which yee have nowe so strongeleye planted, throughout all Ireland, and everyie place swarming with soldyers: shall there be noe end of them: For now thus being mee semeth I doe see rather a Countrie of Warr, then of peace and quiet which yee erst pretended to worke in Ireland, for yf you bring all thinges to the quietnes which yee said, what need then to maintaine so great forces as ye have charged upon yt:" To which Irenaeus (the "peacemaker") replies that he will keep his arms and garrisons until peace is established, which will lead to a stabilizing of prosperity. He alludes to the danger from Spain, but asserts a double aim, "to settle an eternall peace in that Countrie (Ireland), and also to make yt verie profitable to her maiestie, the which I see must be rought in by a stronge hand, and so continewed untyll yt growe into a steadfast course of government." See Cyril Falls, *Elizabeth's Irish Wars* (London, 1950).

Spenser, of course, had chosen a British archetype for the hero of Book V. The fact that Artegall is partly modeled on a native hero, Arthgallo, draws the myth of the social bandit into a British world, making it Galfridian as much as classical or biblical or hermetic (in "Egyptian" style).[30] We have seen that one element in social banditry is the hero's equivocal relation to established order; this political ambivalence is apparent again with Geoffrey of Monmouth's Arthgallo. As a *young* ruler he "made it his business everywhere to smite down the noble and upraise the base; to take away from the rich that which was their own, and to heap untold treasure for himself."[31] Now in Book V Artegall specifically does not do this. But there is a character who would like to follow in Arthgallo's footsteps, the Egalitarian Giant. Since Book V shows its hero learning to be just, we may call this episode of the Giant, "Artegall learning to be just, in dialogue with himself." Spenser does not say, "The Egalitarian Giant is Artegall's *alter ego*," but the legendary source for the hero's life suggests that he is. When Artegall defeats the Giant in debate, he defeats his own pride.[32] This transcendence of a weakness inherent to the role of the justiciar is proper mythologically as well, since we learn from Geoffrey of Monmouth that Arthgallo, having been deposed and then reinstated through the help of his brother, "did so amend him of his former mis-

30. Hermetic interest in magic powers of civilization might be discerned in many parts of *FQ*, but the most significant problems of Hermetic prophecy occur in connection with Isis Church and with the Blatant Beast, which may tangentially be touched by the *Spaccio della bestia trionfante* (1584) of Bruno, which, we could say, reconstellates the vices and virtues. See Frances Yates, *Giordano Bruno and the Hermetic Tradition*, 211–34.

31. *History of the Kings of Britain*, trans. Sebastian Evans; rev. C. W. Dunn (New York, 1958), 61 (book 3, sec. 17).

32. Thus Dunseath argues that "the debate with the giant pits Artegall against one who is symbolic of his greatest enemy—his pride." The psychic drama occurs, as Dunseath shows, in the patterning of a formal debate, which contains the Herculean theme of justice as eloquence. See *Spenser's Allegory of Justice*, 94–111.

deeds, as that now he did begin to abase the baser sort and to exalt the gentler, to allow every man to hold his own, and to do right justice."

Having some of this Galfridian blood in his veins, Artegall has finally to be a reformed character if he will reform others. To insist on the tenuous nature of his hero's virtue, Spenser involves Artegall in an ongoing evolution of justice. He overextends the hero's duties. Artegall is like a sheriff to whom extraordinary power, but also extraordinary jurisdiction, has been granted. He is almost a governor-general, and the allusion to Lord Grey suggests that if Artegall is a sort of supersheriff, his model goes back to the pre-sixteenth-century period. Maitland, who showed that during the sixteenth century the office of sheriff had declined in range and force, giving way to that of the Justices of the Peace —a rule dubbed "Eirenarcha" by its chief apologist, William Lambarde—describes the archetypal sheriff of the twelfth century as little less than a provincial viceroy. "All the affairs of the shire—fiscal, military, governmental, its justice and police—were under his control, and he was the president of the county court."[33] In England, though not in Ireland, such regal powers were increasingly alien to sixteenth-century practice, which explains why they fit Spenser's poem so closely. He is writing of an archaic stage in development, and that stage can only be represented historically by a return to an earlier situation. Equally important to our grasp of Book V, besides this archaism of its mythic history, is the fact that as a viceroy Artegall serves an imperial as well as a local function. He takes the queen's justice overseas, and in this resembles the heroic line of Aeneas. He is a settler—whether one sees in him a mythic figure patterned on Brut, on Hercules, on Aeneas—or a historical figure patterned on Lord Grey de Wilton, who was Elizabeth's viceroy in Ireland during the years

33. F: W. Maitland, *The Constitutional History of England* (Cambridge, 1946), 233. G. R. Elton, *The Tudor Revolution in Government: Administrative Changes in the Reign of Henry VIII* (Cambridge, 1960), shows how administrative bureaucratization altered the king's household until something like the machinery of the modern nation-state was reached during the earlier sixteenth century.

1580 to 1582. In every case the sphere of the hero's authority is yet to be defined by him; it is not quite given to him; he must establish it. This is true in Elizabethan history, as it is true in Herculean myth. We are talking about a place and time where law is an uncontained force.

Without defending Elizabethan imperialism, let us imagine one such place, Ireland, as English governors saw her. Sir Philip Sidney, whose father was one of the more successful Irish viceroys, wrote in his fragmentary "Discourse of Irish Affairs" that lenity was not really possible in such a country, where the people were "not fully conquered." Of such a people he says that "untyll by tyme they fynde the sweetenes of dew subjection, it is impossible that any gentle meanes shoolde putt owt the freshe remembrance of their loste lyberty. And that the Irishe man is that way as obstinate as any nation, withe whome no other passion can prevail but feare besydes their storye whiche plainly painte it owt, their manner of lyfe wherein they choose rather all filthines then any law, and their own consciences who beste know their owne natures, give sufficient proofe of. For under the son there is not a nation, whiche live more tirranniously than they doe one over the other. And truly even in her Majesties tyme, the rebellions of Oneale, and all the Earle of Wormondes brethren, shew well, how little force any gratefull love dothe beare withe them."[34] Living in the waning twentieth century, we see that the Irish "social bandits" wished to be cruel and kind

---

34. *Prose Works of Sir Philip Sidney*, ed. Albert Feuillerat (Cambridge, 192; repr. 1962), 3:49–50. Renwick describes this "time of unusual anxiety" in his edition of the *Vewe*, 223–51. Papal decree declared that Ireland might wage a "just war" against Elizabeth, as stated in "The Proclamation of the Right Honourable Lord James Geraldine concerning the Justice of that War which he wageth in Ireland for the Faith" (1579), in *Cal. Carew MSS.*, I, 400, as given in Constantia Maxwell, *Irish History from Contemporary Sources: 1509–1610* (London, 1923), 169. The papacy exhorted the Catholic Irish "to throw off the yoke of slavery imposed upon you by the English" (*Cal. Carew MSS.*, I, 523: Maxwell, 145.). On the situation of Catholic Englishmen exiled to Spain, see Albert J. Loomie, *The Spanish Elizabethans* (New York, 1963).

to each other on their own terms rather than submit to English rule again. Yet Sidney is typical. He is rationalizing English imperialism. Pouring all the finest military talent of the age into her Irish wars, England still remained unable to "pacify" the Irish. Whether Celtic or Anglo-Norman, Catholic Ireland remained untamed, willing to permit Spain to stage for an attack upon her neighbor, under the guidance and with the support of Rome. We cannot exaggerate the fear of rearguard invasion from Ireland, nor was this fear unreasonable, given Spanish intentions and capabilities.

It is against this background that we must read of Artegall's Herculean task, to do battle with other bandits, for the crown of truly *social* banditry. His mythic plantation of culture is analogous to the actual "plantations" Elizabeth sought to establish in Ireland.[35]

> Though vertue then were held in highest price,
>> In those old times, of which I doe intreat,
>> Yet then likewise the wicked seede of vice
>> Began to spring which shortly grew full great,
>> And with their boughes the gentle plants did beat.
>> But evermore some of the vertuous race
>> Rose up, inspired with heroicke heat,
>> That cropt the branches of the sient base,
> And with strong hand their fruitfull rancknes did deface.

35. For the full panorama of this expansion see A. L. Rowse, *The Expansion of Elizabethan England*, chaps. 3, 4, and 11. Rowse is an enthusiast for the Empire, but this aids rather than hinders his portrayal of the climate of these adventuring years. "Everything happened to them new then, as if for the first time" (158). The story as a whole is just short of unbelievable. Yet Rowse can speak of "that memory of a people which is history." Conquest, on any level, is likely to arouse enthusiasm. Chapman, who had celebrated in Odysseus "the Minds inward, constant, and unconquered Empire," wrote the *De Guiana* (1596), in a blank verse unique among his poems. There he envisions the queen rising from her throne "in the *Thespiads* bright Propheticke Fount." *Poems*, ed. P. B. Bartlett (repr. New York, 1962), 356.

Such first was *Bacchus*, that with furious might
  All th' East before untam'd did overronne,
  And wrong repressed, and establisht right,
  Which lawlesse men had formerly fordonne.
  There Justice first her princely rule begonne.
  Next *Hercules* his like ensample shewed,
  Who all the West with equall conquest wonne,
  And monstrous tyrants with his club subdewed;
The club of Justice dread, with kingly powre endewed.

(V, i, 1–2)

The gardening image of justice locks the myth into step with biblical symbolism, and implies that the hero will have to curb "heroic heat." Throughout Book V there is an interplay of this fearsome rage, one of whose aspects is desire, and the attenuating, softening, gentling restraints of Christian charity. Spenser, like Milton, is aware of the paradox implied in Christian heroism: that to fight for the good as one of the saints is to use a *virtu* which the good itself transcends.[36] Power, even reproductive power, and grace are at odds, and this is nowhere clearer than with the driving quests of the social bandit.

Like every myth of development the Herculean story begins on a "lower" level and rises to a "higher" level: "Such *first* was Bacchus. . . . *Next* Hercules his like ensample shewed"; we learn the first and second stages of a slowly unfolding process, because these contain the seeds of the later history of justice.[37] Although in the strict legal sense the social bandit does not yet deal in "equity law," his actions possess what we may call "natural equity," because he is conceived as a hero with an idea of fair dealings. This "salvage" virtue is apparently natural, that is, it seems integral to the possibility of humane awareness on any level.

36. John M. Steadman, *Milton and the Renaissance Hero* (Oxford, 1967).
37. Alastair Fowler, *Spenser and the Numbers of Time*, 216: "No one can read in Book V for long without being struck by the prominence given to temporal images and to the reckoning of time."

Men learn by making distinctions, according to the dialectical theory of knowledge, and they learn justice in an equally negative way, through the "sense of injustice." Edmond Cahn reminds us that we may not always know what is right, but we usually know what is not right, what is unfair, what is unjust.[38] By defining the response negatively, Spenser is seeking the primitive roots of justice, which can be sought in the actions of the unlegalistic social bandits. (Criminal law itself preserves this primitive response to the unjust by largely operating as a set of restrictive covenants.) The Herculean hero possesses this innate sense that certain actions are unbalanced with regard to a community, that they violate the presumption of Aristotle's equity (*epieikeia*): "In every association there is some rule of justice governing the relationships between the partners, and some friendly feeling is also presupposed."[39] For men to deal as friends with each other they have to restrain rebellious lusts. The *libido dominandi* must be held down, to cooperate with other forces of the soul, under the government of reason. The giants of myth, enemies of justice, exercise no self restraint—their immense size is one emblem of their extremity, and this manifestly "unnatural" bodily aspect betokens their opposition to natural equity.

In this broad prelegal sense equity can have little to do with

38. The idea of justice may be conceived either under the forms of social oneness (equality) or personal oneness (integrity). Edmond Cahn, in *The Sense of Injustice* (New York, 1949; repr. Bloomington, 1964), 15, argued that these two onenesses are reciprocal: "As human integers, men are indistinguishables. This natural fact imposes a limit on the classificatory discretion of positive law. The sense of injustice does not tolerate juridic classes by which the integral status of man is violated. Legal slavery, for example, was doomed to disappear everywhere, for no other reason than that a slave is a man." H. L. A. Hart discusses the legal "guarantees of impartiality or objectivity" in *The Concept of Law* (Oxford, 1961), 156.

39. *Ethics* VIII, 9; cf. Cicero, *De officiis*, I, x; also "Of Friendship" (*Laelius*). See both Fowler, *Spenser and Numbers*, and Thomas Roche, *The Kindly Flame*, on the figure of Concord, which governs the allegory of Book IV.

statutes and sanctions. Its prudence is not yet jurisprudence. Yet, as in the Hercules myth, even before the law is codified, there are times when justice will be adequately done through the scarcely rationalized balance of conflicting claims. Prelegal tyranny may be overthrown. Much of the interest of Book V derives from the fact that, with curious ambivalence, Spenser combines in Artegall certain features of the social bandit and certain features of a more refined, postlegal justiciar. Artegall exists in a fluctuating developmental world, and can judge according to either the natural or the artificial "disposition in virtue of which a just man is said to choose deliberately to do what is just."[40]

Among the various ways in which the social bandit manages to exist in this fluctuating world, one pertains especially to the present argument: as Cicero says in *De divinatione* (I.48), Romulus is the founder of augury and this knowing perspective is demanded by the job of the social bandit. In fact Romulus is said to be a better augur than his twin. The role of religion in ancient Roman politics is a major theme in Machiavelli's *Discourses*, which show that religion permits oracular control of public opinion. Augury and the auspices are an essential ingredient in the early evolution of justice, and Spenser is aware, from having read classical mythography, if not from the *Discourses*, that prophecy can be enlisted to support even the original fraternal crime, by which, having murdered Remus, Romulus is in a position to develop a genuine government. "That Romulus deserves to be excused for the death of his brother and that of his associate, and that what he had done was for the general good, and not for the gratification of his own ambition, is proved by the fact that he immediately instituted a Senate with which to consult, and according to the opinions of which he might form his resolu-

40. Cf. *Ethics*, V, 9, on willing of just action; and further, 1137a, 6–30, on difficulty of just action. See Rosemond Tuve, *Allegorical Imagery* (Princeton, 1966), passim and 61–62, on the relation of Aristotle to Spenser. Tuve reminds us that among ethical influences Aristotle has to stand with Seneca, Cicero, and Macrobius.

tions."[41] It was to extend and reinforce the "right" of these reso-
lutions that Romulus, and to an even greater extent his successor
Numa Pompilius, based the religion of the Roman gentiles upon
"the responses of the oracles, and the tenets of the augurs and
auspices; upon these alone depended all their ceremonies, rites,
and sacrifices."[42] Religion can play such a large political role in
this context because, as Machiavelli said of the Romans, "they
readily believed that the Deity which would predict their future
good or ill was also able to bestow it upon them."[43] Precisely because this is not Christian, in general, and is too close to Puritan
predestination, in particular, the effect of such religiosity is muted
and complicated by the purposes of Book V. Here, as we shall
see, a purely predictive prophet, the Egalitarian Giant, will be
heretical. As a prophetic type Artegall must be closer to the
relativistic present than the all-or-nothing future. Yet the involvement of social banditry in divination leads to many of the
obscurities which this myth of justice must be allowed to express.
Historically, no one "has expounded or ever will expound equity
as a single, consistent system, an articulate body of law."[44] A legal
spirit appears to be the dominant note of equity. Such a spirit animates the first and last moments of just vision, but between Eden
and the Apocalypse lie deserts of legalism.

Legal Codification: The Second Stage of the Myth

AFTER THE ORIGINAL STAGE has passed, the conditions of equity become too complex for any primitive heroism to
do them justice. A second stage in development is marked by the
creation of legal codes, an achievement equally weighed down

41. Niccolò Machiavelli, *Discourses*, in *The Prince and The Discourses*, ed. Max Lerner (New York, 1950, Modern Library ed.),
139.

42. Ibid., 150.

43. Ibid., 150.

44. F. W. Maitland, *Equity* (1909; repr. Cambridge, 1936), 19.

by trouble. Like his contemporaries, Spenser here thinks largely in terms of stability, which is the final goal of codification. But first the laws have to be created, and this is in fact possible only because, with the social bandit's victory over his rivals, there does indeed begin to be a momentary stability. Travel seems safe for a while, when the extortionists Pollente and Munera are destroyed; the mob is dispersed when the Egalitarian Giant is shoved over the cliff. Such victories serve justice in its primitive state, and for Spenser there is no question about the natural right of the victory. But as with all naturally evolving processes there is a doubt about its permanent effects, and at this point the poet, once again following tradition, moves considerably beyond the primitive, archaic stage of social banditry. Nor is Spenser deterred by the foreshortening, reversing, accelerating, and general collapsing of historical time which this advance requires of his poem.

Dumézil, among modern mythographers, has claimed that after the archaic period of the *dux*, our social bandit, must come a period of the *rex*, a magistrate or king whose main aim is not so much primitive victory over malefactors as the stabilization of victories won by others.[45] Instability is the mark of the primitive hero's character, and it is a legacy he passes on to the social world he rudely establishes. To remedy this instability the *rex* seeks to impose a continuous peace and order upon his people through the medium of law, which he will codify. The *rex* is the living symbol of the sources of law, those several fountains of authority on which men draw, to make a law-abiding community.

Plutarch again exemplifies for us the historical and mythic dimensions of this development of justice. Having shown the beginnings with the *Lives* of Theseus and Romulus, he then presents

45. Georges Dumézil, *Mitra-Varuna: Essai sur deux représentations indo-européennes de la souveraineté* (Paris, 1940), and on the work of Dumézil, Bertrand de Jouvenel, *Sovereignty*, trans. J. F. Huntington (Chicago, 1963), 21–23. De Jouvenel notes that the *dux-rex* contrast was drawn by Rousseau in the *Social Contract*, IV, iv, where Rousseau compares Numa and Romulus.

a sequence of four lawgivers, Lycurgus and Numa Pompilius, Solon and Poplicola. Plutarch sees the hidden danger in the triumphs of social banditry, for although he grants that Theseus and Romulus were "by nature meant for governors," he remarks that "neither lived up to the true character of a king, but fell off, and ran, the one into popularity (i.e., demagoguery), the other into tyranny, falling both into the same fault out of different passions."[46] By contrast Lycurgus and Numa enforce an orderly, lawful social system upon their people. "Their points of likeness are obvious: their moderation, their religion, their capacity of government and discipline, their both deriving their laws and constitutions from the gods."[47] This catalogue of virtues, which in the *Lives* of Solon and Poplicola is further refined to an exemplum of all-encompassing wisdom or *sophia*, marks a shift from heroic violence into a calmer, colder, more disciplined life of legal settlement. De Jouvenel has observed that the change is rendered mythologically in the change from an active, aggressive imagery of the sword to the passive, defensive imagery of the shield,[48] shield as sacred guarantee.

Yet in the story of Artegall both sword and shield play a part, and we discover that Spenser has collapsed Plutarch's two mythistorical stages into one somewhat rubbery time scheme. For, as I have already suggested, his hero is both social bandit and lawmaker, as in their ways are Britomart and ·Arthur. On the one hand Artegall possesses the settled wisdom of Solomon (de Jouvenel's chief instance of the *rex*, his Hebrew name meaning "peace" and his justice set off against the social banditry of David), while on the other he has to learn to restrain violence and his own Herculean ambivalence, especially in his encounter with Radigund. This collapse of the two stages into one shows per-

---

46. *Lives*, "Comparison of Romulus with Theseus." For clarity in the comparison I have here used the Dryden translation (Modern Library ed.), 47.

47. Ibid., "Comparison of Numa with Lycurgus," 93.

48. De Jouvenel, *Sovereignty*, 50–51.

haps the actual turmoil under which law comes into existence during a period of rapid political and economic change.[49] For law and justice never can be created without encountering the hazards of power. The ideal, then, is not laws codified into total uniformity and rigor, but a flexible system always responsive to the promptings of man's deeper instincts toward equity.

The first step on the road toward this codified authority is always a trial followed by a judgment, for which Spenser's favorite word is "doom." Thus, Artegall is taught "the depth of rightfull doome" by Astraea, an education seemingly in two halves, the one consisting of weighing right and wrong "in equall ballance," the other consisting of the imposition of equity "according to the line of conscience, / When so it needs with rigour to dispence" (V, i, 7). Presumably, when Britomart "did true Justice deale," after rescuing Artegall and the other male prisoners of Radigund, she too was making judicial decisions on particular cases. Arthur, on the other hand, though preeminently capable of rightful doom, does not impose his own judgments on the Lady Belge, having rescued her, but leaves her "settled in her raine." Arthur's judicial competence oddly seems a little less than Artegall's judging from his behavior at the trial of Duessa, where he is unduly influenced by the pathos and beauty of the stricken queen. But he too owns authority, unless we take an exceedingly skeptical view of his providential role in the poem. Prince Arthur's relative weaknesses as a judge may be the side effect of his having a higher purpose, which is to restore life, to rescue and save, to create, rather than to preserve and order what others have created.

But about Artegall's judicial function there can be no doubt.

49. Hobsbawm, *Primitive Rebels*, 23–24: "But it seems that Robin Hoodism is most likely to become a major phenomenon when their traditional equilibrium is upset: during and after periods of abnormal hardship, such as famines or wars, or at the moments when the jaws of the dynamic modern world seize the static communities in order to destroy and transform them." See Hobsbawm, 23, on the urban transformation of the Robin Hood type after the sixteenth century.

He is trained to make judgments and throughout the poem he offers to make them. We learn that both Sir Sangliere and his victim, the "carefull Squire," freely allowed Artegall to be their referee "and to his doome with listfull eares did both attend." At first "well pleased with that doome was Sangliere," until through the famous device or game of Solomon's Judgment he was shown to be the false lover, whereupon he "disdained much his doome." Such phrases express the idea that Artegall decides controversies by right and with authority, which is so great indeed that men "adore" him for it. Even when one of the parties is displeased, like Amidas and Philtra in their treasure-trove dispute with Bracidas and Lucy, the hero's judicial decision is sufficiently authoritative that it stands: "So was their discord by this doome appeased, / And each one had his right." The higher form of respect for such judgments seems to be adoration; right judgment is a kind of miracle. Britomart can be worshipped, and Mercilla apotheosized in her sovereign majesty, as Regina Britannia:

> All over her cloth of state was spred,
>> Not of rich tissew, nor of cloth of gold,
>> Nor of ought else, that may be richest red,
>> But like a cloud, as likest may be told,
>> That her brode spreading wings did wyde unfold;
>> Whose skirts were bordred with bright sunny beams,
>> Glistring like gold, amongst the plights enrold,
>> And here and there shooting forth silver streames,
> Mongst which crept litle Angels through the glittering gleames.
>
> Seemed those litle Angels did uphold
>> The cloth of state, and on their purpled wings
>> Did beare the pendants, through their nimblesse bold:
>> Besides a thousand more of such, as sings
>> Hymnes to high God, and carols heavenly things,
>> Encompassed the throne, on which she sate:
>> She Angel-like, the heyre of ancient kings
>> And mightie Conquerors, in royal state,
> Whylest kings and kesars at her feet did them prostrate.
>
> (V, ix, 28–9)

At the apex of her miraculous sovereign state Mercilla combines the roles of ruler and judge. She sits upon "a throne of gold full bright and sheene," which, ornamented with gems, is "all embost with Lyons and with Flourdelice," to signify her empire over both England and France. Among the regalia the throne, as Hooker says, symbolizes "sedentary, or judicial power," in contradistinction to the crown, which symbolizes military, and the oil, religious power.[50] So it would appear that Mercilla claims the right to sit in judgment over France as well as England. She does so as president of the Parliament, her country's highest court, where she lays down true precedent. Of all the iconographic details in this epiphany of Mercilla's "majesty imperiall," one stands out, her identification with the sun—with Jupiter therefore—and this reinforces our sense that she can judge, since she enjoys "dreaded soverayntie," "soverayne Majestie," "Majesty and awe" —in other words, the power of supreme authority.

Since the law comes into being when judges like Mercilla and

50. *The Laws of Ecclesiastical Polity*, ed. John Keble (Oxford, 1865), VIII, ii, 13 (vol. 3, p. 353). Spenser's image of Mercilla enthroned beneath a heavenly canopy may be an intentional combination of the ideas Hooker had set forth in his account of the origins of justice and law, in *Ecclesiastical Polity*, I, viii, 5: "Notwithstanding whatsoever such principle [of an essential justice] there is, it was at the first found out by discourse, and drawn from out of the very bowels of heaven and earth. For we are to note, that things in the world are to us discernible, not only so far forth as serveth for our vital preservation, but further also in a twofold higher respect. For first if all other uses were utterly taken away, yet the mind of man being by nature speculative and delighted with contemplation in itself, they were to be known even for mere knowledge and understanding's sake. Yea further besides this, the knowledge of every the least thing in the whole world hath in it a second peculiar benefit unto us, inasmuch as it serveth to minister rules, canons, and laws, for men to direct those actions which we properly term human. This did the very heathens themselves obscurely insinuate, by making *Themis*, which we call *Jus*, or Right, to be the daughter of heaven and earth." Here Hooker is alluding, apparently, to Hesiod's *Theogony*. The throne is emblematically the crossover point between this heaven and earth, as the double sources of the energies of justice.

Artegall decide on actual cases, law is the progeny of trial, as with Mercilla's hearing of the case of Duessa, though there may be no obvious machinery of trial if evidence can be easily given by the contending parties. The greater complication of the mechanism of Mercilla's judgment tells us that this is a case of universal concern, and it also suggests that the process of judgment is itself capable of gradual development, so that changes slowly occur in the means of arraigning the defendant, defining and presenting evidence, pleading the case, and so on. Over time there grows a heightened solemnity in atmosphere, a gradual elevation of the judge to a superior position of awe, with an accompanying formality and decoration of the "high court." This elaborate trial for treason contrasts with the casual setting in which Artegall first passes judgment, against Sangliere, quite without ceremony. Yet even here Artegall demonstrates an evolved procedure; his doom replaces trial by sacrament, by ordeal, and by "bloody fight."[51] The formality of trial seems furthermore to increase as the poem advances, reaching a climax at the court of Mercilla, where Artegall is introduced to the ultimate refinements of a full-scale institutionalized court trial. One main effect of this increased elaboration is psychological: Mercilla judges with felt authority. For authority is a creative force, more spiritual and rhetorical than physical, much reinforced by the brilliant appeal of a state occasion. Mythically Mercilla's authority is presented as a cosmic, solar order and sway, since she is Minervan, a fe-

---

51. Cf. Johan Huizinga, *Homo Ludens: A Study of the Play Element in Culture* (Boston, 1955), chap. 4, passim. Huizinga notes that "the original starting point of the ordeal must have been the contest, the test as to who will win. The winning *as such* is, for the archaic mind, the proof of truth and rightness." Ordeal, a term parallel to *Gottesurteil* (God's judgment) means "nothing more nor less than divine judgment. . . . it might appear as if primitive man believed that the gods showed by the outcome of a trial or casting, which of the parties is right or—what amounts to the same thing—in which direction they have disposed fate. Of course the idea of a *miracle* proving which side is right is only a secondary Christian interpretation."

male Jupiter, Astraea on earth. In general, a gradually ascending authority accorded to the lawgiver would be felt as historically true for the Elizabethan period, inasmuch as Common Law courts, the Court of Chancery—the "court of conscience"—and Parliament as the highest court, all reach new dignity during this epoch.

An ancient power underlies the formality of trial: Themis, who is represented at Mercilla's court in the person of her three daughters, Justice, Good Law, and Peace. Themis may be called an undefined consciousness and habit of orderly behavior, or, as Jane Harrison put it, "the social conscience on which depends social structure."[52] In his *Ancient Law*, Maine observed that "*Themistes*, Themises, the plural of Themis, are the awards themselves, divinely dictated to the judge. . . . they are not laws, but judgments, or, to take the exact Teutonic equivalent, 'dooms.' "[53] The distinction is useful, for the dooms of Artegall, in the plural, *lead to* the establishment of law; they are the movements of law-in-action, rather than law itself. Indeed, Book V seems to be largely concerned with this kind of active, evolutionary lawmaking process.

Yet the Legend of Justice retains many memories of a primitive justice. Maine says, significantly, that "*Nomos*, or law, so great and famous a term in the political vocabulary of the later Greek society, does not occur in Homer." Primary among the forces of social coherence in the earliest political phase is the common celebration of religious rites, and also the conception of law as a social rhythm: "It is certain that, in the infancy of mankind, no sort of legislature, not even a distinct author of law, is

52. Jane Harrison, *Themis: a Study of the Social Origins of Greek Religion* (London, 1912; repr. Cleveland and New York, 1962), chap. 11, where Harrison further observes that "Themis is in a sense prophecy incarnate, but it is only in the old sense of *prophecy*, utterance, ordinance, not in the later sense of a forecast of the future" (482).

53. *Ancient Law: Its connection with the early history of society and its relation to modern ideas*, intro. and notes by Frederick Pollock (1861; repr. Boston, 1963), 13.

contemplated or even conceived of. Law has scarcely reached the footing of custom; it is rather a habit. It is, to use a French phrase, 'in the air.' "[54] Such early law resembles traditional ritual and is constituted by the largely unwritten, orally transmitted customs of men, imitated or carried in oral poetry and folklore. Thus, Lycurgus thought that men should not write down their laws,

54. Ibid., 15. Speaking of "Poetic Diction and Legal Fiction," Owen Barfield observes that lawful forms of action "grew out of the whole history of English social life." He then notes a distinction which parallels that of the advance from a level of social banditry to evolved judicial process, i.e., "a wide difference between those forms of action which had their roots in the feudal system and those which sprang from later and different sources. I think it is true to say that they were different because they were really based on two different ways of looking at human beings in society. You may look at a human being in what I will call the genealogical way, in which case you will conceive of his legal rights and position as being determined by what he *is* rather than by what he may choose to *do*. They will then seem to be determined by the kind of father he had, by the piece of land to which he and his ancestors were attached or which was attached to them, and by its relations to adjoining land attached to other people and their ancestors and descendants. Or alternatively you may look at him in what I will call the personal way, in which case his position will seem to be determined more by the things he himself has chosen to *do* of his own free will. Maine in his *Ancient Law* calls the first way 'Status' and the second way 'Contract,' and he depicts society as evolving from the first towards the second. Broadly speaking, forms of action having to do with the ownership of land had grown up out of the first way, forms of action having to do with the ownership of personal property out of the second way, of looking at human beings." The essay is reprinted in Max Black, *The Importance of Language* (Englewood Cliffs, 1962). Status and contract specify the thematic interest of the Amidas-Bracidas episode in Book V, but the two modes have the wider function of defining the range of vision in poets like Spenser and Shakespeare. The latter is fascinated by the role of contract in human society; his late romances, to be sure, emphasize myths of status. But Spenser keeps these myths central in his poetry. The geophantic myth of Faerieland encloses the stories of human action and interaction, while every hero has a contractual relation to Gloriana and to his own emerging personality.

so as to preserve their good habits in ritual form, through memory and customary imitation. As such, of course, law shares in the cyclical and templar nature of rituals of all kinds, and in the service of this law Mercilla, Arthur, Artegall, or any other judge must obey the timeless dictates of an inherited Themis.

Already, it would appear, Artegall carries a threefold burden as heroic justiciar, and in this legend the poet unfolds the three faces of prophecy. *Retrospectively*, in his Herculean social-bandit role, as destroyer of giants, Artegall brings justice as an unformulated condition. Making his own judgments and creating the habits of themis, he is *at present* shown upholding the customs of the land. Finally, as agency of nomos he goes beyond the enforcement of what is already established and customary, to create new laws which will anticipate *future* contingencies. Elizabethan political science, profoundly influenced and enlivened by the practical successes of Henry VIII in his legal enactment of independence from Rome, and perhaps influenced by continental theorists such as Machiavelli, Botero, and Bodin, could readily accept the sovereign command of the king as the proper source for this third kind of law. To call Gloriana and Mercilla "sovereign" is to give them a lawmaking prerogative which is envisioned, at the court of Mercilla, as the power of the Queen in Parliament.[55] Presumably the wrong use of this power, its dem-

55. Bodin, *Six Books of the Commonwealth*, trans. and ed. M. J. Tooley (Oxford, n.d.), I, chap. 8, p. 32: "From all this it is clear that the principal mark of sovereign majesty and absolute power is the right to impose laws generally on all subjects regardless of their consent." C. J. Friedrich, *The Philosophy of Law in Historical Perspective* (Chicago, 1963), 60–61, shows that Bodin distinguished between law (*jus*) and laws (*leges*). "The law (*jus*) is good and equitable without command, but the laws (*leges*) result from the exercise of the sovereignty of him who commands. For the laws are nothing but the commands of the highest power. Therefore the decisive point is this: law as positive statutory laws must be clearly distinguished from any kind of law derived from morals and equity. This tearing apart of the two sides of law, which until then had always been considered a unity, parallels in its historical import the analogous separation of power poli-

onic parody, produces Radigund's rebellion and tyranny, while the right use marks Britomart's reestablishment of order when that rebellion has been put down. Spenser does not, however, allow unlimited lawmaking power to the sovereign, as would Bodin or, later, Hobbes. His sovereign's commands have sway because they accord with the good will of her Parliament and they fit other patterns of good rule. A general coherence of nature and man and god enables these commands, when blessed by grace as are those of Gloriana, to possess genuine authority.

Artegall's story is in one sense a myth of growing confidence in these sanctions, for that freedom is the psychological requirement of his duty to act as a fair judge. "To prescribe the order of doing in all things, is a peculiar prerogative which Wisdom hath, as queen or sovereign commandress over other virtues"—such is Hooker's formula.[56] Wisdom demands detachment and a sense of divine appointment, for, as another apologist for the Elizabethan establishment put it, "the magistrate is the ordinance of God, appointed by Him with the sword of punishment, to looke straitly to all evill doers. And therefore that that is done by the Magistrate, is done by the ordinance of God, whom the Scriptures oftentimes doth call God, because he hathe the execution of God's office."[57] Here one sees the open possibility of bad faith, but the hope remains that the magistrate will transcend the *lex talionis*, the law of Talus. In part such grace has an intellectual source, for as Artegall argues in his debate with the Giant, "in the mind the doome of right must bee." Bodin held that "natural

---

tics and morals by Machiavelli." On "the morality that makes law possible" see Lon L. Fuller, *The Morality of Law* (New Haven, 1964); Hart, *The Concept of Law*, chaps. 8 and 9; Cahn, *The Sense of Injustice*.

56. *Ecclesiastical Polity*, VIII, 1, in *Works*, 3:33. See Eugene F. Rice, *The Renaissance Idea of Wisdom*, especially 143–47, on the Calvinist view.

57. John Hooper, *Annotations in the Thirteenth Chapter to the Romans*, quoted in J. W. Allen, *Political Thought in the Sixteenth Century* (London, 1928), 126.

liberty" meant "the right under God to be subject to no man living and amenable only to those commands which are self-imposed, that is to say the commands of right reason conformable to the will of God." It follows that "before a man can govern others he must learn to govern himself."[58] Artegall's mental philosophy of right "doome," like Bodin's arguments, owes something to the Stoic and Ciceronian tradition. When he submits to Radigund, Artegall is tested in Stoic courage. But he is also being tested in another Stoic framework, in that Radigund has laws which as pure command must be obeyed, which yet defy the larger dictates of wisdom and reason and in that sense are inequitable.

Cicero, quoting Chrysippus' *Digest*, notes that the Stoic philosopher had identified Jupiter with the law and could do so because for this philosophy "law is highest reason, embedded in nature, which commands what should be done, and forbids the contrary."[59] Friedrich has explained the relation of this natural law and man's communal behavior by saying that "man, in contrast to other living beings, participates consciously in this *ratio* because he himself possesses reason and therefore can understand the laws of nature."[60] Man does not make these laws, since they are eternal and above him; Cicero expressly states that man cannot derive his knowledge of the law from the decisions of the praetors or from the Twelve Tables, but only from philosophy. Now, although for Stoicism the Senecan apotheosis of Hercules caps the most significant achievement of his heroic life, his victory

58. Bodin, *Six Books*, I, 10. See Robert Hoopes, *Right Reason in the English Renaissance* (Cambridge, Mass., 1962). The control of the Body Politic requires a theory of temperance or krasis, on which see Harry Berger, Jr., *The Allegorical Temper*, and William Nelson, *The Poetry of Edmund Spenser*, 123–27 (*ethice* versus *politice*). On medieval theory of reason as organizing principle, see Otto Gierke, *Political Theories of the Middle Age*, trans. Maitland (Cambridge, 1900; repr. Boston, 1959), 22–30.

59. Friedrich, *Philosophy of Law*, 29.

60. Ibid., 30.

over death, he has a more limited meaning within Stoic tradition, which applies directly to Book V and its use of the Herculean archetype.[61] According to Seneca, Hercules conquered the earth, not for himself (*non concupiscendo*), but in order to judge those whom he conquered; he is enemy of the bad, defender of the good, and peacemaker of both land and sea (*De beneficiis* 1.13.3). And for Cicero, in the familiar *De officiis* (3.5.25). Hercules represents *magnitudo*, *comitas*, *liberalitas*, and *iustitia*. Finally, this tradition is focused on the single governing belief that in his apotheosis Hercules becomes *numen* (*es numen et te mundus aeternum tenet*); in other words, he becomes one with the will of the gods, acquiring the majesty of divine assent, as signified in the nod of the head. One cannot help suspecting a pun here between *numen* and (Greek) *nous*, but in any case the divinity of

61. For the following citations I am indebted to Wade Stephens, "The Function of Religious and Philosophical Ideas in Ovid's *Metamorphoses*," unpublished doctoral dissertation, Princeton University, 1957, 32 ff. Joseph Fontenrose, *Python: A Study of Delphic Myth* (Berkeley and Los Angeles, 1959), chap. 12, gives a full account of myths in which Hercules triumphed over death—as in Euripides' *Alkestis*. In connection with this play Fontenrose observes: "The Artemis who, offended by Admetus' neglect of her, filled his bridal chamber with coiled snakes is Pheraia, the great goddess of Pherai, identified with Hekate. She is that goddess of death, called Persephone in the sources, who relents and releases Alkestis in one form of the myth." Spenser's treatment of Britomart, Radigund, and Belphoebe indicates his awareness of this deadly Artemis. There is furthermore a curious ambivalence in the myth of the three Horai, present at Duessa's trial (V, ix). The Horai and the three Charities, or Graces, are somehow connected with the figure of the triple Hekate. *Themis*, 408: "the triple maidens were, to begin with, of earth. One of them like the Semnae, like the Erinyes, holds a coiled snake. The Horae or Seasons of the Moon, her *Moirae*, are preceded by the earlier Horae, the Season's of Earth's fertility, at first two, spring for blossoming, autumn for fruit, then under the influence of a moon-calendar three. These earliest Horae dance as was meet round the old fertility-pillar." Cf. *F.Q.* VI, x.

Hercules in his last epiphany is such that he becomes pure ethereal spirit, transfigured beyond death. Spenser, drawing on Ovid, Cicero, or Seneca, may imagine his Herculean hero Artegall seeking an appropriately philosophical antagonist and finding him in the Egalitarian Giant. Against the Giant, Artegall argues for a divine quality of man's mind, its essential *ratio*, and in this he agrees with the Ciceronian view that "the whole world is a community of gods and men," and that "we are born for justice," that "law is not based on opinion but upon the very nature of man."[62] Each rational man in this Stoic view is equal to all other rational men, and as Friedrich observes, this universalizing view of justice marks a profound shift from the narrower political basis in Plato and Aristotle. Community becomes worldwide and coterminous with reason itself.

The Stoic view of justice leads to a cult of cosmic reason, but here another Spenserian "source" of law is probably at odds with the tendency to extend justice into world community. Spenser, like many of his contemporaries, holds that laws derive in part from love. Sir John Cheke, in a pamphlet authorizing harsh magisterial measures, can still pretend that "Love is not only the knot of Commonwealth, whereby divers parts be perfectly joined together in one politique body, but also the strength and might of the same, gathering together in one small room with order, which, scattered, would else breed confusion and debate."[63] Mercilla, commanding a capital execution, can still be said to maintain "the sacred pledge of peace and clemencie, / With which high God had blest her happie land." Tyrants like Radigund are false *lovers*. Isis, a love goddess, confers *eudaimonia* or happiness on Britomart and Artegall. Law arises, by nature it would seem, out of the desired structure of such loves—the family—and thus the Lady Belge, through all her trials, remains

<hr>

62. Friedrich, *Philosophy of Law*, 30.

63. *Dialogue between Cardinal Pole and Thomas Lupset* (1536), quoted in Allen, *Political Thought*, 141.

devoted to her children, while her two "springals" try to save her. The Order of Maidenhead is a transcendental family structure.[64] The true love of man and woman is parodied by the lust of the crocodile.[65] Love is generalized in the forms of friendship, which Aristotle's *Ethics* and Cicero's *De officiis* had claimed to be the precondition, because it was so spontaneous, of all true justice.

64. On the family as a social order, and basis for political science during this period: R. W. K. Hinton, "Husbands, Fathers and Conquerors," *Political Studies* 15 (1967): 291–300; P. Laslett, *Patriarcha and Other Political Works of Sir Robert Filmer* (Oxford, 1949); for medieval political metaphors of the familial, see Kenneth Burke, *Attitudes toward History* (Boston, 1961), 124–34; also Ernst Troeltsch, *The Social Teaching of the Christian Churches* (London, 1931; repr. New York, 1960), 2:544, 545, 655. In the romance tradition familial order has mythic force: see W. T. H. Jackson, *The Literature of the Middle Ages* (New York and London, 1960), 116–35, especially 134–35 on *Parsival* and Wolfram of Eschenbach's deliberate "insistence on the family." The most important humanist treatise taking the family as the central structural unit of noble life is L. B. Alberti, *I Primi tre libri della famiglia*, ed. F. C. Pellegrini (Florence, 1946); see G. Saitta, *L'Umanesimo* (Florence, 1961), 403–34. Althusius (1603) made family a central concept in his theory of politics; see his *Politics*, ed. and trans. F. S. Carney (Boston, 1964), chaps. 2 and 3.

65. Such ambivalent myth even appears with Geryon. Comes, as noted in *Variorum*, 5:255: "Others have believed by the fable of Geryon, who had many legs, hands, and eyes, governed by one will, was symbolized concord among citizens, which makes them invincible when all those who are just men act in concert, as Plutarch says in his *Politics*." Similarly, what does one make of the fact that Arthur is called "the Cornish Bore" in one of the Merlin prophecies (Thomas Heywood, *The Life of Merlin Ambrosius* . . . [London, 1641], 37), since we might associate Sir Sangliere also with the boar that killed Adonis? Myths of concord seem peculiarly vulnerable. Thus, "those who upheld the chivalric ideal were aware of its falsity, and it is for this reason that—almost from the very beginning—there was a tendency for the ideal to deny itself from time to time in irony and satire, parody and caricature. *Don Quixote* was merely the last, supreme expression of that irony: the line runs through the whole of the Middle Ages." Huizinga, "Historical Ideals of Life," in *Men and Ideas*, ed. and trans. J. S. Holmes and Hans van Marle (New York, 1959), 89.

Finally, this climate of *philia* is the basis of a governing image of the sources of law, the "mystical body of this most noble realm."[66] The familiar body image of the state permits law to be referred to natural processes of growth and decay, of the temple-garden and the waste wilderness.

Law Stabilized: Enforcement, Custom, and Record—
The Third Stage

OUR OWN EXPERIENCE TEACHES us that all the statutes in the world are useless unless enforced, accepted as customary, and kept on record. This third (tripartite) stage in the development of justice is yet more temporally rich, more historically "loaded" than the first two. We are talking about the law as it affects every man in the later eras of civilization. The realities of law are in part now psychologically felt: the good lawmaker hopes to create conditions of social coherence, not tyrannical unity.

Law functions only when it can partly detach itself from physical enforcement, when, through its own clear authority, it sways men to act in accordance with principle. Law then begins to be established as custom, and custom may in turn bind human behavior quite as strictly as any statute. In idealized, purely templar form Canto X of Book II displays the manner in which such inherited and customary behavior is to be contained by a library. Spenser has preceded this Canto of the two chronicles by his figure of "infinite remembraunce," the aged Eumnestes, who is helped by a little boy, Anamnestes, his library page. Eumnestes embodies the spirit of custom, in the sense that, ancient as he is, "yet lively vigour rested in his mind."

---

66. Robert Crowley, *The Way to Health*, quoted in Allen, *Political Thought*, 141. As Allen remarks, with his state-body analogy in hand, Crowley "becomes prophetic." The standard work: Ernst Kantorowicz, *The King's Two Bodies* (Princeton, 1957).

> This man of infinite remembraunce was,
>> And things foregone through many ages held,
>> Which he recorded still, as they did pas,
>> Ne suffred them to perish through long eld,
>> As all things else, the which this world doth weld,
>> But laid them up in his immortall scrine,
>> Where they for ever incorrupted dweld:
>>> (ix, 56)

Eumnestes holds the past by "endlesse exercise," and in Book V there is not enough time for such hermetic, scholarly activities. But the two histories of Book II, Canto X, provide a theory of cultural growth which Book V can then assume. Thus Prince Arthur, having read his Chronicle of Briton Kings,

> At last quite ravisht with delight, to heare,
>> The royall Offspring of his native land,
>> Cryde out, Deare country, O how dearely deare
>> Ought thy remembraunce, and perpetuall band
>> Be to thy foster Childe, that from thy hand
>> Did commun breath and nouriture receave?
>> How brutish is it not to understand,
>> How much to her we owe, that all us gave,
>> That gave unto us all, what ever good we have.
>>> (x, 69)

Guyon's nature and nurture have their history as well, and the doubling of the two chronicles provides a stereoscopic vision of the two time-systems out of which Faerieland makes its legendary and prophetic momentousness.

Spenser would appear to believe that habitual or customary responses provide the basis of the most stable legal system, since they are built into the behavior of each citizen, who is in this sense "inner-directed," rendering police force unnecessary. There are nevertheless obstacles to this kind of stabilization and there are limits to the speed with which it may take root.[67] Bodin, while

---

67. Berger, *Allegorical Temper*, 101–2; summarizing the didactic

maintaining that the prince is the author of statute law, holds that the prince's subjects are the authors of custom, and this latter, broad-based authorship requires a gradually more educated citizenry. Perhaps England has been remarkable in the legalistic awareness of her ordinary citizens; if so, this early helped the settlement of the law.

Book V begins with an account of Artegall's legal education; it treats both Britomart and Mercilla as instructors in law, and throughout it tells the story of Artegall's continuing "experience" —Ralegh's *Maxims of State* speak of an "experiment of his [the prince's] Wisdom and Equity."[68] In one remarkable stanza Spenser presents the dialectical opposite of this benevolent teaching, in the form of Geryoneo's monster, which teaches to destroy, and thus resembles the Theban sphinx:

---

element of the British chronicle, Berger notes four concerns: "(1) the need of a proper heir, the advantage of natural succession especially where native influence has been favorable; (2) supplementation of the natural line by Law; (3) assent of the people to the ruler; (4) vigilance of the Ruler against both domestic and foreign threats." Berger then proceeds to show the ambivalence of the chronicle: "Canto X presents corruption in the soul of a government, through weakness in will or reason. The political anatomy discloses that the weakness of flesh—the contingencies of krasis—may affect kings. Even good and reasonable kings are hampered by a defect in nature whereby they leave no heirs, the wrong heirs, or too many heirs. Neither history as a process nor any man in history possesses the power to redeem, once and for all, the fleshly slime; only Christ can do this. Arthur as a minister of grace, an imitation of Christ, can redeem Britain from subjugation to the Earthly City, but Arthur is mortal and Britain will fall again."

68. Ralegh, *Works* (London, 1751), 1:19. Cf. Francesco Guicciardini, *Maxims and Reflections* (*Ricordi*), trans. Mario Domandi (New York, 1965), 43 (series C, 9): "Let no one trust so much in native intelligence that he believes it to be sufficient without the help of experience. No matter what his natural endowments, any man who has been in a position of responsibility will admit that experience attains many things which natural gifts alone could never attain."

> Much like in foulnesse and deformity
> > Unto that Monster, whom the Theban Knight,
> > The father of that fatall progeny,
> > Made kill her selfe for very hearts despight,
> > That he had red her Riddle, which no wight
> > Could ever loose, but suffred deadly doole,
> > So also did this Monster use like slight
> > To many a one, which came unto her schoole,
> > Whom she did put to death, deceived like a foole.
>
> (ix, 25)

This allusion to Oedipus, besides mentioning the theme of fraud and deceit, recalls an archetypal king whose greatness was the consequence of a wisdom "tried" in answering the riddle of the Sphinx. The Sphinx itself belongs to that familiar horrid tribe of multiform, rebellious, ultimately suicidal tyrants. By answering "her," Oedipus fashioned the base of his own authority, and became the original master of the educated guess. The allusion fixes a bond between governance and wisdom, intelligence and *imperium*, insight and justice. Their troth demands, furthermore, a fatal acceptance of the ultimate Oedipal tragedy.

Some risks are incidental to history itself, and when the hero tries to stabilize the law, he accepts the "terror of history" to its fullest extent. The quest is subject to many tensions and historical reversals. There is tension, for example, insofar as laws and custom change at different rates. "Custom establishes itself gradually over a long period of years, and by common consent, or at any rate the consent of the greater part. Law is made on the instant and draws its force from him who has the right to bind all the rest. Custom is established imperceptibly and without any exercise of compulsion. Law is promulgated and imposed by authority, and often against the wishes of the subject. For this reason Dio Chrysostom compared custom to the king and law to the tyrant."[69] Book V searches for this kingship amidst the threat of

69. Bodin, *Six Books*, 44.

this tyranny. Artegall, who fights against evil fortune in the person of Radigund, and who believes all change is dangerous, nonetheless experiences the variable fortunes of actual political life. He has to argue for a slow improvement of law, in place of radical utopian improvements. He would agree with Bodin's argument that "even when law is patently unjust, it is better to let it lapse gradually than to make any sudden change." We find also that when new laws or new judicial arrangements are required, these too should partake of customary growth, not revolutionary change. For Spenser, as Bodin said, it often seems that "the nature of men is extraordinarily corruptible, and they continually descend from good to bad, and from bad to worse. Their vices slowly establish a hold on them, like the ill humours which gradually invade the body till they entirely possess it. It is therefore necessary at times to make new laws to deal with the situation, but it should always be done very gradually. . . . The ordering of the commonwealth should be modelled on the ordering of the universe. God, the first cause, accomplishes all things gradually and almost insensibly."[70]

Such a conception of cosmic order, which I believe Spenser shares, must assert that the law aspires to a timeless cyclical uniformity, in partial approach to the gradual, insensible closure of a sacred *templum*. For Spenser's era, as for our own, this aspiration collides with the impatient desire to revolt against changeless "establishments." The lawmaker is the highest kind of poet, since his legal fictions are binding upon men in actual life. Stabilization of law largely implies the creation of the right sort of legalistic atmosphere, creation of laws in adequate response to the accidents and movements of history. Perhaps beginning with Sir John Fortescue's *De laudibus legum Angliae* in the fifteenth century, English jurists and humanist scholars might argue that, as compared with France, "the better statute laws of England were the result of a better method of creating law. [Fortescue] emphasized that what brought this about was the work of a parlia-

70. Ibid., 125.

ment representing the people in conjunction with the practice of the Inns of Court conscious of the legal traditions of the land. For such a parliament both interpreted and amended the law."[71]

For Fortescue, historical perspective in interpreting and amending the law follows naturally from a contemplation of native means of generating laws. England's legal tradition is already evolutionary and creative, broadening from precedent to precedent, a fact which bears upon the generative myths Spenser employs throughout Book V. At the same time there is no conflict between generation of new laws and recourse to the "antique image" which holds up archetypal patterns to the hero, and which, as we shall see, leads to a good sort of revolutionary change. A modern historian has said that by 1600 "there was hardly any constitutional movement without its accompanying historical myth. . . . In England, the uniformity or commonness of the law helped to sanctify the myth of the immemorial antiquity of the law."[72]

Sir Edward Coke and other jurists were beginning to assert once again that, to protect the rights of the citizen and subject, legal precedent should always be transcribed in writing. "Legal history for Coke meant contemporary history in the fullest sense," as a modern scholar observes.[73] Earlier in the century Thomas

71. Friedrich, *Philosophy of Law*, 51.

72. F. Smith Fussner, *The Historical Revolution*, 28.

73. Ibid., 30. C. D. Bowen, *The Lion and the Throne: The Life and Times of Sir Edward Coke* (Boston, 1956), 505, gives an account of the *Reports*, which "covering forty years of court cases, had been issued serially from 1600 to 1616. While yet a student at the Temple, Coke had begun to write them, by no means limiting himself to suits which he himself witnessed. . . . No law reports had hitherto been half so comprehensive; Coke must have lived and walked and sat and talked with notebook in hand. At once the books became—as Blackstone indicated in 1785—an internecine authority in the courts of justice." Coke, as Bowen recalls, would not have cases committed "to slippery memory, which seldom yieldeth a certain reckoning. In troth, reading, hearing, conference, meditation, and recordation are necessary." The existence of such reports does not and did not automat-

Starkey had lamented the disorder of law in these terms: "Thys is no dowte but that our law and ordur thereof ys overconfuse. Hyt is infynyte, and without ordur or end. Ther yes no stabyl grounde therin, no sure stay; . . . There is no stabyl grounde in our commyn law to leyne unto. The jugementys of yerys [i.e., the Year Books] be infynyte and ful of much controversy; and besyde that, of smal authorytye. The jugys are not bounden, as I ynderstone, to follow them as a rule, but aftur theyr owne lyberty they have authorytye to juge."[74] This passage, which later proposes a codification in Justianian manner, objects to a misused "recordation." But, as Maitland remarks, "in 1535, the year in which More was done to death, the Year Books come to an end: in other words, the great stream of law reports that has been flowing for near two centuries and a half, ever since the days of Edward I, becomes discontinuous and then runs dry. The exact significance of this ominous event has never yet been duly explored; but ominous it surely is. Some words that once fell from Edmund Burke occur to us: 'To put an end to reports is to put an end to the law of England.' "[75]

Maitland's sense of threat may be exaggerated, yet for the purpose of understanding Spenserian myth, it points in the right direction. One of the built-in themes of Book V is a continuous subterranean reference to its dialectical model, Book II, which shows us directly the function of "recordation." It is no accident

---

ically provide the "Oracle of the Law" with a full theory of the historical course of English Law. Maitland, discussing Blackstone's success in first analyzing the feudal system, says this of the author of the *Reports:* "Coke had no such theory (as that of the feudal system) and because he had none was utterly unable to give any connected account of the law that he knew so well." In "Why the History of English Law was not written," the Cambridge inaugural lecture of 1888, repr. in *Frederick William Maitland: Historian,* ed. R. L. Schuyler (Berkeley and Los Angeles, 1960), 135.

74. Quoted in Maitland, *Historical Essays,* ed. H. M. Cam (Cambridge, 1957), 149.

75. Ibid., 143.

that the Knight of Temperance learns his place in sacred time (the medium of temperance) by studying an idealized History of Faery, while his coadjutor, Prince Arthur, reads a profane chronicle of the just and unjust reigns of English kings. Book V explicitly shows that correct reporting of just and unjust acts and decisions on them is almost as needful as having an inner sense of them. Like Thucydides in describing the revolution in Corcyra, Spenser complains of the failed language of jurisprudence, "for that which all men then did vertue call, / Is now cald vice; and that which vice was hight, / Is now hight vertue, and so us'd of all"[76] (V, Proem, 4). More exactly, however, he refers to the precedent established by his hero:

> Whereof no braver president this day
> Remaines on earth, preserv'd from yron rust
> Of rude oblivion, and long times decay,
> Then this of Artegall, which here we have to say.
>
> (iv, 2)

Later Spenser remarks that men will "report" ill of Artegall, for the precedent of his defeat by Radigund. Now this "report" is not legal record, in Coke's sense, but it bears the same relation to that record which justice bears to law, since the good fame and remembered praise of Artegall is a customary force for the establishment of law. When men hear his praise for what he has established rightly, they have a pattern to emulate, and his story becomes something like philosophy teaching by example.

---

76. As *Variorum*, 5:157 suggests, these lines resemble Shakespeare's *Troilus* 1.3.93–118. But a more immediate parallel is Cicero, *De officiis*, I, x: " 'The height of justice is the height of roguery' is now become a daily and common proverb among us." *The Offices*, trans. John Warrington (London, 1909; repr. 1960), 15. It seems to me likely that Spenser had read Thucydides, who by roughly the middle of the century was available in English, French, German, Italian, and Spanish. See R. R. Bolgar, *The Classical Heritage and Its Beneficiaries: From the Carolingian Age to the End of the Renaissance* (1954; repr. New York, 1964), 524–25.

Exemplary history requires this kind of good report, which more commonly Elizabethans called "fame." We finally learn how important fame is when Artegall encounters his last enemies, the hags Envy and Detraction, whose purpose is to destroy "good report." In the final analysis law and justice are shown to depend upon a right attitude toward truth, which in turn requires respect for fair speech. Justice assumes a prior stability of the linguistic community, on which fame may rest, and then law.

From all the new directions taken by historiography during this period, one seems to predominate in its influence over Book V. This is the marked concern with legal and political norms which historians begin to demonstrate. We know of Machiavelli's importance for scientific theories of statecraft: that his name is almost synonymous with analyses of the state, of the concept of sovereign power, of political initiative and expediency—in short, with power politics. But for Machiavelli the law is a primary concern, and from this concern flows most of his new skepticism and his new science. Gilmore has shown that in the *Discourses on Livy* "recourse is always had to those judgments or to those remedies which have been decreed or provided by the ancients, since the civil law is nothing else than the opinion of ancient jurisconsults, which opinions, when they are arranged in order teach our present jurisconsults to judge."[77] Machiavelli does not blame Christianity for these failures, nor does he believe in the decay of Christian cities through a "proud indolence." Rather, men have failed to rule well because they lack a true theory of history, a lack all the more remarkable in the light of the earlier Italian humanist praise of history. But Machiavelli imagined a flaw in that earlier enthusiasm: "Those who had contemplated the course of history had indeed found examples of virtue and vice, wisdom and foolishness but these had never been reduced to a system; there existed no systematic body of knowledge which could be compared to that accumulated by the commentators on the civil law and this was the focal point of Machia-

77. Myron Gilmore, *Facets of the Renaissance*, 90.

velli's criticism of humanist tradition—a tradition from which he had himself started and upon which he had built but which he found wanting as he reflected on the failures of Italian political institutions to meet the shock of the northern invasions."

This same systematic need to connect history and law appears later in the important *Method for the Easy Comprehension of History* (1566) of Bodin. "His express aim in writing the *Methodus* was the study of universal law, for in the narrative of human affairs, he said, the best part of universal law lay hidden."[78] Bodin's focal point is more or less what we would call constitutional history, although his *Methodus* concerns itself with problems of astrological and climatic influence, theories of chronology, and the like. Like Machiavelli he wants to locate the origins and current centers of political power. He wants history to define the best type of state, a desire which becomes overt in the later *Six Books of the Commonwealth*, translated into English during the earliest years of the seventeenth century. Bodin's views of polity and history coincide with the expansionist ideology of the new sovereign states of Europe, but he is curiously fond of mythological problems, which might have made him congenial to Spenser.[79]

If on this primary level of historical language justice presupposes the continuing envelopment of man by his own recorded laws, judgments, and precedents, the shape this envelopment takes

---

78. *Method*, ed. Beatrice Reynolds, intro., xi.

79. E.g., the *Démonomanie des sorciers* (1580). One is impressed with the importance Bodin accords to the myth of the Four Ages, given his remarkable independence from legend. But Machiavelli draws mythological parallels in his *Discourses* and *The Prince*, while Giovanni Botero, in *The Reason of State* (*Della Ragion di stato*, 1589), trans. and ed. P. J. and D. P. Waley (London, 1956), bk. 1, sec. 5, cites Herculean saga to define the imperialist's risk; "for this reason Hercules, when he wishes to persuade the Romans not to extend their empire beyond Europe, reminds them that 'it had been easier for them to acquire their provinces one by one than to maintain their entire possessions' (Livy, XXXVII, 35)." Cf. Machiavelli, *Discourses*, II, xii, for a parallel myth.

is that of a cultivation of history as famous, heroic exploit. For this period Hakluyt's *Voyages* and Holinshed's *Chronicles* perhaps provide the best models. During the late sixteenth century, when Parliament wins its initiative, lawmaking is a heroic act, and Artegall the lawmaking hero engages in a patently historical allegory. The one thing critics have held against his portrait is the one thing that is most heroic and natural about it, its historic coloration. The same may also be said of Talus, the embodied *lex talionis*, whose personification then as now ought to have engaged the reader's awareness of historical ironies. His function as policeman has to many readers seemed merely repulsive, sadistic, genocidal. But history conceived as myth will not permit quite the same judgments we make of actual history, since in its prophetic aspect this history is, by nature, idealized in certain directions. Thus, Spenser looks at first glance simply reactionary. But at the heart of his epic there is a belief in individual freedom, and there are many sides to this belief which enter Book V through the other five books. Instead of mere sadistic imperialism we have that peculiar ambivalence toward the interaction of force and right which so marks our more modern democratic politics also. It is, I think, a redeeming discomfort and doubt, and it forces historical determinism and all its mechanical images of the way events *necessarily* develop, into a prophetic, that is, an indeterminate, ominous, always promising myth of the past, present, and future. The myth is not determining; it influences and it guides.

Chivalry: The Romantic Vision of Justice

SPENSER IS SUFFICIENTLY a humanist to believe that law exists to serve the higher values of life and spirit. Having set forth the stages by which his myth of justice develops, we need now to trace its higher aims. These are—in order of increasing range—chivalry, culture, and empire. Their scope enlarges in much the same system of transcendent expansion that widens the ideas of beauty in Castiglione's *The Courtier*. Chivalry, to begin with, provides Spenser with a narrative mode he learns from the romantic epic of Italy and from medieval English romances.[80] If he is to create an *experience* of justice, he needs such a narrative method. His sense that chivalry is also a mode of justice permits him to use the lightest, the most charming and romantic literary conventions in the grimmest portion of the whole work.

Ceremonial forms, not horses, are the basis of chivalry. As both the institution and the ideal the poem assumes, chivalry is a ritualized social arrangement where custom is the predominant cohesive force. Britomart, we learn, obeys the "laws of chivalry," and insofar as knighthood is the role of the hero, Artegall also lives by this allegiance. To serve Gloriana is indeed to serve chivalry. In all its violence the cult of chivalric rescue—with its constant overtone of a spiritual salvation—is a stylized social banditry. The chivalric code is a quasi-legal social code which supplies a rudimentary jurisprudence, a customary form whose spirit is courtesy, or better, grace. Book V presents a series of heroic encounters in the style of chivalric adventure, in such a way that each encounter represents a trial and a quest for justice.

80. John Arthos, *On the Poetry of Spenser and the Form of Romances* (London, 1956); Tuve, *Allegorical Imagery*, 360 ff.; Graham Hough, *A Preface to the Faerie Queene* (New York, 1963). Bishop Hurd, author of a series of sermons on the "prophetic style," originated this romance-gothic theory of Spenserian form, in his *Letters on Chivalry and Romance*. Davenant's *Preface to Gondibert* records the neoclassic discomfort in the face of heroic and prophetic inspiration; conceptions of "nature" are changing, and Davenant wishes Spenser had employed his talents in a more decorous way, "upon matter of a more naturall and therefore of a more useful kinde: His allegorical Story, by many held defective in the connexion, resembling, methinks, a continuance of extraordinary Dreams, such as excellent Poets and Painters, by being over-studious, may have in the beginning of Feavers." What is at issue is the question of connectivity in narrative form. For Davenant and for Hobbes's *Answer to Davenant*, see J. E. Spingarn, ed., *Critical Essays of the Seventeenth Century* (Oxford; repr. Bloomington, Ind., 1963), vol. 2.

To set the chivalric tone at once, the judgment of Sangliere introduces the Legend of Justice by shifting Solomonic wisdom from the realm of domestic maternal right to the realm of courtly love. The reader is reminded that justice should be the highest aim of romance. This view is reinforced by the tournament in honor of Florimell—another of Queen Elizabeth's ectypes—where the model trial, on aesthetic and courtly lines, links Artegall with Guyon, who suddenly reappears here to regain his horse, the emblem of chivalry. Florimell's vindication bespeaks the triumph of natural beauty and therefore of natural law, and this bizarre beauty contest is specifically called a "game" by Spenser, to indicate the role of play in the chivalric tournament. For such is the mythic meaning of a tourney—justice as play, and therefore as the archetypal festive imitation of a divinely free and fortunate pattern. The tourney establishes the "true measures of honour," the very English ideal of a fair fight, fair play, and the like, and this gamesomeness of justice confers a touch of beauty on the hero's quest: Artegall seeks the beautiful resolution of a measured debate. The act is also recreative: men try their strength, their grace, their skill, their right, and when the fight is over and a comic recreation has taken place, they go out to do battle in a real world. This tourney in Book V looks back to classical epic, where the equivalent is the athletic contest, which in Homer and Vergil is the ritual celebration of life itself. For Spenser, as for his classical models, the tourney takes place in sacred time. Hooker, describing the manner of celebrating church festivals, gives the best account of this last and highest mode of time. "The sanctification of days and times is a token of that thankfulness and a part of that public honour which we owe to God for admirable benefits, whereof it doth not suffice that we keep a secret calendar, taking thereby our private occasion as we list ourselves to think how much God hath done for all men, but the days which are chosen out to serve as public memorials of such his mercies ought to be clothed with those outward robes of holiness whereby their difference from other days may be made sensible. But because time in itself as hath been already proved can receive no alteration, the hallowing of festival days must consist in the shape or countenance which we put upon the affairs that are incident to those days."[81] In like manner heroes wear their emblematic armor here to notify mankind of their heroic purpose, a purpose which later they will uphold in the profane world; their failure to be always armed—as when Sir Burbon leaves his shield behind—will mark a loss of faith in the chivalric ideal.

For Artegall this ideal is all important, though he is a "salvage" knight, gifted naïvely with a sense of natural justice. He too must enter the chivalric tourney, whose custom is the social equivalent of natural law. Chivalry teaches the hero to justify himself through service. Regarding society as bound together in mutual bonds of love, chivalry fixes and regularizes the momentary success of law as a more permanent pattern of heroic triumph. Finally chivalry can ritualize law, because service means the continuous rededication of the hero to an endless warfare against the forces of night, darkness, winter, deceit, cruelty, lust.

Beyond Justice: The Culture Bringer

Book V, and with it the whole of *The Faerie Queene*, widens further in mythographic scope when chivalry brings culture to the ideal commonwealth. The hero seeks the growth of the state, which in Aristotelian terms can be studied "just as one studies the growth of a tree."[82] This organic purpose

81. *Ecclesiastical Polity*, V, lxx, 1. In V, lxx, 4, Hooker says that the festival recuperation of the Sabbath is an image of heaven itself. Burckhardt first stressed the role of festivals (*Civilization of the Renaissance in Italy*); we have now the monumental collection of essays, *Les Fêtes de la renaissance*, I and II, ed. Jean Jacquot; A. M. Nagler, *Theatre Festivals of the Medici: 1539–1637* (New Haven, 1964); C. L. Barber, *Shakespeare's Festive Comedy* (Princeton, 1959).

82. As noted by Richard Wollheim, "Aristotle's Politics," in *The Listener* (26 Sept. 1963), 467. In *Politics*, I, ii (1252b) Aristotle compares this growth to that of "a man or a horse or a family."

had been shown in the Proem, where the poet describes the Age of Saturn:

> No warre was knowne, no dreadfull trumpets sound,
> Peace universall rayn'd mongst men and beasts,
> And all things freely grew out of the ground.

This *eirenarcha* or rule of peace can only succeed a formative period when social banditry, then law, then equity create a climate for abundance. This must be a fertile climate of good faith. Following Vergil, Spenser writes of an ideal *pax britannica* whose hope is to restore the *saturnia regna*.

The hero able to go beyond law and justice is a culture bringer, a Theseus, a Hercules, an Osiris. Lucius Apuleius in *The Golden Ass* had shown an Osiris whose jurisprudence guaranteed justice. But Plutarch in the *Isis and Osiris* drew a more copious portrait. There, as Hegel summarized the matter, Plutarch credited Osiris and Isis with "the introduction of agriculture, the invention of the plough and the hoe, for Osiris controls not only the useful itself—the fertility of the earth—but, moreover, the human means of making earth useful. He also gives men laws, a civil order and a religious ritual; he thus places in men's hands the means of labor and secures its result. Osiris is also the symbol of the seed which is placed in the earth and then springs up, as also of the course of life. Thus we find a heterogeneous duality—the phenomena of Nature and the Spiritual—woven together into one knot."[83]

83. G. W. F. Hegel, *The Philosophy of History*, trans. J. Sibree (New York, 1956), 209. Diodorus of Sicily (Loeb Classics ed., London, 1935), II, 343: "The Egyptians, for example, say the god who among them bears the name Osiris is the one whom the Greeks call Dionysus. And this god, as their myths relate, visited all the inhabited world, was the discoverer of wine, taught mankind how to cultivate the vine, and because of this benefaction of his received the gift of immortality with the approval of all. But the Indians likewise declared that this god was born amongst them." Apollodorus, II, notes that the conflation of Dionysus and Osiris is implied by the statement that Io "set up an image of Demeter, whom the Egyptians called Isis, and

Euhemeristic interpretation ties this myth to actual historical time, preserving the ratio of the sacred and the profane, the cycle and the line. If the marriage of Artegall and Britomart occurs at a true Maygame, their union will presume the annual revival of the Osirian king. At the ancient festival of Osiris "the Pharaoh as the potential Osiris probably underwent a ritual death in order to be resuscitated by Horus and Isis as the living king in his Horus manifestation. Hence the declaration, 'thou beginnest thy renewal, beginnest to flourish again like the infant god of the Moon, thou art young again year by year, like Nun at the beginning of the ages, thou art reborn by renewing thy festival of *Sed*.' Thus the king as the centre of the social structure was ritually regen-

---

Io they likewise called by the name of Isis," since the relationship throughout is that of Mother Goddess and her own son, the Dying God. Plutarch *Isis and Osiris*, and Herodotus, II, 42–44, note the conflation. See Jean Przyluski, *La Grande Déesse: Introduction à l'étude comparative des religions* (Paris, 1950), 82–83. On the tree as cosmic center: Mircea Eliade, *Patterns in Comparative Religion*, chap. 8; Paracelsus, *Selected Writings*, ed. Jolande Jacobi (New York, 1951), 101–7; Gilbert Durand, *Les Structures anthropologiques de l'imaginaire: Introduction à l'archetypologie générale* (Grenoble, 1960), 365–70. The Dionysian cult of Dionysos Dendrites places the tree in the center of the universe. See H. Jeanmarie, *Dionysos: Histoire du culte de Bacchus* (Paris, 1951), 12; J. G. Frazer, *The New Golden Bough*, ed. T. H. Gaster (New York, 1961); and, in a Renaissance context, R. E. Hallowell, "The Mating Palm Trees in Du Bartas' 'Seconde Sepmaine,'" *Renaissance News* 17 (1964): 2, 89–94. See also on the Osiris-Dionysus complex, Isabel Rathborne, *The Meaning of Spenser's Fairyland*, 79–80, showing the appearance of the duality of the two gods in Berosus: "The Egyptian Empire of the just Osiris, ruling all the world except for the Babylonian kingdom, the Trojan realm from which came the pious Aeneas, the British kingdom founded by Brutus, whose descent from Dardanus and Aeneas made him a worthy progenitor of the mighty Arthur—these kingdoms . . . were contemporary in foundation and parallel in development with the Jewish state, prototype of the Christian Church, and could hardly have been regarded as evil by a poet for whom Church and State were united under a single head, whose ancestry he celebrates in his fairy genealogy." On hierogamy, see Theodore Gaster, *Thespis: Ritual*,

erated in the Osirian rites."[84] And, we may add, in this way Artegall's Osirian kingship is to be renewed in something resembling
the equinoctial celebration of the birthday of the Eyes of Horus.
Horus is the "lion of great might" who is born of the dream union
of Britomart-Isis and Artegall-Osiris. Horus, Fowler has said,
signifies "not only the political generation of an 'hour' or era of
justice through the mingling of righteousness and peace, justice
and equity; but also more largely, the creation of time by the
interaction of sun and moon."[85]

Modern scholarship supplies yet another explanation of Spenser's choice of an Egyptian myth, instead of the more obvious
Greek myth of Dionysus. "Since the fertility of the crops and
the cattle was bound up with the person of the king, Pharaoh in
his Horus manifestation as the ever-living son of his deified father
(Osiris) was the principal actor as the dynamic centre of the
nation. The rites, therefore, were communal rather than individ-
ualistic in character, thereby differing from their Hellenic coun-

---

Myth and Drama in the Ancient Near East (New York, 1961), 413–
15; E. O. James, *Comparative Religion* (New York, 1961), 94–95. On
the Mother Goddess and Egyptian Mystery: A. J. Festugière, *Personal
Religion among the Greeks* (Berkeley and Los Angeles, 1960), chap.
5; W. J. Tarn, *Hellenistic Civilization* (New York, 1961); 354–59;
Moses Hadas *Hellenistic Culture* (New York, 1959), 182–97; H. J.
Rose, *Religion in Greece and Rome* (New York, 1959), chap. 4,
"Egypt"; Robert Briffault, *The Mothers: The Matriarchal Theory of
Social Origins*, abridged ed. (New York, 1963), chap. 23, "The Great
Mothers"; Erich Neumann, *The Great Mother* (New York, 1955).
Egyptian history and myth show Osiris and Isis as actual monarchs;
see Henri Frankfort, *Kingship and the Gods* (Chicago, 1948); L.
Cerfaux and J. Tondriau, *Le Culte des souverains: Un concurrent du
Christianisme dans la civilization greco-romaine* (Tournai, 1957).
Plutarch, *Isis and Osiris*, sec. 10, remarks that Osiris is represented by
an eye and a scepter, "whereof the one signifies foresight, the other
power." "In many places also, they exhibit a statue of Osiris in the
human shape, erecting the genitals, on account of his generative and
nutritive character" (sec. 51).

84. E. O. James, *Comparative Religion*, 111.
85. Fowler, *Spenser and Numbers*, 216.

terparts. Their purpose was to secure the well-being of the community, not the salvation of the initiate. Behind the drama lies the primitive conception of the divine kingship, the Osiris-Horus myth symbolizing the course of the agricultural year and the renewal of the seasons, in the form recurrent in the Ancient East as exemplified in the Babylonian story of Tammuz and Ishtar or the Phoenician Adonis."[86] Artegall likewise is initiated into the cyclical process of merciful renewal only that he may assume new power for a whole community—the Egyptian source gives overwhelming stress to this kingly role. Prince Arthur aside, Artegall is the most public-spirited hero of *The Faerie Queene*, and while all Spenser's heroes are types of the dying god through their *imitatio Christi*, Artegall is most openly the communal hero, as Spenser knew when he chose to follow Plutarch's *Isis and Osiris*. James has observed in this source a confusion perfectly suited to the kind of poem Spenser is writing. For while in the older Egyptian texts Osiris is "the dead king" or the "king of the dead," and this suits Rathborne's argument about Fairieland, Plutarch thinks of him in second-century terms, so that touches of the Isiac mysteries rub off on Artegall's mythic ancestor. Artegall experiences the faintest vestige of sacrificial dismemberment (symbolically this occurs when he is "disarmed quight"), associating him vaguely with the Tammuz-Adonis type.[87]

86. James, *Comparative Religion*, 111–12. Fowler observes "Britomart's anxiety about Arthegall's delay prompts her to look for him, and thus to re-enact the yearning search for Osiris."

87. On the sparagmos see Frazer, *New Golden Bough*, pts. 4 and 5; Northrop Frye, *Anatomy of Criticism*, 148, 192–93, 222. The mythic dismemberment of Osiris by Typhon is a destruction *by the sea*. Isis appears allied to the sea, because her powers relate to matter, as it "turns itself into and embraces all things—light, darkness, day, night, life, death, beginning, end, whereas that power of Osiris has no shadow or variation but one, simple, the image of light; for pure is the final cause, and free from mixture the Primal and Intelligible" (*Isis and Osiris*, 77.). Saint George, in *F.Q.* I, is *Georgos*, the hero of earth, *terra firma*, on which see Nelson, *Poetry of Spenser*, 150–53. For mythic valuation of earth: E. O. James, *Seasonal Feasts* (New York,

Culture, as it goes beyond legal forms, also goes beyond agriculture. It includes the sum of energies, behaviors, habits, products, styles, pains, pleasures, hopes, and fears of a world. The one attribute which culture must have is studied social order of some kind, embodied in a sense of historical selfhood, and to this attainment the culture bringer attends. Spenser thus imagines the role of Artegall's counterpart, Lord Grey de Wilton. As Elizabeth's Lord Lieutenant in Ireland, Grey was required to "pacify" the Irish and to maintain English plantations in economic and political security. Since the office of Lord Lieutenant was a continuing one as long as the English Crown remained in Ireland, the allegory looks backward to include other former lords, perhaps Sir Henry Sidney and Sir John Perrott. Simultaneously the poem looks forward, and Artegall's difficulties anticipate later troubles of other actual viceroys. The Osirian myth attempts to show on the plane of sacred time what is encountered by such actual, profane princes of the realm. Perhaps here more clearly than with the justice-bringing aspects of the role, we find that the Osirian ruler is an ambiguous vatic type.

1963), 20–55; M. P. Nilsson, *Greek Folk Religion* (New York, 1940), 22–41. The earth, when cultivated, allows rebirth; the sea, harvested without any seeding or cultivation of its wealth, yields its own endless riches. Thus the Proem to Book V begins with the Flood, of which, as archetype, Eliade has said: "Almost all the traditions of deluges are bound up with the idea of humanity returning to the water whence it had come, and the establishment of a new era and a new humanity. They display a conception of the universe and its history as something 'cyclic': one era is abolished by disaster and a new one opens, ruled by 'new men.' This conception of cycles is also shown by the convergence of the lunar myths with themes of floods and deluges; for the moon is by far the most important symbol of rhythmic development, of death and resurrection. . . . I am not sure that one can call it a pessimistic conception of life. It is rather a resigned view, imposed simply by seeing the pattern made by water, the moon and change." *Patterns in Comparative Religion*, 210. See D. C. Allen, *The Legend of Noah*, 83, on identification of Noah with Saturn, Deucalion, and Hercules.

In the first place he is neither god nor man, but both. Ancient, medieval, Renaissance, and modern mythographers have agreed that the Dionysus-Osiris-Hercules type belongs to a quasi-human, quasi-divine archetype. Whereas the Olympian gods are completely gods, whose divinity is underscored because their actions are often (in Homer) humanly comic, the younger gods, of whom Dionysus is the perfect exemplar, belong to both worlds, human and divine, and their followers "become the god" in the mysteries.[88] The cult here does not maintain distance between deity and devotee; it identifies them (thus providing the original basis of ritual drama) at the moment of ecstasis. Euhemerism merely exaggerates this divine-human identification, having given it a political meaning.

There is an equally important confusion of sex among these younger deities, for they are all partially feminine. (Cartari's Bacchus provides one Renaissance example of the duality.) Hesiod and the antique mythographers tell us that the coalescence of sex represents and expresses a primal human desire for unity and fertility, since as an androgyne the god can without a consort procreate perfectly by simply including the other sex within himself.[89] When we think Hercules and Dionysus are *weakened*

88. W. J. C. Guthrie, *Orpheus and Greek Religion: A Study of the Orphic Movement* (London, 1935), 112. Again, of Dionysos, "The ultimate aim was union with the god, by the attainment of ecstasy and the sacred meal to become oneself a Bakchos." At the height of the ritual the initiate was called Bakchos. George E. Mylonas, *Eleusis and the Eleusinian Mysteries* (Princeton, 1961), 155, observes that "the role of Bacchos became more important after the Persian invasion of Xerxes, since it was believed that the youthful God helped the Greeks against the barbarians in the battle of Salamis." Thus history and myth mingle in the Dionysian-Osirian archetype.

89. *F.Q.*, IV, x. Marie Delcourt, *Hermaphrodite: Myths and Rites of the Bisexual Figure in Classical Antiquity* (London, 1961); Nelson, *Poetry*, 236–55; Fowler, *Spenser and Numbers*, 163; Cheney, "Spenser's Hermaphrodite and the 1590 Faerie Queene," (*PMLA*, 1971, in prep.). A. J. L. Busst, "The Image of the Androgyne in the Nineteenth Century," in *Romantic Mythologies*, ed. Ian Fletcher

by effeminacy, we are only partly right, since the heart of their myths is a belief that by combining the two sexes, as happens in ritual transvestism, the poets and priests of antiquity could maintain a myth of total fertility.[90] Spenser elsewhere uses the myth of the hermaphrodite to express the same principle of generation.[91]

Together Artegall and Arthur reenact the story of Hercules in several episodes recalling the Twelve Labors, but the most prominent episode recalls his servitude to Omphale. Spenser's account of the battle with Radigund, which Artegall in a sense wins, may derive from the ninth labor, the attack on the Amazons, even though Artegall does not challenge Radigund because he wants a magic garment. Yet she is an Amazon queen like Penthesilea or Hippolyte, and when in the original myth Hercules wins the trophy from Hippolyte, he takes the spoils to Omphale, whose analogue Radigund in fact is. Radigund combines elements of both the Amazon queen and the Lydian queen Omphale, which seems proper inasmuch as Diodorus records an Amazon queen, "filled with pride at her many victories," constraining men to spin and serve as women, while in the

---

(London, 1967), 63: "The union of a couple, then, is not the fusion of two distinct entities, but the revelation of an underlying unity: and the androgyny which symbolizes this union reveals a pre-existent androgyny [in reference to Novalis]."

90. Cartari, translated by Richard Linche as *The Foundation of Ancient Fiction. Wherein is lively depictured the images and statues of the gods of the ancients, with their proper and particular expositions* (London, 1599), notes "that Bacchus was oftentimes depictured and drawne forth in his Statues and Images, clothed with womens garments, and in effeminate habite." (Sig. Y–iii) He concludes that "the clothes and garments of women, so said to be on Bacchus, signifie, that the inordinate taking of wine weakeneth and debillitateth the naturall forces and powers of a man, making him feeble, unconstant, and strengthlesse, like a woman."

91. As in *F.Q.*, 1590 ed., III, xii, 44–47, of which Lewis and also Roche have observed that the Bible authorizes the metaphor: "For this cause shall a man leave his father and mother, and shall be joined unto his wife, and they two shall be one flesh."

Omphale-Iole myth we have the older archetype of such tyranny.[92] Natales Comes had justified the terrible story of Hercules' imprisonment as a lesson told by the ancients "to warn us that a good man must be ever on the watch; for if he turns his eyes from virtue but a moment," he will fall.[93] On the moral and legal plane these stories enforce a certain heroic anxiety, the same anxiety which pervades *The Faerie Queene* at large. But the Omphale story also suggests a much older and more interesting generative myth: her name "denoted the *centre* of the human body, the intersection of its two axes, the *root* of life, the *cord* which binds the child to its mother and which represents the destiny of each one of us."[94] The *omphalos* furthermore is the center of the cosmos, the archetypal place of rest, renewal, and sacred temporality. To serve Radigund-Omphale is to return to a travesty of the *locus amoenus*. When Britomart saves Artegall from his apparent effeminacy, he has already participated in the transvestite female mystery, so that now he can maintain himself "not as effeminate, but in the full power of his double nature."[95] Here sexuality implies an *eros* on the level of the Demiurge in the *Timaeus*, "that sovereign cause of becoming and of cosmic order."

Having said that during the *Saturnia regna* "all things freely grew out of the ground," the Proem fixes for the rest of Book V an equivalence between virtue and vice and the seeds, the *logoi spermatikoi*, of human action. Canto I at once advances this theme.

> Though vertue then were held in highest price,
>   In those old times, of which I doe entreat,
>   Yet then likewise the wicked seede of vice
>   Began to spring which shortly grew full great,

92. Spenser substitutes Iole for Omphale, perhaps following Boccaccio. See *Variorum*, 5:203.
93. Comes 7.1. See *Variorum*, 5:203.
94. Delcourt, *Hermaphrodite*, 24.
95. Ibid.

> And with their boughes the gentle plants did beat.
> But evermore some of the vertuous race
> Rose up, inspired with heroicke heat,
> That cropt the branches of the sient base,
> And with strong hand their fruitfull rancknes did deface.
>
> (i, 1)

Spenser the Vergilian identifies both Bacchus and Hercules with the "vertuous race," and he parodies georgic imagery whenever Talus wields the iron flail. The flail as an instrument of harvest time "thresht out falsehood, and did truth unfold"; "did thresh so thin,/ That he no worke at all left for the leach"; "began to lay about,/ From whose sterne presence they [the followers of Grantorto] diffused ran,/ Like scattered chaff, the which the wind away doth fan." More complicated is that final allusion to Talus's destructive winnowing, for in the end it actually becomes a kind of seed sowing. As Artegall approaches his last encounter, the scouts of Grantorto come out to meet him before he and Talus can establish a beachhead.

> But ere he marched farre, he with them met,
>   And fiercely charged them with all his force;
> But Talus sternely did upon them set,
>   And brusht, and battred them without remorse,
>   That on the ground he left full many a corse;
> Ne any able was him to withstand,
>   But he them overthrew both man and horse,
> That they lay scattred over all the land,
> As thicke as doth the seede after the sowers hand.
>
> (xii, 7)

This mingling of generation and destruction is furthermore present whenever sun and moon appear. Both Britomart and Radigund are likened to the moon. While Artegall and Arthur are, like Osiris, heroes of the sun, their enemies equally serve the sun, but as a destructive force. The Soldan is a desert sun, Geryoneo's arms are branches that grow profusely but are evil in their generation. So in his defeat they are "pruned from the native tree, and cropped quight." Like other poets, Ralegh for example, Spenser uses the imagery of flowers to imply beauty, which means a kind of unsullied order. Thus in a purely political context the Lady Belge is described:

> Her name was Belge, who in former age
> > A Ladie of great worth and wealth had beene,
> > And mother of a frutefull heritage,
> > Even seventeene goodly sonnes;[96] which who had seene
> > In their first flowre, before this fatall teene
> > Them overtooke, and their faire blossomes blasted,
> > More happie mother would her surely weene
> > Then famous *Niobe*, before she tasted
> *Latonaes* childrens wrath, that all her issue wasted.
>
> > > > (x, 7)

Niobe, the archetypal image of the grieving mother, is a familiar figure of abortive maternity; she must be saved; the hero's quest here and in other parts of *The Faerie Queene* is to rescue the givers of life. In Ovidian parody of Florimell, the abused females of this book are identified with various flowers, like the widowed city in the Book of Lamentations. Belge is lily-white; Burbon's lady, France, is naturally called Flourdelis; Irena is compared to the favored flower of love.

> Like as a tender Rose in open plaine,
> > That with untimely drought nigh withered was,
> > And hung the head, soone as few drops of raine
> > Thereon distill, and deaw her daintie face,

96. The seventeen sons of **Belge** are the seventeen provinces constituting the Netherlands before their conquest by Spain. Gough (*Variorum*, 5:317) says that the two Springals are probably "to be equated with the provinces that took the lead in the revolt of the Netherlands, namely, Holland and Zealand, although Upton was of the opinion that they represented the Marquess of Havre and Adolf Meetkerche, whom the States sent as special envoys to England in 1577."

> Gins to looke up, and with fresh wonted grace
> Dispreds the glorie of her leaves gay;
> Such was *Irenas* countenance, such her case,
> When *Artegall* she saw in that array,
> There wayting for the Tyrant, till it was farre day.
>
> (xii, 13)

Irena becomes Flora, whose rescue is nothing less than her resurrection from the dead.

Yet Spenser's heroines are not always types of Persephone. In fact he distinguishes two cultures, the one perhaps an original innocent one, identified with the green world, the other a man-made civilized one. When Belge meets Prince Arthur, who in imitation of Hercules is going to destroy Geryoneo, she laments the loss of her cities and towers, those towers that like Nimrod rise above the common run.

> Ay me (sayd she) and whether shall I goe?
> Are not all places full of forraine powres?
> My pallaces possessed of my foe,
> My cities sackt, and their sky-threating towres
> Raced, and made smooth fields now full of flowers?
> Onely these marishes, and myrie bogs,
> In which the fearefull ewftes do build their bowres,
> Yeeld me an hostry mongst the croking frogs,
> And harbour here in safety from those ravenous dogs.
>
> (x, 23)

Though Arthur reassures her, he concludes ominously: "and if all fayle, yet farewell open field: / The earth to all her creatures lodging lends," as if to say they can take refuge in caves, or in the grave. Even despite his troubled feelings about the pride of courts, Spenser believes that the "sky-threating" city is the basis of culture—which significantly he maintains in his two marriage odes. While the untamed natural world may breed flowers, it also breeds ewftes and frogs and all the other night creatures cursed in the *Epithalamium*. Gloriana has built Cleopolis the city of fame to wall out all wild things. Her subject Artegall must progress from his own "salvage" justice to a courtly, civil justice. The natural culmination of Book V, as Cheney has argued, is the Legend of Courtesy, where justice is rendered in its highest form: courteous order.[97]

Beyond Culture: Idealized Imperialism

JUSTICE EXPANDS in its implications into empire—and one wonders if courtesy would not have implied a restriction upon empire. Certainly, as we reach the widest scope of mythic justice in Book V, we reach Spenser's greatest range of risk. Nowhere else is his vision so suspicious, at least to the modern reader.

Yet he has to follow his logic, and hope to redeem the imperial myth (like his other myths of power) by creating a covert analogy between his poem and the vision created by his poem. Very simply, before we try to account for political ideas in the poem, we have another problem to face: that insofar as any great and complex poem is a unity, it is also something of a political metaphor—it is a nation or state, in some sense—and thus Spenser is finally writing a poem which, expressing ideas and aspirations and happenings occurring outside itself, also is a cosmogonic allegory whose main intent is to watch its own coming into being. For the culture defined by *The Faerie Queene* is finally a life within the poem itself, and, as Durling has shown, the poet's *persona* periodically asserts his creative power.[98] The poem is a kind of dragon, with one lazy eye open to survey the lengthy undulations of its own body. By the time the critic grasps the full range of its allegory, he finds himself lapped in vision, as if its world were more real than any world outside it.

97. Donald Cheney, *Spenser's Image of Nature*, 176–95.
98. Robert M. Durling, *The Figure of the Poet in Renaissance Epic*.

Under such conditions of entanglement there is no wonder that our criticism of Spenser seems frequently awkward and naïve and, in the case of Book V, where the inner reality is "historical" in part, so easily confused. Book V raises the question of mode more acutely than does any other book, and to give a tentative account of typologized history here seems all the more important since, through Britomart's story, Book V becomes a continuation of Books III and IV, fully employing "the sequence of time as a symbol and organizing force."[99]

The Proem to Book V makes it quite clear that its final theme is the expansive power and rule of Gloriana, a rule "resembling God in his imperiall might," while her "magnificke might and wondrous wit [i.e., wisdom]," carries beyond her own borders, filling foreign nations with dread. Since for Elizabethans the idea of the British Empire is still rather vague, it seems significant that Spenser calls Gloriana "that soveraine Queene, that mightie Emperesse,/ Whose glorie is to aide all suppliants pore,/ And of weake Princes to be Patronesse." Her imperial crown evidently entitles her to meddle in the affairs of other states.[100] It equally invites her to aid and comfort them if they come asking for help, and in this latter function there is a type of equity, since she will mercifully help them against unwanted tyrants.

The terms "empire" and "imperial" have an ancient history, however, and this reminds us of a more militant purpose: before its complete adoption by Augustus Caesar, the praenomen *imperator* "originally was, and for some time still remained, a military title conferred by acclamation on a high-ranking commander after victory."[101] The *imperator* was he who *prepared against* the enemy, was thus truly a general, and even earned the credit of "providing for" victory. Although *imperium* comes finally to mean the dignity, authority, supreme command, or

99. Roche, *Kindly Flame*, 60.
100. See Richard Koebner, *Empire*, chap. 3.
101. Koebner, *Empire*, 6.

absolute sway by which the *imperator* rules, the term nevertheless is always tinged with an overtone of social banditry, if only
because Rome had gained her world rule through military conquest. Thus, the other meaning of empire—an extensive territory under the sway or control of a given ruler, or an aggregate
of states under such control—is normal in the Roman context.
Indeed, this remains a useful meaning of the word *imperium*,
uniting, as it does, separate geographic and political notions.
Henry VIII inevitably argued that "this realm of England is an
Empire," because his declaration of independence from Rome
included an assertion of territorial integrity which became ever
more prominent during successive treason trials of spies who
came from overseas or who, although Englishmen, served foreign
governments.

For the epic poet this assumption of the "empery" of England
helps to conventionalize the epic form: the imperial myth reaches
back to the Vergilian typology and to Roman prehistory. For
Sallust, when Romulus was described as transforming the original "loose and amorphous multitude . . . into a civil society," this
meant the creation of an empire, through the hero's conscious
and deliberate statecraft. "This act, which is ascribed to a (mythical) herofounder or lawgiver, consists of imposing upon the
assembled elements the characteristic forms of the *polis* or the
civitas, i.e., of civilized life. But, in the nature of things, the
original source of these forms must itself be 'formal,' since otherwise it could not discharge its function. Accordingly, it may be
described (in the terminology of Sallust) as *imperium legitimum*.
To such a principle, as represented in prehistorical kings, the
historian attributes 'the conservation of freedom and the increase
of public good.' "[102] This development we have identified with
the labors of the true social bandit, the *dux*, whose aim is to im-

102. Quoted in C. N. Cochrane, *Christianity and Classical Culture*
(New York, 1957), 104–5. The passage is from *The Conspiracy of
Catiline*, available in Sallust, *The Jugurthine War; The Conspiracy of
Catiline*, trans. S. A. Handford (Penguin ed., 1963), 173.

pose the law of force, and the stabilizer or *rex*, whose aim is to impose the force of law. After this expansion of order is accomplished, there is only one higher stage left, the "constitution of religions," which is also the work of the lawmaking *rex*, Numa Pompilius for Rome, Solon for Athens, Solomon for the Children of Israel.

It is clear that although the constitution of religions brings a higher order than that of the social bandit, there can be an equal amount of conflict in reaching the higher state. European history in the sixteenth and seventeenth centuries tells a tale of the most savage religious passions, which only the cunning of the *politique* could hope to control, and then only by playing the game of religious compromise, as did Henry of Navarre or Elizabeth herself. It was precisely those men who appeared most passionately religious whose political and militant behavior was most extreme. We must ask, therefore, whether the imperialist reality of this period does not contradict the peacemaking myth as received from Vergil, Plutarch, or the Roman historians. On the Continent events do not suggest a clear advance from social banditry to ecumenical harmony. But in the case of England there is a measure of accuracy in Spenser's historical allegory, for the attitudes of Book V well represent the ambiguity of Elizabeth's political behavior. She was so unwilling to come out strongly and irrevocably in any constitutional changes made through statute that one historian has said, "Among all great rulers it is the distinction of Elizabeth to have shown how much may be achieved by simply allowing full play to the influence of time."[103] She did have negative capability in politics, and its consequence was to give her empire the advantages of flexible policy with all the splendor of *imperium legitimum*. She avoided political giganticism and rigor. By contrast, the various tyrants who are represented in Book V are shown to pretend, falsely, to

103. J. R. Seeley, *The Growth of British Policy* (Cambridge, 1897), 1:247, quoted in E. H. Harbison, *The Age of Reformation* (Ithaca, 1961), 122.

the glory and majesty of empire, which are attributes, finally, of the sun itself as it rides westward overhead. A central purpose of Book V was to show that through her equity Elizabeth checked the tendency toward imperial absolutism. Mercilla's trial of Duessa takes place in what amounts to a parliament, and in this framework the monarch could not, except symbolically, assume absolute right in imitation of Julius Caesar.

Nor, historically, does Elizabethan imperialism commit England to the military conquest of the European mainland. Elizabeth's meddling with France, the Low Countries, and Spain falls rather under the head of political intervention. Camden portrayed her as the Augustan creator of a *pax britannica:* "Thus sate she as an heroical Princess and Umpire betwixt the Spaniards, the French, and the Estates. . . . And true it was which one hath written, that France and Spain are as it were Scales in the Balance of Europe, and England the Tongue of the Holder of the Balance."[104] This judgment in effect agrees with the modern views of Neale, Mattingly, and others. Elizabeth avoided the fatal error diagnosed in Mattingly's *Renaissance Diplomacy:* "In wars of ideas the sense of proportion, like the knack of compromise, is easily lost. Europe had to wade in blood for nearly a century before it could be persuaded that states with different (not really so very different) ideologies need not necessarily destroy each other. It had to spend a longer time and do itself graver injury before its rulers learned that their subjects could live at peace together in one kingdom, professing different faiths. . . . The religious wars nearly wrecked the diplomatic institutions with which Europe had been trying to adjust its quarrels."[105] Such dogmatic tragedies Elizabeth mainly avoided. "Successful diplomatic negotiations require that the parties involved can at least imagine a mutually satisfactory settlement, that neither assumes

104. Camden's *History* (1577), 223, quoted in Fussner, *Historical Revolution*, 241.

105. Garrett Mattingly, *Renaissance Diplomacy* (Boston, 1955), 194–96.

that the only permanent solution is the total destruction of the other. As long as conflicts between states are about prestige or profit or power, grounds of agreement are always accessible to sane men. But the clash of ideological absolutes drives diplomacy from the field."

Such is the background to Elizabeth's handling of Philip II and to Spenser's allegory of the Soldan, Geryoneo, and Grantorto. In Canto VIII Samient may stand for the capacity to bring disputants together, to make them one, or similar. She is an ambassadress bringing Mercilla's call for aid against the subversive Soldan. In historical fact, no woman ever acted such a part, but in mythic terms a woman, schooled in equity, might well represent a quality of "samience," a *homonoia* or universal likemindedness. This spirit of concord was first envisaged, we are told, by Alexander the Great, who tried "to break down not merely the physical but also the ideological barriers which had hitherto separated Greek from barbarian, and to erect a new concept of human excellence, the excellence of the cosmopolitan or citizen of the world."[106] This would be too much to claim for Elizabeth, particularly since her voyaging servants, Drake, Hawkins, and the rest—real-life social bandits—maintained piracy on a worldwide scale. Yet the pattern of compromise and concord was an Elizabethan style, which makes it worth noticing that Spenser, not altogether inconsistently, condemns Sir Burbon (Henry of Navarre) for abandoning his faith—even though the apostasy was an act of the highest *politique* diplomacy. Paris, Henry is reputed to have said, was surely worth a Mass. Yet on the level of religious conviction perhaps Elizabeth would have drawn the line before committing Henry's daring switch; she

106. Cochrane, *Christianity*, 88. Tarn holds similar views—see his *Alexander the Great*. Jean-Pierre Vernant, *Les Origines de la pensée grecque* (Paris, 1962), 87, shows that the notion of *homonoia* is ancient among the Greeks, that it derives from the legal and judicial establishment set down by Solon (the mythic parallel to Solomon): "*Homonoia*, or concord, is a 'harmony' obtained by proportions all the more exact because Solon gives them a quasi-numerical form."

could afford to think so, anyway, because England was so un-like France in its general political and religious acceptance of the Reformation. In Book VI, where, as Cheney observes, "di-plomacy is less a technique than a symbol,"[107] the poet always assumes that the basis of diplomacy (or courtesy enacted on a political or international scene) must be, for England, the English Reformation.

Diplomacy and the balancing of power in Europe were not unaccompanied by the use of armed force, and to justify this aggression Spenser invoked the idea of freedom. Milton, more than Spenser, is our Renaissance poet of liberty. But Miltonic libertarianism grows from a double root, from the poet's polit-ical and religious convictions, and also from his literary inheri-tance, which, being Spenserian as much as anything else, includes a heavy debt to Book V, which after all unfolds the major theme of *Paradise Lost*. While working on a much smaller scale, having shown the religious liberation of England in the Legend of Holiness, Spenser now proceeds to show that England, to protect herself, will intervene to liberate others. Her own liberation is again a major theme in the defeat of the Soldan, an allegory chiefly remarkable for its allusion to the providential order of the battle and for its dialectical play on the role of the Terrible Mother, here called Adicia, or Injustice. The Soldan's chariot horses stampede, out of control, like the galleons of Medina Sidonia blown by the "protestant wind." Their Phaeton-like re-bellion against the curb of authority shows that the Soldan is not truly Sol but his demonic parody.[108] Similarly, accusations of

107. Cheney, *Spenser's Image*, 185. The background to the prob-lem of cooperation, diplomacy, and concord is the prior attitude of tolerance or intolerance, on which see A. J. Klein, *Intolerance in the Reign of Elizabeth, Queen of England* (Boston, 1917), passim.

108. There is a curious illustration by Breughel, showing Phaeton falling and a sea battle occurring simultaneously (see Dover edition of Breughel's prints). Christian poetry draws analogies between the Fall of Man and Phaeton's fall—which is a rebellion—e.g., Giles Fletcher, *Christ's Victory and Triumph* (1610) st. 7. But the Ovidian

murder, incontinence, adultery, and impiety mask the real drive of the arraignment of Duessa, that is, to convict Duessa of treason against a realm which under Henry VIII had declared itself independent of Roman Catholicism and, thereby, of Spain.

When a country defends its own territorial or political integrity in such manner, the term "imperialism" may not apply as we use the word nowadays. But it would apply to the expedition of Arthur to liberate the Lady Belge from Geryoneo, since that action sent English forces overseas. Leaving aside the ineffectual scope of Leicester's military aid, the support of the Netherlands has a significance out of all proportion to the merely military side of the picture. For the revolt of the Netherlands against Spanish dominance had been and would continue to be the great model of Protestant freedom, for Europe, for Englishmen, and two centuries later for Americans looking at their own Revolution.[109] To help the Lady Belge meant to help the cause of liberty itself. Spenser gives to this episode some of his finest writing, expounding a monstrously ornate allegory of tyrannical power, a nightmare vision of the Duke of Alva's inquisitionary rule. To suggest the historical point of the Geryoneo myth, let us recall that on 16 February 1568 the Inquisition had condemned every single inhabitant of the Netherlands to death, with a few stated exceptions.[110] The mythic home of Geryoneo's father was Cadiz, and it seems fitting that Drake (whom Spaniards called "the Dragon," *El Draque*) twice sailed into Cadiz,

---

myth (*Metamorphoses*, II, 1–366) seems to parallel the prior story of the Flood (*Metam.*, I, 253–347), each story showing a primal rebellion, a near destruction of life on earth, followed by a rebirth.

109. J. N. Figgis, *Political Thought from Gerson to Grotius* (New York, 1960), chap. 8, "The Netherlands Revolt." Peter Geyl, *Encounters in History* (New York, 1961), "Motley and his *Rise of the Dutch Republic*," observes that ironically the revolt was *not* "a triumph of Liberalism, of Enlightenment, of Democracy." But this is demythologizing criticism, and of no force against mythological, romantic historiography.

110. *Variorum*, 5:252.

attacking the monster in his lair. A providential note hovers over this allegory, when we recall that Geryon is the final Herculean victim. Geryon and Geryoneo are creatures of death, of the setting sun, of the west. If Arthur is a prince of the sun, like Artegall, Geryoneo is another demonic parody of the sun king.[111] We have noticed the recurrent resurrection theme in the Belge episode; the sun revives the drooping flower, "that earst was dead, restor'd to life againe." Liberation then means freedom in the sense of redemption from death; it also means political restoration of ancient rights.

Poetically considered, imperialism in Book V reaches a climax with the rescue of Irena from Grantorto, and here we also reach an area of essential critical difficulty. For to justify the imperialism of this liberation is to justify the allegory of the whole book, whose prior analyses of Justice lead up to and are included in this final battle. Canto I had told us at once that Artegall would "restore" Irena's right to her, and here the familiar analogy to a withered Rose reminds us later that with the arrival of her champion Irena will be brought back to life. The final heroic episode shows a heightened attention to the passage of time, and the reader is told the actual timetable for the battle with Grantorto. He threatens that if the champion of Irena does not present himself within a fixed number of days, she will die. Artegall's arrival marks a precise moment in time (historically, the moment when Grey began his lieutenancy), and his resurrection of Irena is vaguely messianic. That it does not bear final apocalyptic sway over history is precisely the irony Spenser wants to achieve with his Envy and Detraction. But in principle

111. Dunseath, *Spenser's Allegory*, 70–71: "Artegall's true movement in his quest is from east to west, the movement of the sun, or reason, Plato's motion of the *same* [from the *Timaeus*]. . . . Whenever one of these chosen men deviates from his symbolic westward course, he falls in nature—Plato's motion of the *other*, representing the passions . . . Because Artegall, as a type of Hercules, emblematically bears the burden of all just men, he achieves an inward state of peace at the end of his quest."

the rescue is a final one, born of true justice and good will. Elizabeth, like Henry VII and her father, sought a restoration of English rule in Ireland, a rule which had decayed steadily since the days of Edward I and which even the Poynings statutes failed to bring back.[112] Whatever we think of the English case, from the Tudor angle it appeared to be a restoring of ancient English rights. The precedent of earlier rule, to which Spenser refers in his Machiavellian *Vewe of the Present State of Irelande*, was held sufficient to "justify" this return.

Ireland, of course, holds a special place in Spenser's poetry, not merely because he wrote of it allusively in his poems and directly in the *Vewe of the Present State*. Ireland appears to have been for him a pastoral, holy land, which provided him with a visionary perspective on England. It was a place of distance, a place of contrast, of the salvage man, where on the hill of Arlo Mutabilitie was once judged by the gods. It might hope to be rich and prosperous, like "fruitfullest Virginia." For such reasons Ireland is the landfall of the allegory of justice. Ireland is Irena, the land where peace should reign, and the poet might imagine his sovereign uttering the words of Acts 24:25, "When I have a convenient season, I will call for thee." Yet his *Vewe of the Present State* saw the situation more soberly. Its language was prophetic: "It is the fatall destynie of that land, that noe purposes whatsoever are mente for her good will prosper or take good effecte, which whether yt proceed from the verie *Genius* of the soyle, or influence of the starrs, or that almightie god hath not yett yppointed the tyme of her reformacion, or that he reserveth her in this unquiet state still, for some secreete scourge which shall by her come unto England, yt is harde to bee knowen but yett much to be feared."[113]

This Ireland enjoyed no lasting peace, yet it was the "home"

---

112. Agnes Conway, *Henry VII's Relations with Scotland and Ireland, 1485–1498, with a Chapter on the Acts of the Poynings Parliament, by Edmund Curtis* (Cambridge, 1932), 143.

113. *Vewe*, in *Variorum*, 8:39–231.

to which Colin Clout returned. Like other Renaissance poets
Spenser lived a "life of allegory," first in politics and service to
the state, then in poetic works. There is Spenser's own history
and the history of his time, and both histories fill the pages of
The Faerie Queene with a spirit of expansion and imaginative
conquest. History is Platonically the shadow of the ideas the
poem intends to allegorize, and its historical allusions are *figurae*
born of those ideas. From this typological perspective if from no
other we should expect Spenser himself to fuse the two realms
of imperialism, the political and poetical. As an officer of Elizabeth's *imperium*, as the friend of Sidney and Ralegh, he knew
political life, and Book V reflects his cruel assessment of its realities, but purely as a poet and an image maker, as Bonfont, he
builds another empire which he calls Faerieland, where his subjects are of many orders and his authority large. If it is not absolute authority, this only proves the point. For Spenser is the
true Machiavel among poets; he deploys the daemonic energy
of *ragion di stato* in the control of his principate. His "hart-
ravishing knowledge" is not always stable. Yet, as readers of the
Aeneid have felt that its form and character study fit the theme
of imperial glory which is its aim, the same congruity may be
observed in Spenser, if on a more symbolic, digressive basis.
What we finally observe is that Homer, Vergil, and then Spenser
(through the medium of Ariosto and Tasso) create worlds which
they dispose imperially. The epic poet is the provider, unlike
the dramatic poet who slices into a small segment of a situation.
On this cosmic scale of creation, as we shall see, the poet also
disposes of time through the problematic images of temples and
labyrinths, truths and errors, vision and experience.

V

Error and Experience

 O FAR WE HAVE EXAMINED THE LEGEND OF JUS-
tice as a myth of historical and national devel-
opment. Even though there are countercur-
rents, Book V can be said to narrate a steady
shift from primitive, prelegal conditions (the
world after Astraea's departure) to evolved
legal and political establishments (where Artegall and Arthur make war on foreign powers).

The second subject of this developmental fugue is the strengthen-
ing link between justice and historical perspective. Another level
of interpretation now suggests itself, and, through it, a return to
the central problem of prophecy. This is the level on which
Book V creates a mythic present. The temple/error nexus describes many moments in the developmental scheme, but it finally
describes a state of mind and action which the poem locates
"now and in England." The poet looks back and forward, "recoursing to the thinges forepaste, and divining of thinges to
come," but Spenser's ultimate aim is to tie the present into this
single knot of prophecy and then, by making "a pleasing Analysis of all," to untie the knot into its significant temporal strands.

On this analytic level *The Faerie Queene* throughout deals

with error as a divisive, digressive, diversionary movement away from the "right line" of truth. As justice, the right line describes a steady political course, and, as we shall see, political error is presented in images of uncertain, shaky movements. This spatial allegory is familiar to all political scientists—spatial terms are among the most frequent we use to describe political actions. On the whole, critics of Spenser have allowed that *for him* rebellion and other lesser political errors are undeniably "bad," while Artegall's rectitude is undeniably "good." This propagandistic, naïve allegory has given rise to the troubled reputation of Book V. It has repelled many liberal minds, while among Spenser's allegorical creations Talus seems always to have been notorious. Yet precisely because Book V appears in the garb of Elizabethan propaganda, we must defend its more speculative aims. These involve the complications of the temple/error linkage.

The chief complication might be called the "necessity of error." Its doctrinal Christian aspect is the Fortunate Fall, the idea that a certain "felicity" or grace came to man only because his original error permitted his later redemption.[1] This necessity transcends fate; it is providential. Now, with the exception of mystical theology and ascetic nihilism, almost no philosophy lacks this kind of necessary category for error. Every system, as system, requires a means of proving its truth, and this trial inevitably involves error. We can reformulate our problem, then: experience is complicated by the "necessity of *trial* and error." Error provides the negative terms of an experimental method, and in human affairs this method is simply called "experience."

In English letters the poet who most fully analyzes the relation of error and experience is Milton, though the problem recurs throughout the romantic tradition, especially in Wordsworth, exploiting temple/error relations as its mythographic basis. A major claim made in this tradition is that doctrinal certitude

1. As described in A. O. Lovejoy, "Milton and the Paradox of the Fortunate Fall," in *Essays in the History of Ideas* (1948; repr. New York, 1960).

should not be allowed to censor experience in the false desire to avoid error by a "cloister'd virtue." The same desire to include experience in the virtuous life informs Spenserian myth. We have seen that the ideas of temple and maze interact typologically. If *The Faerie Queene* is by its concentric form a templar vision, its flowing narrative is the image of error and experience. The implication follows that error can be contained by the temple. The templar structure gives meaning to the labyrinthine ways of Faerieland. Ultimately, then, the temple/error union is defined by the six books as a whole, and to the extent that error and experience are the "content" of the six books, these must end by not ending.

Rebellion or Revolution: The Tragic Frame

I⊤ MAY BE THAT SPENSER wrote his Mutabilitie Cantos, not in order to get another book launched, but because he needed to stand away from his immense epic, to criticize it from the perspective of a philosophic allegory, "the noblest and most pregnant of its kind."[2] If the figure of Talus introduces time as the radical of justice, the drama of Mutabilitie works out a basic distinction between rebellion and revolution. The fact that not all rebellions are revolutions leads to a tragic conclusion: that with all his will to change things for the better, man cannot always reform as he wishes, or keep his reformation intact when it has happened. Spenser moderates this tragedy (or irony, at any rate) by defeating the rebellion of Mutabilitie; this defeat follows not from her annihilation but from her contain-

2. S. T. Coleridge, "On the Prometheus of Aeschylus," in *Essays and Lectures on Shakespeare and some other Old Poets and Dramatists* (London, Everyman ed., 1907), 334. For a sustained philosophical argument showing the connections of rebellion with Shakespearian tragedy: *Fools of Time: Studies in Shakespearean Tragedy* (Toronto, 1967), by Northrop Frye. Frye gives great weight to the History plays.

ment within a larger order. We need to consider the cantos briefly before arguing that, for every phase in the building of the temple, there is an analogous phase in the unbuilding of error.

In the Mutabilitie Cantos Spenser proves an ultimate cosmic constancy by denying the suit of the Titaness in the trial held on Arlo Hill. The language of the trial is so precisely legal that we are entitled to discern in it a legislation of the whole order of nature and destiny. Sherman Hawkins holds that the pageant of months and seasons does not, as Mutabilitie would claim, prove the changefulness of things, but rather their permanence in change, their capacity to be continually reborn in fresh versions of their archetypes.[3] The trial asserts a triumphant belief in the divinely ordered cyclicality of sacred time. Nature's calendar is redeemed immediately by the poet's visionary pageant, and ultimately by the Redeemer himself, since "it is the Incarnation which gives meaning to the cycle of time and direction to man's striving."[4]

Yet a more frontal issue in these cantos is the political allegory of rebellion. For the Titaness is primarily a rebel, and her cosmic designs are implications of her rebellion. Assuming that the cosmos is the largest possible image of political order, we can move inward from Mutabilitie's insurrection, applying its lessons of cosmic error to the field of human politics, which is the subject of Book V. In the course of our reading, we discover, as Hawkins suggested, that there is a radical difference between rebellion and revolution, since the latter displays the perfect form of the cyclical motion of the seasons and of the life process. By mistaking this difference, Mutabilitie forfeits her right. Spenser has often been accused of gratuitously stepping outside his framework in the stanzas of the "imperfect" seventh canto. He does not change ground there, as a close examination shows, but he

3. Sherman Hawkins, "Mutabilitie and the Cycle of the Months," in *Form and Convention in the Poetry of Edmund Spenser*, ed. William Nelson, 76–102.
4. Ibid., 95.

does extend his purview. More important, he also *begins* the Cantos on a detached basis, since it is a *prima facie* contradiction for Mutabilitie, a rebel, to go to court in defense of her rebellion. There can, in the Elizabethan context, be no appeal from the grounds of rebellion. She can, in law, only seek to prove she is not a rebel.[5] She cannot justify rebellion as such, and the language Spenser employs throughout, by insisting on its legalism, provides a set of terms whose meaning, apparently, is not known to Mutabilitie. For us, and to a lesser extent for her, the trial is an exploration of the way in which injustice is erroneous.

> Ne shee the lawes of Nature onely brake,
> > But eke of Justice, and of Policie;
> And wrong of right, and bad of good did make,
> > And death for life exchanged foolishlie:
> Since which, all living wights have learn'd to die,
> And all this world is woxen daily worse.
> O pittious worke of MUTABILITIE!
> By which, we all are subject to that curse,
> And death instead of life have sucked from our Nurse.
>
> > > > > (vi, 6)

The Fall of Man here is viewed politically. When the Titaness rebels against the established power of Jove, "rule and dominion to her selfe to gaine," a standard Elizabethan political theory is made explicit: Mutabilitie has attacked the sovereignty of Cynthia, Jove, and all the petty gods who rule under the sway of Natural Law. Cynthia (whose personification at once involves Elizabeth) has her "soveraigne seat / By highest Jove assign'd," while Jove claims to possess sovereign power "by Conquest of

5. J. W. Allen, *Political Thought in the Sixteenth Century*, II, ii, "The Doctrine of Non-resistance." "Even the Elizabethan Puritans, rebels as they were logically and potentially, never claimed a right of rebellion" (132). See James K. Lowers, *Mirrors for Rebels: A Study of Polemical Literature* (Berkeley and Los Angeles, 1953), relating to the 1569 Northern Rebellion, especially chap. 6, "The Doctrine in Nonpolemical Literature."

our soveraine might, / And by eternall doome of Fates decree,"
and he describes his rule as containing "the Empire of the
Heavens bright," thus identifying himself with the sun's glory.[6]
When he sits in council surrounded by the congregation of the
Olympians, he assumes "his principall Estate," from which he
hands down decrees and sovereign judgments. He can cite the
famous cases in which rebels against him, including Prometheus,
had been condemned to everlasting pain. Mutabilitie is allowed
to plead her case with all the "large evidence" she can muster,
but the case is moved to "Natur's Bar," where finally the goddess Nature gives judgment against the Titaness. Nature, even
on Mutabilitie's own statement, is a "sovereign goddess," which
more than any other detail indicates the political relevance and
originality of the Cantos. For whereas natural law remains a
powerful theoretical source of authority, as evidenced in the
Laws of Ecclesiastical Polity, it is usually counterpoised during
this period against the authority of the sovereign prince, because
this latter source owes little to the natural order of the hierarchical worldview, to *Lex Naturae*, and owes everything to
"reason of state."[7] To call Nature a sovereign is to equate organic order and princely power within a system of authority.
This myth fits the Tudor establishment, where sheer force triumphed and, as a modern historian puts it, if anyone asked which

6. On the solar identification of Arthur and Artegall, see Alastair
Fowler, *Spenser and the Numbers of Time*, 214–21.

7. On "reason of state," Enrico Castelli, *Christianismo e ragion
di stato: l'umanesimo e il demoniaco nell'arte* (Rome, 1953) and Gerhart Ritter, *The Corrupting Influence of Power* (Hadleigh, Essex,
1952); Friedrich Meinecke, *Machiavellism: The Doctrine of Raison
d'Etat and Its Place in Modern History* (New Haven, 1962); Felix
Raab, *The English Face of Machiavelli: A Changing Interpretation*
(London, 1965); Edwin Greenlaw, "The Influence of Machiavelli on
Spenser," *Modern Philology* 7 (1909): 187–202; Greenlaw, *Studies in
Spenser's Historical Allegory* (Baltimore and London, 1932), chap. 4;
and more general, Mario Praz, *The Flaming Heart* (New York, 1958),
90–145. On political foreknowledge, Robert Orr, "The Time Motif
in Machiavelli," *Political Studies* 17 (June 1969), no 2, 145–59.

king is the one appointed by god to rule as king-in-parliament, "the Tudor answer was pragmatic: whoever happens to be recognized as king."[8] Such also is Jove's right of conquest. It joins hands with an undefined "eternall doome of Fates decree" on the one hand, and parliamentary consent on the other. For modern readers this may seem an untidy arrangement; the myth of "king-in-parliament" remains, however, an arrangement that worked for the Tudors because they managed to give it a messianic aura, though its trials were not over at the death of Elizabeth;[9] indeed its pragmatism left open a number of extremely dangerous issues of constitutional order.

In the Mutabilitie Cantos the sovereignty of Nature is subject to a yet higher law, that of the eternal Christian God, under whom a settled pyramid of authority, as it becomes ever more absolute, maintains an ever wider base of contractual obligation. Jove's sovereignty is "mixed," expressing both norm and command. Nature's sovereignty is a perfect expression of reason, since she is the ultimate fecund neutral, both male and female. Only God's authority is absolute, and it causes "the poet's" dreamy wonderment, which we feel in the tonal change occurring in the last two appended stanzas, where the narrator disengages himself from the anonymous, or rather, conventional, account of the trial, withdrawing into his own mental closet, to muse upon what he has envisioned. He sees that the attack of Mutabilitie is a defiance of the secure fortresses of order.

More important, her first items of evidence are random, jagged mutations in the natural world: men and beasts fighting and enthralling each other (as she would enthrall all nature), storms and upsets of calm in every realm, shifts of races—"the

8. G. R. Elton, intro. to J. N. Figgis, *The Divine Right of Kings* (1914; repr. New York, 1965), xxiv.

9. On the messianic ruler: *The New Cambridge Modern History*, vol. 2, *The Reformation*, 441–50; A. P. D'Entrèves, *The Medieval Contribution to Political Thought* (Oxford, 1939), 95–116; also, on Hooker, 117–42; E. T. Davies, *The Political Ideas of Richard Hooker* (London, 1948), 1–26.

fish, still floting, doe at randon range"—wild quarrels of times, of seasons, of elements, of events. This flux is change according to chance and *fortuna,* and as such it is the most tyrannical change, being the most unpredictable. But then, though she does not realize what has happened, the great peripeteia occurs, and Mutabilitie becomes the "victim of a vast dramatic irony."[10] Proud and blind to her own illogical disposition, Mutabilitie brings forward the pageant of the seasons to prove a general mutability, and this evidence destroys her case. Such seasonal forms of cyclical revolution do not uphold the claim of change as random alteration. Quite the contrary. Ritual change is circular and thus perfect, and its revolutionary form is one of "dilation," a term meaning the continuing fulfillment of the idea of a thing. There are forces of disruption in the march of the months, with their apparent lusts and pleasures, but these, like all of Nature's children, "doe worke their perfection so by fate." The natural elements "doe their states maintaine," and while the poem has reached the verge of cosmic extension precisely here, its word "states" throws the judgment of Dame Nature back into the primitive political vocabulary which was basic to the trial in the first place.

Broadly then, the Cantos have defined what Hawkins calls a "hierarchy of powers." Highest is Nature's surrogate providential sway—she speaks for the eternal God in human and natural terms, her sapience being the knowledge of "heavenly beauty." Beneath her rule is Jove's sovereign power, a cosmic destiny, ritually apparent in the cycles of nature, symbolizing and maintaining a princely court of order and rebirth. The lowest rule, whose power Spenser cannot deny, works in a spirit of rebellious opposition to Jove. Mutabilitie controls through accidents, random exertions of the personal will, fickle Machiavellian *fortuna.*[11] Her Titanic, indeed Satanic, energy is not with-

10. Sherman Hawkins, "Mutabilitie and the Cycle of the Months," in William Nelson, *Form and Convention in the Poetry of Edmund Spenser,* 87.

11. Machiavelli, *Discourses on Livy,* 1.9. See Bertrand de Jouvenel,

out its tragic grandeur, and all those changes in man's estate which are wrought through his will-driven *virtu* possess the same grandeur If it is correct to associate Mutabilitie's domain with the rule of Fortuna, then these cantos may be said to show the limits of man's creativity as a political being. He will create at random, if, following Mutabilitie's lead, he rebels against custom. Rebellion will change things, but will not achieve their continual rebirth. The life principle lies elsewhere, in the rolling courses of natural recurrence, and only by attaining to harmony with that recurrence will the prince escape from profane time.

The Proem to Book V speaks of the heavens' "revolution," but Spenser does not suggest that the "rowling" motion spells death and decay—on the contrary, it is the original and true order of the universe. Human political disorder is given astrological causes in the disruption (the *anakuklesis*) of this original, ordered, circular motion.[12] Time and a planetary wandering have made "contrarie constitution / Of all this lower world, toward his dissolution." The tone of this proem is vaguely ironic, but so also is the tone of the Mutabilitie Cantos, perhaps because each work seeks to portray a divine comedy and each is colored by Renaissance doubt and melancholy. Spenser must write in an ambivalent political and ideological climate, where

---

Sovereignty, 48. See G. R. Levy, *Religious Conceptions of the Stone Age* (original title *The Gate of Horn*) (New York, 1963), pt. 4, chap. 2, "Mythical Foundations of the Mainland Cities"; Levy, *The Sword from the Rock: An Investigation into the Origins of Epic Literature and the Development of the Hero* (London, 1953); Martin Braun, *History and Romance in Graeco-Oriental Literature* (Oxford, 1938), chap. 1—in all these works a contrast is drawn between the constructive and the destructive act.

12. Alexander Koyré, *From the Closed World to the Infinite Universe* (New York, 1958), 163–71. On *anakuklesis*, Fowler, *Spenser and Numbers*, 42, 192 ff.; F. R. Johnson, *Astronomical Thought in Renaissance England* (Baltimore, 1937). Pope Gregory XIII had reformed the calendar in 1582 to correct the retrogradation of the equinox. "Wandered" in V, Proem, 4:7; 5:5, is a technical term for planetary shifts, Greek *planetes* meaning "wanderer."

the term "revolution" is not yet fixed in its modern political sense of the complete overthrow and replacement of an established form of government. This terminological shift seems to have begun seriously to occur only after 1660, or perhaps not until after the Glorious Revolution of 1688.[13] Before this the term seems more neutral and more likely to connote regular movement around an axis, the absolute, as opposed to relative, motion which is created by rotation around a point. In Drayton's phrase this movement is "kindest revolution" (*Endimion and Phoebe*, 382). Hooker (V, lxx, 9) gives the Sabbath as an instance of a "revolution," this being a newly established form of recurrent "perpetual homage" to God, following the Old Testament law of Moses, but now fixed by Christ according to the New Law. The term "revolution," therefore, does not during this period suggest the violence and novelty of political upheaval, though one glimpses the later meaning in its first ambiguous stages of formation. Rather, revolution suggests those movements of the planets and seasons which Mutabilitie sought to enlist as evidence for random change, but which turned out to prove the absolute motion of eternal Natural Law. "Revolt," on the other hand, early has its modern sense of insurrection or rebellion, so that an overtone—a potentiality for violent disorder—touches even the idea of circular return.[14] "Whatever is good,"

13. See Merritt Hughes, *Ten Perspectives on Milton* (New Haven, 1965), "Milton as a Revolutionary," 240–76. The typological is a revolutionary mode, and in this sense Milton the archetypal revolutionary poet: See Northrop Frye, "The Typology of *Paradise Regained*," in *Milton: Modern Essays in Criticism*, ed. A. E. Barker; Frye, *The Return of Eden*; also Harold Bloom, *Blake's Apocalypse* (London, 1963), chap. 5, "Revolution and Prophecy," and chaps. 11–12, on Milton and Jerusalem; David Erdman, *Blake: Prophet against Empire* (Princeton, 1954).

14. OED gives 1560 as first date for "revolt," 1600 for the modern sense of "revolutions." Shakespeare, who uses "revolt" often for rebellion ("The king is merciful, if you revolt," etc.), seems to confine the

Nelson has said in connection with the Cantos, "is not simply good but by its very nature potentially evil."[15]

Rebellion, we conclude, is an act of disruptive self-assertion whereby hostile forces align themselves with social unrest or political disaffection. As such, rebellion promises violence, novelty, temporary improvements in social life; it promises, but may not achieve, a permanent reconstitution of political order. Only when rebellion shifts into genuine revolution does this remaking of order occur. At that moment rebellion, as such, must die. Speaking of the French Revolution, Arendt has written: "If foundation was the aim and end of revolution, then the revolutionary spirit was not merely the spirit of beginning something new but of starting something permanent and enduring; a lasting institution, embodying this spirit and encouraging it to new achievements, would be self-defeating. From which it unfortunately seems to follow that nothing threatens the very achievements of revolution more dangerously and more acutely than the spirit which has brought them about. Should freedom, in its most exalted sense as freedom to act, be the price to be paid for foundation?"[16] No exit from this puzzle is suggested by Book V, but the threat itself is abundantly documented in

---

sense of "revolution," which he uses only four times, to mean a complete circuit or oscillation. Thus, *Henry IV, Part II*, III, i, 45–53:

> O God! that one might read the book of fate,
> And see the revolution of the times
> Make mountains level, and the continent,—
> Weary of solid firmness,—melt itself
> Into the sea! and, other times, to see
> The beachy girdle of the ocean
> Too wide for Neptune's hips; how chances mock,
> And changes fill the cup of alteration
> With divers liquors.

15. Nelson, *The Poetry of Edmund Spenser*, 304.
16. Hannah Arendt, *On Revolution* (New York, 1963), 235.

its myths of daemonic political energy seeking change and then requiring to be held in bounds.

The two phases of rebellion and revolutionary foundation, like the two kinds of banditry, remain theoretically if not always practically distinct from each other. During the Elizabethan era, for a civil servant like Spenser, spending much of his active life in Ireland, the chance of a successful transition from the first to the second phase seems unlikely, and he attacks the revolutionary-looking Egalitarian Giant because he believes such rebels cannot achieve the foundation they promise to their followers. As for the other rebels in Book V, they are unambiguously tyrannical. Yet even so, Spenser knows philosophically that revolution itself is benign—he after all is trying to defend the Protestant Reformation.

Truth informs genuine revolution, according to the biblical typology of the marriage of Redcrosse and Una, and once again the archetype of rebellion as the demonic parody of revolution may be discerned in the Mutabilitie Cantos. Mutabilitie champions error because her policies, her enthronement "on high," would pervert the natural processes of renovation. These natural changes, symbolized most fully and persuasively in the Gardens of Adonis and the Marriage of the Rivers, are the benign metamorphoses that we found basic to Ovidian typology. Spenser never asserts that human life is free of death and time, but only that death and time may be redeemed by the wedding of Love and the Soul, and thus "brought back" to a degree of ideal perfection through the Ovidian transformations occurring in the Gardens of Adonis. Their mutability is patterned on the death of Christ, which is the change of changes, the basis of the Transfiguration. Yet even this complete and absolute mode of translation is subject to the errors of demonic parody. As an *imitatio Christi* may be an *imitatio Diaboli*, Mutabilitie asserts her "right to rule," not to increase the general sense of cosmic justice and community of love, but to alienate men and creatures and things from each other. She would deny the sacred community implicit in the Ovidian-Christian vision; she would deny that

> ... so all things excellent begin,
> And eke enrooted deepe must be that Tree,
> Whose big embodied braunches shall not lin,
> Till they to heavens hight forth stretched bee.
>
> (III, iii, 22)

This templar image, grounded in Christ's statement "I am the vine and ye are the branches," gives the correct idea of a just stability, and it is made organic—that is, capable of Ovidian-Christian metamorphosis—in the famous lines of Book III:

> That substance is eterne, and bideth so,
> Ne when the life decayes, and forme does fade,
> Doth it consume, and into nothing go,
> But chaunged is, and often altred to and fro.
>
> (vi, 37)

The sacred world tree with its ever-renewing leaves and widening branches presents a sort of paradox, of the kind we have already met, in the conjunction of the ideas of cyclical and linear time. To counter the despotism of linear time Spenser adduces two higher laws: the final sovereignty of the Eternal God of Sabbath Sight, and the immediate and present reality of anagogic vision, that fourth sense of meaning which opens a window on our wandering experience of life. This experience, hopefully, is to be continually reborn. "The New as restoration involves a problem; although it is restoration, it is *in process*; thus, it is always ambivalent, a mixture of essential fulfillment and non-fulfillment."[17] The logic of this mixed condition is a generation

17. Paul Tillich, "The Importance of New Being for Christian Theology," in *Man and Transformation*, ed. Joseph Campbell (New York, 1964), 166. I believe my argument is in substantial agreement with the position taken by Harry Berger, Jr., in "The *Mutabilitie Cantos:* Archaism and Evolution in retrospect," in his *Spenser: A Collection of Critical Essays*, on "new being" and truth; G. B. Ladner, *The Idea of Reform: Its Impact on Christian Thought and Action in the Age of the Fathers* (Cambridge, Mass., 1959), 138–43.

from opposites, a roughly Platonic process of endless rebirth from contraries.

Error then is the unredeemed experience of this process, and throughout the Mutabilities Cantos and the rest of *The Faerie Queene* images of the burning heat of the desert, or the wasteland, are the facades of error in an unredeemed world. The equation of the benign vision with a vision of life, or organic process, thus puts a heavy burden on all images of growth and sexuality, and to these, as we shall see, Spenser devotes special care in his mythography of rebellion.

Betrayal: Origins of Injustice

THE DEMONIC PARODY of the hero's naïve equity when he first establishes the rudiments of a natural justice, like the demonic parody of any other radical good, has to go very deep for its source. Among the myths of the origins of injustice a poet can draw on, perhaps the most primitive is the myth of betrayal. According to such a myth, the first crime is a betrayal, and all attempts to create broad injustices are violations of trust. Dante expresses this principle in the structure of his Inferno, where the deeper and more terrible the crime, the greater the violations of the bonds of man and God. The lesser crimes break no basic confidence. At the pit of hell, on the contrary, God has imprisoned traitors, the foulest betrayers. Crime in that system is proportional to the degree of deceit, or, in another formula, to the degree that force is united with and strengthened by fraud.[18] The latter, in order to achieve its end, presupposes initial trust, and it is exactly such trust that struc-

18. See on "force and fraud," Jane Aptekar, *Icons of Justice*, passim. Joseph Mazzeo, *Renaissance and Seventeenth-Century Studies* (New York and London, 1964), 90–144, shows the sequence of thought linking Dante and Machiavelli. See also A. H. Gilbert, *Dante's Conception of Justice* (Durham, N.C., 1925).

tures the crimes of the rebel against the state. In Book V Spenser treats at least three violations of trust as types of treason: in the trial of Duessa, the judgment of the Egalitarian Giant, the defeat of Radigund. In each case the poet assumes that treason is *radically* subversive.

In his *Primitive Rebels* Eric Hobsbawm has shown that the common end of the social bandit's relatively short career is "by betrayal."[19] This can be explained socially and economically as a result of his relation to those whom he would help; the peasantry will protect him against the police, but by the same token they can betray his unwritten security. On the other hand, one senses that the betrayal has a tragic dimension not quite covered by the historian's deterministic account; the betrayal comes partly from an envious response to the social bandit's hubris and

---

19. E. J. Hobsbawm, *Primitive Rebels*, 14: "Oleksa Dovbush, the Carpathian bandit of the 18th century, was betrayed by his mistress; Nikola Shuhaj . . . by his friends. Angelo Duca (Angiolillo), c. 1760–84, perhaps the purest example of social banditry, of whose career Benedetto Croce has given a masterly analysis, suffered the same fate. So, in 1950, did Salvatore Giuliano of Montelepre, Sicily, the most notorious of recent bandits, whose career has lately been described in a moving book (G. Maxwell, *God preserve me from my friends* [1956]). So, if it comes to that, did Robin Hood himself. But the law, to hide its impotence, claims credit for the bandit's capture or death: the policemen shoot bullets into Nikola Shuhaj's dead body to claim the kill, as they did, if Gavin Maxwell is to be believed, into Giuliano's. The practice is so common that there is even a Corsican proverb to describe it: 'Killed after death, like a bandit by the police.' " In connection with Talus it seems important that "the peasants in turn add invulnerability to the bandit's many other legendary and heroic qualities. Angiolillo was supposed to possess a magic ring which turned away bullets. Shuhaj was invulnerable because—theories diverged—he had a green twig with which he waved aside bullets, or because a witch had made him drink a brew that made him resist them; that is why he had to be killed with an axe. Oleksa Dovbush could only be killed with a silver bullet that had been kept one year in a dish of spring wheat, blessed by a priest on the day of the twelve great saints and over which twelve priests had read twelve masses."

magnificence. The fact that bandit and social bandit are almost indistinguishable should alert us to the tragic causes of betrayal. A purely human failure may underlie the more systematic structures by which betrayal creates radical injustice. There is a suggestion, for example, that in his history plays Shakespeare was creating what Frye has called "tragedies of order," through the extensive treatment of a hubristic pride which drives men to follow and then to betray their leaders.

Before examining the three cases of betrayal in Book V, we should also consider the general question of the rebel's "right" to betray his sovereign (the so-called "right of rebellion"). In so doing we shall discover that in a political arena we can ascribe complete trustfulness and trustworthiness to no single party. Spenser here is quite like Shakespeare, who has to assume the status quo of the Tudor establishment, though this assumption introduces complications in the history plays where our sympathies are strongly for Hotspur and the other rebels—especially after we have heard Falstaff describe the cold-blooded cruelty of Prince John of Lancaster; similarly in Book V, many readers feel sympathy for Duessa/Mary.[20] But this is exactly the

20. Perhaps Irving Ribner is too strict in his reading of Tudor policy when he says that "Tudor doctrine [as instanced by Cheke's *Hurt of Sedition*] held unequivocally that no subject had the right to judge the king and certainly not to refuse to serve him on the basis of his judgement." The complication arises only because this doctrine always was countered by a strong propagandist aim of making the sovereign into an object of love as well as service in the modern sense. "Service," in the medieval sense, implied love. Ribner continues: "Yet that is precisely what Macduff does. There is no evidence in *Macbeth* that Shakespeare accepted without reservation the Tudor doctrines of divine right and passive obedience to tyranny. What evidence we have seems to indicate that his long consideration of the subject had led him finally to quite contrary conclusions." *The English History Play in the Age of Shakespeare*, 259. The point is: the Tudor line forced equivocation upon any serious person who thought about obedience, and Shakespeare's dramatic medium permitted him to show all the complexities of feeling that were possible under Tudor and Stuart rule.

point: by Spenser's time the revolution of government under the Tudors has to be assumed, taken for granted politically; it is a fait accompli. The successful rebellion of Henry VII (which led to his victory at Bosworth Field in 1485) has turned into a rightful revolution. It was blessed by divine providence; so it has assumed the mantle of Astraea, and will enjoy the rightful harvest.

Where Book V is problematic, it shows that new rebellions may seek to undo an achieved harmony (Tudor or other), and it casts two sorts of doubt on the possibility of these latter-day rebellions achieving the status of the revolutionary cycle. First, the ideal new state may of itself propose an evil plan, so that its stability, once found, will be a tyranny of some kind. Second, the process of reaching that final stability, even if it might be thought inherently desirable, would initially entail such political chaos that the state could not survive the transition. In practice this second claim against rebellion as the road to revolution might well come first for Elizabethan politicians. Of the numerous attempts, realistic or fantastic, at unseating the reigning monarch of England during this century, few could claim to have a very stabilizing effect or purpose; few aimed at more than the replacement of the monarch by another ruler more suited to the rebel's religious allegiance. English Reformation politics were rarely untouched by religious issues, particularly since Spain and Rome could not afford to let these alone. Burghley himself, in his *Execution of Justice in England*, claimed that Her Majesty's Government persecuted "none that savour not of treason," no matter what their religious views, but he probably said this because he wanted it understood that religious views could easily lead a man into treasonous ways he originally did not intend but for which, by law, he could be apprehended and executed. The dangers of disobedience were everywhere apparent to Protestant advisers to the queen, particularly after the papal bull of 1570, which excommunicated her and called upon her Catholic subjects to rebel against her. Burghley saw clearly that "this bull was the ground of rebellion in England and Ireland," and that "so many as should have obeyed that wicked warrant . . . should have been in their hearts and consciences secret traitors."[21] Under such a strain it was only natural that Elizabeth's government made obedience to the Crown the cornerstone of all its policies. Even though Elizabeth might permit men their privacy of conscience, her government assumed their absolute political loyalty.

The history of Elizabeth's reign reads like one long, recurrent cycle of spy stories. Twice in Book V Spenser shows that one requirement of political betrayal was political deception. From the moment when, in 1574, the Jesuits decided to support the Douai mission to England, the Commons were instructed to believe that such spies were "creeping into the howses and familiaryes of men of behaviour and reputation, not only to corrupt the realme with false doctrine, but also under that pretence to stir sedition."[22] Sedition required spying, and in the

21. Conyers Read, *Lord Burghley and Queen Elizabeth* (New York, 1960), 251–54. The relevant Second Treasons Act (13 Eliz. C.2 [1571]) appears in *Crown and Parliament in Tudor-Stuart England: A Documentary Constitutional History*, ed. P. L. Hughes and R. F. Fries (New York, 1959), 113–16. Burghley's tract is available as a good modern text: Robert M. Kingdon, ed., *The Execution of Justice in England* [by W. Cecil] and *A True, Sincere, and Modest Defense of English Catholics* [by William Allen] (Ithaca, 1965). For background to these pamphlets, see Thomas G. Law, *A Historical Sketch of the Conflicts between Jesuits and Seculars in the Reign of Queen Elizabeth with a Reprint of Christopher Bagshaw's 'True Relation of the Faction begun at Wisbich' and Illustrative Documents* (London, 1889), i–cxxvii.

22. Mildmay's speech in the Commons, 25 Jan. 1581, quoted in Stanford E. Lehmberg, *Sir Walter Mildmay and Tudor Government* (Austin, Texas, 1964), 193. Sir Thomas Elyot, in *The Boke of the Governour*, III, vi, had argued the connection of treason and betrayal: "That which in Latin is called *Fides* is a part of justice and may be diversely interpreted, and yet it finally tendeth to one purpose in effect. Sometime it may be called faith, sometime credence, other whiles trust [and as the latter involve equity law]. Also in a French term it is named loyalty. And to the imitation of Latin it is often called fidelity. All which words, if they be entirely and (as I might say) exactly

persons of Dolon and Malengin Book V represents this source of political error. Dolon comes from the *Iliad* originally, perhaps through Boccaccio. In Greek the name means "fraud" or "craft"; as the latter it is applied to Odysseus. In the *Iliad* Dolon is a spy who loses face in the heroic scale of honor by assuming a disguise.[23] In Book V he tries to waylay Britomart on her journey to rescue Sir Artegall from Radigund's false law.

Curiously, the name Dolon has more refined legal connotations. In law there is a concept of *dolus malus*, deliberate fraud, which is always an attempt to undermine good faith. Furthermore, in Roman law "the spirit of *aequitas* is opposed to *dolus malus*, and the form of *dolus malus* is *subtilitas*, or adherence to the strict letter of the law, in order to make it the means of an unscrupulous advantage. The essence of the wrong complained of is not that it is illegal, but that it is too legal."[24] This description perfectly accounts for Sir Artegall's entrapment by Radigund, as we have seen. Here the allegory (in the order in which we read it, after the entrapment has taken place but before Britomart rescues Sir Artegall) implies that, unlike Sir Artegall, Britomart can *experience* the error of *dolus malus* in an experimental fashion so that, unlike him, she will not fall into the trap of excessive legalism.

---

understood, shall appear to a studious reader to signify one virtue or quality, although they seem to have some diversity. As believing the precepts and promise of God it is called faith. In contracts between man and man it is commonly called credence. Between persons of equal estate or condition it is called trust. From the subject or servant to his sovereign or master it is properly named fidelity, and in a French term loyalty." Elyot entitles the chapter, "Of faith or fidelity, called in Latin *fides*, which is the foundation of justice."

23. *Iliad*, X, 345 ff. W. B. Stanford, *The Ulysses Theme: A Study in the Adaptability of a Traditional Hero* (New York, 1964), 13, says that when the term *doloi* is applied to Odysseus, it means simply "devices," and is neutral in tone; "To become derogatory it needs a pejorative epithet," e.g., *dolus malus* as opposed to *dolus bonus*. See Stanford, chap. 2, n. 17.

24. C. K. Allen, *Law in the Making*, 5th ed. (Oxford, 1962), 379.

Similarly, on a more intense level, before Sir Artegall can assist at the trial of Duessa, or even perhaps enter Mercilla's court, Talus has to destroy Malengin. Dolon had been "a man of subtill wit and wicked minde,/ That whilome in his youth had bene a Knight," who with his three wicked sons had devised "full many treasons vild." The four are plainly conspirators, one of them, Guizor, perhaps identifiable as the same Duke of Guise who engineered the Saint Bartholomew's Day Massacre. Unlike them the "wicked villaine" Malengin, who appears to be identified with the renegade Irish who resisted the Elizabethan governors and troops, turns into a monstrous chthonic embodiment of the principle of deceit itself. Spenser calls him "Guyle," and we learn that his lair lies at such "a dreadful depth, how deepe no man can tell;/ But some doe say, it goeth downe to hell" (V, ix, 6). Like other deceivers Malengin is light, quick, "smooth of tongue, and subtile in his face." Commenting on the fact that "the character of Malengin and his methods of attack resemble those of the Irish kerns and galloglasses, as they appeared to their English enemies," Gough continues, "there is an unconscious irony in the selection of the most atrocious chapter in English history as an example of the virtue of justice."[25]

The irony is compounded, however, if we draw back to a larger perspective on the example. We learn that to catch Malengin Artegall himself uses guile, sending the maiden Samient ahead to lure Guyle into the open. In his cave, Malengin is "ugly as sin," like Duessa stripped, and he appears to be a travesty of a good pastor; he is also a false "fisher of men" (ix, 11). He has a "guileful pype" to charm the birds with, and he catches his prey with a net. The poem attains a sinister delicacy when, having distracted Samient's "intentive mind," Malengin throws the net over her head "like a puff of wind." What follows has suggested the malign powers of Proteus the shape-shifter. To evade capture, Malengin turns himself successively into a fox, a bush, a bird, a stone, a hedgehog, and finally a snake.[26] This meta-

25. *Variorum*, 5:233.
26. The chain of images parallels the style of statutes against trea-

morphic chain leads at last to Satan, who like a snake indeed "goeth down to hell." Yet Talus can overtake the serpent, and his flail can break its bones "as small as sandy grayle." The sequence follows the type of cosmogonic myth making so common in Spenser, whereby the origin of an evil is sought in a natural process exaggerated to the last degree. What had been technical deceit with Dolon is here rendered on an archetypal basis, with Malengin the monstrous epitome of espionage and guile. The allegory has to precede the meeting with Mercilla, who is a "most sacred wight, most debonayre and free," because absolute justice can only be reached after the experienced trial of a contrary absolute, which, we find, is not force, but fraud. Force cannot betray; fraud can. Ironically, Book V shows that Artegall can betray Britomart.

One thing results if betrayal is the ultimate origin of injustice: the basis of justice in trust is a metaphysical basis, opposed to the physical basis in police force. If injustice radically comes from or through betrayal, then injustice is subject not primarily to police correction but to a reformation of thought about the natural bonds of society. Such is the theory Spenser holds. The obvious emphasis on treason in Book V has often been called the bias of an Establishment poet. But it follows directly from a theory independently valid, both as political or human truth and as poetic truth.

---

son (as of other complex crimes) where, typically, we get the following: "and such compasses, imaginations, inventions, devices, or intentions or if any of them shall maliciously, advisedly, and expressly utter or declare by any printing, writing, ciphering, speech, words, or sayings, or if any person or persons whatsoever . . . shall maliciously, advisedly, and directly publish, declare, hold opinion, affirm, or say by any speech, express words or sayings, that our said Sovereign Lady Queen Elizabeth during her life is not or ought not to be Queen of this realm of England and also of the realms of France and Ireland . . ." (SR, IV, 526: 13 Elizabeth, c.1), quoted in Hughes and Fries, *Crown and Parliament*, 114a. The coverage of terms, of course, follows usual legal "form."

Duessa's Trial: Testing the Legal Code

THE IDEA OF LEGAL TRIAL is the foundation stone of the law as codified justice, for, without testing, such justice would remain imprecise in its statute form. Duessa (or some figure like her) has to appear in Book V to permit the myth of testing the code. Mythistorically, of course, since she is a figure of Mary of Scotland, she enters the poem for more obvious reasons. Conspiracies surrounding Mary Stuart, using her, with or without her knowledge, were a continuing source of political instability, which led eventually to her execution—it would appear, against Elizabeth's personal wishes. Duessa's trial blames lust for causing the treason, that is, it blames a perversion of love. If Malengin deceived by sleight of hand, Duessa deceives by her beauty, a beauty and charm possessed by Mary herself. Duessa anticipates the Delilah of Milton, and her crime is more terrible than that of Malengin. Dupes of the latter are "foolish"; of the former, accomplices in "vyld treasons, and outrageous shame" (ix, 40). Spenser accuses Duessa of seeking to overthrow a royal throne so that she might get the crown herself "and triumph in their blood, whom she to death did dryve."

The case against Duessa is so complete as to be unbelievable except in the overheated context of a treason trial. *Zeal* and *Kindomes Care* begin the proceedings:

> Then gan Authority to her to appose
>   With peremptorie powre, that made all mute;
>   And then the law of *Nations* against her rose,
>   And reasons brought, that no man could refute;
>   Next gan *Religion* gainst her to impute
>   High Gods beheast, and powre of holy lawes;
>   Then gan the Peoples cry and Commons sute,
>   Importune care of their owne publicke cause;
> And lastly Justice charged her with breach of lawes.
>
>   (ix, 44)

What seems superogatory, when crowded into the space of a single stanza, needs to be justified as the "analysis" of a typical Elizabethan response. The prosecutor Zeal, who seeks to "aggravate the horror of her blame," simply talks the language of his time (and doubtless of our time as well). Treason is not murder; not blasphemy; not madness; not betrayal of all that is good; not seditious libel; not subversion of the law—but all these combined. Treason is supercrime; as the defender of the state against traitors, Talus is supercop. Pity, respect, threats, honor, and grief have nothing to do with such a level of absolute criminality. Thus, in a sense, we might question whether this degree of rebellion against the right is a mode of error. Strictly speaking, Duessa, a queen, cannot be a rebel; but her cohorts in the allegory, Murder, Sedition, Incontinence of Life, Adultery and Impiety, are all rebels against one mode of discipline or another. She therefore is served by rebels, and we do need to relate her crime to the idea of error. Perhaps only on the highest level, as analogue to the Fall of Man and his "first disobedience," can the relation be drawn. There is some warrant for this in the stress laid on Duessa's adultery.[27] That her lovers Blandamour and Paridell are the Earls of Northumberland and Arundell may or may not be true, but in the bond between lust and treachery, as between love and loyalty, there is a poetic truth which Shakespeare's *Hamlet* later attempted to dramatize. The prosecutor presents only the standard rhetoric for displaying this truth. His arguments versify what had been heard from every pulpit in England in the Homily of 1571, *Against Disobedience and Wil-*

27. On charges of adultery against Mary Queen of Scots, see J. E. Phillips, *Images of a Queen*, 43–48, 64–65, 70, 83, 89–95, 201–2. See also John Bruce, ed., *Letters of Queen Elizabeth and King James VI of Scotland* (London, 1849), 37–49. Elizabeth refers to the Babington conspiracy (1586) as a plot to murder her, a design that "rose up from the wicked suggestion of the Jesuits" (38). In defending the execution of Mary, Elizabeth speaks of her own "long danger" and the "bloudy invention of traitors handz," "sinister whisperers," and "busy troblars of princis states" (44–45; Letter of about 1 Feb. 1586–87).

ful Rebellion: "He that nameth rebellion, nameth not a singular and one only sin, as in theft, robbery, murder and such like; but he nameth the whole puddle and sink of all sins against God and man, against his prince, his country, his kinsfolks, his friends and against all men universally; all sins, I say, against God and all men heaped together, nameth he that nameth rebellion."[28] This is propaganda, and with the commination of rebellion goes another homiletic prediction that "ye shall not find that God ever prospered any rebellion against their natural and lawful prince."[29] Underlying all this rhetoric against revolt is a firm belief that disruption of the state is a mortal sickness, caused by a political "poison." Rebellion's source lies in the sinful soul and infected will of man, and mythographically the model source is the poisonous entrails of the Dragon Error or the "puddle of contagion" left by the destruction of Geryoneo's monster, or

28. Sermon III, quoted by J. W. Allen, *Political Thought in the Sixteenth Cenutry*, 132. The danger of rebellion is capital in the sense that every large-scale rebellion implies that the "legitimate" government is a tyranny. Therefore much controversy is spent on the right to revolt against tyranny, e.g., Juan de Mariana, *De rege et regis institutione*, chap. 6, considers "whether it is right to destroy a tyrant." Davies, in *Political Ideas of Hooker*, 22, holds that none but the Anabaptists allowed private persons to rebel. Thus Cranmer, in his "Sermon on Rebellion," quoted by W. S. Hudson, *John Ponet: Advocate of Limited Monarchy* (Chicago, 1942), 123: "Hearken, and fear the saying of Christ, *He that taketh the sword shall perish with the sword*. To take the sword, is to draw the sword without the authority of the prince. For God in his Scriptures expressly forbiddeth all private revengeing, and hath made this order in common weals, that there should be kings and governors, to whom he hath willed men to be subject and obedient." On Althusius' development of a doctrine of resistance to tyranny see C. J. Friedrich, *The Philosophy of Law in Historical Perspective*, 63–65; *Politics of Johannes Althusius*, ed. Carney, chap. 38, "Tyranny and its remedies."

29. Sermon IV, Allen, *Political Thought*, 132. In Sidney's *Arcadia* (1590) Evarchus says that the lives of Pyrochles and Musidorus were "contaminated with so many fowle breaches of hospitality, civility and virtue." *Prose Works* of Sir Philip Sidney, 4:383.

the "pond" of blood pouring from the body of Grantorto. Such images credit rebellion with the power of infecting the body politic, and associate it with labyrinths of watery and earthly chaos, with Lerna and Stygian Lake.

The precise technique of rebellion involves at least three forces: war and violence, fraud and treachery, envy and rumor. Earlier in the century Elyot's *Governor* had held that of all injuries that which is done by fraud is most horrible and detestable, not in the opinion of man only, but also in the sight and judgment of God. For unto Him nothing may be acceptable wherein lacketh verity, called commonly truth, He Himself being all verity."[30] And early in the following century Sir Francis Bacon was to maintain that libels, licentious discourses against the state, "false news often running up and down to the disadvantage of the state," were all the evil preludes of seditions to come. Following Vergil, who related evil fame to lusts of the giants, Bacon continued: "Seditious tumults and seditious fames differ no more but as brother and sister, masculine and feminine."[31] For Spenser the equivalent views are couched in terms

30. Elyot, *Boke of the Governour*, III, iv. One gets an idea of the tone of those times from the correspondence of Matthew Parker and Sir Nicholas Bacon (*Correspondence*, ed. John Bruce [Cambridge, 1853], 60–61), in 1559: "At my last being at London, I heard and saw books printed, which be spread abroad, whose authors be ministers of good estimation: the doctrine of the one is to prove, that a lady woman cannot be, by God's word, a governour in a Christian realm. And in another book going abroad, is matter set out to prove that it is lawful for every private subject to kill his sovereign . . . if he thinks him to be a tyrant in his conscience, yea, and worthy to have a reward for his attempt." And Parker adds: "what lord of the council shall ride quietly minded in the streets among desperate beasts?" Machiavelli saw clearly enough that the prince would be both feared and loved, if successful, but that "of all princes, it is impossible for a new prince to escape the reputation of cruelty, new states always being full of dangers"—and he quoted the *Aeneid* to support the view.

31. Essay, "Of Seditions and Troubles." Bacon observed that an ominous "equality" of times was propitious to rebellion. "Shepherds of people had need know the calendars of tempests in state; which

of biblical typology: "wicked driftes of trayterous desynes, / Gainst loyall Princes . . . all this cursed Plot."

Duessa, like Mary in Elizabeth's own crude verses, is "the daughter of debate," the whore of Ate who is "glad of spoyle and ruinous decay." Everywhere in *The Faerie Queene* human behavior is intermeshed with the uses of language; the poem is eternally critical in this sense, but here, through the concept of seditious libel, Spenser expresses the most practical results of symbolic action. He shares the view expressed in the *Arcadia*, where the rebels are identified as a wave of disruptive noise; among other things, they are "an unruly sorte of Clownes whiche lyke a vyolent flood were carryed, they them selves knewe not whether . . . like enraged beastes." Suddenly, while Philisides sings an echo song to Dorus, "the horrible Cryes of

---

are commonly greatest when things grow to equality; as natural tempests are greatest about the *Equinoctia*. And as there are certain hollow blasts of wind and secret swellings of seas before a tempest, so are there in states." This evil equinox is a demonic parody of the true *kairos* of Book V, where, as Fowler has tried to show, the episode in the Temple of Isis marks an equinoctial celebration, which draws together several main themes. "In the first place, the equinox is a supreme cosmic example of Equity. The 'like race' of the luminaries is run, we are told, in *equal* justice. The natural laws of compensation invoked by Artegall find here their grandest manifestation, in the balancing of night and day, winter and summer . . . a just proportion is maintained. Secondly, from a schematic point of view, the equinox expresses the nature of the zodiacal signs allotted to Book V, Virgo and Libra. Virgo is the constellation in which the autumnal equinoctial point actually lay in Spenser's time, while the sign Libra, more directly, is the 'equall divider of the Day and Night.' Thirdly, the symbolism comprehends Britomart's Minervan role: as guardian of Aries, Minerva was known as the 'ruler of the equinoctial circle.' Finally, since the precessional period and the *annus magnus* are one and the same, the equinox is an earnest of the eventual return of the Golden Age of justice. Britomart's commitment to equity and justice at Isis Church, which gives rise to the dream of a new political era, rebuts the superficial meaning of the poem, but confirms its deeper implication." *Spenser and Numbers*, 219.

the madd multitude gave an untymely Conclusyon to his passionate Musick." Finally, it is with noise, the perversion of fair
speech, that their revolt begins: "There was no matter theyre
eares had ever hearde of, that grewe not to bee a Subject of
theyre wyny Conference. . . . At lengthe the Princes person fell
to bee theyre Table talke, and to speake lycencyously of that,
was a tickling poynte of Corage to them, a proude worde did
swell in theyre stomackes, and disdaynefull reproches to great
persons had putt on a shadowe of greatenes in theyre little
myndes: Till at lengthe the very unbrydeled use of wordes having increase fyer to theyre myndes (whiche thoughte theyre
knouledg notable bycause they had at all no knouledg, to Con-
dempne theyre owne wante of knowledge) they discended to a
direct myslyke of ye Dukes living from among them."[32] Cleophila bravely diverts the rebels from their violent onslaught by
wielding their antithesis, which is not armed force, but eloquence;
with her fine words and argument she persuades them to rally
to the Duke and turn on their own most obdurate leaders. Persuasion, the ancient Greek *peitho*, is the humanist ideal in politics and thus here and in Spenser is opposed to rebellion, which
begins as "the Confused Rumor of a mutinus multitude." This
is an age of instant political scandal, *le bruit qui court*, fostered
by pamphleteering, ballad making and plain talking. Shakespeare
is not unusual in presenting his chorus, Rumor, as a Blatant Beast
who rides out to fill men with the motives of rebellious acts:[33]

> Upon my tongue continual slanders ride,
> The which in every language I pronounce,

32. I quote from the *Old Arcadia*, reprinted in Sidney, *Prose
Works*, 4:120–21. The rebellion in Arcadia is worked into Book II
of the *New Arcadia* (1590), where Cleophila becomes Zelmane, and
where, although her speech to the rebels is elaborated, the chief change
seems to be an increase of detail in the realism of identifying the rebels
as persons and graphic stereotypes, and in realizing the character of
Zelmane herself.

33. *Henry IV, Part II*, Prologue, Act I.

Stuffing the ears of men with false reports.
I speak of peace while covert enmity
Under the smile of safety wounds the world.
And who but Rumor, who but only I,
Make fearful musters and prepared defense
Whiles the big year, swoln with some other grief,
Is thought with child by the stern tyrant war,
And no such matter? Rumor is a pipe
Blown by surmises, jealousies, conjectures,
And of so easy and so plain a stop
That the blunt monster with uncounted heads,
The still-discordant wavering multitude,
Can play upon it. But what need I thus
My well-known body to anatomize
Among my household? Why is Rumor here?

In the Globe Theatre? In England? In the discordant wavering multitudes of all men? Chronicling rebellion, Book V, like the *Henry* plays, must account for the failure of truth in demagogic politics. There is always in such works a half hidden commentary on the relation of poetry to propaganda, and on the relation of true law to the wandering of "false reports."

The Egalitarian Giant: Shaking the Foundations

After laws had been codified, the myth of justice saw them growing into customs of acceptance and enforcement and true record. Antithetical attacks upon justice would strike precisely at the law as a stabilized system, and this is exactly what happens in the virtuoso debate between Artegall and the Giant. The Giant boasts, Artegall reasons, and each makes rhetorical appeals to a theory of distributive justice. Artegall defends the stable foundations of law by an appeal to ancient writ. Some readers have associated the Giant with the antinomian sect of Anabaptists, and yet his radical primitivism is of wider scope than theirs. He has a large following of ignorant simple folk and is "admired much of fooles, women, and boys." The vulgar mob hovers round his giant shape, certain in their "great expectation," "for well they hoped to have got great good, / And wondrous riches by his innovation." He is *for them* a social bandit with chiliastic aims promising them a golden age of plenty and wealth, which will come when their former rulers are destroyed as tyrants. The Giant betrays his followers even more fearfully than he upsets the state. The allegory may reflect the memory of Munster under the cruel reign of John of Leyden, a wild sequence of events, the subject of a major episode in Nashe's *Unfortunate Traveller* and a familiar theme in conservative tracts. The Anabaptists of Munster had shown themselves exceptional even for their own sect; they were not merely rebels against property rights and the world of the flesh; they became the passionate victims of their own radical leaders.[34] It may be that Anabaptism influences the Giant's discourse, and perhaps we are meant to associate his drowning with their rebaptism, through a ferocious travesty of the sacrament. But the important point for our interpretation of justice and history is to grasp the main form of the Giant's expectations. It appears that he has no genuine theory of revolution, and his rebellion is a still born child of mere force.

The Giant argues that the world is awry, which appears to be the poet's own view, as expressed in the Proem. But the Giant argues that *ab origine* the world was "created smooth and round,

34. *Variorum*, 5:336–45, F. M. Padelford, "Spenser's Arraignment of the Anabaptists"; Norman Cohn, *The Pursuit of the Millennium* (New York, 1961), chaps. 10, 11, 12; R. H. Bainton, *The Reformation of the Sixteenth Century* (Boston, 1952), chap. 5; F. H. Littell, *The Origins of Sectarian Protestantism* (New York, 1964). As A. G. Dickens, *The English Reformation* (New York, 1964), 236, observes: "So-called Anabaptists can be found to represent Arianism, Socinianism, Pelagianism, Manichaeism, Docetism, Millenarianism, mysticism and communism. Their varied programmes embrace almost every imaginable reform from pacifism to polygamy."

like a ball or an egg,"[35] and now ought to be leveled to give all men their equal share of wealth, of "treasure," Bacon's fourth pillar of the state. The Giant dislikes the course of nature, and his reforms would remake Natural Law. He does not believe that this law is eternal, and he misunderstands the basis for a just distribution of wealth, which is, according to ancient and Elizabethan thought alike, proportional rather than egalitarian. The hierarchical principle supposes an uneven, hilly distribution of goods, because on that scale not all men are of equal merit, and their ownership must be always in ratio to their true, essential properties. This relationship between real property and a man's self as the aggregate of his "properties" may not be as clear here as in Dante, where the thieves are horribly metamorphosed, to show their unnatural redisposition of property, but nevertheless Spenser would say that the final stage of the egalitarian rebellion would be to change man's nature itself. And this God forbids, through natural law. Most of Artegall's argument follows the familiar lines of *Lex naturae*, but as we have already seen with the Mutabilitie Cantos, Spenser allies natural law with the "soveraine power" of God, which ordains that law. The Giant thus must be revolting against God, since he wants to remake the cosmos. If only he were right, we might call him a transcendental social bandit. But at that level of change Spenser wants to have nothing to do with him. This is rather the demonic parody of social banditry, raised to a cosmogonic plane. Like Mutabilitie, who also sought justice, the Giant rebels against a constitution authority which is already coherent, logical, and legitimate. His success similarly would lead to tyranny, although perhaps not into Mutabilitie's continuous state of rebellion masquerading as genuine revolution.

Of the many objections to the Giant's program the one that concerns us here is his attempt to rewrite the history of the world, to accelerate the slow ordering and unfolding of time as

35. Nelson, *Poetry of Spenser*, 258.

a variegated fulfillment. "Expectation" is the key word for his appeal to the masses, and his millenarian zeal betrays the temporal hoax he would play on them. For he would have them believe that he (not God) can give them a New Jerusalem of their own, a private, treasure-centered utopia, in which the simpler goals of a Robin Hood have been long forgotten.[36] Their hope is not equalization and amelioration—and we should know that Spenser hated poverty—but rather a flattening out of historical time which corresponds to their flattening out of space. They would destroy the process of dilation which Nature had prescribed for Mutabilitie. Acting as if the Giant were God, they would try to encapsulate history, to stop time, to end providence. It is tempting to believe that the simile of Talus chasing the mob, comparing him to a falcon, is a similitude with Christ, but we need not go so far, since the point has already been made that "the base blood of such a rascall crew" has only monstrous progeny. There is no indication that the Giant and his followers understand the

36. Hobsbawm, however, shows that social banditry has a strong millenarian tinge. Lazzaretti, the "Messiah of Monte Amiata," wrote a *Rescritti Profetici*, surrounding his actions by prophetic omens and *predictions* of a better world to come. His death reads rather like that of the Egalitarian Giant. The millenarian predictions have a kinetic effect: "If a sudden vast mass movement could be stamped out of the ground, if thousands could be shaken out of the lethargy and defeatism of centuries by a single speech, how could men doubt that great and world-overturning events would soon come to pass?" *Primitive Rebels*, 64. More broadly, "the kinds of community which produced millenarian heresies are not the ones in which clear distinctions between religious and secular things can be drawn" (66). Finally, millenarianism rises most often when sudden irruptions of new economic and political forces create a rapidly changing climate, against which the old traditional societies are ill equipped to stand. "The irruption of modern capitalism into peasant society, generally in the form of liberal or Jacobin reforms (the introduction of a free land-market, the secularization of church estates, the equivalents of the enclosure movement and the reform of common land and forest laws, etc.) has always had cataclysmic effects on that society" (67).

redemptive history of Christian man, in which good and evil, plenty and poverty, are mixed by divine mystery. For them, as for the older brother, Bracidas, in Canto IV, "tract of time"[37] does not suggest a providential history, whose alterations and dilations are the norm, but only a materialist time span in which total power should give them control over a leveled utopian world.

Mythographically the energy of the allegory derives in part from the underlying theme of a natural interchange between elements. Besides allusion to the elemental giant of Daniel 2, this physical allegory focusses on a war between the land and "the enchafèd flood," present here because of the setting of the scene and the Giant's final shipwreck. The poet returns to this land-sea balance in Canto IV and, more historically, in the allegory of the defeat of the Armada. Even the destruction of the other mob attacking Sir Burbon touches on this theme, since Talus, pursuing the rascall many, "ne ceassed not, till all their scattred crew / Into the sea he drove quite from that soyle, / The which they troubled had with great turmoyle." The rebellious mob and their champions return always to the sea, the chaotic element.[38] If the land is the element where God's providence is manifest more surely, the more so in England's case because she is ringed with ocean, the sea is the province of Fortuna, who is the Giant's guide in his foolhardy enterprise. (The sea is also an infinite ocean of living forms, whose energy needs always to be harnessed, as Troynovant tamed the River Thames.) To this extent, as follower of fortune, the Giant is a Machiavellian *politique*, unscrupulous as he is legalistically argumentative. He acts in bad faith. His program of a millenarian age of gold for himself and his friends is an attack on Christian revelation.

37. Cf. *Paradise Lost*, V, 498: "improved by tract of time."

38. W. H. Auden, *The Enchafèd Flood; or the Romantic Iconography of the Sea* (New York, 1967), especially chap. 1, "The Sea and the Desert." Also, for the Christian traditions of this iconography, D. C. Allen, *The Legend of Noah*, 1–91, passim.

Radigund: Betrayal of Chivalry

THE ULTIMATE BOND of society in the ceremonial
Spenserian narrative is "heroic love," and the tyranness Radigund,
by perverting the ideal of loyal service and devotion, is giving
chivalry over to the forces of chaos. She is repeatedly identified
with Fortune (and the Moon), and Artegall's submission to her
is Fortune's victory. It is a Machiavellian defeat. To the extent
that chivalry is the poetic system of "historical ideals" which
subtend the actual political life of this period, the attack upon
chivalry subverts justice on the plane of propaganda and ideological rhetoric. Radigund would "give a bad name" to the
chivalric ideal.

Sexual meanings are primary in this section of the poem, and
they unite Artegall's heroic quest with his personal destiny as
the lover of Britomart. The crime is rape, the victim a man instead of a woman. Another woman must punish Radigund, to
conform to the Herculean pattern of retaliation, and the final
design of this rescue is to restore the family to its proper balance.
Politically speaking, the hierarchically ordered family is the
Natural Law model of the state (and gives the up-to-date Bodin
one model of sovereignty, following patristic lines), and in this
arrangement the female must be subordinate. Again the rebellion in the *Arcadia* provides a revealing parallel. Addressing the
rebels, Cleophila says not a word about their rebellion in itself
until she has disposed of the obvious fact that she is a woman.
"With a brave unabashed Countenance" she begins her speech:
"An unadvysed thinge yt is, and I thincke, not heretofore seene,
O *Arcadians*, that a woman shoulde give Counsell to men, a
Straunger to the Contrey people, and that lastly in suche a
presence a private person as I am shoulde possess the Regall
throne? But the strangenes of youre action makes that used for
vertue, whiche youre vyolent necessity imposeth, for certeynly
a woman may well speake to suche men, who have forgotten

all manly government."[39] During this period the presence of women on European thrones gives Cleophila's speech and Spenser's allegory a special point. Primarily, however, sexuality enters the political poem because it is a main interest of chivalry, whose laws parallel the good laws of custom; here Artegall, shorn of his manhood, is equally shorn of his knighthood. Finally, from Britomart's position, owing to her role as justiciar—chastity itself being a kind of temperance and sexual prudence—the allegory must show her relation to her own violence, namely the potential Radigund in her, so that she may experience this violence and reject it for her ultimate marriage to an Osirian lover. Because the poem must demonstrate that secrecy and privacy are not identical, that justice and private conscience coincide, its allegory of love allows the poet to show how Radigund employs deceit to gain her unjust ends, sharing the guile of Dolon and Malengin. Treachery begins at home. One victim is Sir Terpine, whose name suggests turpitude. One gloss on this episode might be the remark of Sir Edward Coke at the Norwich Assizes: "Partialitie in a Judge is a Turpitude, which doth soyle and staine all the action done by him." In the debate between lust and discipline the Herculean hero must choose the harder road, nor can he, like Sir Burbon, blame his own case on the "forgerie" of female beauty. Such beauty is a natural gift, to be used well or ill, but never denied its place in nature. When the Vergilian hero fails to discipline himself, like Artegall in responding to Radigund, he loses the benefit of his own power, which has to harmonize with his epic fate.

Book V may thus be seen, from one angle, as a narrowing cone of myth whose broadest circle is the whole physical universe, bound by natural law, whose narrowest, in microcosm, is the family unit, and then, even more radically, the male-female relation. This narrowing of a mythos of justice to the erotic sphere is entirely in accord with Ovidian typology, where heroic *eros* must always play a major dynamic role. But, as I have noted,

39. Sidney, *Prose Works*, 4:123.

it also accords with the legalistic practice of statutes against treason, which insist that it is natural for subjects to "love" their sovereign. A further virtue of focusing political myth in this way is the fact that, by so doing, the poet makes Christian and Pagan myth coherent, since not only Augustine and Aquinas, but Hesiod and Plato also, could regard love as the force by which a divine mover supported life in the universe. Then, in the Dantesque manner, the definition of treason as betrayal of trust provides a human analogue to the cosmic rebellion.

Rage: Ambiguous Energies of Culture

THE MERE FACT that the social bandit and culture-bringing hero are full of the energy to create gives them a corresponding liability: they may destroy with that same energy. We find a disturbing similarity between the psychology of rebellion and that of culture bringing. Spenser, vitalistically, psychologizes the sources of rebellion by identifying them with a primitive, or at least classical, notion of fury (*mania*). All rebellions are competitions between rival forms of charisma, but at the heart of Book V, in the middle of the Temple of Isis, Spenser shows how such a rivalry may be structured on a deeper level. Rebellion must have energy—*virtu* of some kind—and conversely the aim of justice and order will be to contain energy. Love is an energy of state, but of disorder and rebellion the energy is rage. It may take many forms, pride, lust, wrath, envy, fanaticism, madness, but in all forms its main characteristic is fury. Rage is a revealing term. It implies fury and impetuous violence, the madness of the mad dog (and Englishman?). Whence there derive more interesting senses: the term has overtones of dreaming (through the Middle French, *resver*) and more obviously with raving. There is in every rage a delirium that puts the rabid mind out of touch with reality, though it may leave him with an ecstatic truth of vision. Thus, as with other notions of power treated by *The Faerie Queene* (or the *Orlando Furioso*, for that matter), energies of this nature are not so different from benign energies: to dream may be good or evil, and only the prophet can tell the difference.[40] For him alone is rage the demonic parody of the fair dream of love. The aged nurse Glauce can reassure Britomart that her "raging smart" is normal enough, but only a seer could interpret Spenser's dream of the origins of rebellion, that curious digression about earth, wine, and the Titans' blood, which we read just before we are told that Britomart and the priests of Isis sleep on the ground beside the altar of the Goddess.

> For other beds the Priests there used none,
>> But on their mother Earths deare lap did lie,
>> And bake their sides uppon the cold hard stone,
>> T'enure themselves to sufferaunce thereby
>> And proud rebellious flesh to mortify.
>> For by the vow of their religion
>> They tied were to steadfast chastity,
>> And continence of life, that all forgon,
> They mote the better tend to their devotion.

> Therefore they mote not taste of fleshly food,
>> Ne feed on ought, the which doth bloud containe,
>> Ne drinke of wine, for wine they say is blood,
>> Even the bloud of Gyants, which were slaine,
>> By thundring Jove in the Phlegrean plaine.
>> For which the earth (as they the story tell)
>> Wroth with the Gods, which to perpetuall paine
>> Had damn'd her sonnes, which gainst them did rebell,
> With inward griefe and malice did against them swell.

40. Orlando's madness, in the *Furioso*, is both a cause and a condition of error, e.g. "ch'in questo inferno tormentandosi erra" (XXIII, 990); "Pel bosco erro tutta la notte il Conte" (XXIII, 993)—Harington rendered the latter line, "Thus wandering still in ways that have no way . . ." The same translator renders "furore" as "rage." In Shakespeare rage is usually the hot, dry passion of anger, but he knows of the Maenadic rage, e.g., *Midsummer Night's Dream*, 5, 1, 49.

> And of their vitall bloud, the which was shed
>> Into her pregnant bosome, forth she brought
>> The fruitfull vine, whose liquor blouddy red
>> Having the mindes of men with fury fraught,
>> Mote in them stirre up old rebellious thought,
>> To make new warre against the Gods againe:
>> Such is the powre of that same fruit, that nought
>> The fell contagion may thereof restraine,
> Ne within reasons rule, her madding mood containe.
>
> (V, vii, 9–11)

As we should expect with a moon goddess, Isis gets her power from the earth; her priests lie at night on the earth mother's lap, which suggests their sexual service to her—a travesty, since they are copied from the eunuch priests of the Syrian Goddess, whose name, *galloi*, may connect them with Artegall.[41] They lie on the ground to mortify their "proud rebellious flesh," a phrase with Pauline overtones, though it also implies something like political ambition. When they swear allegiance to the cult of chastity, this allows a higher marriage to take place. As Christ was married to the Church, in apocalyptic symbolism—for example, the apocalyptic reading of the Song of Songs—so these priests are married to "steadfast chastity and continence of life."

The strange thing here is that the *aitia* of justice and rebellion are but two facets of the same myth of an original gigantomachia. Dionysus pacifies the East, but his wine stirs up maenadism and "rebellious thought." Myth presents us with a crossroads, like the crossroads where Hercules is said to have paused before finally choosing the active, heroic, stoical life. The giant, the bandit, the male aggressor, call him what we will, can either become the enemy or the friend of the gods. But as their enemy he allies himself with the earth, often with the original furies, the female deities of earth and night. The "old rebellious thought" of the Titans is stirred by the draught of "liquor blouddy red," and this

41. *Variorum*, 5:214–20.

connects Bacchus with rebellion. Wine and the bacchic mood raise the man's pride, but they take away his manhood. They distort the manly purpose. Thus in the *Arcadia* Cleophila had been able to shame the rebels for misusing their "manfull weapons" and their "valyant mens Corages," for having "forgotten all manly government." Sidney had been careful to detail the origin of the rebellion in Arcadia, and his account squares with the vision in Book V, Canto vii: "But, before I tell yow what became thereof, mee thinckes yt reason yow knowe what raging motion was the beginning of this Tumulte: *Bacchus* (they say) was begotten with Thunder, I thinck that made hym ever synce so full of sturr, and debate, *Bacchus* in deede yt was wch sounded the first Trompett of this rude Allarum, a Maner the *Arcardians* had, to solempnize the Princes byrthe dayes with banquetting together."[42] The rebels gather at a ceremonial feast: "As largely as the quality of ye Company coulde suffer a barbarus opynion to thincke, with vyce, to doo honor, or with activity in beastlynes to shewe abundance of Love. This Custome beeyng general . . . there beeyng chafed with wyne," the rebels began their "wyny Conference," shouting and railing, since "Raylings was coumpted the fruite of freedom." We have seen that Sidney's fable ascribes the rebellious act to a misuse of speech; but we could go further, to say that here, as in Spenser, rebellion is a kind of madness, brought on by a rage which in its original form is bacchanalian. The strength, the enthusiasm, the creative energy, and the excess of the social bandit have to be taken together in a cluster. One result of the bacchic *aition* of justice is that it must share the dangers of a bacchic *aition* of rebellion, and this in turn means that the hero may court the subversion of his own manhood, a large measure of which is his prudence and self-control. Hercules' imprisonment by Omphale, Artegall's by Radigund, Samson's by Dalilah, Antony's by Cleopatra—all require the hero's loss of masculinity. For this reason, when Britomart recovers from her battle with Radigund (a duel replete with suggestive erotic dou-

42. Sidney, *Prose Works*, 4:120.

ble entendres), and after she has rescued her lover from his misplaced obedience, she reestablishes the bond of justice and male dominance:

> For all those Knights, which long in captive shade
>> Had shrowded bene, she did from thraldome free;
>> And magistrates of all that city made,
>> And gave to them great living and large fee:
>> And that they should for ever faithfull bee,
>> And them sweare fealty to *Artegall*.
>> Who when him selfe now well recur'd did see,
>> He purposed to proceed, what so be fall,
> Upon his first adventure, which to him forth did call.
>
> (V, vii, 43)

Britomart has earned the ritual adoration due to Isis and in her Isiac purity can restore male Osirian rule, having established her own sphere of power, which is the guardianship of sexual innocence. Through her chastity she can preserve chivalric fealty, which holds a promise of fertility. Again we come to this conclusion rather as the heroine and hero come to it, after error and experiment, after learning the destructive side of the psyche, after identifying the forces of social and political disruption with that destructive side.

The Fall Into History:
Undercutting the Imperial Ideal

TIMELESS CYCLES OF GROWTH promise an eternal return. But empire is built, and in historical time, so that the tragedy of empire is its affirmation of eternal cities, the sun never setting, while that very affirmation is being made *in* history. History surrounds, and man as imperial hero is trapped "within the compass of a pale." Spenser, however, shared the Christian beliefs that could salvage something from this grim view. Potentially he could hold that the energies of rebellion were, under providence, of good use. Like Milton after him, Spenser in *The Faerie Queene* exploits the necessity of error, including the notion that with the *felix culpa* man entered human historical time. In arguing that throughout the Mutabilitie Cantos Spenser's principal concern is less with the polar abstractions of "the purely dark" and "the purely bright," but with "the real world lying between them," Nelson has well observed that the Cantos intend to define a significant *present:* "The cosmos before Mutabilitie's foolish exchange of wrong for right and death for life, and Arlo Hill before Faunus' fatuous pursuit of forbidden knowledge provide the standard by which the state of the present may be known. Similar reference points are to be found in each of the books of *The Faerie Queene*, realms free of the evil and darkness which perturb and obscure this life. The unsullied state is Eden before the Old Dragon besieged it, the golden world in which Astraea dwelt, Belphoebe's pavilion and the Garden of Adonis, the glorious history of Fairyland about which Guyon reads in the House of Alma, the Acidalian Mount, or, vaguely, that 'antique age yet in the infancie / Of time' when 'loyall love had royall regiment' (IV, viii, 30). The happy states may be Biblical, chivalric, poetic, or philosophic in inspiration; they are alike in that they are neither the unchanging serenity of heaven —that is, the New Jerusalem—nor the dark confusion of the mundane."[43]

Because with the Fall man enters history, a myth of the Fall like the Cantos will inevitably serve the purpose of defining the historicity of error in the temple/error relationship. The prelapsarian *locus amoenus* is always a temple, its fallen state an image of error. Spenser presses his argument in the Cantos toward the elusive problem of the nature of time itself, and he makes mythical sense of this mystery because he doubles the image of error. Two falls occur here, and they both create profane time. Spenser goes out of his way to show that rebellion actually generates history, insofar as history means profane time. At the climax of the

43. Nelson, *Poetry of Spenser*, 302.

trial Mutabilitie invokes an equation between this shape of time and her species of change.

> When these were past, thus gan the *Titanesse;*
>> Lo, mighty mother, now be judge and say,
>> Whether in all thy creatures more or lesse
>> CHANGE doth not raign and beare the greatest sway;
>> For, who sees not, that *Time* on all doth pray?
>> But *Times* do change and move continually.
>> So nothing heere long standeth in one stay:
>> Wherefore this lower world who can deny
> But to be subject still to *Mutabilitie?*
>
>> (vii, 47)

Picking up the irony of the pun on "still," Jove's summing up holds, on the contrary, that

>>> . . . Right true it is, that these
>> And all things else that under heaven dwell
>> Are chaung'd of *Time,* who doth them all disseise
>> Of being: But, who is it (to me tell)
>> That *Time* himselfe doth move and still compell
>> To keepe his course? Is not that namely wee
>> Which poure that vertue from our heavenly cell,
>> That moves them all, and makes them changed be?
>> So them we gods doe rule, and in them also thee.

The debate has reached a plane higher than that on which it began, for now the court must decide whether, besides ruling change, Jove or Mutabilitie rules time. Again, random versus recurrent change will be the grounds of the dispute, and Jove whose sun pours daylight down without intermission will win the argument. While profane time can legally "disseise" sublunar things of their present forms, this metamorphosis does not imply entropy *sub Jovem.* To say that Mutabilitie generates a real debate over time is only to say that her own principle of being implies a theory of time as the dimension of entropy, whereas another theory finally controls her entropic power. This hierarchy appears clearly, humanized and brought down from cold cosmic heights, in the digression of the Faunus episode.

Arlo Hill is not only a very exactly placed setting for the trial of Mutabilitie's treason, but Spenser gives it a curious history in the poem. It had originally been a scene of holiday, where Diana sported and hunted and refreshed herself. It was an Edenic playground, where time was sacred and indeed where the ritually recurrent games of the goddess made the hill her temple. Faunus' rebellion against Diana's privacy contravened the highest taboo which can surround a king or deity, and placed a ban on the sacred space of Arlo Hill, reducing it to a mere historical existence. It fell, as Eden fell, though it could be restored, as Eden might. Its fall is a declension into history:

> Since which, those Woods, and all that goodly Chase,
> Doth to this day with Wolves and Thieves abound:
> Which too-too true that lands in-dwellers since have found.

We are suddenly brought down hard to the Ireland Spenser knew and which he would have hoped to rescue from its own sufferings.

Several patterns of the fall of the *templum* into history were available to an Elizabethan reader, so the fall of Arlo would seem to him typical. The Christian Fall would be the archetype, but Hesiod had described the revolt of the Titans and the withdrawal of Aidos and Nemesis, "with their sweet forms wrapped in white robes," from the company of men. Book V employs a variant on Hesiod, in its depiction of Astraea's withdrawal, the immediate source being Natalis Comes. Coinciding with the loss of an original "shamefastness" or innocence, is man's entrance into the quarrelsome arena of history, the iron age.

Expelled from paradise, man enters profane time. The iconography of this shift is by no means monolithic, but two elements in it seem constant, the primal rebellion against authority, and a fraternal crime of some sort. After the Fall, Cain murders Abel, Romulus murders Remus, Theseus betrays Ariadne (whom Bacchus saves) and causes the death of his father, Aegeus, Shakespeare's Bolingbroke murders Richard by the hand of Exton, who for his crime must now "with Cain go wander through the shades of night." Having projected the fraternal crime onto Exton, Bolingbroke can exclaim with suitably lighthearted gloom: "Lords, I protest my soul is full of woe, / That blood should sprinkle me to make me grow." Later, as King Henry, he will make a promise of pilgrimage to the Holy Land, to wash off the stain of the death of his "brother." That he never actually makes this pilgrimage is a most important fact to Shakespeare, for it means that a curse will hang over the royal house throughout King Henry's reign. Continued rebellion is the legacy of this un-purified "poison." In principle, however, Henry is right to believe that he will die purified and that his rebellious act will prove to be a blessed liberation from tyranny, as he has had to pretend it is.

For King Henry's crime is Romulus' archetypal city-founding crime, whose reason is to put an end to random change and to create a significant history. Artegall is not unlike Henry, in that he too puts down all the competition and he too ends his political career with a strong sense of failure, a yearning to be free of the cares of his political life. The tension, the unfinished shaping, the "threatening influence" of the Blatant Beast, all these premonitions are an acceptance of the curse that hung over the Tudor establishment, the unanswered question: is the monarch's right to rule fixed only because backed by power, or is it genuine right? Book V treats political error as the labyrinth it really is; all Sir Artegall's assertions aside, the Book has presented sufficient material on both sides to indicate the paradoxes of justice and force. Book V recognizes the terrible Promethean joke that men are saved only *after* they are lost, never before. That is the meaning of the equation of error and experience.

V I

The Temple of Truth

he *Faerie Queene* HAS MANY TEMPLES, IN OUR sense of a sacred space where the vision of time is redeemed and clarified. At each "house of instruction" a hero or heroine takes on the power of an archetype: holiness, temperance, chastity, or whatever. Such temples are variously houses, palaces, castles, gardens, islands, theaters, pavilions, sacred mountains, but Book V, Canto 7, goes out of its way to insist that "Isis Church" is a templum by using the exact latinate term, as Book IV had previously spoken of "Great Venus Temple."[1] It is possible that among the various *templa* of *The Faerie Queene* Isis Church most clearly exemplifies the dynamic nature of such images.

Britomart Comes to Isis Church

CANTO VII INCORPORATES two separate but closely related actions: the visit to the Temple of Isis and the defeat of

1. Harry Berger, Jr., "Two Spenserian Retrospects: The Antique Temple of Venus and the Primitive Marriage of Rivers," *Texas Studies in Literature and Language* 10, no. 1 (1968): 8–13.

Radigund. The latter depends upon the former, insofar as through her "strange visions" Britomart is instructed in her sacred destiny, which includes the defeat of the "monstrous regiment of women." The formal invocation to the Temple points to one main theme, the definition of the ideas underlying the concept of right. The invocation looks forward to the sacral nature of the ensuing vision:

> Nought is on earth more sacred or divine,
>> That Gods and men doe equally adore,
>> Then this same vertue, that doth right define:
>> For th' hevens themselves, whence mortal men implore
>> Right in their wrongs, are rul'd by righteous lore
>> Of highest Jove, who doth true justice deale
>> To his inferiour Gods, and evermore
>> Therewith containes his heavenly Common-weale:
> The skill whereof to Princes hearts he doth reveale.
>
> (vii, 1)

Primarily the poet asserts the unconditional, Jovial nature of justice, which exists in a heaven, comprising a source or model for human judgments. Then too the invocation reminds the reader, as had the Mutabilitie Cantos, that the logic of law requires that even in heaven there be a hierarchy of powers, revealed in the ranks of "inferiour Gods." This decorum applies syncretically to the hierarchy of Christian angels and suggests that, granting the typological parallel, there can be no modern democracy in the "heavenly Common-weale." The divine model is a monarchic containment, which, however, by insisting on its own hierarchical structure, insists on a complexity of "inferiour" orders. This is not exactly a monolithic dictatorship. The terms "common-weale" and "Princes" suggest at once the Elizabethan compromise, where the monarch trusts and protects her loyal subjects who in some sense give her a divine providential reason for ruling. Since the justice of Jove is "righteous," it recalls the religious sanctions for political rule accepted throughout this period, and its character as "lore" places the definition of right in a learned context: the dictates of justice are matters of record and true memory. They have a temporal dimension, like the Common Law. Finally, they are a sacred body of knowledge and wisdom; they are handed down to mortal princes through revelation, and like all Christian revelation, handed down only to those whose "hearts" are open. This is not a question of pure intellect and mental decision, but of love and feeling. Only a human heart, in fact, can be the perfect repository of Jove's righteous lore; human justice needs to be conceived in human terms.

> Well therefore did the antique world invent,
>> That Justice was a God of soveraine grace,
>> And altars unto him, and temples lent,
>> And heavenly honours in the highest place;
>> Calling him great *Osyris*, of the race
>> Of th' old Aegyptian Kings, that whylome were;
>> With fayned colours shading a true case:
>> For that *Osyris* whilest he lived here,
> The justest man alive, and truest did appeare.

> (vii, 2)

By adopting the euhemerist tradition that Osiris was originally a man and not a god, Spenser drives his myth into the humanistic sphere where justice takes the form of action. Osiris ruled by what is sometimes called "divine kingship," that is, in a role that fused the human and divine in the single person of the monarch. Men raise altars and build temples to honor the divine king, because he is more than mortal; he has two bodies, one mortal, the other eternal. As always, Spenser's language is here drawn with unobtrusive precision from the matrix of his fable: as the kings of England ruled by "the grace of God," so Osiris in one respect is "a God of soveraine grace." He enjoys the stability of real justice—he speaks *ex cathedra*. But the stanza reminds us that Osiris sojourned on earth only a limited time, after which he was, like Hercules, translated to the heavens. This temporary sojourn marks the specifically typological nature of this myth, for the Osirian rule provided types of all human justice, "with fayned colours shading a true case," so that his semi-divine *umbra* was the Christian or Platonic "shadow of divine things." Only a hero on this model can "appeare" as the "truest" prince. Appearance, conversely, is redeemed by such divine kings, and while the king may live earthbound, dictating human judgments in a mutable world, he shares in the divine every time he enters the temples that enshrine his divine essence. The same human-divine monarchy characterizes the divine queen, Isis, whose partnership with Osiris—derived by Spenser largely from one of the most complex essays in comparative religion composed in antiquity, Plutarch's *Of Isis and Osiris*—besides giving her equal status in rule, gives her kingly consort a divine virtue which Spenser seems clearly to associate with the female, Equity. We learn that Isis too enjoys the worship of grateful mortals.

> His wife was *Isis*, whom they likewise made
>   A Goddesse of great powre and soveraity,
>   And in her person cunningly did shade
>   That part of Justice, which is Equity,
>   Whereof I have to treat here presently.
>   Unto whose temple when as *Britomart*
>   Arrived, she with great humility
>   Did enter in, ne would that night depart;
> But *Talus* mote not be admitted to her part.
>   (vii, 3)

Even the fact that Osiris has a "wife" brings the vision momentarily down to earth; her clemency is attached to "great powre and soveraity." Spenser again touches on his favorite theme of the creativity of thought and action, by remarking that when men contemplate a mysterious being like Isis, they can only "shade" her meaning "cunningly." Britomart meanwhile is responsive to the sacral moment; she is about to be initiated into the Isiac mysteries; her humility is her card of identity, while Talus, rude and opposed to equity by his iron nature, is not even admitted to the temple. Talus would profane the temple.

> There she received was in goodly wize
> > Of many Priests, which duely did attend
> > Uppon the rites and daily sacrifize,
> > All clad in linnen robes with silver hemd:
> > And on their heads with long locks comely kemd,
> > They wore rich Mitres shaped like the Moone,
> > To shew that Isis doth the Moone portend;
> > Like as Osyris signifies the Sunne.
> For that they both like race in equall justice runne.
>
> (vii, 4)

Much has been said about the Priests of Isis, in part because Spenser appears to be toying with the iconography of their appearance, drawing their long hair from a source other than Plutarch, probably to identify them with the *galloi*. Upton's comment was and remains instructive, showing, as always with his sensitive reading, a grasp of Spenserian ambiguity: "Spenser never thinks himself tied down to exactness in minute descriptions: he has an allegory and a mythology of his own, and takes from others just as suits his scheme. Tis very well known that the Aegyptian priests wore linnen robes, (that is, agreeing with Spenser's account) and were bald, quite contrary to what Spenser says, Juvenal 6.533: 'Qui grege linigero circumdatus, et grege calve.' But Spenser does not carry you to Aegypt; you stand upon allegorical and Fairy Ground. He will dress therefore the priests of Justice, like the priests of Him, the assessors of whose throne Justice and Judgement are, Psalms 89:14; 97:2. In the prophet Ezekiel 'tis said (44:20), 'the priests shall be clothed with linnen garments': yet 'tis ordered (44:20), 'they shall not shave their heads (nor suffer their locks to grow long).' The original command seems to intend that a distinction should be kept up between the Jewish and Aegyptian priests even in their dress.

See Leviticus 21:5."[2] This reminds us that the typology of the scene requires a mixture of "Egyptian" hermetic material with the biblical patterns of Old Testament prophecy, and while there are other reasons for identifying the priests as "long haired" and therefore vaguely feminine, Upton's response is initially the right one. The lunar association of Isis must surround her with the glow of female mystery, like that of the Syrian Goddess. Whether we are to imagine the mitred priests as belonging to a perfect Christian sect, the bishops of the primitive church, is perhaps less important than seeing that they serve a goddess hierarchically equal to Osiris. The marked emphasis on the equality of the "race" the two deities run falls where it should, because it defines the rectified error of human wanderings according to a redeemed pattern of "equall justice." "Race" also connotes the astral movement of the heavenly bodies, thus drawing our thought back to the Proem of Book V and forward to the continuing images of the sun, as Arthur enters the poem to aid Artegall, in the defeat of the vicious, burning sun of the Soldan.[3] To run an equal race in this sense means to enjoy the permanence of the revolutions of the starry spheres, and there is some suggestion that equity is, on the highest and most abstracted plane of myth, simply the absolute equation—the marriage—of male and female divine principles. The canto has begun with a reminder that justice stems from a hierogamy.

> The Championesse them greeting, as she could,
>   Was thence by them into the Temple led;
>   Whose goodly building when she did behould,
>   Borne uppon stately pillours, all dispred
>   With shining gold, and arched over hed,
>   She wondred at the workemans passing skill,
>   Whose like before she never saw nor red;

2. *Variorum*, 5:217.
3. Alastair Fowler, *Spenser and the Numbers of Time*, chaps. 5 and 12, on pentadic numerology and the cosmic symbolisms of Book V.

>   And thereuppon long while stood gazing still,
>   But thought, that she thereon could never gaze her fill.

>   Thence forth unto the Idoll they her brought,
>   The which was framed all of silver fine,
>   So well as could with cunning hand be wrought,
>   And clothed all in garments made of line,
>   Hemd all about with fringe of silver twine.
>   Uppon her head she wore a Crowne of gold,
>   To shew that she had powre in things divine;
>   And at her feete a Crocodile was rold,
>   That with her wreathed taile her middle did enfold.

>   One foote was set uppon the Crocodile,
>   And on the ground the other fast did stand,
>   So meaning to suppresse both forged guile,
>   And open force: and in her other hand
>   She stretched forthe a long white sclender wand.
>   Such was the Goddesse; whom when *Britomart*
>   Had long beheld, her selfe uppon the land
>   She did prostrate, and with right humble hart,
>   Unto her selfe her silent prayers did impart.

>   To which the Idoll as it were inclining,
>   Her wand did move with amiable looke,
>   By outward shew her inward scence desining.
>   Who well perceiving, how her wand she shooke,
>   It as a token of good fortune tooke.
>   By this the day with dampe was overcast,
>   And joyous light the house of *Jove* forsooke:
>   Which when she saw, her helmet she unlaste,
>   And by the altars side her selfe to slumber plaste.

>   (vii, 5–8)

During the course of these stanzas the density of imagery increases, and a technique of repetition asserts the governing

concept of Britomart's ritual initiation. In the Vergilian context of her heroic quest she is notably the "championesse" of chaste love, but the tone of the fifth stanza arises out of another concern, Hermetic interest in the artifact of the temple. "Building" here is an admirable mode of existence, drawing attention to the labors of the cunning craftsman, whose "passing skill" creates objects of worship. The gilded ceiling of the temple, "arched over hed," suggests the primitive equation between the "sky-god" Jove and the vault of the heavens, while the pillars of the building (anticipating those of the Mutabilitie Cantos, viii, 2) resemble a colossus bestriding the earth. Yet for Britomart the creative skill that went into making the temple is drowned in her own naïve, innocent religious awe; using the metaphor of thirst, Spenser conveys the idea of assimilating the deity, *l'accueil du divin*. Britomart's awareness ("But thought") that she can never gaze her fill of the sacred space distinguishes her from the contemplative hero;[4] she knows she lives, rightly, in a world of action, and she will never have the occasion to rest long enough to contemplate all the beauty before her eyes.

This rapture steals away all conscious detachment, and Britomart confronts an "Idoll" whose ornamental dress provides the archetype for the dress of the priests, drawing our attention once again to the "cunning hand" of the artist, not only because Spenser wants to distinguish the real from the artificial, but also because he wants to praise the balance of art. This idol making is to be contrasted with the spurious art of the Bower of Bliss; of itself, without recourse to its ethical context, the cunning hand of art will be neither good nor bad. Its ends and uses determine such value, and in this instance the royal, sovereign crown of gold signifies a true locus of justice, like the crown in turreted form

4. Varro, *On the Latin Language* (*De lingua latina*), trans. R. G. Kent (Loeb Classics ed., Cambridge, Mass., 1958), VII, sec. 5–10, gives origins for *templum* and associated terms. He derives *templum* here from *tueri, attueri*, to gaze at, to attend to closely; this idea survives in our *contemplate*. The etymology is false. Varro opposes *templum* to *tesca*, or desert.

that appears in the Cartari image of Cybele.[5] The hollow crown is a microcosmic fortress.

More puzzling to the commentators, and of greater moment, is the iconography of the Crocodile. In terms of the allegory of power this beast is directly glossed in stanza 7, where its abasement stands for the suppression of "forged guile, / And open force," those twin repressive powers demanded by Machiavelli's *The Prince*. If the prince is to succeed, he must use both powers (as Artegall does), and must know how to control them. Here the difference is that a goddess, a female deity, is in control; and although for the moment we learn only that Isis, through the image of her divinity, acts this role, we are soon to ascribe a surrogate control of force and fraud to the heroine Britomart. So far the allegory speaks only of Isis' power over the crocodile, and ascribes it with traditional political symbolism to her scepter-like wand. The term "wand" soon picks up stronger political overtones, but for the moment it lifts the scene into a magic circle. Thaumaturgy belongs with the concern for art working, because art and magic in the Hermetic tradition are cooperative activities. Without any incongruity, the "inclining" of the Idoll resembles science fiction, and the reader is drawn into an atmosphere of oracles and omens. Like a delphic sybil, the idol nods amiably, "by outward shew her inward sence desining"—and once again Spencer repeats a contrast between outward, aesthetic appearance and inner truth. The word "desining," which could so easily have sinister overtones, here is curiously reassuring, owing to its unexpected application to the movements of the Isiac oracle. Britomart's good fortune, thus forecast, shares in the benignity of the Idol's designs.

During this brief scene of adoration the behavior of Britomart tells us again that she is a creature of action, whose prayers are silent. She abases herself on the ground and easily goes to sleep on the ground. She is at home here; on other occasions she had refused to unlace her helmet. The unlacing points graphically to the

5. Fowler, *Spenser and Numbers*, plate 16a.

nature of the experience: for Britomart this is an initiation into her womanhood. In the chaste presence of the priests, at the side of the altar, she reveals the only sign that she is a woman, her beautiful long hair. Even the word "slumber" comes in to render the calm of her mind, drowned already in its own astonishment. As the light goes out in the greatest temple, Jove's House, the lesser Temple of Isis darkens and sleep returns to the earth. We have already examined the *aition* of rebellion that surges from the depths of the scene at this moment; the abstinence of the priesthood, so readily shared by Britomart, admits the connection of the Isiac cult with "mother Earth," and complicates the lunar symbolism of Isis. Yet this is normal to such myths—lunar deities are always tied closely to myths of terrestrial powers, as the female herself is tied to the symbolism of earth. Over and over in these three ensuing stanzas the poet drives home the paradoxical nature of the Herculean-Dionysian archetype. The castration of the *galloi*, models of the Spenserian priests, with their vaguely female costume, reminds us that rage and lust are the forces that bring about the Ovidian flux of metamorphoses, which must be tamed in a Pythagorean asceticism. Yet what the priests achieve imperfectly through their withdrawn self-discipline, Britomart achieves apparently by nature.

> There did the warlike Maide her selfe repose,
>> Under the wings of *Isis* all that night,
>> And with sweete rest her heavy eyes did close,
>> After that long daies toile and weary plight.
>> Where whilest her earthly parts with soft delight
>> Of senceless sleepe did deeply drowned lie,
>> There did appeare unto her heavenly spright
>> A wondrous vision, which did close implie
> The course of all her fortune and posteritie.
>
> (vii, 12)

The vision specifically foretells the heroine's prophetic destiny, including the fate of her "posteritie," that is, her own heroic children and their progeny. At precisely this moment, therefore, we shall expect the heaviest concentration of typological modalities. The poet will compress into four stanzas the whole prophetic history of Britain, and for his purposes every matrix will contribute its share to the poetic language.

> Her seem'd as she was doing sacrifize
>   To *Isis*, deckt with Mitre on her hed,
>   And linnen stole after those Priestes guize,
>   All sodainely she saw transfigured
>   Her linnen stole to robe of scarlet red,
>   And Moone-like Mitre to a Crowne of gold,
>   That even she her selfe much wondered
>   At such a chaunge, and joyed to behold
> Her selfe, adorn'd with gems and jewels manifold.
>
> (vii, 13)

Something very remarkable and subtle is occurring here: we might call it the crossing from one mental state into a deeper state, from waking to dream. Spenser is almost systematic in his adherence to ideas of appearance, vision, and seeming, to indicate the wondrous sight that constitutes the prophetic moment in its purest form. We move from the drowsy slumber "under the wings of Isis," the brooding wings of peace that lasts "all that night," and gradually we enter a transition phase of consciousness (or so Spenser imagines the inception of the dream, for he does not initially speak of the end of the dream and its "flight into the unconscious"). During this transition phase the vision only "seem'd" to Britomart; it appears to her *as if* something strange were happening to her; her dream is a prophetic similitude only. Its import is complete transfiguration, but when Britomart is depicted as wondering at "such a chaunge," we are led to believe that the dream comes to her with such force that she imagines she is awake, seeing the Transfiguration of herself from the garb of priestess to the enrobed splendor of the Goddess. She appears to herself as if she were a figure in a masque, as the words "all sodainely" indicate, the phrase being a commonplace of masque and pageant. Her apotheosis is objective and impressive;

only its mode of revelation is enigmatic, and that fact leads to the ensuing need for priestly interpretation of her dream. But in the meantime (with some misgivings) we may say that the vision occurs *somehow*, by a masquing magic, and it lifts the heroine into a storm of truly templar dimensions.

> And in the midst of her felicity,
>> An hideous tempest seemed from below,
>> To rise through all the Temple sodainely,
>> That from the Altar all about did blow
>> The holy fire, and all the embers strow
>> Uppon the ground, which kindled privily,
>> Into outragious flames unwares did grow,
>> That all the Temple put in jeopardy
> Of flaming, and her selfe in great perplexity.
>
> With that the Crocodile, which sleeping lay
>> Under the Idols feete in fearelesse bowre,
>> Seem'd to awake in horrible dismay,
>> As being troubled with that stormy stowre;
>> And gaping greedy wide, did streight devoure
>> Both flames and tempest: with which growen great,
>> And swolne with pride of his owne peereless powre,
>> He gan to threaten her likewise to eat;
> But that the Goddesse with her rod him backe did beat.
>
> Tho turning all his pride to humblesse meeke,
>> Him selfe before her feete he lowly threw,
>> And gan for grace and love of her to seeke:
>> Which she accepting, he so neare her drew,
>> That of his game she soone enwombed grew,
>> And forth did bring a Lion of great might,
>> That shortly did all other beasts subdew.
>> With that she waked, full of fearefull fright,
> And doubtfully dismayd through that so uncouth sight.
>
> (vii, 14–16)

We may properly begin a brief comment on these central stanzas of the whole of Book V by observing that they rest on a bad pun —Britomart is "dismayd" because, although she is troubled and distraught by her dream, she is deflowered in that dream. This perfect instance of Spenser's crucial bad puns will alert the reader to the odd, puppeteering tone that animates so many of the poet's great moments. By joking in his rustic way, he alleviates the excessive tension and anxiety implicit in his omens of destiny.

The stanzas move Britomart from a state of slumbering, delicious, self-absorbed "felicity" through the experience of sexual intercourse to childbirth. "Felicity," from the obscure root that produces *fela* (the breast), and *female*, is a peculiarly rich word here, and cannot fail to recall the ambivalence of the *felix culpa*, and such remote images as the *Arabia felix*, the milk giving paradise opposed in myth to the *Arabia Deserta*. Felicity is the enjoyment of grace, theologically considered, and this too is a ground from which the vision proceeds.

A hint of masquing arises in the phrase "from below," but more important is the play on *tempest* and *temple* which structures the meaning of Britomart's sacred impregnation. For she will not give birth to the Lion of England without divine life being breathed (inspired) into her. The wind of the holy fire and tempest has power, that is, the sheer power, to destroy; it is "outrageous" with the same rage that animates the proud makers of all things, a rage that can destroy and must be transformed into the "blessed rage for order." On the other hand, the fire "kindled privily," by which perhaps the poet means that it is a secret flame proper to a celebration of the mysteries. It belongs to the sacred precincts of the temple. This meaning would appear to be justified by Spencer's sources, where the cult of Isis articulates a secret female mystery. The fire, from the perspective of Vergilian prophecy, is the vestal hearth fire of the Virgin Astraea, while within the biblical tradition Spenser is recollecting his earlier prefiguration: the "housling fire" kindled at the marriage of Una and Redcrosse (I, xii, 27). The fourteenth stanza gathers some of its momentum from a threatening equation of temple and tempest, and by the ninth line Britomart's perplexity reflects a real danger to the sacred shrine; the same sacred time that gives the shrine its permanence in change also structures the sudden coming of the storm, which is an ominous tempest, of the kind Shakespeare uses to frame the action of his play. *The Faerie Queene*, like other major mythological works, had begun with such a storm, the tempest that drives Redcrosse into the Wood of Error. A similar threat occurs here, and yet here we are led directly from the threat of the tempest to the contained blessing of the sacred enclosure. Though the Temple is put in jeopardy —that is, threatened with division, as well as danger—something about it prevents the storm from devouring the *templum*. This something is surely the fact that inside the temple there is a hierarchy of powers larger than any forces nature can put forward, while the tempestuous wind, "from below," from the realm of the Eumenides, is the archetype of imprisoned chthonic forces. The fact that hierarchy reigns here finally overcomes the heroine's perplexity; otherwise we might say of her, as of Redcrosse, God help the man so wrapt in error's train. Yet the bower is "fearless," and the storm wakes the Crocodile, who now becomes more and more the symbol of masculine sexuality.

Stanza 15 raises questions about the meaning of the Goddesse's (Britomart's) rod, but it begins with a clearly sexual use of the image of eating. The Crocodile, like the helical serpent of the prophet Serapis, impregnates the goddess with the sacred breath of life, which he can devour; he can take in both heat and spirit, "both flames and tempest."[6] He takes in the tempest. Having as-

6. The crocodile is richly dowered with symbolic meanings: deceit, wisdom, eternity, prophecy are among its attributes. Besides Jane Aptekar, *Icons of Justice*, see W. M. Carroll, *Animal Conventions in English Renaissance Non-religious Prose (1550–1600)* (New York, 1954), 97, for a summary of attributes culled from prose sources. With Herodotus (II, 69) Plutarch (*Isis and Osiris*, 381.75) held that "the crocodile, certainly has acquired honour which is not devoid of a plausible reason, but he is declared (by the Egyptians) to be a

similated the natural life force, he then, fascinated by the scepter of the Goddesse, turns gently to her and in their "game" plants the sacred seed, an inspired breath, in her body. The rough implication seems to be that the creation of the Temple, that is, its perfectability through the marriage of its fertile female deity and her felicity, depends first upon the intaking of the tempestuous sexual rage. Without this rebellious male force, no procreativity. Very soon the word "game" is to recur, when Britomart rescues her wandering lord from Radigund's prison, and accuses him of playing a wanton "Maygame." For that demonic parody of the act of love, this is the true form, and here notably the male force is much the more powerful, much more in need of restraint and containment. But here, too, disciplinary containment has the only shape that can be benign—"she soone enwombed grew." Growth takes place in a matrix, and the Spenserian ideal of the restraint of power is always at bottom a species of impregnation, as his notion of truth is always that of a sacred troth or copulation.

The fearful response of Britomart to her own dream is naturalistically one of the finer things in Spenser, and entirely in accord with his usual finesse when dealing with states of consciousness. Less learned in iconographic lore than Spenser's readers, she wants to reveal her melancholy doubts to the High Priest. We withdraw with her from the inner, intellectual realm of the dream temple, into the larger rooms of the new day, lit by the sun "up-lifted in the porch of heaven hie." (17:4) She tells her dream to the High Priest, "as well as to her mind it had recourse," and he in turn is equally astonished,

> And with long locks up-standing, stifly stared
> Like one adawed with some dreadfull spright.
> So fild with heavenly fŭry, thus he her behight.
>
> (vii, 20:7–9)

---

living representation of God, since he is the only creature without a tongue; for the Divine Word has no need of a voice." Loeb Classics ed., Plutarch's *Moralia*, V, 173.

This weird "stowre" recalls the fainting fit of Merlin when he foresees the time of Elizabeth, and recalls to us that what for Britomart is only a dream, to the interpreter is a prophetic vision, which he proceeds to explain to her:

> Magnificke Virgin, that in queint disguise
>   Of British armes doest maske thy royall blood,
>   So to pursue a perillous emprize,
>   How couldst thou weene, through that disguized hood,
>   To hide thy state from being understood?
>   Can from th' immortall Gods ought hidden bee?
>   They doe thy linage, and thy Lordly brood;
>   They doe thy sire, lamenting sore for thee;
> They doe thy love, forlorne in womens thraldome see.
>
> The end whereof, and all the long event,
>   They doe to thee in this same dreame discover.
>   For that same Crocodile doth represent
>   The righteous Knight, that is thy faithfull lover,
>   Like to *Osyris* in all just endever.
>   For that same Crocodile *Osyris* is,
>   That under *Isis* feete doth sleepe for ever:
>   To shew that clemence oft in things amis,
> Restraines those sterne behests, and cruell doomes of his.
>
> That Knight shall all the troublous stormes asswage,
>   And raging flames, that many foes shall reare,
>   To hinder thee from the just heritage
>   Of thy sires Crowne, and from thy countrey deare.
>   Then shalt thou take him to thy loved fere,
>   And joyne in equall portion of thy realme:
>   And afterwards a sonne to him shalt beare,
>   That Lion-like shall shew his powre extreame.
> So blesse thee God, and give thee joyance of thy dreame.
>
> (vii, 21-23)

At this explanation Britomart is relieved and goes forward on her mission, having rewarded the priests with "royall gifts" for their goddess. By this time, since in her own dream she became the goddess, she is able to reward *herself* in her complete acceptance of the vision. For just as her gifts to the goddess must properly be "royal," so she herself is a "magnificke Virgin," an Astraea returned to earth to rescue her child, student, lover, and future husband, Artegall. Perhaps the dominant note in the priest's interpretation is Galfridian, since it insists on the truth of her lineage, what Tillyard called "the myth of pedigree." In terms of its sexual dynamic we learn very little about the dream in the priestly interpretation. That has already been made clear enough. But the High Priest underlines the political import of the dream, in an allegorical equation of storms with all the rebellions that we have found Artegall opposing. This political destiny may be read on its highest plane as a predicted state of Augustan peace, and therefore the vision looks forward to the liberation of Irena, who must be made free if she is to have "joyance" of her dream. "Joyance" here, of course, means fulfillment in the sense of a happy childbirth, but it looks beyond the political reality of a sound royal succession to a state of almost metaphysical happiness. True, the major source of political unrest during the period is precisely that which the Temple of Isis attempts to resolve, the succession to the Crown. And Spenser does not mean that Elizabeth will have to marry and have a son for England to survive. He means that the spirit of such a procreative act will have to inspire whoever rules England, and to the extent that Gloriana sends her knights on good quests, she has sons, many lions to serve her Court of Maidenhead. What may not exist in actual fact, may still exist in visionary truth, and the latter may do more good to the kingdom than the fragile permanence of merely physical rebirth.

If one seeks the Hermetic aspects of the Temple, they are to be found in the priestly interpretation, which brings "egyptian" lore, the most secret and arcane lore in all magic philosophy, into line with local myth. The lion is commonly identified with Horus. Fowler has shown that the numbering of elements in Book V gives a central, pivotal, we might say equilibrating, position to the Temple and to the immediately succeeding rescue of Artegall, which seems to be a direct yield of Britomart's empowering vision. This too is Hermetic. But the radical myth here is simply the well-known equivalence of Christ and Osiris, an adjunct to the equivalence between Christ and Hercules, Christ and Dionysus. Through the copresence of such apparently conflicting interpretations Book V gains its special richness, since here, we might say, Christ has a human, heroic spouse; like the Church Militant of patristic lore, Britomart is a political heroine, Britain's *Venus Armata*[7] playing the role of Deborah or Judith. Critics have noticed that Spenser here is using a consistently enjambed style of prosody, and the feeling of continuity and driving flow it creates, along with a rather austere legal and mythic language, full of repetitions and ritual incantations (e.g., 21:7–9), creates an impression of enormous mythic urgency.

The final meaning of this episode has more to do with time and temporal extent than with anything else. For Britomart learns things external to her own person; she learns her *moira*, what it is to be a "magnificke virgin," espoused to a magnificent justiciar, who yet is bound in prison. The Temple scene breathes the air of expectant temporality, much as if it were a court masque celebrating a hymeneal rite.

Equity: The Prophetic Heart of Justice

FROM WHAT WE HAVE SEEN, the conclusion is inescapable that a pure *lex talionis* could have no prophetic significance. A wrathful or automatic meting out of "dreadful dooms" could contribute nothing to a developing sense of national or spiritual destiny. On the other hand, equity, which is the theme of the most intense *kairos* in Book V, does provide typological meaning. The High Priest tells Britomart that her dream is a

7. On the iconography of Venus here, see Roche, *The Kindly Flame*, passim; Kathleen Williams, *Spenser's World of Glass*, 96–102.

vision of a benign destiny for Britain. This alone endows the episode with prophetic force. But Spenser has a deeper perception: equity is the prophetic essence or reduction of the law.

The episode in the Temple shows Britomart passing through three stages of a female mystery: her initiation, her coronation, and her marriage. We have dwelt on the first, and it suffices only to remark that the dream and its interpretation are also visionary emblems of the actual coronation ceremony which installs the prince in his royal function. The Archbishop by ancient custom presents two emblems to the prince, and their double meaning clarifies the doubleness of the image of the "wand" and the Crocodile. First the Archbishop says: "Receive the Scepter, the signe of Kingly Power, the Rod of the Kingdomes, the Rod of Vertue, that thou mayst governe thy self aright, and defend the holy Church and Christian people committed by God unto thy charge, punish the wicked and protect the juste, and lead them in the way of righteousnesse; that from this temporal kingdome thou mayst be advanced to an eternall kingdome by his goodnesse, whose kingdome is everlasting."[8]

For the second presentation, in which the monarch is given a scepter with the Dove of Peace carved on it, the Archbishop says: "Receive the Rod of vertue and equity. Learn to make

---

8. These parts of the Coronation Service (in the case of Charles I) come from *The Manner of the Coronation of King Charles the First of England at Westminster, 2 Feb. 1626*, ed. Christopher Wordsworth (London, 1892). That we still have a hierogamy is apparent from the benediction: "O Lord the Fountaine of all good things . . . Establish him in the Throne of this Realme, Visite him with the encrease of children, Let justice spring up in his daies and gladnesse, let him reigne in thine everlasting Kingdome. Amen." See E. C. Ratcliff, *The Coronation Service of Queen Elizabeth II* (London and Cambridge, 1953), 13: "Queen Elizabeth I was the last English Sovereign whose Coronation Service was in Latin. The rite of *Liber Regalis* was used for her, as it had been used for her sister, Mary I. The fact that these two Sovereigns were Queens required no alteration of the rite. One ceremony alone had to be omitted: the Spurs were not put upon their heels. For the rest, all was done as for a King."

much of the godly and to terrify the wicked, Shew the way to those that goe astray, Offer thy hand to those that fall, Represse the proud, Lift up the lowly, that our Lord Jesus Christ may open to thee the dore, who saith of himself, I am the dore, by me if any man enter, he shall be safe; And let him be thy helper, who is the Key of David, and the Scepter of the house of Israel, who openeth and no man shutteth, who shutteth and no man openeth, who bringeth the captive out of prison where he sate in darknesse, and in the shadowe of death, that in all things thou maist follow him, of whom the Prophet David saith, Thy seat, O God, endureth for ever; The Scepter of thy kingdome is a right Scepter, thou hast loved righteousnesse and hated iniquity, where God, even thy God hath anointed thee with the oile of gladnesse above thy fellows, ever Jesus Christ our Lord." Immediately after this pronouncement a *Te Deum* is sung, and in fact the monarch has become sole ruler, the Davidic King of England.[9] When to the scepter and the oil (which symbolizes the *religious* power of the monarch) there is added an orb symbolizing the imperial command of earth, the regalia are complete, and the equation of Davidic kingship with the Isis-Osiris archetype is also complete. The Archbishop has by this time prayed for the increase of the monarch's children, or, in Elizabeth's case, for the prosperity of her realm. Now, in the old words, the queen "shall rise and, receiving again her Crowne, and taking the Scepter and Rod into her hands, shall repair to her Throne."[10] With this final act she is seated in the place of royal power and wisdom. Her throne is the figurative basis of her sovereignty, her *status*, her "sedentary power." John of Gaunt's prophecy envisions England as a "royal throne of kings."

9. G. Tibault, commenting on G. Kernodle, "Déroulement de la procession dans le temps ou espace théâtrale dans les fêtes de la renaissance," in *Les Fêtes de la renaissance*, ed. Jacquot, 1:454: "With regard to festivals in which the people participate, we must not forget the great assemblies of the populace like those of a *Te Deum* which celebrate victories. They are important because they unite the sacred with the profane."

10. Ratcliff, *Coronation Service*, 61.

If coronation leads forward to the sacred period of a happy rule, the sacred marriage also guarantees the "Reconciliation of the Four Daughters of God." This marriage of the virtues, bringing together Truth, Justice, Mercy, and Peace, is accomplished largely through the possibility that Mercy has power to weld states and kingdoms. Mercy is the form taken by equity at the Court of Mercilla, and Mercy was the essential attribute of the Christian god, whose "justification" was the one divine virtue that a prophetic theology had always required. Cranmer's *Homily of Salvation* describes the connection of Justice and Mercy with "the forgiveness of man's sins and trespasses in such things as he hath offended. This justification or righteousness which we so receive by God's mercy and Christ's merits embraced by faith, is taken, accepted and allowed of God for our perfect and full justification."[11] Mythically, without regard to the commonplace of the Reconciliation, marriage guarantees a temporal fulfillment through childbirth, and childbirth in turn always carries with it a sense of innocence, when the baptised child is blessed by divine grace. This messianic promise, which is equally Christian and Vergilian (from *Eclogue IV*), incarnates the possibility that the harsh virtues of Truth and Justice will join hands with the loving virtues of Mercy and Peace, while peaceful rule itself will be the seedbed of all kinds of fertility and "joyance."

Initiation, coronation, and the sacred marriage are three aspects of one continual mystery. Their merging in the Temple seems to have arisen from the overarching idea of equity, which itself implies the merging of other virtues, in the manner of the Reconciliation. But the believability of this merging results, in part, from a formula that we can best call psychological.

Britomart's dream shows her undergoing a change of mind, through which she recognizes the attitude of equity. She acquires a new mental framework. By identifying her with Isis, Spenser makes it possible for her to defeat the masculine, violent, inequitable aspect of her own Amazonian nature. She thereby

11. E. G. Rupp, *The Making of the English Protestant Tradition* (Cambridge, 1966), 174.

defeats the inner monstrosity of her own ambivalent nature—
that same monstrosity to which, at a crucial moment, Spenser refers in the Mutabilitie Cantos, when he recalls Alanus' *Complaint
of Nature*.[12]

Traditional thinking on the nature of equity will clarify this
psychological change. Especially in English law equity is described as the "conscience of the law." This view had been implicit in Aristotle's idea that the law should be conscious of its
own errors. Certainly the notion is developed in Chancery, the
Court of Equity. "If we look for one general principle which
more than any other influenced equity as it was developed by
Chancery, we find it in a philosophical and theological conception of *conscience*. The term was from an early date familiar to
English lawyers. In the Common Law courts of the thirteenth
and fourteenth centuries, we hear a good deal, in many connections, about 'conscience,' 'good faith,' 'reason,' 'conscience and
law,' 'the law of conscience,' 'law and right,' 'law, right, and good
conscience,' 'right and reason,' 'reason and good faith'; of 'equity'
we hear very little. In the practice of Common Law, we hear
still more about *conscience* from an angle of view which attempts, though with only partial success, to be scientifically dialectical."[13] By this dialectic Allen means the development of
equity in the sixteenth-century treatise of Saint Germain, *Doctor
and Student*. "St. Germain's preoccupation is with *equity in general*, the faculty, sublimated in conscience, of discerning between
good and evil and inclining towards the good."[14] In Book V
equity is precisely "the faculty, sublimated in conscience"—
Artegall's (and Astraea's) "line of conscience." The sublimating
process interests Spenser, as with all patterns of good action. He
wants to determine the sacral-psychological source of any virtue, and for equity this source is the conscience of the hero.
When Artegall and Arthur come to Mercilla's court, they wit-

12. *F.Q.*, VII, vii, 9.
13. C. K. Allen, *Law in the Making*, 389–90.
14. Ibid., 391.

ness a public exhibition of this sublimated power. Mercilla presides over a "court of conscience," to borrow the common Elizabethan epithet for Chancery, an epithet which might equally be applied to Parliament sitting as the highest court. Such courts aim to go beyond the barriers of mere legal convenience. They do not thereby soften the law into dereliction. In the words of a 1609 treatise on equity, Mercilla's. court would give "a ruled kind of justice . . . allayed with the sweetness of mercy."[15] Only a court of conscience could decide whether Mary's *de jure* right of immunity as a monarch of the realm of Scotland should override her *de facto* intrigues, her *mala fides*. The case was not simply moral, or legal, but lay astride the boundaries of the two realms of equity and law and was to be judged accordingly.

Blackstone, writing in the eighteenth century, looked back over the evolution of equity and denied its functions to any single court, even to the Court of Chancery, its official home.[16] Instead he saw that a public conscience had permeated all English life and law and could be found at work in all sorts of Common Law judgments of crimes and civil disputes. This generalization of equity implies something which Spenser would approve,

15. Quoted, ibid., 391.

16. F. W. Maitland, *Equity*, 18: "No, we ought to think of equity as supplementary law, a sort of appendix added on to our code, or a sort of gloss written round our code, an appendix, a gloss, which used to be administered by courts especially designed for that purpose, but which is now administered by the High Court of Justice as part of the code. The language which equity held to law, if we may personify the two, was not, 'No, that is not so, you make a mistake, our rule is absurd, an obsolete one'; but 'Yes, of course that is so, but it is not the whole truth. You say that A is the owner of this land; no doubt that is so, but I must add that he is bound by one of those obligations which are known as trusts.'" On the notion of equity I have used: Maitland, *Equity;* Maitland, *Constitutional History of England;* C. K. Allen, *Law in the Making;* Edmond Cahn, *The Sense of Injustice;* F. S. Cohen, *Ethical Systems and Legal Ideas* (Ithaca, 1959); D. J. Boorstin, *The Mysterious Science of the Law* (Boston, 1958); Henri Lévy-Ullmann, *The English Legal Tradition: Its Sources and History,* trans. M. Mitchell (London, 1935).

the citizen's personal share in the public virtue. For he would fashion a gentleman, as well as a state. The individual must participate in the larger function. Artegall shares in the conscience of the law through Britomart and Mercilla, who redeem his judgment.

Conscience provides a psychological basis for equity through its balancing functions; the mind in its conscience is undivided, has no doubt about standards, judges equably. But it also achieves self-consciousness, and this leads the hero to take part in a historical destiny. Without an awareness of the continuing complications of judgments, that is, of their ever-changing conditions, the mind is incapable of seeing into the future or taking part in a significant movement through historical time. This historicity of conscience is enshrined in the legal formulation of equity as a corrective to the law. By insisting on this meaning of equity, Spenser gives to his Legend the direction of a legitimate prophecy.

The social bandit disposed of a natural equity, relying on his own native sense of fairness. Yet after the development of legal codes the primitive justice of the social bandit gives way, as we have seen, to formulations which themselves may impose a kind of bureaucratic or legalistic tyranny on the citizen. To correct this situation equity plays a major part. Aristotle early phrases the problem as follows: "When the law states a universal proposition, and the facts in a given case do not square with the proposition, the right course to pursue is therefore the following. The legislator having left a gap and committed an error by making an unqualified proposition we must correct his omission; we must say for him what he would have said himself if he had been present, and what he would have put into law if only he had known. . . . The nature of the equitable may accordingly be defined as a correction of law where law is defective owing to its universality."[17]

17. *Ethics*, V, 10 (1137b). Cf. C. J. Friedrich, *The Philosophy of Law in Historical Perspective*, chap. 7, "Law as Historical Fact: the Humanists"; Guido Kisch, "Humanistic Jurisprudence," *Studies in the*

Aristotle describes the psychology of this corrective prudence in a metaphor: "The law is aware that there is a possibility of error; but the law is none the less correct."[18] Emblematically justice preserves her impartial adherence to universal forms by wearing a blindfold over her eyes, but as de Jouvenel says, "It has often been said that justice is blind; let us go so far as to agree that to be just she must be myopic."[19] Jurisprudence demands that we defend the law against the idea that no regularized propositions whatever will be relevant to the human condition. The possibility that exceptional cases will lie beyond the applicability of given laws should not, in Aristotle's view, dissuade us from believing in the need for law. He admits only that the universality of law carries an inherent defect of rigid irrelevancy. Although he grants that "there are matters on which it is impossible to lay down a law, and for which the use of a decree is thus necessary," he fixes our attention on the just man himself, "a man who is not a martinet for justice in a bad sense, but ready to yield a point even when he has the law on his side. This is the state of character which constitutes a spirit of equity; and the spirit of equity is thus a sort of justice, and not a separate state of character."[20]

Though names for this spirit may change from culture to culture, its guiding idea seems to be a willingness to modify rigid principles to suit varying historical circumstances. Thus, through

---

Renaissance 8 (1961): 71–87; L. C. Stevens, "The Contributions of French Jurists to the Humanism of the Renaissance," *Studies in the Renaissance* 1 (1954): 92–105; Myron Gilmore, *Humanists and Jurists*, chaps. 1 and 4; Giuseppe Saitta, *L'Umanesimo*, chap. 6.

18. Maitland, *Equity*, 19. Josef Pieper, *The Four Cardinal Virtues* (New York, 1965), 3: "nothing less than the whole ordered structure of the Occidental Christian view of man rests upon the pre-eminence of prudence over the other virtues." See R. J. Dorius, "Prudence and Excess in Richard II and the Histories," in *Discussions of Shakespeare's Histories*, ed. R. J. Dorius (Boston, 1964), 24–40.

19. Bertrand de Jouvenel, *Sovereignty*, 163.

20. *Ethics*, V, 10.

the intricacies of Maine's argument that equity (*aequitas*) allowed the Romans to blend two legal systems—the *Jus Gentium* (law of nations) and the *Jus Naturae* (law of nature)—there runs the belief that an equitable solution to a quarrel always provides "an equal or proportionate distribution."[21] Maine believes that "the Latin word '*aequus*' carries with it more distinctly than the Greek '*isos*' the sense of levelling." The Egalitarian Giant tries to remake the laws of the universe (instituting a new law of nature and nations), and travesties the aim of equity. Spenser makes it clear that the Giant is a travesty when Artegall, in effect, is called a tyrant. The Giant considers himself an equitable judge, remaking law in the image of a perfectly symmetrical, but disproportionate, nature. The Giant would destroy the basis of equity, man's capacity to be "scandalized by false proportions,"[22] for no ratios would be left after his reforms were done. Yet both Artegall and the Giant appeal to Nature. Only their views of "due proportion" differ.

For Spenserian criticism it may be wise to recall a deep affinity between the original idea of nature, upon which is built the medieval legist's natural law, and the idea of justice. "To elucidate the meaning of such a term as justice, built and vested with associations by an historical process of social thought, we shall do well to go back to its origin and the root from which it has grown. That root, which appears in many branches and has been prolific of many growths, would seem to be the notion of 'joining' (as in the Latin *jungere* or the Greek *zeugnunai*); of 'binding,' or 'fitting,' or 'tying together.' Justice is thus, in its original notion, the quality or aptitude of joining: it ties together whatever it touches. Primarily it ties *men* together, by the common

21. Otto Gierke, *Political Theories of the Middle Ages*, 76: "the *Ius Gentium* [in medieval thought] (thereby being meant such Law as all Nations agreed in recognizing) was regarded as the sum of those rules which flowed from the pure Law of Nature when account was taken of the relationships which were introduced by that deterioration of human nature which was caused by the Fall of Man."

22. De Jouvenel, *Sovereignty*, 153.

bond of a right and 'fitting' order of relations, under which each has his position in the order and receives his due place (*suum cuique*); each has rights as his share of the general Right pervading and constituting the order; and each *jura* is the exemplification and concrete expression in his own case of the general *jus*."[23] By a process of evolution, *justitia* becomes *jus*, justice is translated into law, and in an even larger perspective "justice is a joining or fitting together not only of persons, but also of principles." This description recalls ancient ideas of nature. Nature (*physis* or *cosmos*) constitutes an order. In ancient and medieval theory a natural order is a means of maintaining a universe. Nature implies unity in diversity. The term connotes the proportional, rational joining of the myriad splinters of our physical selves and surroundings, all of which seek, in the long run, to exist in harmonious coexistence.[24] The grand syzygy of justice finds a pattern, as the law of nature recognizes, in the harmony of the universe.

Violations of this harmony become the target of the "natural sense of justice," the so-called *vulgaris aequitas*, which in fact is not unlike the *lex talionis*. "But here we have to ask who it is who retributes, and what it is that 'pays back.' It is not the injured person who retributes or pays back; it is not even the whole community of persons, considered simply as persons. It is the mental rule of law which pays back a violation of itself by a violent return, much as the natural rules of health pay back a violation of themselves by a violent return. The *lex talionis* does not mean that the person or body of persons you hurt shall hurt you in return: it means that the order you disturb will disturb you in

23. Ernest Barker, *Principles of Social and Political Theory* (Oxford, 1961), 168; also 94.

24. Friedrich Solmsen, *Aristotle's System of the Physical World* (Ithaca, 1960); Leo Spitzer, *Classical and Christian Ideas of World Harmony;* John Hollander, *The Untuning of the Sky: Ideas of Music in English Poetry 1500–1700* (Princeton, 1961); Gretchen Finney, *Musical Backgrounds for English Literature: 1580–1660* (New Brunswick, 1967).

order to restore itself."[25] This casts a new light on the figure of Talus. We are inclined too often to equate his retaliations with the will of the hero, Artegall, instead of relating them correctly to the "mental rule of law." The close line which divides Talus from the monsters he represses follows from the fine line in men's minds, whenever they seek an impersonal justice. For to go outside oneself to a sanctioning law, is to court the risk of denying one's humanity and one's parentage in universal, natural error.

To the degree that Talus's retaliations keep the law consistent with itself, they minister to the logic of justice. But since conditions may change, the logic has to change, and, as Spenser suggests several times, Talus himself is a destroyer as well as the grim reaper of Time's harvest. Without the ameliorating counterinfluence of equity and conscience (which Talus entirely lacks), there can be no survival of justice through time. Equity creates the possibility of a living, spirited law, a law responsive to season. The absolute necessity of an idea of rebirth for any typological vision requires here the operation of equity, which Spenser understands as a readiness to look again for the spirit within the letter of the law. Equity, with the spirit of the Redeemer, looks for the New within the Old Law, a prophetic search. Calvin's *Institutes* (IV, viii, 7) describes this relationship in such a way as to link the vision of the Old and New Testaments: "Then there followed the prophets, through whom God published new oracles which were added to the law—but not so new that they did not flow from the law and hark back to it. As for doctrine, they were only interpreters of the law and added nothing to it except predictions of things to come. Apart from these, they brought nothing forth but a pure exposition of the law. But because the Lord was pleased to reveal a clearer and fuller doctrine in order better to satisfy weak consciences, he commanded that the prophecies also be committed to writing and be accounted part of his Word. At the same time, histories

25. Henry Maine, *Ancient Law*, 44.

were added to these, also the labor of the prophets, but composed under the Holy Spirit's dictation. I include the psalms with the prophecies, since what we attribute to the prophecies is common to them. . . . Therefore, that whole body, put together out of law, prophecies, psalms, and histories, was the Lord's Word for the ancient people. . . . Now therefore, since Christ, the Sun of Righteousness, has shone, while before there was only dim light, we have the perfect radiance of divine truth, like the wonted brilliance of midday. For truly the apostle meant to proclaim no common thing when he wrote, 'In many and various ways God spoke of old to the fathers by the prophets; but in these last days he has begun to speak to us through his beloved Son.' " So different a theologian as Hooker can in the same vein say that "the chief and principal matter of prophecy is the promise of righteousness, peace, holiness, glory, victory, immortality, unto every soul which believeth that Jesus is Christ, of the Jew first, and of the Gentile (Rom. i. 16)."[26] The resolving power of Christian mercy underlies this vast promise.

In sum, equity is templar, while the *lex talionis* resembles the labyrinthine, even irrational, experience of error. Equity temporalizes the *lex talionis* in a dimension of sacred time, just as Britomart's vision sets her quest in a significant providential scheme, so that her revenge on Radigund surpasses the insatiable rage of the jealous lover and enters the sphere of cosmic restitution. So also with the trial of Duessa: mercy as the highest form of equity gives truth to that trial; as revenge, pure and simple, the trial would be selfcontradictory. If the Temple requires joy, the sacred "repose in the desire for an object," then it will require *misericordia*, the appeasement of the cruelty of justice. Spenser's myth here is strong, whatever may have been his personal motives. He knows that without such equity and mercy at its mythic center, the Legend of Justice will lack the historicity which must be the ground plan for its typological justice.

26. Hooker, Sermon V, in Keble ed., *Works*, 3:663.

A Gift to Sir Calidore

No sooner has Sir Artegall restored Irena to her
people, led her with "meete majestie / Unto the pallace, where
their kings did rayne, / [and] did her therein establish peace-
ablie," than the weary champion meets "two old ill favour'd
Hags," "Two griesly creatures," Envie and Detraction, who attack him and all he has stood for. Not only do they rail against
the Herculean Artegall, but they have a servant monster, the
Blatant Beast, who also attacks him. For Book V the effect is
graphic: justice suffers a backlash. Spenser suggests that Envy
and Detraction are on the loose partly because Artegall and Talus
do not complete the reformation of Irena's Commonweal: "But
ere he could reforme it thoroughly, / He through occasion called
was away, / To Faerie Court." The mere fact that Artegall has
not done his full work, (Grey had not succeeded in Ireland) enables Envy's cloud to dim the luster of his fame.[27] Perhaps, had
the work been done, even Envy would have failed; the implication being also that envious men are never equitable, will never
grant partial success to the struggling ruler. Yet as soon as he steps
on the shore of his native land, Artegall is attacked. Much speculation has surrounded this allegory and the interpretation of the
Blatant Beast.

Though clearly nothing troubled Spenser more than what
he took to be the defamation of Lord Grey, the loyal defense of
his patron does not quite account for one aspect of the Beast's
meaning. The Beast seems to embody the bestiality of defama-

27. Chaucer, in *The Parson's Tale*, is orthodox enough when he
says that envy is the "worste synne that is." Others have particular
targets, but "certes, Envye is agayns alle vertues and agayns alle good-
nesses . . . thanne is Envye a synne agayns kynde." Envy is both a
resentment against others' prosperity and a delight in harming others,
and Chaucer's Parson derives all the types of "bakbityng" therefrom.
The end of the cycle of sin is the growth of "murmure" and discord,
"that unbyndeth alle manere of freendshipe."

tion, as his name suggests, and since courtesy, the theme of Book VI, implies honor and fame, we should expect Sir Calidore to deal harshly with this terrible legacy from Sir Artegall's quest. Even so, the Beast's cruelty seems to have something essentially verbal about it; his "blatting" is a deformed kind of speech, the blasphemous perversion of eloquence. The irony here is that in Arcadia speech ought to be clear, lively, and truthful, so that death in Arcadia takes, among other forms, the character of monstrous utterance. To be bitten by the Beast is to suffer a wounded "name," to experience true courtesy is to experience one's "good name." Furthermore, Spenser carefully aligns this sense of the Beast with the idea of error. In the stanzas that open Book VI, Canto IX, the poet tells us that, as poet, he can rescue Sir Calidore from the evil of ill fame because his poem can stand above the wanderings of its hero, who is caught in the endless pursuit of the monster.

> Now turne againe my teme thou jolly swayne,
>   Backe to the furrow which I lately left;
>   I lately left a furrow, one or twayne
>   Unplough'd, the which my coulter hath not cleft:
>   Yet seem'd the soyle both fayre and frutefull eft,
>   As I it past, that were too great a shame,
>   That so rich frute should be from us bereft;
>   Besides the great dishonour and defame,
> Which should befall to *Calidores* immortall fame.
>
>   (VI, ix, 1)

We learn that the bard has, however, a clear notion of Sir Calidore's activities: "Full many pathes and perils he hath past, / Through hills, through dales, through forests, and through plaines." He has indeed been "restless." And with good reason.

> So sharpely he the Monster did pursew,
>   That day nor night he suffred him to rest,
>   Ne rested he himselfe but natures dew,
>   For dread of daunger, not to be redrest,
>   If he for slouth forslackt so famous quest.

Him first from court he to the citties coursed,
And from the citties to the townes him prest,
And from the townes into the countrie forsed,
And from the country back to private farmes he scorsed.

From thence into the open fields he fled,
　　Whereas the Heardes were keeping of their neat,
　　And shepherds singing to their flockes, that fed,
　　Layes of sweete love and youthes delightfull heat:
　　Him thether eke for all his fearefull threat,
　　He followed fast, and chaced him so nie,
　　That to the folds, where sheepe at night doe seat,
　　And to the litle cots, where shepherds lie
In winters wrathfull time, he forced him to flie.

(ix, 3–4)

While it is wrong to limit the meaning of the Beast to a space he travels about in, that endless chase of the monster does suggest that, like false rumor, the Blatant Beast wanders at will, restrained by none. His loyalty to the kingdom of death is perhaps implied by his being driven to secret safety "in winters wrathfull time," which in turn is the "season" of Christ's birth. Spenser ends the Legend of Courtesy with a full-scale identification of the Beast with the evil mouth of hell, whose open jaws appear "like the mouth of Orcus griesly grim." In the ensuing catalogue of the Beast's vicious weaponry, we learn that he is an obscene mass of tongues, some of beasts, "but most of them were tongues of mortall men, / Which spake reprochfully, not caring where nor when." Next we are told that his tongues mingle the tongues of serpents, spitting poison and blood, ravenously; the Beast "spake licentious words and hatefull things / Of good and bad alike, of low and hie, / Ne Kesars spared he a whit, nor Kings" (xii, 28). The Beast shares the fury of the "hell-borne Hydra," once put down by Hercules; and a little later, Spenser compares the Beast to Cerberus, muzzled by Hercules again. For a while the muzzled Beast follows Sir Calidore like "a fearefull dog," and everyone marvels at this submission of evil and at the prowess of such a knight. We almost begin to believe that such a victory has occurred in the time the poem refers to, the historical time when the Beast defamed Sir Artegall as Lord Grey, until we realize that all this happened *in illo tempore*, after the Golden Age had ended and Astraea had left earth for heaven. From the Fall until the present time of the poem's creation the Beast is abroad and destroying everywhere he can. As the poem ends we are left in no doubt whatsoever that Spenser regards the Blatant Beast as the particular enemy of poetry and of himself as poet.

> So now he raungeth through the world agayne,
>> And rageth sore in each degree and state;
>> Ne any is that may him now restraine,
>> He growen is so great and strong of late,
>> Barking and biting all that him doe bate,
>> Albe they worthy blame, or cleare of crime:
>> Ne spareth he most learned wits to rate,
>> Ne spareth he the gentle Poets rime,
> But rends without regard of person or of time.
>
> Ne may this homely verse, of many meanest,
>> Hope to escape his venomous despite,
>> More then my former writs, all were they clearest
>> From blamefull blot, and free from all that wite,
>> With which some wicked tongues did it backebite,
>> And bring into a mighty Peres displeasure,
>> That never so deserved to endite.
>> Therefore do you my rimes keep better measure,
> And seeke to please, that now is counted wisemens threasure.
>
> (xii, 40–41)

The irony is complete; in his last parting invocation to his own rhymes the poet counsels them to flatter and deceive, to meet fraud with fraud. He seems to be saying to Lord Burghley or more probably to the Court: You get what you deserve if I flatter you, for you have harbored the Beast. The accusation refers the Legend of Courtesy back to the preceding Legend, since one basis of Justice had been truth and respect for truth. The Beast speaks un-truths, but it is even more monstrous, in the poet's view, that the medium of his own verses, his own "dear native tongue," should be so debased. Not only, then, does *The Faerie Queene* end grimly, but it ends with an allegorical implication that Envy, "the enemy who drives Truth from England,"[28] will prevent the triumph of truth as the daughter of time. We are told that when Truth is pictured in emblem as *filia temporis*, "her enemies are Envy and Hypocrisy . . . and Fraud and Slander, Error and Falsehood."[29] This triumphant rage of the Blatant Beast has strong

28. S. C. Chew, *The Virtues Reconciled*, 77. See also Chew, *The Pilgrimage of Life;* Honor Matthews, *Character and Symbol in Shakespeare's Plays: A Study of certain Christian and Pre-Christian Elements in their Structure and Imagery* (Cambridge, 1962), pt. 2, "Two Daughters of God: The Conflict between Justice and Mercy." The Reconciliation is often conceived as a festive meeting; thus Jean Bodin, *Method for the Easy Comprehension of History*, trans. and ed. Beatrice Reynolds, chap. 6, 288: "peace, fitting the harmonic ratio in the most remarkable way, is the most excellent and best objective of empires and states. Nor do I think that those ancient lawgivers had any other goal when they united their citizens by means of public banquets." Bodin instances Cretan gatherings ordered by Minos, Lycurgan feasts at Sparta, Plato's symposium, Moses' *skenopegia* and great *pasach*, "which the Greeks corruptly called *pascha*," the Christian love feasts, the Romans' *caristia*, the Venetian festivals, and finally the "mutual drinking bouts" of the Swiss—to which we might add the "Annuall feaste" of the Faerie Queene herself. Festive rejoicing was the public celebration of the coronation contract, by which, in effect the prince swore to achieve the reconciliation of the Four Daughters. Thus, in the Coronation Service of Charles I the oath had two such parts: "Sir, will you keepe peace and godlye agreement entirely according to your power both to god and the holye church, the cleargye and the people," and, "Sir will you to your power cause lawe, justice, and discretion, in mercye and truth to be executed in all your judgments." From *The Manner of the Coronation of King Charles the First of England at Westminster, 2 Feb. 1626*, Christopher Wordsworth (London, 1892).

29. Chew, *Virtues Reconciled*, 88. Slander and calumny are closely associated, the latter a favorite Renaissance motif on account

millenarian overtones; it suggests the triumph of Antichrist. But in the meantime Spenser has referred the triumph to the hazardous act of making an epic poem. He may be trying to define the preconditions of a betrayal of poetry itself.[30] In treason trials, slander was customarily associated with the treasonous spread of foreign propaganda, and here it could well be that the Bestial slander is equally subversive in the realm of ordered, measured speech.

If so, slander is the enemy of vatic language. The poet himself prevents his reader from limiting the role of slander to social and political occasions; it now includes the fame of the poet, and soon, if even he can joke about writing only to please, it may kill the truth of the poem whose purpose, "with fayned colours shading a true case," is to restore a lost oneness and delight. Unmeasurable, like death, the Beast is a creature of Babel. In one of those fine, odd puns that cannot fail to amuse the serious reader, Spenser once associates the Beast directly with rebellion. When it

---

of the famous painting of Apelles, showing Denunciation and Spite dragging a victim before a judge, who listens to Ignorance and Suspicion, while Truth, in the background, averts her eyes. See E. Ph. Goldschmit, "Lucian's *Calumnia*," in D. J. Gordon, ed., *Fritz Saxl: 1890–1948* (London, 1957), 228–44. On the association of the Invidia, Hercules' last opponent, with the Hydra, see T. K. Dunseath, *Spenser's Allegory of Justice*, 232 and plate 3, showing Veen's *Emblemata Horatiana* for the same. The iconography is more fully discussed in Aptekar, *Icons of Justice*, 201–17.

30. Consider, together, the two following statements, which extend the poetic significance of the allegory of blasphemy and envy. (1) "The high poetry, the bombast, of Marlowe and kindred Elizabethans is not shaped to express what is, whether a passion or a fact, but to make something happen or become—it is incantation, a willful, self-made sort of liturgy." C. L. Barber, "The form of Faustus' fortunes good or bad," *Tulane Drama Review* 8, no. 4 (1964): 117. (2) "It is interesting that Faustus' last despairing attempt to appease his angry God, by offering to burn his books, echoes Envy's sentence: 'I cannot read and therefore wish all books burned' (II, ii, 128)." Robert Ornstein, "The Tragic Theology of 'Dr. Faustus,'" *PMLA* 83, no. 5 (1968): 1385n.

attacks Sir Artegall, barking and baying "with bitter rage and fell contention," all the woods and rocks begin to shake and tremble with dismay, "and all the aire rebellowed againe" (V, xii, 41). Spenser seems almost to believe that the most grievous injustice is this storm of bitter words, "most shamefull, most unrighteous, most untrue." He cannot vaccinate his poem against the disease carried by the Blatant Beast; language itself is the primary medium of error and betrayal. Book VI returns to the first encounter of Book I. If the reader wants to believe the Arcadian setting in Book VI is a kind of poetic homecoming, the presence of the Beast fouls the homecoming—*et in Arcadia ego*. On this basis alone, even leaving aside the notable clumsiness of Sir Calidore, who keeps breaking time, interrupting the dance, Book VI is the most ironical part of *The Faerie Queene*. Irony, perhaps, is appropriate to a visionary poem that refuses all simple apocalyptic and millenarian modes, as the heresies of the prophetic tradition to which it belongs.

Looking Back

SPENSER'S POETICAL THEFTS are sometimes so bizarre in their collage that they create a surrealistic distance between the old and the new context. One difficulty we may have in defining Spenserian "irony," whether at the close of Book VI or more generally, is that it inheres in the intermediate position *The Faerie Queene* occupies among European epics. All epic after Homer had been to a degree "secondary epic," dependent on the Homeric model even when departing from it. This dependency reached a new height with the Italian romantic epic, and then a further development with Spenser. Spenser, furthermore, seems to have intended that his readers remain aware of *source*, that is, of the secondariness of his epic, as a quality in itself. The gradual transformation of sources is one thing; the frequently "superb disregard" Spenser displays in distorting his sources almost beyond recognition—that is another. In the latter process Spenser elicits wonderment or puzzlement about the status of his narrative as epic, as traditional heroic poem, with traditional accoutrements. It is not easy to define this bemused response to the poem, but it seems to involve a kind or a degree of irony.

Recently Donald Cheney has reminded us that critics could well give more attention to "the Chaucerian tradition, since Spenser in so many ways demonstrates his indebtedness to his master, both for his merging of sacred and profane quests and for his sense of solemn comedy."[31] Scholars have perhaps overstressed the Italianate origins of romance in Spenser. Chaucer matters a great deal to him because, quite simply he and Chaucer are both English and share analogous problems of literary influence. Equally important, as Cheney seems to suggest, both poets believe in the prophetic moment; with Chaucer, its force is announced in the opening lines of the General Prologue, where the poet presents the temple/error nexus in classic form. Finally, both poets create an atmosphere approaching irony and yet somehow withstanding it. David Worcester has said that Chaucer's "ironical manner . . . diffuses an air of genial skepticism and penetrating humor through his major writings."[32] Spenser is not so warm, but his "solemn comedy"—very strong in the Mutabilitie Cantos—is also a pervasive air, a scarcely definable "sense." This is worth considering for a moment. Cicero is said to have been the first to observe that irony could be a pervasive life style, and he instanced Socrates. This is not dramatic irony but "the irony of detachment." "By this we mean the attitude of mind held by a philosophic observer when he abstracts himself from the contradictions of life and views them all impartially, himself perhaps included in the ironic vision."[33] Spenser is too involved in prophetic aims to be impartial, but he has detachment,

31. In an address to the International Spenser Conference, held at the University of New Brunswick, Fredericton, New Brunswick, September 1969.

32. David Worcester, *The Art of Satire* (Cambridge, Mass., 1940), 98, quoted by Norman Knox, *The Word "Irony" and Its Context, 1500–1755* (Durham, N.C., 1961), 18.

33. G. G. Sedgewick, *Of Irony Especially in Drama* (Toronto, 1948), 13, quoted in Knox, *The Word "Irony,"* 20.

and his narrative persona is an *eiron*, Colin Clout. Where Colin Clout differs from the Socratic and even the Chaucerian mood, though less from the latter, is in his melancholy. A saturnine manner marks the earliest published poems and the last. Like English weather, it presses down on the work that made Spenser famous, the *Calender*, and within that structure darkens the eclogue which E. K. (or the editor, at least) thought "farre passing his reache, and in myne opinion all other the Eclogues of this booke," the November Eclogue, where Spenser wittily rimes "verse" with "hearse."

Such melancholy, which is not cavalier, not even Ariostan, is in fact the consequence of a perception of tragedy in the midst of romance. One can have tragedies on every level of fictional mode, as Frye has shown, whether it be the death of a god in myth, or the death of a salesman. When tragedy enters romance, however, the effect is exactly what we should expect with Spenser, and it is *not* irony. Frye's general formulation suggests that when we call Spenser "ironical" we are trying to label a mood that is very close to, but not identical with, irony.[34]

Whatever this mood is to be called, it gathers steadily throughout Books V and VI. Artegall, for example, begins in exemplary romantic fashion, teaching the wild creatures of the forest, "far from companie exilde." But as we have seen, he leaves archetypal nature behind, to enter the sphere of human "companie." In so doing, he becomes a tragic hero in a romantic world. At the close of Book V he is an isolated figure. But alienation within romance is precisely that special case of a tone close to, but not identical with, irony. What normally would have the destructive force of an ironic separation is present here, death is present here, though it is oddly reserved. "The hero's death or isolation thus has the effect of a spirit passing out of nature, and evokes a mood best described as elegiac. The elegiac presents a heroism unspoiled by irony."[35] The poem takes such a tone toward Artegall's (and

34. Northrop Frye, *Anatomy of Criticism*, 33.
35. *Anatomy of Criticism*, 36–37, the source for this and the following quotations from Frye.

Lord Grey's?) failure: "Yet he past on, and seem'd of them to take no keepe" (xii, 42.8). Again the general account in the *Anatomy* points in the right direction. "The inevitability in the death of Beowulf, the treachery in the death of Roland, the malignancy that compasses the death of the martyred saint, are of much greater emotional importance than any ironic complications of hybris and hamartia that may be involved."

Rhetorical or dramatic precision have only a limited place in the deeper structure of Spenserian myth, superficially interesting as they may be from moment to moment. The reader will have noticed that Frye here does not say "the inevitability *of*" or the "treachery *of*" the death of Roland. Frye's "in" is significant, for it reminds us that the forces of romance and its elegiac constraints when tragedy enters romance are natural forces and constraints; they are weatherlike. In a hagiography, when men martyr a saint we are not allowed much concern for their economic, political, or other purely human motives and complexities; rather, a "malignancy . . . *compasses* the death." (How otherwise, of course, could a victim become a saint, unless in his death his sacred virtue were made to shine forth as a natural phenomenon?) Spenser was not unaware of the fatalistic background to his epic, that in the apotheosis of the Faerie Queene he was imagining a fatal, female reign. This, and so many other modes of inevitability, constrain him to look back over his poem with elegiac melancholy. "The elegiac is often accompanied by a diffused, resigned, melancholy sense of the passing of time, of the old order changing and yielding to a new one; one thinks of Beowulf looking, while he is dying, at the great stone monuments of the eras of history that vanished before him. In very late 'sentimental' form the same mood is well enough caught in Tennyson's *Passing of Arthur*." When Spenser looks back, he expresses this "diffused, resigned, melancholy sense of the passing of time, of the old order changing and yielding to a new one." But when he looks back, what does he immediately see, if not the monument to that old order, his own poem? What with Tennyson, the second great English imperialist poet, became a sentimentalized passing of Arthur, was with Spenser a genuinely elegiac vision. Milton no doubt perceived this as he pondered the Spenserian legacy he had, as epic poet, inherited. Spenser, on the other hand, had reached a point, in Book VI, where he was able to inherit his own poem. But we need not go so far. The elegiac mood that comes to pervade *The Faerie Queene* encompasses both the poem and the worldview it contains. Spenser knows the tears of things and shares the Vergilian panoramic melancholy so well described by Greene, Parry, and others in the studies on which Berger has drawn in his theoretical account of Spenserian retrospection.

The "introversion of the elegiac"[36] does not prevent the narrative from spinning itself out at great length, but changes our view of the spinning process. Book VI, Berger has suggested, presents the hermetic, "secret discipline" of poetic vision, much narrower than the theological and moral visions of Books I and II, and yet in its highly focused way equally essential to the poem at large. Through this poetical perspective we learn that Spenserian heroes are chiefly *percipient* actors, whose interest lies in their projection of varying settings. The atmosphere is increasingly full of suspicion. In earlier Books *The Faerie Queene* presented an optimistic analogy between its own expansion and the expansion of empire.[37] Britain's power would spread, and the poem

---

36. *Anatomy of Criticism*, 43.

37. In his chapter, "All in *Paradise Lost*" [*Structure of Complex Words*, 101–4] Empson exemplified "emotive theory" by Milton's "all." Empson found 612 uses, or about once in every seventeen lines, with some dense agglomerations in passages of lament or penitence. "It [all] seems to be suited to his temperament because he is an absolutist, an all-or-none man." Spenser's usage is in its way much more remarkable, and I believe it implies a marked change in his view of imperial expansion (with its poetical cognates of visionary possessiveness). In Book I: approximately 360 (about once in every fifteen lines, and more evenly distributed throughout the Book than throughout *Paradise Lost*); in Book II, 154 times. Variation of semantic range is wide enough, e.g., from trivial uses ("and over all a blacke stole shee did throw") to loaded ones ("sole king of forrests all," "all earthly thinges," "All which compacted made a goodly Diapase). Such "om-

would dilate to convey this expansion. It is the ancient Horatian and Vergilian problem: what is the good of empire, if it forces men to overextend themselves? "What is nearest us touchest us most," said Dr. Johnson, at a time when the Empire was already a political reality. While empire remained a largely imaginative construct, it could inspire prophetic exuberance, with no mechanical operation of the spirit. But as soon as its *libido dominandi* became fact, whether in political or in poetical domains, imaginative freedom was endangered.

Spenser allows the threat to emerge, but he does not directly resist or overcome it. Some readers have been disappointed that *The Faerie Queene* is not more uniformly optimistic. By accepting the gradual emergence of elegiac introversion, which amounts to a kind of metamorphic instability within the mythography, we get closer, I suspect, to Spenser's aim. By turning inward, which indeed had always been his tendency, he saved the life of his poem. In this he dimly anticipated the poetical career of Milton, whose *Il Penseroso* associated prophetic powers with the mood of melancholy. Milton appears to have believed that the great

---

nifics" express the fullness of the cosmos and the *pleroma* of Christian time. But note that there is a sudden disappearance of "all" after Book II. The mere count is extraordinary: Book III *three* uses (two of which occur in the Proem); Book IV *two;* Book V *six;* Book VI *zero;* and in the Mutabilitie Cantos *zero*. It may not be possible to explain these statistics, but I would argue that the avoidance of "all" marks a conscious resistance to elegaic introversion. Only by conscious attention could Spenser have so completely done away with a word that is almost synonymous with the elegiac mode. Granted that "all" is a key-word for biblical exegesis: e.g., Donne: "There is no one word so often in the Bible, as this *Omne, All*. Neither hath God spread the word more liberally upon all the lines of this Booke, then he hath his gracious purposes upon the soules of men" ([Potter and Simpson, eds., *Sermons*, VII, no. 9, ll. 390–93], quoted by Joan Webber, *Contrary Music: The Prose Style of John Donne* [Madison, 1963], 140). But these omnifics, which reflect the encyclopedic nature of the Bible as a world-book, are intensified in elegiac poetry, where classical as well as Christian mythography is at play.

Typically, we find "all" in *The Phoenix and the Turtle* ("Grace in

epic vision could not come from a merely technical imperial expansion over vast territories. This was for him a problem of intense personal significance, since he was by nature and training one of the most learned poets in the English tradition. If syncretism is a major requirement for Spenser, it is far more taxing in the case of Milton. The Miltonic choice has a special importance to later poetic tradition, for he early holds that the only legitimate route toward true poetic vision will be a return to the self, by introspection and introversion, by rejecting the external pleasures of *L'Allegro*. Prophecy thrives on the mystery of *turning inward*, on the sense that the self can achieve Ovidian metamorphoses, for whatever can turn inward may also turn outward.

---

all simplicity"); *Daphnaida* ("Which all the world subdued unto it"); *Astrophel:*

> Woods, hills and rivers, now are desolate,
> Sith he is gone the which them all did grace:
> And all the fields do waile their widow state,
> Sith death their fairest flowre did late deface.
> The fairest flowre in field that ever grew,
> Was *Astrophel;* that was, we all may rew,
> What cruell hand of cursed foe unknowne,
> Hath cropt the stalke which bore so faire a flowre?
> Untimely cropt, before it well were growne,
> And cleane defaced in untimely howre.
> Great losse to all that ever him did see,
> Great losse to all, but greatest losse to mee.
>
>   (25–36)

Finally, *Lycidas:* "And all their ecchoes mourn" (41); "And perfet witness of all-judging *Jove*" (82); "Throw hither all your quaint enameled eyes" (139); "And purple all the ground with vernal flowres" (141); "Bid *Amarantus* all his beauty shed" (149); "To all that wander in that perilous flood" (185); "And now the Sun had stretch'd out all the hills" (190). The word projects personal loss as a universal trauma, with which all nature empathizes and suffers as one vast being. What then can the extirpation of "all" imply, but the poet's reaction against a force very deep in his own nature?

The imitators of Spenser, while recognizing the danger of a mechanical expansion of poetic cosmologies, could not solve the problem, either because their views were superficial or regressive. The creation of a Purple Island does restrict the compass of a world, and so does the Castle of Indolence, but in both cases we get a return to a neomedieval or gothic allegory. By contrast Milton asked what was the inner drive of the expansive Spenserian vision, which he found in that introverted, elegiac, prophetic strain—the atmosphere which steadily asserted itself more strongly as *The Faerie Queene* progressed.

No simple account of the links between major poets will satisfy the critical historian, but Spenser and Milton do join hands in one particularly generative linkage. Between Spenser and Milton, Shakespeare intervened, and this fact has not been sufficiently pondered. By comparison the "Spenserians" were of negligible influence. For it was through Shakespeare's example of dramatic economy, maintained in works like *Antony and Cleopatra* and *The Tempest*, that Milton learned how to create what may be called "transcendental forms," forms which have the content of expansionist and expansive poems, but hold this content within relatively more economical bounds, thus gaining in intensity, virtuosity and élan.[38] These virtuoso forms, of which Milton's first major essay was the Nativity Hymn and second and for him more important, *Comus*, are powerfully expressive. They retain the introversion of the elegiac, even while they project a bright new world. Similarly, the very personal utterances of *Lycidas* give it more exuberance than a marriage ode, or, alternatively, turn it into an epithalamium by which the poet himself is "married to immortal verse." The Miltonic freedom required the mastery of melancholy, the "heightened self-awareness" that could lead a poet to "attain / To something like prophetic strain." The

38. Cf. C. S. Lewis, *Studies in Medieval and Renaissance Literature* (Cambridge, 1966), where, reviewing Robert Ellrodt, *Neoplatonism in the Poetry of Spenser* (Geneva, 1960), Lewis associates symbolic overload with the syncretism of "Pagan Mysteries in the Renaissance." Edgar Wind had described a poetry and art whose claims to attention

early seventeenth century might be called "the age of Burton's *Anatomy*," and to that extent it is also a period of rapid stylistic change. Black humor and the grotesque often go with the new Saturnian wisdom, whose complexities demand the plastic independence of mannerism and the baroque, as well as the imagistic musculature of metaphysical verse. The drama has its share of the new semantic instability, and we could look for it in plays like *The Revenger's Tragedy* or *The Malcontent*. In every case, wherever poets display the fashionable melancolia of the Jacobean period, we find a prophetic, not to say apocalyptic, style of poetic diction. In plays, as in nondramatic verse, the prophetic strain transfigures the heavy "melancholy demon" of medieval tradition into "an ideal condition, inherently pleasurable, however painful—a condition which by the continually renewed tension between depression and exaltation, unhappiness and 'apartness,' horror of death and increased awareness of life, could impart a new vitality to drama, poetry and art."[39] This is the new "fullness and force" Coleridge discovered in *The Tragedy of Hamlet*.

---

were extravagant. As Lewis puts it, "The aim is to load every inch of the canvas and every stanza of the poem with the greatest possible weight of 'wisdom,' learning, edification, suggestion, solemnity, and ideal beauty. Symbols that are on different levels or come from very different sources are not logically harmonized with great care; they are plastically harmonized in the pictorial design or the narrative flow." The logic of Milton has always attracted scrutiny, and recently a full-scale reading by D. H. Burden, *The Logical Epic: a Study of the Argument of Paradise Lost* (Cambridge, Mass, 1967). The attempt to press rhetoric into critical service, in reading Spenser, is connected with this same interest in logic. For such purposes, Kenneth Burke's notion of the "caricature of courtship," in *Rhetoric of Motives* (New York, 1955), 233–44, would seem a useful starting point.

39. Raymond Klibansky, Erwin Panofsky and Fritz Saxl, *Saturn and Melancholy: Studies in the History of Natural Philosophy, Religion, and Art* (London, 1964), p. 3, "Poetic Melancholy and Melancholia Generosa," 233. See also Thomas Greene, "The Flexibility of the Self in Renaissance Literature," in *The Disciplines of Criticism: Essays in Literary Theory, Interpretation, and History*, ed. Peter Demetz, Thomas Greene, and Lowry Nelson, Jr. (New Haven, 1968).

In part the dramatists of the late Elizabethan and Jacobean periods reflect a climate of apocalyptic emergency, a doomsday fever that finds even the slightest event ominous, "relevant," and "meaningful." Much of the excitement of *Hamlet* comes from this expectant atmosphere. But with the force there is also a fullness, and it is here that Spenserian poetics, which may influence the drama through Marlowe, contribute so much to later poets. For Spenser achieves unprecedented resonance—which was probably what struck the first, excited readers of *The Shepheardes Calender*. His words have weight; they settle into space like solid objects; they give a "local habitation" to ideas. We have seen how Spenser makes a dialectical platform for this localization of language, through his many sided ambiguities of the temple/labyrinth relationship.

Perhaps the feeling that poetic diction has a specific gravity, or real density, comes from the use of paradox where one least expects it—in the magical flow of verse. In the twentieth century Eliot and a whole school of poets, critics, and scholars discovered this weightiness in the wit and paradox of the metaphysical poets. Among the romantics, one cannot help instancing Keats, whose advice to Shelley, to load every rift of his verse with bars of gold, was an ironic reference to the Cave of Mammon: "Embost with massy gold of glorious gift, / And with rich metall loaded every rift." During the eighteenth century various reactions against metaphysical mannerisms do set in, but one suspects that with all the public rejection of the more tortured metaphysical conceits, there remains an unshakable belief that high poetry is always paradoxical, one way or another, so that the case might be made for a relocation of the mode of paradox, always arranged so that current fashions of thought could find their expression through the appropriate paradoxical manner. (Thus, with the Augustans, wit is eminently social and satirical.) If, then, poetic diction gains its "fullness" from a "secret wit," it is important that the Spenserian level of paradox—in the sense of an allegorical "level of meaning" —differs from that of the metaphysicals. The difference, of course, is hard to establish, and we are not surprised to find it so.

Without ascribing any special value to the terms, we can say that the Spenserian *discordia concors* runs *deeper* than that of Donne, and is correspondingly *simpler*. Spenser's metaphysical wit exists on a mythographic level, spun out of the temple/error union or out of some variant of that bond. For this reason, as C. S. Lewis so often suggested, the forces of Spenserian narrative are like the forces of nature; they are presocietal. In a word they are cosmological. One side effect of this poetic vision is its inherent musicality, its narrative blankness. Throughout *The Faerie Queene* there is an obvious lack of what might be called novelistic detail. This lack is so far from being a failing of the poem that it seems necessary to Spenser, if he is to create the mental space of his Faerieland. The model for such narrative emptiness is the chart or map, whose art was a rapidly developing Elizabethan interest. Expansions of horizon and the mythography of experiential quest give substance to the empty map and fill its spaces with the ornamental figures of monsters, magic castles, nymphs, sea creatures, ships and other symbols of the unknown. Readers of romance in every age will recognize the magic of such mapping. The questing mind fills the area between the places, while the places—quite unreal as places we might have been to—are islands of hope in a landscape of wonder. On its naïve levels romantic poetry is always cartographic to this extent, because the seeker demands a mental space, a referential vacuum, to fill with his own visions. A more Donnean metaphysical poetry, or a more novelistic and satirical poetry, crowded as they are by the realities of social life, will prevent this excursion into the untrodden regions of the mind. Furthermore, such realities tend to undercut belief in the magic of the English language, as, to borrow a German phrase, a thing in itself. This magic is naïve. One tests it readily by reading *The Faerie Queene* aloud. Its force assures Spenser his fundamental influence upon later English poetry and gives him a place in the studies of almost every subsequent English poet of any fame. He gives weight, value, and resonance to poetic diction and thus guarantees the survival of an art of poetry.

Index of Names:
Traditional Sources

Adams, Robert, 31
Agrippa d'Aubigné, 118
Alanus de Insulis, 280
Alberti, L. B., 8, 23, 178
Althusius, Johannes, 178, 238
Apollodorus, 138, 151, 193
Apollonius, Rhodius, 92, 112,
    138–39
Apuleius, Lucius, 93, 193
Aquinas, Saint Thomas, 74, 249
Ariosto, Lodovico, 78, 89, 98, 99,
    137, 214, 296; *Orlando Furi-
    oso*, 249–50
Aristides, Aelius, 151
Aristotle, 53, 143, 162, 163, 177–
78, 192, 282–83
Augustine, 22, 85, 121, 249

Bacon, Sir Francis, 239, 244
Berosus, 194
Bible: Acts, 213; I Corinthians,
    4; Daniel, 66–67, 141–42, 246;
    Ezekiel, 67, 263; Genesis, 152;
    Isaiah, 67; Jeremiah, 67, 137;
    Lamentations, 202; Leviticus,
    264; Psalms, 60, 69; Revelation
    (Apocalypse), 61, 66, 69;

Romans, 287; Song of Songs,
    251
Blackstone, Sir William, 185, 281
Blake, William, 10, 35, 37, 49, 51,
    136
Boccaccio, Giovanni, 68, 80, 92,
    149, 233
Bodin, Jean, 66, 67, 124, 141, 145,
    155, 156, 173, 174, 175, 182,
    188, 292
Botero, Giovanni, 173, 188
Bovillus, Carolus, 110, 111
Breughel, Peter, 210
Browne, Sir Thomas, 18, 124
Bruno, Giordano, 124, 125, 157
Burckhardt, Jacob, 192
Burke, Edmund, 185
Burton, Robert, 302
Butts, Thomas, 37

Calvin, John, 286
Camoens, Luis de, 115
Campanella, Tommaso, 66, 72
Cartari, Vincenzo, 154, 198, 199,
    267
Castiglione, Baldassare, 190
Castle of Indolence, 301

Caxton, William, 107, 112
Chapman, George, 40, 160
Chaucer, Geoffrey, 3, 84, 85, 99,
   101, 114, 125, 130, 150, 288, 295
Cheke, Sir John, 177, 230
Chrysippus, 175
Cicero, 48, 162, 163, 175, 176,
   177, 178, 186,
Coke, Sir Edward, 184–85
Coleridge, S. T., 42, 96, 217, 302
Collart, Jean, 104
Comes, Natalis, 140, 178, 200,
   256
Cranmer, Thomas, 238, 279
Crowley, Robert, 179

Daniel, Samuel, 32, 39, 106
Dante, 35, 46, 50, 77, 86, 89, 113,
   114, 115, 137, 228, 244
Davenant, Sir William, 190
Davies, Sir John, 11, 125, 126,
   238
Davison, Francis, 94
Dee, John, 108, 109, 110, 111
Dekker, Thomas, 107
Denham, Sir John, 45
Descartes, René, 8
Digby, Sir Kenelm, 122, 123, 130
Dio Chrysostomos, 148, 182
Diodorus Siculus, 151, 154, 193,
   199
Don Juan, 130
Donne, John, 4, 14, 26, 47, 60, 75,
   299, 304
Drayton, Michael, 16, 33, 45, 62,
   95, 97, 224
Dryden, John, 94, 166
Dyer, Sir Edward, 109

Elyot, Sir Thomas, 232–33, 239
Ennius, 77
Erasmus, Desiderius, 68
Euripides, 151, 176

Ficino, Marsilio, 116
Filmer, Sir Robert, 178

Fletcher, Giles, 210
Fletcher, Phineas (The Purple
   Island), 301
Fortescue, Sir John, 183
Foxe, John, 67, 89
Fraunce, Abraham, 94, 152

Gascoigne, George, 107, 116
Gay, John, 147
Geoffrey of Monmouth, 92,
   106–21, 275
Germain, Saint, 280
Giorgione, La Tempesta, 17
Golding, Arthur, 9, 91, 92
Gregory VIII (pope), 223
Greville, Fulke, 59
Guicciardini, Francesco, 181

Hakluyt, Richard, 189
Harington, Sir John, 250
Harrison, William, 149
Hawes, Stephen, 85
Hazlitt, William, 51
Hegel, G. F. W., 22, 23, 193
Heraclitus, 104, 105
Herbert, George, 19, 47
Hermes Trismegistus, 125
Herodotus, 48, 194, 272
Herrick, Robert, 17
Hesiod, 136, 138, 140, 142, 169,
   249, 256
Hobbes, Thomas, 174, 190
Holbein, Hans, 102
Hölderlin, Friedrich, 105
Holinshed, Raphael, 149, 189
Holyday, Barten, 143
Homer, 40, 76, 78, 171, 191, 198,
   214, 294; Iliad, 17, 78, 81, 98,
   138, 233; Odyssey, 78–79
Homily Against Disobedience
   and Wilful Rebellion, 237
Hooker, Richard, 65, 71–72, 74,
   128, 169, 174, 191–92, 220–21,
   224, 238, 287
Hooper, John, 174
Hoopes, Robert, 175

Horace, 82, 299
Hurd, Richard, 11, 150, 190

Isidore of Seville, 104, 105

Joachim of Flora, 141
Johnson, Samuel, 299
Jonson, Ben, 6, 17, 33, 99, 103,
    105, 107
Juvenal, 263

Keats, John, 303
King, Henry, 24

Lactantius, 140, 155
Lambarde, William, 158
Langland, William, 3
Linche, Richard, 199
Livy, 91, 188
Locke, John, 20
Lucian of Samosata (*Calumnia*),
    293

Machiavelli, Niccolo, 91, 163,
    164, 173, 174, 187, 188, 220,
    222, 228, 267
Macrobius, 76, 151, 163
The Malcontent, 302
Malory, Sir Thomas, 34, 109
Mariana, Juan de, 238
Marlowe, Christopher, 28, 293,
    303
Marsilius of Padua, 89
Marvell, Andrew, 33
Milton, John, 27, 28, 46, 47, 49,
    51, 82, 106, 112, 115, 120, 128,
    131, 161, 210, 216, 224, 236,
    254, 298, 300, 301, 302;
    L'Allegro, 300; *Comus*, 14, 79,
    117, 126, 301; *Lycidas*, 115,
    300–301; *On the Morning of
    Christ's Nativity*, 47, 301;
    Paradise Lost, 7, 28, 30, 61,
    246; *Paradise Regained*, 61;
    Samson Agonistes, 59
Mirror for Magistrates, 39

Misfortunes of Arthur, 109
More, Sir Thomas, 68, 185

Nashe, Thomas, 243
North, Sir Thomas, 151
Novalis, 199

Orosius, 66
Ovid, 16, 25, 70, 78, 90–106, 115,
    138, 140, 176–77, 202, 210–11,
    226–27, 268, 300

Paracelsus, 194
Parker, Matthew, 239
Parmenides, 104
Parsival, 178
Peele, George, 62
Petrarch, 85
Philo Judaeus, 46, 91
Pico della Mirandola, 126
Pindar, 151
Plato, 100, 103, 104, 105, 177, 212,
    214, 249, 262, 292; *Cratylus*,
    100–105; *Timaeus*, 200
Plutarch, 48, 93, 149, 150, 151,
    152, 153, 165–66, 178, 193, 194,
    195, 196, 207, 262–63, 272–73
Pomponazzi, Pietro, 72
Ponet, John, 238
Ptolemy, 124
Pythagoras, 91–93

Ralegh, Sir Walter, 24, 39, 115,
    181, 202, 214
The Revenger's Tragedy, 302
Reynolds, Henry, 122–23
Rousseau, J. J., 165

Saint Ambrose, 60
Saint Bernard, 70
Saint Bonaventure, 50
Saint Luke, 47
Saint Paul, 4, 69, 251
Sallust, 206
Saxton, Christopher, 31
Scaliger, J. C., 53
Selden, John, 95, 97

Seneca, 151, 163, 176–77

Shakespeare, 13, 28, 51, 149, 172, 186, 224, 230, 237, 241, 250, 256–57, 272, 283; *Antony and Cleopatra*, 94, 301; *Hamlet*, 237, 302–3; *Henry IV, Part II*, 225, 241; *Macbeth*, 54, 230; *Merchant of Venice*, 30, 126; *Midsummer Night's Dream*, 250; *The Phoenix and the Turtle*, 299; *Richard II*, 17, 68; *The Tempest*, 26, 51, 301; *Troilus and Cressida*, 186

Shelley, P. B., 10, 303

Sidney, Sir Philip, 7, 8, 53, 70, 78, 124, 159, 214, 238, 241, 252

Socrates, 295

Sophocles, 151

Spenser, Edmund: *Amoretti*, 44, 112; *Astrophel*, 35, 300; *Colin Clouts Come Home Again*, 30; *Daphnaida*, 300; *Epithalamium*, 121, 122, 203; *Letter to Ralegh*, 59, 76–78; *Mutabilitie Cantos*, 12, 57, 70, 86, 217, 244, 254, 260, 266, 280, 295; *Prothalamium*, 127; *The Shepheardes Calender*, 29, 42, 71, 127, 296, 303; *Tears of the Muses*, 27; *Vewe of the Present State of Ireland*, 40–41, 48, 156, 213

Stair Ercueil (Life of Hercules), 142

Starkey, Thomas, 185

Swift, Jonathan, 147

Sylvester, Joshua, 28, 148

Tacitus, 91

Tasso, 35, 55, 78, 99, 107, 137, 214

Taylor, Jeremy, 64

Tennyson, 297

Thucydides, 156, 186

Titian, 17, 49

Traherne, Thomas, 60

Upton, John, 202, 263

Valerius Flaccus, 115

Varro, 104, 266

Vergil, 53, 76–91, 101, 103, 117, 119, 140, 148, 191, 193, 201, 206–7, 214, 239, 248, 266, 279, 298–99; *Aeneid*, 17, 76–90, 92, 214, 239; *Eclogue IV*, 148

Vertue, Henry, 60

Vinci, Leonardo da, 116

Wagner, Richard, 14

Warner, William, 39, 117

Wolfram of Eschenbach, 178

Wordsworth, 35, 216

Xenophon, 50, 78

Index of Names:
Modern Sources

Abrams, M. H., 116
Allen, C. K., 223, 280–81
Allen, D. C., 7, 68, 78, 140, 197, 246
Allen, J. W., 128, 174, 177, 179, 219, 232, 238
Allt, Peter, 49
Alpers, Paul, 11, 25, 28, 29, 32, 42, 61, 100, 103
Alspach, R. K., 49
André, Bernard, 107
Andrews, K. R., 109
Aptekar, Jane, 9, 140, 228, 272, 293
Arendt, Hannah, 225
Arthos, John, 190
Auden, W. H., 246
Auerbach, Erich, 65, 71

Bainton, R. H., 243
Baker, Herschel, 40
Baltrusaitis, Jurgis, 102
Barber, C. L., 192, 293
Barfield, Owen, 172
Barker, A. E., 224, 285
Bartlett, P. B., 160
Berger, Gaston, 22

Berger, Harry, Jr., 8–9, 13, 23, 44, 45, 55, 64, 73, 86, 87, 110, 175, 180–81, 227, 259, 298
Bevington, David, 42
Black, Max, 172
Bloom, Harold, 6, 224
Boas, George, 87
Bolgar, R. R., 91, 186
Boorstin, D. J., 281
Borges, J. L., 9, 16
Bowen, C. D., 184
Bowra, C. M., 77
Braun, Martin, 223
Briffault, Robert, 195
Brink, C. O., 104
Brinkley, Roberta, 107
Bruce, John, 237, 239
Buber, Martin, 65
Bultmann, Rudolf, 65
Burden, D. H., 302
Burke, Kenneth, 22, 35, 178, 302
Bush, Douglas, 112
Busst, A. J. L., 198
Butterfield, Herbert, 65

Cahn, Edmond, 162, 281
Cambridge, H. M., 185

Campbell, Joseph, 227
Carey, John, 115
Carney, F. S., 178, 238
Carroll, W. M., 272
Cassirer, Ernst, 7, 72
Castelli, Enrico, 220
Castor, Grahame, 7
Cerfaux, L., 195
Chambers, E. K., 107
Chatman, Seymour, 28
Cheney, Donald, 94, 95, 140, 198, 204, 210, 295
Chew, S. C., 140, 143, 144, 292
Christie, J. D., 32
Clements, R. J., 95
Cochrane, C. N., 206, 209
Cohn, Norman, 243
Collingwood, R. G., 39
Commager, Henry Steele, 82, 91
Conway, Agnes, 213
Craig, Martha, 100, 103, 104
Croce, Benedetto, 229
Crum, Margaret, 24
Cullmann, Oscar, 72
Curtis, Edmund, 156, 213
Curtius, E. R., 17

Dannenfeldt, K. H., 124
D'Arcy, M. C., 65
Davies, E. T., 221
Davis, John, 124
Dawley, P. M., 65
Delcourt, Marie, 198, 200
Demetz, Peter, 302
D'Entrèves, A. P., 221
Di Cesare, M. A., 76, 77
Dickens, A. G., 243
Diel, Paul, 112, 113
Dodd, C. H., 38
Domandi, Mario, 181
Dorius, R. J., 283
Dowden, Edward, 32
Driver, T. F., 65
Duckworth, G. E., 77, 91
Dumézil, Georges, 165
Dunn, C. W., 157

Dunseath, T. K., 9, 48, 137, 139, 145, 152, 157, 212, 293
Durand, Gilbert, 194
Durling, R. M., 94, 204

Edie, J. E., 105
Edwards, Calvin, 98
Eliade, Mircea, 14, 17, 21, 33, 37, 120, 194, 197
Eliot, T. S., 3, 9, 10, 31, 32, 88, 89, 99, 115, 127, 303
Ellrodt, Robert, 301
Elton, G. R., 158, 221
Empson, William, 29, 103, 131, 298
Erdman, David, 224
Evans, Sebastian, 157

Falls, Cyril, 156
Farnell, C. G. S., 140
Farrer, Austin, 4
Festugière, A. J., 195
Feuillerat, Albert, 159
Figgis, J. N., 211, 221
Finney, Gretchen, 285
Fixler, Michael, 59
Flaceliere, Robert, 77
Fletcher, Ian, 198
Fontenrose, Joseph, 176
Fowler, Alastair, 11, 35, 95, 115, 121, 122, 123, 124, 128, 161, 162, 195–96, 198, 220, 223, 240, 264, 267, 275
Fowler, H. N., 105
Frankfort, Henri, 195
Fraser, Douglas, 16
Frazer, J. G., 194, 196
Freccero, John, 35, 48, 50, 137
Friedrich, C. J., 173, 175, 177, 184, 238, 282
Fries, R. F., 232
Frye, Northrop, 8, 11, 13, 35, 41, 59, 117, 131, 146, 196, 217, 224, 230, 296–97
Fuller, Lon L., 174
Fussner, F. S., 39, 184

Gairdner, James, 107
Gaster, T. H., 52, 194
Gennep, Arnold van, 17
Geyl, Peter, 211
Giamatti, A. B., 35
Gierke, Otto, 175, 284
Giet, Stanislas, 65
Gilbert, A. H., 228
Gilmore, Myron, 39, 91, 187, 283
Gilson, Etienne, 69
Gordon, D. J., 293
Gough, A. B., 118, 234
Greene, Thomas, 298, 302
Greenlaw, Edwin, 64, 86, 220
Grosart, A. B., 149
Guépin, J. P., 139
Guthrie, W. J. C., 198

Hadas, Moses, 91, 195
Haller, William, 68
Hallowell, R. E., 194
Hamilton, A. C., 78
Handford, S. A., 206
Hanning, R. W., 117
Hanson, R. P. C., 65, 71
Harbison, E. H., 207
Hardison, O. B., 39, 107
Harrison, Jane, 171
Hart, H. L. A., 162, 174
Hawkins, Sherman, 140, 218, 222
Heaton, E. W., 66
Hebel, J. W., 33
Heidegger, Martin, 105
Hibbard, Howard, 16
Hieatt, A. K., 121, 122
Hill, Christopher, 39
Hinton, R. W. K., 178
Hobsbawm, E. J., 147, 153, 167, 229, 245
Hodgen, Margaret T., 78
Hollander, John, 285
Hooke, S. H., 142
Hough, Graham, 190
Hudson, W. S., 238
Hughes, Merritt, 224

Hughes, P. L., 232, 235
Huizinga, Johan, 170, 178
Hutchinson, F. E., 47

Iredale, Roger O., 151, 152

Jackson, W. T. H., 178
Jacobi, Jolande, 194
Jacquot, Jean, 107, 192
James, E. O., 195, 196
Jeanmaire, H., 194
Jewkes, W. T., 114
Johnson, F. R., 223
Jouvenel, Bertrand de, 165-66, 222, 283-84
Joyce, James, 37
Judson, A. C., 156

Kafka, 9, 90
Kaufmann, Walter, 22, 23
Kantorowicz, Ernst, 179
Keble, John, 169
Keen, Maurice, 154
Kent, R. G., 266
Kermode, Frank, 42, 73, 89, 95
Kernodle, G. R., 278
Keynes, Geoffrey, 37
Kingdon, Robert M., 232
Kinser, Samuel, 118
Kisch, Guido, 282
Klein, A. J., 210
Klibansky, Raymond, 39, 302
Knight, W. F. Jackson, 32
Knowles, David, 121
Knox, Norman, 295
Koebner, Richard, 108, 205
Koonce, B. G., 85
Koyré, Alexander, 223
Krouse, F. M., 59

Ladner, G. B., 91, 227
Lampert, E., 65, 71
Laslett, P., 178
Law, T. G., 232
Lehmberg, S. E., 232
Lenkeith, Nancy, 77

Lerner, Max, 164
Levy, F. J., 39
Levy, G. R., 223
Lewalski, Barbara, 59, 60
Lewine, M. J., 16
Lewis, C. S., 12, 13, 34, 35, 41, 52, 54, 55, 60, 96, 199, 301, 302, 304
Littell, F. H., 243
Lloyd, M., 115
Loomie, A. J., 159
Loomis, R. S., 140
Lotspeich, H. G., 140
Lovejoy, A. O., 87, 216
Lowers, J. K., 219
Löwith, Karl, 39, 65
Lumiansky, M., 109

MacKay, L. A., 48
Madsen, W. G., 59
Maine, Sir Henry, 171–72, 284, 286
Maitland, F. W., 158, 164, 185, 281, 283
Malkiel, Yakov, 104
Mann, Thomas, 9
Manuel, Frank, 39, 46
Martin, L. C., 18
Mattingly, Garrett, 69, 208
Maxwell, Gavin, 229
Mazzeo, Joseph, 228
Meek, T. J., 65
Meinecke, Friedrich, 220
Merrill, R. V., 95
Miles, Josephine, 28
Millican, C. B., 108
Moore, C. H., 77
Mulligan, R. W., 74
Murrin, Michael, 9
Muscatine, Charles, 99
Mylonas, George E., 198

Nadel, George H., 39
Nagler, A. M., 192
Neale, J. E., 144, 208
Nelson, Lowry, Jr., 302

Nelson, William, 11, 55, 76, 90, 95, 101, 112, 121, 140, 175, 196, 198, 218, 225, 244, 254
Neumann, Erich, 195
Nicoll, Allardyce, 40
Nilsson, M. P., 197
Nims, J. F., 92

O'Connor, Daniel, 22
O'Kelly, Bernard, 98
Orgel, Stephen, 94
Ornstein, Robert, 293
Orr, Robert, 220
Osenburg, F. C., 140
Osgood, C. G., 68

Padelford, F. M., 138, 243
Panofsky, Erwin, 49, 94, 140, 143, 148, 302
Parks, G. B., 31
Parry, Adam, 298
Partridge, Eric, 14, 114
Paton, H. J., 39
Patrides, C. A., 39, 59, 77
Pellegrini, F. C., 178
Phillips, J. E., 144, 237
Picasso, Pablo, 103
Pollock, Frederick, 171
Porteous, N. W., 67, 142
Porter, Howard, 81
Poulet, Georges, 22
Pound, Ezra, 99
Praz, Mario, 220
Proust, Marcel, 9
Przyluski, Jean, 194

Quin, Gordon, 142

Raab, Felix, 220
Raglan, Lord, 21, 47
Ratcliff, E. C., 277–78
Rathborne, Isabel, 39, 85, 86, 88, 194, 196
Raymond, I. W., 66
Read, Conyers, 232
Renwick, W. L., 159

Reynolds, Beatrice, 67, 188
Ribner, Irving, 109, 230
Rice, E. F., 7, 110, 111, 174
Rice, W. G., 114
Richards, I. A., 100
Ritter, Gerhart, 220
Robbe, Grillet, Alain, 9
Robinson, H. W., 5, 38, 65, 70, 71
Roche, Thomas, 72, 94, 162, 199, 205, 276
Rollins, H. E., 40, 83
Rose, H. J., 195
Rouse, W. H. D., 151
Rowse, A. L., 111, 160
Rudenstine, Neil, 53
Rupp, E. G., 279
Ruthven, K. K., 103

Said, Edward, 73
Saitta, Giuseppe, 178, 283
Saxl, Fritz, 140, 143, 302
Schoele, Adalbert, 140
Schuyler, R. L., 185
Sedgewick, G. G., 295
Seeley, J. R., 207
Sessions, Barbara, 114
Seznec, Jean, 114, 142, 148
Shepherd, Geoffrey, 8
Sibree, J., 193
Simon, Marcel, 148
Simpson, E. M., 60
Sinclair, J. D., 113
Skinner, John, 65
Smith, G. G., 7, 78
Smith, Hallett, 149
Smith, Morton, 91
Solmsen, Friedrich, 285
Spingarn, J. E., 190
Spitzer, Leo, 21, 53, 285
Stanford, W. B., 233
Steadman, J. M., 61, 161
Stephens. Wade, 176
Stevens, L. C., 283
Stevens, Wallace, 3, 9
Stevenson, D. L., 111

Sugden, H. W., 29
Summerson, John, 21

Tarn, W. J., 195, 209
Tayler, Edward, 123
Taylor, E. G. R., 31
Taylor, René, 16
Taylor, Rupert, 65
Thévenaz, Pierre, 105
Tibault, G., 278
Tillich, Paul, 227
Tillyard, E. M. W., 275
Tondriau, J., 195
Tooley, M. J., 173
Tooley, R. V., 31
Traglia, Antonio, 104
Trattner, W. I., 111
Troeltsch, Ernst, 178
Tuve, Rosemond, 11, 163, 190

Ullmann, Henri Lévy, 281

Valéry, Paul, 9
Veit, Walter, 140
Vernant, Jean-Pierre, 209
Vian, Francis, 138, 151
Viarre, Simone, 91
Vuillaud, Paul, 65

Waith, Eugene, 148
Waley, P. J. and D. P., 188
Walker, D. P., 72
Warnke, F. J., 4, 24
Warrington, John, 186
Waters, D. W., 31
Webber, Joan, 47, 299
Weinberg, Bernard, 66
Welsh, Alexander, 20
Werkmeister, W. H., 39
Whitaker, V. K., 63
White, Helen, 68
Whitman, Cedric, 81
Wickham, Glynne, 107
Willey, Basil, 7
Williams, Arnold, 100

Williams, Kathleen, 116, 139, 276

Wind, Edgar, 17, 49, 301

Witherspoon, A. M., 4, 24

Wittkower, Rudolf, 16, 21

Wollheim, Richard, 192

Worcester, David, 295

Wordsworth, Christopher, 277, 292

Wright, T. L., 109

Yates, Frances, 124, 157

Yeats, W. B., 3, 6, 9, 10, 48, 125, 131

Index of Subjects: General

Aevum, 95
Ages of man and world, 142, 188.
  See also Golden age; Iron age
Alchemy, 110, 120–21
Alexander the Great, 148, 209
"All" (frequency in *FQ*), 298–
  99
Allegory of Prudence, 49
Alva, Duke of, 211
Anabaptists, 242–43
Anakuklesis, 223–24
Anamorphoses, 102
Androgyne, 97, 198–200
Apocalyptic thought, 4–5, 13,
  31, 35–36, 57, 61–62, 67, 70,
  81, 84, 89, 92, 164, 212, 294,
  302–3
Archaism, 8, 9, 100, 103, 158. *See
  also* Retrospective vision
Arithmological stanza, 20, 123
Astrology, 146
Augury, 163. *See also* Politics
  and prophecy
Authority, 19, 146, 159, 167, 169–
  74, 181–83, 205, 214, 220–21

Babington conspiracy, 237

Bacon, Sir Nicholas, 239
Balance of power, 136, 139, 208,
  210, 282. *See also* Power
Banalization, 112–13
Bandit. *See* Social banditry
Betrayal, 228–42, 247–49, 294
Betrothal, 20–23, 267–80
Betweenness, 49–51, 53
Bible: New Testament, 59, 69,
  73, 92, 286; Old Testament, 38,
  41, 59–76, 92, 101, 117, 125,
  224, 264, 286
Biblical matrix of prophecy, 59–
  76, 136–37, 142, 199, 254
Body image, 79, 80, 179, 200, 273
Bonds of society, 179, 192, 200,
  228, 232–33, 284. See also *Jus*
Britain, 85–86, 89, 106–20, 194,
  274. *See also* England
Bureaucratized justice, 138, 158,
  282

Cadiz, 211
Caesar, Augustus, 205
Caesar, Julius, 208
Capitalism and social banditry,
  245

Castles, 16, 79
Cecil, William, Lord Burghley, 108–9, 231–32, 291
Ceremony, 20, 21, 52, 190, 247
Chancery, court of, 171, 280–81
Charlemagne, 107, 110
Charles V of Spain, 114
Chastity, 97, 248–53, 266
Chivalry, 29, 178, 189–92, 247–49. *See also* Courtesy
Christian vision, 59–76, 97
Chronicles, 180–81, 186
Circle (image of), 14, 21, 24, 40, 57, 58, 72, 97, 106, 127, 223
City, 16, 17, 31, 43, 59, 69, 135, 181, 204–7. *See also* Foundation
Cleopatra, 252
Closure of epic form, 18, 57, 87, 183, 204
Codes of justice. *See* Laws, codification of
Coke, Sir Edward, 248
Collage, 76, 102–3, 294. *See also* Echo
Command, as source of law, 173–75, 205
Common Law, 171, 185, 261
Commons, House of, 232, 236
Commonweal, 260. *See also* Parliament
Community, ideas of, 22, 38, 44, 177, 196, 245
Compromise, 207–10, 260
Conditional immortality, 92
Conscience, 21, 137, 167, 171, 280. *See also* Chancery; Equity
Constantine, Emperor, 89
"Constitution of religions," 207. *See also* Foundation
Constitutive vision, 43–44
Contagion, 238–39, 251
Contemplative life, 21, 63, 169, 266. *See also* Vita activa
"Contract" as social norm, 172

Coronation, 275–79, 292
Cosmogony, 92, 136, 146, 204
Courtesy, 190, 204, 210, 288–94
Courtly love, 189–92
Crete, 138, 292
Crown, 278. *See also* Coronation
Culture bringers, 110, 192–214, 249–53
Custom, 179–82, 190, 242, 248
Cybernetic control, 81–82. *See also* Guyon
Cyclical conceptions of history and time, 42, 74–75, 90, 93–94, 145–46, 173, 194, 218, 222, 227, 253

Davidic kingship, 277–78. *See also* Divine kingship
Demiurge, 200
Demonic parody, 34–37, 98, 226, 244
Desert, 29–30, 228. *See also* Labyrinth
Destiny, 90, 116, 118, 213, 222, 275, 277. *See also* Fate; Providence
Digressions, 119
Dilation, 245
Diplomacy, 208–10
Direction, myths of, 29, 41, 42, 84, 282
Discordia concors, 46, 60, 304
Displacement of myths, 99
Distributive justice, 147, 242–44
Divine kingship, 196, 261
Dolus malus, 233
Dooms, 167, 171, 174–75, 221, 274, 276. *See also* Trial
Drake, Sir Francis, 108, 209, 211
Dux, 165, 206

Earth, 268
Echo, 106, 114
Eden, 63, 64, 139
Education, 50, 167
Edward I of England, 185, 213

Egyptian mythology, 49, 124–25, 142, 157, 193–96, 263–64, 272

Elect, idea of the, 9, 65, 72, 117

Elegiac tone, 296–97

Elizabeth I of England, 41, 64–72, 86–89, 108, 124, 144, 149, 156, 191, 207–9, 213, 219, 232, 235–37, 240, 274–75, 277–78. *See also* Gloriana

Eloquence, 157, 289, 293

Empire, 89, 118, 204–14, 220. *See also* Imperialism

Energeia, 53

Energy, 53–56, 249–53

England, 17, 41, 64, 72, 106, 109, 124, 158, 183–85, 207–8, 210, 215, 231, 237, 242, 246

Entrelacement, 11, 13

Equinox, 240

Equity, 147, 161–64, 173–74, 181, 193, 205, 208, 233, 240, 262–64, 276–87

Erotic epyllion, 16

Errantry, 29, 58

Error, 7, 27, 43, 64, 75, 82–83, 119, 127–31, 214–57, 283–89, 292–94

Escorial, 16

Espionage, 144, 206, 232–34, 248

Essex, Earl of, 40

Etymology, 103, 105, 143

Euhemerism, 194

Evolution of justice, 87, 88, 183–84

Exemplary history, 187

Expansionist thought, 111, 115, 131, 188–89, 207, 214, 304

Experience, 23, 44, 115, 181, 190, 215–57

Faerieland, 72, 86, 88, 90, 142, 172, 180, 214, 254, 263, 304. *See also* Labyrinth; Place; Space; Temple

Faerie Queen, The. See separate index

Fall of man, 24, 41, 46, 50, 90, 115, 141, 210, 216, 219, 237, 253–54, 271

Fame, 84, 85, 86, 88, 126, 187, 204, 289

Family, 178, 248

Fate, 77, 89, 216, 297. *See also* Destiny; Providence

Female mystery, 271, 277

Fertility, 251, 253, 268

Festivity, 20, 21, 52, 191–92, 292

Fides, 232–33. *See also* Bonds of society; *Jus*

Flail, 141–42, 201

Flood, 78, 197, 211

Flowers, 202–3, 212

Fluctuating development of justice, 146–54, 163–64

Flux, 103–5

Force, 228, 235, 272

Forest, 16, 25–26, 29, 32. *See also* Labyrinth

Fortune, 32, 110, 222–23, 246–47

Foundation of states, 17, 77, 108, 151, 158, 192–204, 206, 225, 249–53, 266

France, 118, 183, 202, 208, 210

Fraternal crime, 256–57

Fraud, 144, 232–35, 248, 267, 292

Freedom, 36–37, 71, 118, 128, 159, 174–75, 189, 206–12, 225

French Revolution, 225

Futuristic prophecy, 3, 4, 38, 65–66, 73, 121, 164, 220, 242–46

Galfridian matrix, 106–21. *See also* Geoffrey of Monmouth

Garden, 11, 15, 18, 27, 33, 46, 70, 95, 161, 179. *See also* Plantation

Genealogy, 172, 194, 275. *See also* Progeny

Genius, 45, 213. *See also* Place

Giants and giganticism, 141,

Giants and giganticism—*Cont.*
150–51, 162, 174, 207, 243–46,
250–51
Gilbert, Humphrey, 109
Glorius Revolution, 224
Glory, 59, 97, 125–26, 214. *See
also* Gloriana
Godfrey of Boulogne, 107
Golden age, 107, 125, 139, 143,
148, 150, 240, 243, 291
Golden fleece, 33, 113–15
Grace, 190. *See also* Courtesy
Grey de Wilton, Arthur, Lord,
158, 197, 212, 288, 291, 297
Grindal, Archbishop, 65, 71
Growth of justice, 189, 192, 228,
273. *See also* Harvest
Guise, Duke of, 234
Gyre, 10, 62, 82, 131. *See also*
Spiral

Harmony ("love") in politics,
81, 128, 161, 177–78
Harvest, 141–44, 146, 201, 286.
See also Growth of justice
Hatton, Christopher, 77
Havre, Marquess de, 202
Hawkins, Sir John, 209
Henry VII of England, 213, 231
Henry VIII of England, 108,
117, 173, 206, 211
Henry of Navarre (Henry IV
of France), 118, 148, 207, 209
Hermeticism, 49, 121–30, 157,
266–67, 275–76
Hermetic matrix of prophecy,
121–29
Heroic energy, 53–56, 248, 252.
See also Rage
Hierarchy, 260, 272
History and historicism, 5, 6, 37–
45, 70–71, 84–85, 88, 90, 106,
110, 117, 125, 136, 179, 189,
197, 214, 244, 254–56, 282–87
Holiness. *See* Sacred

Home, 17, 28, 63, 79, 80, 128, 211,
213, 271, 294. *See also*
Nostalgia
Homonoia, 209. *See also* Samient
Horizon, 14, 30
"House of instruction," 259. *See
also* Temple

Imitatio Christi, 196, 226
Imperator, 205–6
Imperialism, 50, 78, 88, 110, 115,
158–74, 182, 189, 204–14, 253.
See also Empire
Imperium, 115, 182, 206–7, 214
Incarnation, 90, 218
Initiation, 50, 266, 277, 279
Inquisition (Spanish), 211
Inspiration, and prophecy, 5, 7,
44
Instrument of the law, 138, 146
"Introversion of the elegiac,"
298–99
Ireland, 34, 54, 106, 118, 156–60,
197, 213, 226, 231, 288
Iron age, 138–42. *See also*
Golden age; Talus
Irony, 212, 222, 234, 289, 294–96

James I of England, 237
Jesuits, 232
John of Gaunt, 278
John of Leyden, 243
Joyeuse entrée, 52
Judgment, 170, 185. *See also*
Dooms
Jus, 169, 173, 285
Jus Gentium, 284
Jus Naturae, 284
Justices of the Peace, 158–59

Kairos, 45, 46, 72, 73, 74, 240, 276
Knots, 74, 177. *See also* Bonds of
society
Krasis, 64

Labor, 89, 90

Labyrinth, 6, 9, 11–12, 24–34, 89, 117, 131, 214, 257, 303. *See also* Errantry; Error; Profane; Wandering

Law enforcement, 173–74, 179–89

Law of nature, 284

Laws, codification of, 138, 164–79, 260

Leicester, Earl of, 109, 211

Lex Naturae, 220, 284

Lex talionis, 141, 152, 174, 189, 247, 276, 285–87. *See also* Talus

"Linear" theory of time, 41, 73, 74, 194, 227

Logos. *See* Word

Looking back, 146, 294–303. *See also* Retrospective vision

Low Countries (Netherlands), 118, 202, 208, 211

Loyalty, 232–33. *See also* Treason

Machiavellian politics, 41, 213–14, 246–47

Magic, 120, 125, 129, 157, 275, 304

Magistrate. *See* Law enforcement

Magnetic compass, 82–83

Male dominance, 253–54, 279–80

Maps, 40, 304

Margaret of Burgundy, 107

Marian martyrs, 68, 73

Marriage, 128, 277. *See also* Betrothal

Mary, Queen of Scots, 144, 230, 236–42

Mary Tudor, Queen, 277

Masque, 51–53, 96, 269–71, 276

Mass, 22

Mastery of melancholy, 301–3

Mastery of time, 120–21

Maternity, 202, 268

Meetkerche, Adolf, 202

Memory, 6, 56, 85, 130, 179, 261. *See also* Record

"Mental rule of law," 286

Mercy, 279, 287. *See also* Mercilla

Messianism, 73, 212, 221

Metamorphosis, 9, 90–106, 234–35, 269–70, 300

Metaphysical wit, 302–4

Microcosm, 16, 20, 30, 248

Mildmay, Sir Walter, 232

Millenarian (millennial) speculation, 3–4, 37–45, 53, 64, 68, 78, 243–46, 293–94

Ministry, 19, 250, 263–64, 268, 273–75

Mirror, 4, 108, 110, 116, 120

Moment, 6–7, 45–53, 74, 89, 94–95, 113, 126, 135, 262. *See also* Betweenness

"Monstrous regiment of women," 260

Moon, 251, 263–64, 268–69

Mountain, 15, 16

Mountjoy, Lord, 40

Mount Oeta, 113

Mundus, 15–18. *See also* Temple

Munster, 243

Musical symbols, 126–27, 145, 304

Naïve equity, 228

Naming, 96, 101

Narrative, 7, 13, 43–44, 54–55, 72, 75, 80, 97, 106, 190, 295

Natural law, 191–92, 244. See also *Lex naturae*

Natural sense of justice, 282–85

Nature, 220, 222. *See also* Natural law

Neoplatonism, 23, 50, 70, 124, 128

Nomos, 171, 173. *See also* Laws, codification of

Nostalgia, 28, 54–55. *See also* Home

Number symbolism, 121, 130, 264. *See also* Hermetic matrix

Oil (coronation symbol), 278
Oracles (pagan), 47
Orb, 16, 278
Ordeal, trial by, 170
Outlaw. *See* Social bandit

Pageant, 51–53, 96, 269
Paradise, 16, 36, 60, 63, 95, 256. *See also* Temple
Parliament, 169, 171, 173, 184, 189, 208, 221, 281
Parody, 34–37, 98–106, 226, 244
Participle, 28–29
Pastoral, 23, 115, 148
Peace, 53, 112, 128, 145, 156–61, 165–67, 176–79, 192–204, 207–13, 275–79. *See also* Irena
Peasants Revolt, 154
Pedigree, myth of, 172, 194, 275. *See also* Genealogy
Perrott, Sir John, 197
Perspective, 4, 34, 37, 59–60, 64, 81, 102, 146, 163, 184
Persuasion, 240–42
Philip II of Spain, 209
Piety, 89–90
Piracy, 156. *See also* Social banditry
Place, 23, 45, 113, 303–4. *See also* Genius
Planetary motion, 223. *See also* Labyrinth; Wandering
Plantation, 25, 160, 201
Pléiade poetics, 7
Police, 138–42, 235, 237
Positive law, 162
Power, 55, 161, 187, 204. *See also* Balance of power; Energy; *Virtu*
Precedent, 184–86
Primitivism, 87, 242
Proem, 47, 146, 193, 197, 200, 205, 223, 243, 264. *See also* Threshold

Profane, idea of the, 15, 24–34, 42, 60, 95, 197, 254–56. *See also* Labyrinth
Progeny, 253, 268. *See also* Genealogy
Progressive theory of history, 70–73, 87, 90
Propaganda, 216, 238, 242, 293
Prophecy (general), 5, 38, 45–53, 114, 136, 171, 215, 269, 277, 286–87, 294, 299, 302, and chaps. 2–4 throughout
Prophesyings, 64, 65, 71
Protective labyrinth, 32–33
Protestantism, 19, 63, 72, 210–11, 226, 231
Providence, 42, 44, 59, 63–64, 68, 71, 74–75, 101, 110, 115, 136, 150, 167, 210, 212, 216, 231, 246, 260. *See also* Redemptive history
Proximity of bandit and social bandit, 155
Puns, 99–101, 114, 271, 293
Puritans, 41, 61, 164, 219, 268

Quest, 53–56, 64, 74, 190. *See also* Narrative

Rage, 249–53, 271, 294. *See also* Heroic energy
Ragion di stato (reason of state), 188, 214, 220
Reason, 175–77, 221
Rebellion, 70, 128, 141, 146, 152–53, 156, 174, 210–11, 216–49, 251–53, 268, 293–94
Rebellion in Arcadia, 240–41, 252
Rebirth, 93–95, 143, 211, 222, 228, 275, 286
Recognition, 13, 43, 259–77
"Reconciliation of the Four Daughters of God," 143–44, 279, 292
Record and report, 185–87, 242, 261. *See also* Memory

Redemptive history, 79, 190, 212, 218, 246, 286. *See also* Providence

Reformation, 19, 59–76, 210, 231–33

Regalia, 16, 169, 278

Regiomontanus, 4, 70

Renaissance, 18, 23, 30, 39, 57, 72, 91–92, 98–99, 105, 108, 115–16, 129, 144, 214

Repetition, 22, 40, 223

Reticulation, 18, 44

Retrospective vision, 8, 13, 45, 87, 173

Return motif, 86, 107

Revolt, 224–25

Revolution, 14, 78, 183, 217–49, 264

Rex, 165–66, 207

Right of rebellion, 219, 230

Right reason, 175–77

Ring, 14. *See also* Circle

Romantic epic, 3, 6, 43, 79, 99, 119, 190, 294

Romantic vision, 6, 13, 52, 118, 150, 189–92, 296, 304

Rome (ancient literature, customs, religion), 48, 117–18, 163–64, 207, 284

Roman Catholicism, 63, 118, 159, 173, 211, 231

Rosamond's bower, 32. *See also* Labyrinth

Sacred, the, 15, 22, 33, 95–96, 191, 194, 218, 269, 295

Sacred marriage, 273, 279

Sacrificial dismemberment, 196

Saint Bartholomew's Day Massacre, 234

Saturnia regna, 200. *See also* Peace

Scepter, 273, 278

Scythe, 142–44

Sea, 30, 196, 246

Season, 52, 286, 290. *See also* Moment

Secondary epic, 294

Sheriff, 155–58

Shield, 17, 166, 192

Shrine, 14, 127. *See also* Temple

Sidney, Sir Henry, 197

Slander, 292–93

Sleeping Arthur, 86, 107

Social banditry, 107, 113, 146–64, 206–9, 226, 229–30, 243–44, 249, 282

Socrates, 100, 295–96

Sortes Vergilianae, 7–8

Sources (mythic), 54, 56, 103, 294–95

Sovereignty, 169, 173–74, 187, 220–21, 227, 244, 261

Space, 14, 21, 23, 30, 113. *See also* Labyrinth; Temple

Spain, 31, 160, 202, 208, 211, 231. *See also* Spanish Armada

Spanish Armada, 4, 31, 69, 246

Spenserian Stanza, 52, 124, 127, 130–32

Spiral, 16, 49. *See also* Gyre

Stabilization, political, 165, 179–89, 207, 222, 231, 242

Status, myth of, 172, 278

Stoicism, 175–77

Succession (royal), 71. *See also* Genealogy; Progeny

Sun, 138, 143, 208, 212, 220. *See also* Artegall; Arthur

Sword, 166, 174

Syncretism, 6, 72, 90, 113, 143, 301

Tableau vivant, 52

Te Deum, 278

Temperate, 21, 35, 186, 248. *See also* Temple; *Templum*; *Tempus*

Tempest, 21, 24, 26, 270–73. *See also* Temple; *Templum*

Temple, 6, 9, 11–23, 58, 60, 80–

Temple—*Cont.*
81, 89, 106, 114, 120, 127, 130,
137, 146, 154, 179, 183–84, 214,
218, 227, 256, 259–304. *See also*
Paradise

Temple/error nexus, 11–56,
215–17, 304

Templum, 21, 114, 130, 183, 256,
266. *See also* Temple

Tempus. See also Temple; Time

Terrible Mother, 210, 247–53

Theatre, 4, 15, 52, 95

Threshold, 45, 47–49, 75, 97. *See
also* Proem

Throne, 169

Time, 5, 21, 22, 95, 137–46, 161,
205–7, 244–46, 253–57, 259,
276, 286, 292. *See also* History
and historicism

Timelessness, 10, 57, 253

Time-serpent, 49

Titans, 251

Tolerance, 207–10, 260

Topocosm, 52–53

Tournament, 191–92

Tragedy, 182, 217, 296–300. *See
also* Irony

Transfiguration, 269–73. *See
also* Metamorphosis

Transformations (parodic), 34–
37, 93. *See also* Metamorphosis

Treason, 118, 170, 206, 228–42,
247–49, 256–57

Trial, 50, 128, 170, 236–42. *See
also* Dooms

Trinity, 49

Triumph, 144, 292

Troth, 20–23, 182, 267–80. *See
also* Truth

Troy, 112, 117–19, 135

Trust, 228, 235, 249

Truth, 4–5, 7, 20, 23–24, 27, 38,
62, 74–75, 113–16, 141–44, 201,
214, 227, 259–304. *See also*
Troth; Trust

Tudor monarchy, 108, 117, 125,
213, 220–21, 230–31, 257

Turning inward, 299–300

Typology, 5–6, 37–44, 57–132,
141, 150, 205–6, 214, 217, 224,
226, 262, 269, 276, 287. *See also*
History and historicism

Tyranny, 141, 150, 159, 174, 179,
207, 226, 231, 244

Umbra, 262. *See also* Typology

Vergilian matrix, 76–90

Veritas filia temporis, 143–44

Virtu, 53–56, 249–53

Vision, 3, 5, 8, 21, 37, 44, 52, 63,
64, 68, 87, 129, 204, 214, 246,
275, 294, 304

Vita activa, 50, 63, 266–67

Vocation, 3, 10, 37–38, 71, 117

Voyaging, 40, 82, 111. *See also*
Expansionist thought

Vulgaris aequitas, 285. *See also*
Equity

Wandering, 12, 24, 26, 27, 29, 30–
31, 34–35, 41, 43, 50, 54, 58, 83,
97, 127, 223, 227, 250, 264, 289.
See also Errantry; Error;
Labyrinth

War, 142–48, 192–204. See also
Imperator; Imperialism

Waste houses, 34–36, 96. *See also*
Labyrinth

Wasteland, 28–32, 228. *See also*
Labyrinth

Waves, 27

Whitgift, John, 65

Wilderness, 29, 60, 136, 179. *See
also* Labyrinth; Wasteland

Wine, 252. *See also* Bacchus

Wisdom, 4, 166, 174–75, 182, 191.
See also Reason; *Sapientia*

Women on European thrones,
247–48

Word, The, 22, 37–38, 42, 44, 68,
273, 286–87

"World" (frequency in *FQ*), 94

Index of Subjects:

From THE FAERIE QUEEN

Allegorical Figures
  Adicia, 210
  Adonis, 178
  Adultery, 237
  Aesculapius, 139
  Amidas, 168, 172
  Amoret, 96–7
  Anamnestes, 179
  Antaeus, 80
  Archimago, 62
  Artegall, Sir, 88, 109, 110, 116,
    119, 120, chaps. 4, 5, and 6
    passim
  Arthur, 43, 53, 63, 80, 84, 86,
    88, 98, 107, 108, 110, 119, 138,
    140, 144, 166–67, 173, 178,
    180, 186, 194, 199, 201, 203,
    211–12, 215, 220, 280, 297
  Astraea, 124, 125, 140, 167, 171,
    215, 231, 254, 256, 271, 275,
    291
  Ate, 240
  Authority, 236
  Belge, Lady, 142, 177, 202–3,
    211–12
  Belphoebe, 119, 176, 254
  Blandamour, 237

Blatant Beast, 157, 257, 288,
    290
  Bonfont, 144, 214
  Bracidas, 168, 246
  Braggadochio, 128
  Britomart, 62, 88, 97, 108, 109,
    110, 115, 116, 119, 120, 138,
    166–68, 176–77, 181, 190,
    195, 201, 233, 240, 247–48,
    250, 259, 287
  Brutus, 89
  Burbon, Sir, 118, 192, 209, 246,
    248
  Busirane, 36, 96
  Calidore, Sir, 129, 288–94
  Chrysaor, 141
  Circe, 79
  Colin Clout, 106, 126, 296
  Crocodile, 265, 267, 270, 272,
    277
  Cupid, 94
  Cymochles, 27, 82
  Cynthia, 219
  Despair, 63
  Detraction, 187, 212, 288
  Diana, 16
  Dice, 145

[323]

Dolon, 144, 233–34, 248
Duessa, 62, 144, 145, 170, 208, 211, 229–30, 234, 236–42, 287
Dwarf, 24
Egalitarian giant, 67, 139, 147, 153, 157, 177, 226, 229, 242–46, 284
Eirene, 145
Envy, 187, 212, 288
Errour, 26, 61, 75, 238
Eumnestes, 85, 179
Eunomie, 145
Faerie Queene, 59, 63, 98, 297. *See also* Gloriana
Faunus, 254, 256
Florimell, 30, 93, 102, 191, 202
Fortuna, 26
Furor, 36
Geryon, 178, 212
Geryoneo, 181, 201, 203, 209, 211–12, 238
Glauce, 110, 119, 250
Gloriana, 59, 119, 126, 172–74, 190, 203, 205. *See also* Faerie Queene
Graces, 126, 129, 176
Grantorto, 209, 212, 239
Gryll, 81
Guizor, 234
Guyon, Sir, 18, 29, 43, 78, 79, 80, 82, 84, 85, 114, 191, 254
Heavenly Contemplation, 15, 43
Hermaphrodite Venus, 95
Hours (Horai), 145, 176
Impiety, 237
Incontinence of Life, 237
Irena, 136, 202–3, 212–13, 275, 288
Isis, 177, 251, 279
Kingdomes Care, 236
Lion, 270, 271, 274
Lucifera, 62
Lucy, 168
Malbecco and Hellenore, 98, 119

Maleger, 80
Malengin, 144, 234–35, 248
Mammon, 35
Marinell, 93
Mercilla, 145, 168–71, 173, 177, 181, 234, 279, 281
Merlin, 70, 95, 97, 107, 111, 116–17, 119–20, 178, 274
Murder, 237
Mutabilitie, 213, 217, 254–56
New Jerusalem, 15, 31
Order of Maidenhead, 110, 178
Orgoglio, 62
Palmer, 29
Paridell, 98, 237
Phaedria, 30
Philotime, 79
Philtra, 168
Priests of Isis, 250, 263, 273–76
Proteus, 37, 93–94, 234
Psyche, 94
Pyrochles, 27, 62, 82
Radigund, 109, 149, 166, 174–76, 183, 199–201, 229, 233, 247–48, 252, 260, 287
Redcrosse, 19, 20, 24, 28, 33, 43, 44, 50, 61–64, 75, 82–85, 88, 146, 196, 226, 271
Repentaunce, 96
Reproch, 96
Round Table, 108–110
Saint George, 43, 88, 146, 196. *See also* Redcrosse.
Samient, 209, 234
Sangliere, Sir, 168, 170, 191
Sansjoy, 62
Scudamour, 97
Sedition, 232, 237
Shame, 96
Soldan, 31, 201, 209, 210
Talus, 136, 137, 201, 217, 229, 234–37, 245, 263, 286, 288
Terpine, Sir, 248
Themis, 145, 169, 171, 176
Timias, 119

Trompart, 101, 128
Una, 20, 24, 27–28, 33, 62–64,
     75, 226, 271
Venus, 101, 276
Zeal, 236, 237

Allegorical settings
   Acrasia's Bower, 80
   Arlo Hill, 106, 213, 218, 254,
      256
   Bower of Bliss, 35–36, 79, 266
   Cave of Despair, 35
   Castle of Alma, 12, 18, 64, 79,
      81, 85, 254
   Cave of Mammon, 79, 303
   Cleopolis, 84, 203
   Court of Maidenhead, 74, 275
   Eden, 74, 164, 254, 256
   Garden of Adonis, 12, 18, 70,
      93–95, 226, 254
   House of Busirane, 35
   House of Holiness, 12, 15, 50,
      63, 75
   House of Pride, 62–63, 80
   Idle Lake, 82
   Marriage of Rivers, 9, 45, 52,
      95, 226, 259
   Maske of Cupid, 96
   Mercilla's Court, 146
   Mount Acidale, 12, 127, 254
   New Jerusalem, 69, 84, 245,
      254
   Temple of Isis, 12, 240, 259–76
   Temple of Venus, 9, 12, 45,
      259
   Troynovaunt, 246
   Wood of Error, 24–27, 58, 61

Mythic and historical analogues
   Abel, 256
   Achilles, 17, 79, 88, 98, 116,
      139, 147
   Adonis, 196
   Aegeus, 256
   Aeneas, 17, 77, 79, 81, 88, 101,
      107, 135, 158, 194
   Aidos, 256

Albion, 149, 151
Amazons, 199
Antichrist, 293
Antony, 147, 149, 252
Argonauts, 115
Ariadne, 256
Artemis, 176
Arthgallo, 157
Arthur, King, 107
Bacchus, 147, 148, 149, 153,
     161, 198–99, 201, 252, 256
Beowulf, 297
Bolingbroke, 256–57
Cain, 140, 142, 256–57
Calypso, 79
Cerberus, 290
Chiron, 139
Christ, 149, 181, 224, 226–27,
     251, 276, 290
Chronos, 143
Cronus, 140
Cybele, 267
Daedalus, 32, 37
David, 53, 75, 166, 278
Deborah, 276
Delilah, 236, 252
Demeter, 193
Deucalion, 197
Diana, 256
Dionysus, 153, 193, 194, 195,
     198, 251, 276
Father Time, 143, 144
Galloi, 251, 263, 268
Gideon, 115
Hephaestus, 110
Hercules, 76, 80, 107, 110, 113,
     115, 137, 139, 142, 143, 147,
     148, 149, 151, 152, 153, 155,
     157, 158, 161, 175–76, 177,
     188, 193, 197–98, 199, 201,
     203, 212, 248, 251, 261, 268,
     276, 290, 293
Hercules of France, 148
Hermophrodite, 200
Hesperides, 33
Hippolyte, 199

Horus, 194–96, 275
Hydra, 290
Io, 193
Iole, 149, 200
Isis, 193, 194, 196
Israel, 41
Janus, 48, 50
Jason, 112, 113, 114, 115, 139
Jove (Jupiter), 171, 175, 221–
    22, 255, 260–61, 268
Judith, 149, 276
Kronos, 143
Libra, 240
Lycurgus, 166, 292
Mars, 142, 143, 148
Medea, 138
Moses, 136, 292
Mother Goddess, 195
Nemesis, 256
Neptune, 225
Nimrod, 203
Nine Worthies, 107
Noah, 197
Numa Pompilius, 164, 165,
    166, 207
Odysseus, 28, 37, 79, 81, 88,
    114, 233
Oedipus, 182
Omphale, 149, 152, 199–200,
    252
Orcus, 290
Orpheus, 112, 113
Osiris, 142, 147, 149, 150, 153,

190–98, 201, 248, 261–62,
    274, 276
Persephone, 176, 203
Penthesilea, 199
Phaeton, 210
Poplicola, 166
Prometheus, 220
Pythagorean, 124, 125, 126,
    128, 129
Remus, 163, 256
Robin Hood, 147, 154, 155,
    167, 245
Roland, 297
Romulus, 150, 151, 163, 164,
    165–66, 206, 256–57
Rumor, 241
Samson, 147, 149, 252
Sapientia, 111
Saturn, 140, 143, 193, 197
Sciron, 153
Serapis, 49
Sol, 210
Solomon, 166, 168, 191, 207,
    209
Solon, 166, 207, 209
Sphinx, 181, 182
Syrian Goddess, 251
Talos (see Talus), 138–39
Theseus, 33, 113, 150, 151, 152,
    153, 155, 165–66, 193, 256
Triple Hekate, 176
Ulysses, 36
Virgo, 240